Gods, Kings,
and
Tigers

The Art of Kotah

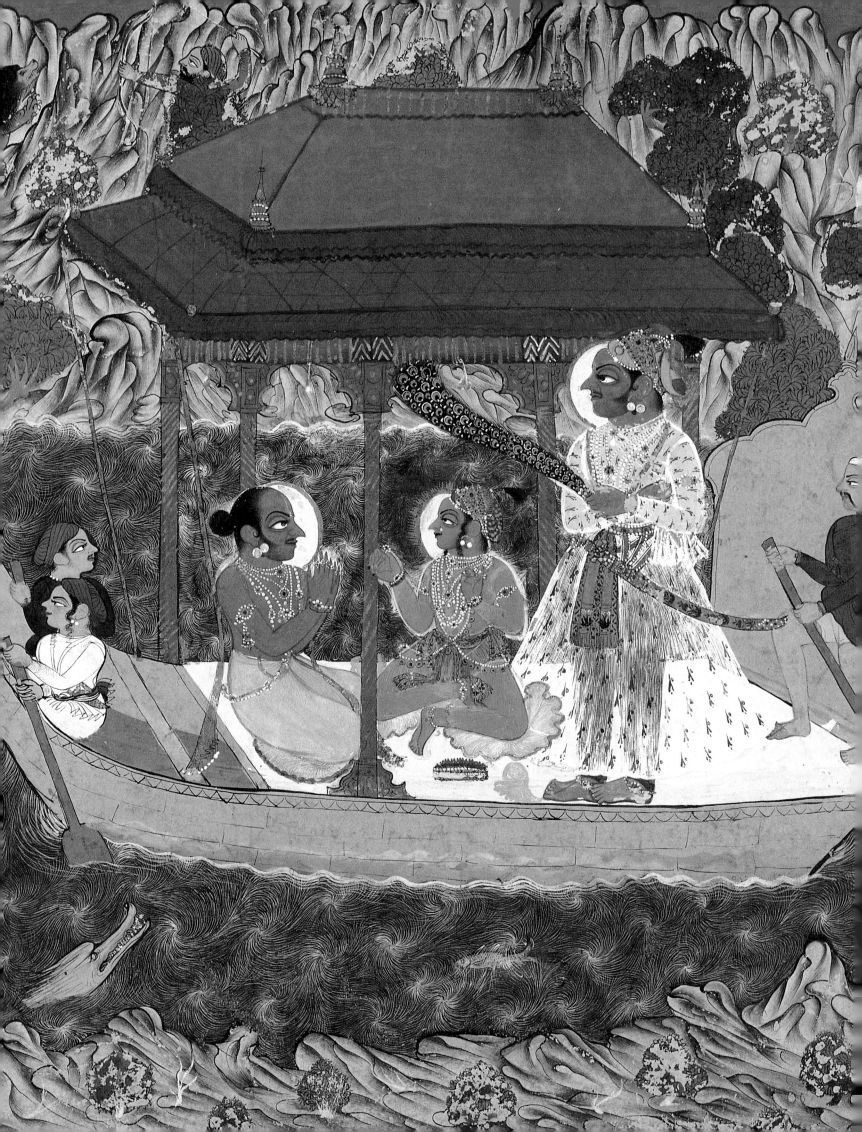

Gods, Kings, and Tigers

The Art of Kotah

Edited by Stuart Cary Welch

Essays by
Stuart Cary Welch, Joachim K. Bautze, Craigen W. Bowen,
Norbert Peabody, and Woodman Taylor

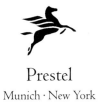

Prestel

Munich · New York

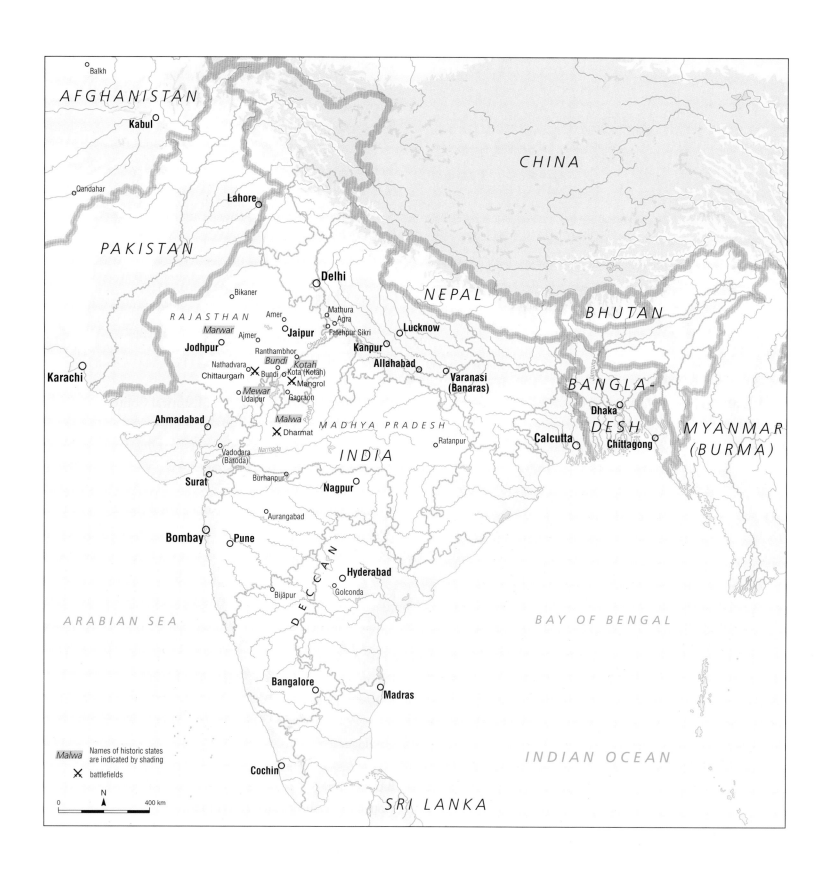

AFGHANISTAN

Balkh

Kabul

Qandahar

Lahore

PAKISTAN

Karachi

CHINA

Delhi

Bikaner

RAJASTHAN

Amer

Marwar

Ajmer

Jaipur

Jodhpur

Ranthambhor

Nathadvara

Bundi

Kotah

Chittaurgarh

Bundi

Kota (Kotah)

Mangrol

Mewar

Udaipur

Gagraon

Malwa

Dharmat

Ahmadabad

MADHYA PRADESH

Ratanpur

Vadodara
(Baroda)

Narmada

INDIA

Burhanpur

Surat

Nagpur

Aurangabad

Bombay

Pune

Hyderabad

Bijāpur

Golconda

ARABIAN SEA

BAY OF BENGAL

DECCAN

Bangalore

Madras

Mathura

Agra

Fatehpur Sikri

Lucknow

Kanpur

Allahabad

Varanasi
(Banaras)

NEPAL

BHUTAN

BANGLA-

Dhaka

DESH

Calcutta

Chittagong

MYANMAR
(BURMA)

INDIAN OCEAN

Cochin

SRI LANKA

Malwa   Names of historic states
         are indicated by shading

✕   battlefields

0   400 km

N

Foreword

As the modern nation of India prepares to celebrate fifty years of independence, we are especially pleased and proud to present this comprehensive exhibition of the visual arts from the important royal court of Kotah in the northern state of Rajasthan.

Created in 1631 when the Mughal emperor Shah Jahan divided the Rajput kingdom of Bundi and gave the newly established kingdom to Madho Singh, the second son of Bundi's ruler, Kotah quickly became one of the most powerful Rajput states, with a strong economy and vibrant cultural traditions. Particularly emphasized was painting, especially images of secular topics for the intimate viewing pleasure of rulers and their courtiers, as well as large paintings on cloth for public viewing. Among the most important themes depicted in the paintings were the conveyance of the divine authority of rulers and depictions of important courtly events, such as battles, hunting expeditions, marriages, and even political alliances. The unique stylistic qualities of Kotah painting are evidence of the mutual influences of Mughal and Rajput artistic traditions that made Kotah one of the most exciting Rajput artistic centers of its day. Indeed, the complex beauty of the arts of Kotah derives in great part from the dynamic interaction between different political, religious, and cultural forces that shaped and reshaped premodern Indian art.

The works of art in the exhibition have been selected from two collections that once constituted the Kotah royal collection and are all works known to have been commissioned, owned, and used by the royal court. These are the Rao Madho Singh Trust Museum, Fort Kotah (housed in the Kotah royal palace), and the personal collection of H.H. Maharao Brijraj Singh, current head of the Kotah royal family. We are greatly honored to be able to reunite these works and exhibit them for the first and perhaps only time outside India. They offer the rare chance to experience the rich artistic production from a single Rajput court.

Exhibitions as complicated as this one are a long time in the making, and *Gods, Kings, and Tigers: The Art of Kotah* is no exception. Its curator, Stuart Cary Welch, curator emeritus of Islamic and later Indian art at the Arthur M. Sackler Museum of the Harvard University Art Museums, first conceived the idea of such an exhibition in the late 1960s. Numerous other exhibition projects intervened until the late 1980s, when the Asia Society and the Harvard University Art Museums agreed to co-organize the exhibition. Since then, we have worked together closely to present the exhibition and publish the catalogue, and their strengths are the direct result of our close and profitable cooperation.

At the Asia Society and Harvard, numerous individuals have contributed much to the success of the exhibition. At Harvard, they include, besides Stuart Cary Welch, Craigen W. Bowen, the Art Museums' Philip and Lynn Straus conservator of works of art on paper, who has studied the materials and techniques of Kotah painters over many years and who presents her findings in this catalogue; Rosaline deButts, coordinator of special exhibitions; Rebecca Wright, manager of grants and traveling exhibitions; Maureen Donovan, registrar; and Danielle Hanrahan and her staff, exhibitions; at the Asia Society, Caron Smith, associate director and curator; Joseph N. Newland, publications manager; Amy V. McEwen, registrar; Merantine Hens-Nolan, publications and exhibitions; Tucker Nichols, exhibitions; and Linden Chubin, public programs.

Financial support for the exhibition, no less crucial to its success, has been provided by generous grants from the National Endowment for the Humanities, the National Endowment for the Arts, Corning, Inc., the Metropolitan Life Foundation, and the Joseph H. Hazen Foundation. Additional funding for the presentation at the Asia Society has been provided by the Woodcock Foundation and the Chatterjee Group. Support for the Asia Society Galleries exhibitions and education programs has been provided by the Friends of Asian Arts, The Starr Foundation, The Armand G. Erpf Fund, and the Arthur Ross Foundation. We are truly grateful to them, just as we are to our lenders, the Rao Madho Singh Trust Museum, Fort Kotah, and H.H. Maharao Brijraj Singh, to whom we are especially indebted for his interest in and personal commitment to the project, which nourished the exhibition over its many years of planning and execution. B. P. Singh and Ashok Vajpeyi of the Department of Culture of the Government of India have been instrumental in securing permission for the loans of these extraordinary works, and we are grateful for their support. Finally, our thanks go to our catalogue authors and team of curatorial advisors: Stuart Cary Welch, Joachim K. Bautze, Craigen W. Bowen, Norbert Peabody, and Woodman Taylor, who helped shape the exhibition at a crucial planning stage; and to Eberhard Fischer, director of the Museum Rietberg in Zurich, who joins us in presenting this exhibition to an international public.

We hope that the resulting exhibition and publication meet the expectations of all of these friends and supporters, and that it pleases the eyes and excites the imagination of the many visitors who will see it in Cambridge, New York, and Zurich, just as it has pleased all of us who have worked so many years to bring the extra-ordinary art of the royal court of Kotah to the public's attention.

JAMES CUNO

Elizabeth and John Moors Cabot Director
Harvard University Art Museums

VISHAKHA N. DESAI

Vice President for Cultural Programs
Director of the Galleries
Asia Society

Preface

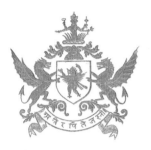

I am very happy that the exhibition *Gods, Kings, and Tigers: The Art of Kotah* is taking place, and that this accompanying catalogue is being published. This is a dream come true for me. It has been nearly ten years since my friend Stuart Cary Welch first discussed this idea with me; since then, the seed planted by him and sustained by us both has grown, and it is a matter of great satisfaction that it has now finally borne fruit.

The exhibition is from the royal collection of the maharaos of Kotah. It provides a rich sampling of the heritage of Kotah and the consummate skills of its master painters. The blossoming of the Kotah school of painting was an important milestone in the history of medieval Indian art. While drawing its main inspiration from the imperial atelier of the court of the great Mughals, it also freely assimilated the style and themes of essential Hindu art forms from Gujarat, wherein lies its genius and genesis. As each princely court took up the art of painting, it slowly but surely developed its own native style and distinctive features. Starting in about 1648 c.e., the Kotah atelier slowly evolved and crystallized in its own inimitable style, reaching the zenith of vitality and excellence in the late eighteenth century.

The hunting scenes set in the rich forests of Kotah are unparalleled in the Indian art world. The artists had full royal patronage and freedom. They painted what they saw, and the spirit was left free, resulting in an exuberance of expression. There was nothing fanciful in the way these master painters depicted nature. The stones, cliffs, hills, trees, rivers, and wildlife, including the majestic tiger, are all shown practically as nature made them. I was privileged to see all this — the wonderful habitat in all its glory and the plentiful wildlife it contained. Alas, all that is now more or less wiped out, in a lamentable tale of unchecked destruction of wildlife and widespread ecological devastation.

Apart from the hunting scenes, two other special features of the Kotah atelier are worthy of mention. One is the wonderful manner in which the artists drew elephants. They captured the majesty and the rhythm of movement along with the power of these great beasts. This is something quite extraordinary. The other feature is the remarkably attractive manner in which the human face was drawn and painted, conferring extreme delicacy and beauty on women and a certain handsomeness on men.

It is not possible for me to extol all the other virtues and features of the Kotah artists in this preface; I trust these will be dealt with at length by the authors of the essays and entries in this catalogue each of whom, of course, has his or her own opinions on the subject. I would only like to add that the second and last flowering of this art took place in the mid nineteenth century, before this glorious tradition sadly came to an end.

The artists (*chatera*s) depicted life as they saw it, creating an authentic pictorial record of the cultural milieu, the pride and passion of the ruler-patrons, and their colorful times. It is a sublime experience to behold the vignettes so cleverly drawn and painstakingly painted, showing such mastery of technique and perfection of treatment. These artists rendered scenes as they brightly visualized them, from our epics and mythology and from the pages of our great romantic literature. The adoration and worship of the gods and goddesses, with their rituals and festivals; the seasons and the *Ragamala*s, "garlands" or families of musical modes (*raga-ragini*s); the splendor of the royal court and its king; the regal processions and state visits; and the brilliant action-packed battle scenes — all formed an important part of their repertoire. This was a vast kaleidoscope that called for an equally colorful treatment.

The past was a different era, with its own values. Things were done differently, but with great grace and gentility, accompanied by dignity and decorum. The ruler had a close personal relationship with the people; he was involved in their lives and very accessible. I am lucky to be old enough to have seen and experienced all this, albeit in a slightly modified, modern form. I retain cherished memories of those bygone days — an era of dazzling grandeur and splendor, of innate grace and elegance.

I am sure that this exhibition and catalogue will provide an opportunity for many to have a better understanding of the art and the style of life in Kotah in those olden days. All this would not have been possible without the funding provided by the United States Government and private sources; the help and understanding of James Cuno, director of the Harvard University Art Museums; the interest shown by Vishakha N. Desai, vice president for cultural programs and director of the galleries at the Asia Society; the permission accorded by the Government of India for the loans; and, lastly, the labor of love invested by a select group of friends and experts, namely Stuart Cary Welch, Craigen W. Bowen, Joachim K. Bautze, Norbert Peabody, and Woodman Taylor, as well as Horst Metzger — all lovers of Kotah and its art.

BRIJRAJ SINGH
Maharao of Kotah

Acknowledgments

This book and the exhibition it catalogues were inspired by two devotions: the first, to Kotah art, initiated in my adolescence when Alice and Nasli Heeramaneck showed me the great Kotah painting now in Cleveland (published by Linda Leach on the cover of her 1986 catalogue of Indian paintings in that museum); the second, to Maharaj Kumar (now H.H. Maharao) Brijraj Singhji Bahadur of Kotah and his family, friends for forty years. Always hospitable and generous, Brijraj Singh — descended from those who found, supported, and directed Kotah's artists — has been the guiding spirit of *Gods, Kings, and Tigers: The Art of Kotah*. Over four decades, in addition to his generosity and kindnesses to those of us who have worked on this catalogue and exhibition, he hospitably welcomed several generations of my students. I am also grateful to Baljit Singh, director of the Rao Madho Singh Trust Museum, Fort Kotah, and to its trustees, for lending the pictures and objects that made this exhibition possible. Takur Jaswant Singh, whose translations of inscriptions, historical information, and renditions of Kotah songs helped and charmed, deserves our collective gratitude. Profound thanks are due to my wife, Edith, and our family, who accepted my frequent disappearances into the world of art. For help in Paris, I am grateful to George and Lois de Menil and to John Tain. Our late friend W. G. Archer, art historian, curator, anthropologist, poet, and author of the first monograph on the art of Kotah, also deserves our gratitude, as does his *chela* and successor, Robert Skelton. At Harvard, we are indebted to James Cuno for his invaluable support of a complex project, to Jane Montgomery and her staff of registrars, to Danielle Hanrahan and the force of talented designers, to Rosaline deButts for her effectiveness as exhibition coordinator, to Shokoofeh Haeri Kafi, to Gauvin Bailey, and to Wheeler M. Thackston, who allowed me to quote from his forthcoming translation of Emperor Jahangir's memoirs. In New York, I am especially thankful to Vishakha N. Desai and to Joseph N. Newland, Merantine Hens-Nolan, Vajra Kilgour, and Molly Aitken, without whose devoted, intelligent, diplomatic, and energetic editorial work our publication would not exist. Without Craigen W. Bowen, a fellow author whose collaboration has extended far beyond her specialty, the exhibition could not have been held. And the catalogue would not exist without the other sagacious fellow authors: Joachim K. Bautze, Norbert Peabody, and Woodman Taylor (known at Kotah as "Muralidhar" — "the man with the flute"). Thanks are due, too, to my friends Howard Hodgkin, Horst Metzger — the exhibition's "godfather" — and Jagdish and Kamla Mittal, for the privilege of illustrating wonders from their collections. For organizing this, the first exhibition dedicated to Kotah, how grateful I am to Harvard University, and to the Asia Society!

STUART CARY WELCH

Curator Emeritus of Islamic and Later Indian Art
Arthur M. Sackler Museum
Harvard University Art Museums

Note to the Reader

All attributions and dates in the captions to the catalogue entries are by Stuart Cary Welch. Translations and transliterations of inscriptions, unless otherwise noted, are by Joachim K. Bautze, who also provided information about where the pictures have been published.

A simplified system of transliterating foreign-language terms has been used in the text. In the interest of presenting unfamiliar material as simply and clearly as possible, English has been used in preference to Sanskrit, Hindi, or Harauti, the dialect precursor of Hindi spoken and written in Kotah. On first occurrence, foreign-language terms appear in transliteration in parentheses after the English translation: for example, "milkmaids (*gopis*)." Variant spellings reflect the use of all three languages or dialects, as well as changes of traditional spellings over time; "Kotah," for example, is a historical spelling for the state now known as "Kota." The forms of titles for the rulers of fiefdoms, principalities, and kingdoms — such as "rao" and "maharao," "raja" and "maharaja," "rana" and "maharana" — also varied from place to place. These differences have been retained.

Transliterations of inscriptions found on the paintings, with diacriticals, are in the Appendix on page 222. All inscriptions are in Devanagari (also known as "Nagari") script, unless otherwise noted.

Works reproduced as figures in essays are from India, unless otherwise identified.

The Ruling Hara Line of Kotah

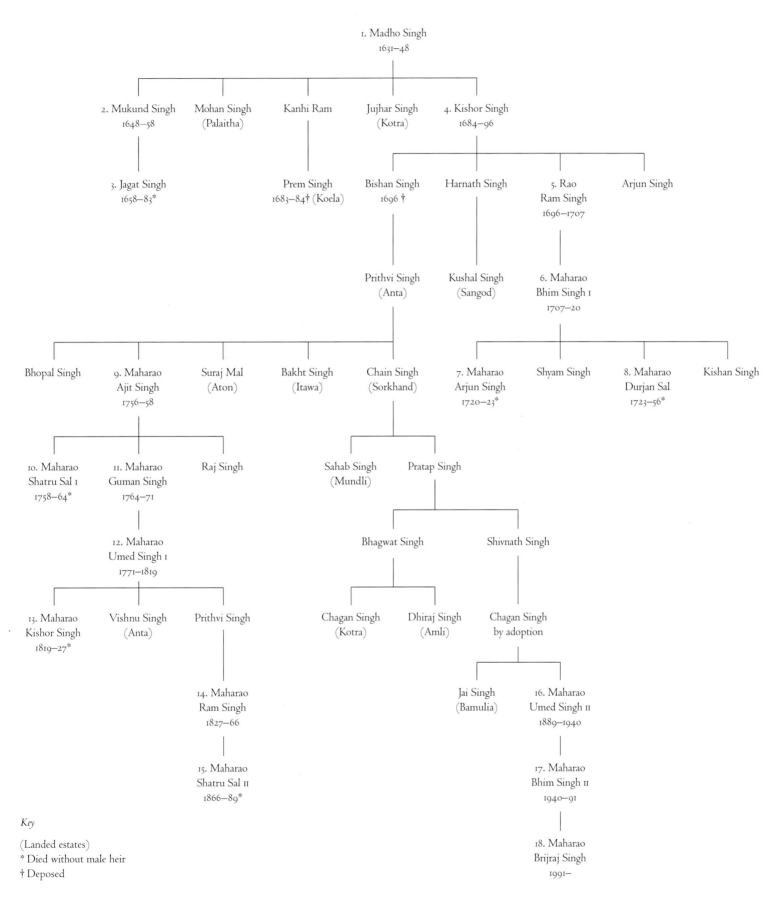

1. Madho Singh
1631–48

2. Mukund Singh
1648–58

Mohan Singh
(Palaitha)

Kanhi Ram

Jujhar Singh
(Kotra)

4. Kishor Singh
1684–96

3. Jagat Singh
1658–83*

Prem Singh
1683–84† (Koela)

Bishan Singh
1696 †

Harnath Singh

5. Rao
Ram Singh
1696–1707

Arjun Singh

Prithvi Singh
(Anta)

Kushal Singh
(Sangod)

6. Maharao
Bhim Singh I
1707–20

Bhopal Singh

9. Maharao
Ajit Singh
1756–58

Suraj Mal
(Aton)

Bakht Singh
(Itawa)

Chain Singh
(Sorkhand)

7. Maharao
Arjun Singh
1720–23*

Shyam Singh

8. Maharao
Durjan Sal
1723–56*

Kishan Singh

10. Maharao
Shatru Sal I
1758–64*

11. Maharao
Guman Singh
1764–71

Raj Singh

Sahab Singh
(Mundli)

Pratap Singh

12. Maharao
Umed Singh I
1771–1819

Bhagwat Singh

Shivnath Singh

13. Maharao
Kishor Singh
1819–27*

Vishnu Singh
(Anta)

Prithvi Singh

Chagan Singh
(Kotra)

Dhiraj Singh
(Amli)

Chagan Singh
by adoption

14. Maharao
Ram Singh
1827–66

Jai Singh
(Bamulia)

16. Maharao
Umed Singh II
1889–1940

15. Maharao
Shatru Sal II
1866–89*

17. Maharao
Bhim Singh II
1940–91

Key

(Landed estates)
* Died without male heir
† Deposed

18. Maharao
Brijraj Singh
1991–

STUART CARY WELCH

Kotah's Lively Patrons and Artists

Background and Setting: The Kotah Rajputs and Their Fort

Locale and setting, as well as people and events, shape artistic style. Kotah art would be drastically different had it not been created in the context of — if not within — Kotah's magnificent fort, which must have existed many centuries before a dynamic Bundi prince, Madho Singh (b. 1599; r. 1631–48 C.E.), established his court there. This complex was not only strategically placed at a scenic bend of the Chambal River; it also adjoined some of the finest hunting grounds in all of India. Now a forty-minute drive from Bundi, it was formerly half a day's ride on horseback, and a much longer trip — at three miles per hour — by elephant. For Madho Singh, it was sufficiently far from his ancestral dynastic capital at Bundi to encourage freedom and self-reliance, but close enough for contact when needed.

The charismatic, energetic Madho Singh was a characteristic founder — an ambitious man, born to lead, happiest in the midst of his own people. Although the historical record tells us that Kotah was granted independence from Bundi by the Mughals in 1631, it is likely that Madho Singh had established his court at Kotah somewhat earlier.

As a Hara Rajput of the Chauhan clan, descended from India's ancient Aryan invaders, Madho Singh was a leader of the traditional second Hindu caste, the Kshatriyas. His role, therefore, was to defend those of the first caste, the priestly Brahmans, and to look after those of the third and fourth castes: the Vaisya, who were business people, and the Sudras, who were agricultural workers. In addition, because the area of Kotah — in 1948, 5,725 square miles — abounded in tribal Bhils, whose ancestors probably laid the foundations of Kotah's fort, it was up to him and his successors to see to it that these casteless aboriginals, with their own traditions and leaders, remained in harmony with all the others.

Kotah Fort was the state's pivot. Its massive walls, intricate interior spaces, and courtyards seem not to have been designed and built, but to have grown organically to satisfy the requirements of its occupants over many centuries. Exploring the fort in its present form reveals a great deal about both the Rajputs and the town of Kotah, which was founded in 1264 C.E. Primarily, the fort was a spiritual center, containing several household shrines and providing shelter and protection for nearby temples, houses, and bazaars. To fulfill religious responsibilities and to serve family and community, it was a formidable stronghold, symbolic of the ruler's armed might as well as the center of his government, from which he ruled the many thousands of people who inhabited the princely state. At the main gate, the arrival of distinguished personages was heralded by the vigorously melodic fanfare of musicians, performing on drums, trumpets, and oboes (*shahnais*). On entering, visitors face an early medieval sculpture of Lord Ganesh, of the family of Lord Shiva, sacred to learning and — appropriately — to beginnings. In addition to shrines sacred to the Kotah divinities, the fort contains public and private audience halls and spaces for trials, celebrations, and the reception of local and foreign dignitaries. On most occasions, royal hospitality was extended; the large halls and courtyards were within reach of the royal kitchens and pantries, which were capable of preparing, delivering, and serving food and drink for hundreds of guests at a time. A superb early complex, perhaps Madho Singh's inner audience hall, is enriched by fine, early pierced stone windows, foliate red sandstone ornament, and an impressive throne platform.

The fort also contains two family complexes — the men's quarters (*mardana*) and the zenana, for women and children — each with its own shrines, baths, kitchens, larders, personal storage places, and servants' quarters. The ruler and his senior wives occupied their own royal apartments. Like the other public and private areas, these were connected by a network of narrow corridors and staircases zigzagging through the massive stone walls to myriad chambers (some of them adorned with wall paintings), courtyards, and gardens. Each was artfully located for warmth, coolness, sunlight, shade, dryness or moisture, breezes, and views. Some of these spaces encourage thoughtful, meditative tranquility, others amorousness, merriment, or serious conversation.

Much of the lower floor of the fort is devoted to stables for elephants and horses — each with its own staff of grooms and menials — and to storage: massive quantities of food — particularly grain — and water were required to weather a siege. Arms and armor were kept, refurbished, and probably manufactured in special areas. Godowns for textiles and costumes were staffed by

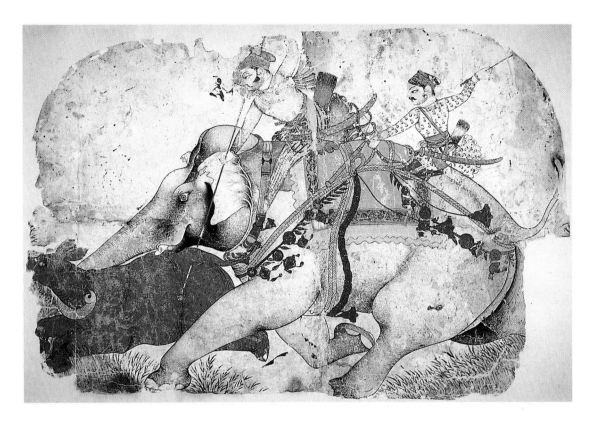

clerks, tailors, and seamstresses who combined the duties of museum curators, couturiers, and dry cleaners. Protected from insects by neem leaves, textiles were wrapped in white cotton and shelved. Jewels and jeweled objects were stored in particularly well-guarded chambers. State documents and unillustrated manuscripts also had their places, superintended by librarians, scribes, and guards. Religious texts, ritual objects, and the many embroidered and painted sacred textiles were maintained by a staff of pandits in the service of the household gods.

Paintings were kept in the airy, dry picture storeroom (*pothikhana*), where they were piled on massive stone shelves. Paintings and drawings were usually wrapped in cotton bandannas to protect them from insects, dampness, and light. The bundles were arranged according to topic and size. Many shelves were devoted to sets portraying Hindu divinities and saints and to illustrations of Hindu classics, such as the *Gita Govinda, Bhagavad Gita, Ramayana, Mahabharata,* and *Madhavanala Kamakandala-chaupai. Ragamala*s — sets of musical modes or "garlands of melody" — and the *Barahmasa*s (Twelve Months) were nearby. Another section was taken up by illustrated histories, astronomical and astrological works, medicine (human and veterinary), erotica, studies of animals — especially of horses and elephants — geography, and local and world history. All of these were available to the ruler, his family, and favored members of his establishment and guests. For a Rajput's continuing traditional education, they were among the essential sources.

Also instructive and enjoyable were paintings and drawings showing Kotah places and events: forts, palaces, pavilions, battles, festivals, marriages, darbars (court gatherings), hunts, polo games, and receptions of fellow rulers and other eminences. Many of these pictures include portraits of the raos and maharaos, their families, courtiers, staff, and guests. Large numbers of single portraits were also commissioned and collected; although most of these depict Kotah people, they include important personages from other Rajput states, the Mughal emperors and members of their courts, Marathas, and others whose lives touched on Kotah.

Each picture was inscribed with vital information, either on the recto or the verso, or on both. They were also numbered and occasionally enriched with comments accumulated over years of viewing. Like books in library stacks, they remained in storage most of the time and were brought out only when requested. On such occasions, they were examined, enjoyed, and commented on by the ruler and his family, friends, and guests.

At present, the Kotah collection includes several hundred paintings and drawings, ranging in size from tiny sketches to such vast pictures on cloth as *Maharao Ram Singh's Visit to Delhi* (cat. 65). Among them, a small number were painted elsewhere than at Kotah, and came as gifts or loot, or by purchase. These include a superb and perfectly preserved mid-seventeenth-century musical modes set from Malwa, several Bundi paintings, fine Maratha, Devgarh, and Jodhpur portraits, and a few folkloristic mandalas and other subjects. Conspicuously absent are examples from the Mughal and Deccani courts — a surprising omission considering the political and cultural ties between these two important polities and Kotah.

Kotah's Eminent Artists

In 1957, the painting *Rao Ram Singh of Kotah Pursuing a Rhinoceros* was sighted among many hundreds of cast-off Indian pictures heaped atop a large table (fig. 1). A paper conservator's nightmare, its surface was abraded; the rhinoceros's mask and most of the elephant's posterior had been worn away. Worse, part of the rump and hind legs of the elephant had been reverently but clumsily replaced. Like an overused dollar bill, the picture had been folded and refolded so often that a "cross" of paper losses threatened to sunder it into four pieces. Nevertheless, the painting's composition, with its mighty, fire-eyed elephant and gracefully whiplashing bell-ropes, demanded attention. Three years later, it enlivened the cover of an Asia Society exhibition catalogue, Sherman Lee's *Rajput Painting*.[1]

Such discoveries inspire searches for more of their kind, and very soon other drawings and paintings assignable to the same hand came to light. Among them were two small drawings of fish, geese, and three dragons, which stimulated speculation about their artist's life and training (fig. 2). The dragons imply links to distant Tabriz, the western Iranian center of culture and trade with China, Europe, and India. During the fifteenth and early sixteenth centuries, Tabriz artists drew and painted large numbers of snorting, romping dragons, derived from imported Chinese ceramics, metalwork, and embroideries acrawl with statelier members of the saurian family.[2]

But why should an artist working at Kotah in the late seventeenth century be so aware of fifteenth-century western Iranian dragons from Turkman Tabriz? History explains, transporting us through space and time to several centers of the Turko-Indo-Iranian world — first to the Deccan, where we meet Sultan-Quli, founder of the Muslim dynasty at Golconda. This aspiring soldier and statesman was born in western Iran to a princely Qara-Quyunlu, or "Black Sheep," Turkman family, who had been replaced by the Aq-Quyunlu, or "White Sheep," Turkmans. After suffering further persecution when Sultan Yaqub came to power in 1478, twenty-year-old Sultan-Quli and his uncle, Allah-Quli, were dispatched by Sultan-Quli's father to India to recoup the family fortunes by trading in horses.

Although Allah-Quli and Sultan-Quli brought valuable presents to help smooth relations with local rulers, they were ill-received in northern India. They ventured southwards into the Deccan, where they fared better, especially at Muhammadabad-Bidar, the still-glorious capital of the Bahmanid sultans. According to legend, young Sultan-Quli gained royal favor in the hunting field. His prowess was honored by a sultanly gift of 150 Arab, Turkish, and Iraqi horses, each with a golden saddle. He was also granted the title of Khawas Khan, and to provide for his herds and himself he received the lucrative estate (*jagir*) of Kurangal. Another legend claims that his success stemmed from making wise investments for ladies of the royal household; yet another ascribes it to saving the life of the king. For whichever reason, in 1496 he was appointed governor (*tarafdar*) of Tilangana and assigned the great fort at Golconda. Always loyal to the Bahmanids, Sultan-Quli, by now titled Qutbul Mulk, abstained from proclaiming himself a sultan, even when the territories of the collapsing Bahmanids were divided

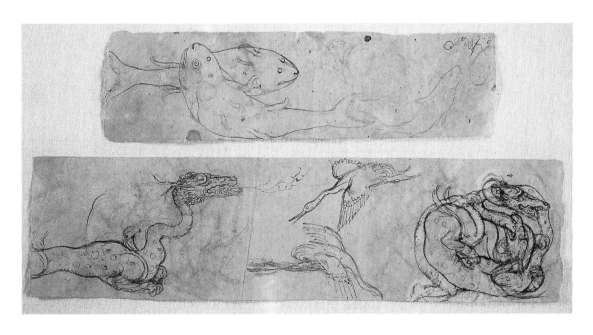

Figure 2
Fish *and* Geese and Three Dragons, *attributed to the Kotah Master, c. 1700, Kotah. Black and red line on paper, (top) 3.4 x 13.7 cm, (bottom) 4.6 x 18.7 cm. Private collection in the Arthur M. Sackler Museum, Harvard University Art Museums, Cambridge, Massachusetts.*

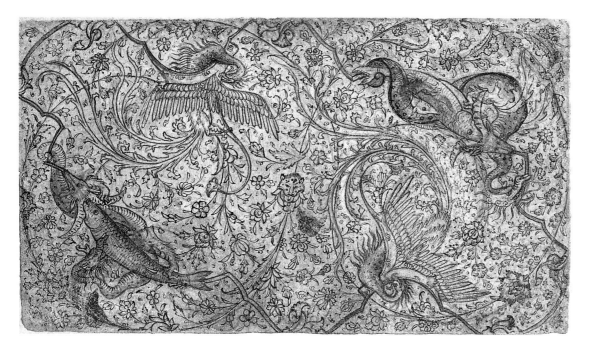

Figure 3
Inhabited Arabesque, *late sixteenth century, Deccan, Golconda. Reddish black ink with touches of white line on paper, 11.4 x 6.4 cm. Jagdish and Kamla Mittal Museum of Indian Art, Hyderabad.*

into five independent dynasties — the Imad Shahis of Berar, Nizam Shahis of Ahmednagar, Barid Shahis of Bidar, Adil Shahis of Bijapur, and his own, the Qutb Shahis of Golconda.[3]

Over the years, the sultanate of Golconda prospered, and its rulers distinguished themselves as enlightened and energetic patrons of every art. Invariably, their pictures and objects combined elements from Iran with those of the Deccan, blending imported Muslim and indigenous Hindu elements. This exciting synthesis is represented by a small, lyrical drawing of inhabited arabesques in Hyderabad (fig. 3).[4] The drawing underscores the extraordinary energy, finesse, and fantasy of Golconda art and looks ahead to the equally exciting works of art that emerged from the diffusion of its contagiously appealing style.

History warns that great success can cause trouble. The lucrative diamond mines, trade, and fertile lands that fueled Golconda's artistic flowering also aroused envy. Toward the end of his reign, the ever-expansive Mughal emperor Akbar (r. 1556–1605) initiated military campaigns against Golconda and the other Deccani sultanates. After his death, his ambitions were kept alive by the continual, wearying campaigns of his successors, until, toward the end of the seventeenth century, his great-grandson Emperor Aurangzeb (r. 1658–1707) finally weakened and defeated his southern rivals.

Because Hindu Rajputs served as officers in the imperial armies of the Muslim Mughals, heroic Kotah warriors, including the rulers Madho Singh (r. 1631–48), Jagat Singh (r. 1658–83), and Kishor Singh (r. 1684–96), spent many years — and spilled much of their blood — in the Deccan. There, at the imperial base camps, first at Burhanpur and later at Aurangabad, a remarkably catalytic cultural synthesis took place. Mughals and Rajputs — each accompanied

by family, court, staff, and armies — learned not only to appreciate one another's arts and traditions but also to admire those of the artistically inventive Deccanis. Because Rajput coffers were filled both from the imperial exchequer and by lavish gifts doled out to imperial generals by enemies eager to delay the inevitable Mughal triumph, these warrior-connoisseurs could afford to cultivate the arts of peace.[5]

Akbar's and his successors' Deccani campaigns in the sixteenth and seventeenth centuries prompted increasing numbers of Deccani artists and craftsmen to seek the security of north Indian employment. Toward the end of the seventeenth century, with the defeats of Bijapur and Golconda seemingly imminent, they flocked to Aurangabad, the Mughal enemy's military outpost, which had become a bustling metropolis. If a Mughal or Rajput enriched by his share of the imperial spoils needed a poet, theologian, philosopher, cook, musician, weaver, metalworker, or artist, he could choose from an eager array of talent trained at Bijapur or Golconda. It seems most likely that at Aurangabad, Jagat Singh of Kotah encountered, admired, and offered employment to the artist whom I call the "Kotah Master," whose work shows powerful influences from both Golconda and Aurangabad.[6]

A portrait attributable to the Kotah Master shows the patron enthroned like a sultan in a formal garden, accompanied by lady attendants (fig. 4).[7] As though riding the full moon, he occupies a golden throne on a round marble platform set in a lush formal garden. Near the lower border, a majestic sarus crane displays every graceful plume to his ladylike inamorata, metaphorically extolling Jagat Singh's magnetism. The bird's impassioned gestures are as expressive as those of Rao Ram Singh's hurtling elephant (fig. 1). As finely painted as a Persian or Golconda miniature, this joyous play on symmetry, burgeoning with flowers and spouting fountains, turns a moment of royal Kotah ease into paradise on earth.

The Kotah Master's apparently simple but in fact exceedingly subtle and difficult technique — essentially opaque watercolor, or gouache, on paper — is part of an artistic legacy from India, Iran, and beyond. Rooted in the ancient classical and Eastern worlds, it was almost identical not only to the technique of every other traditional Turko-Indo-Iranian miniature painter but also to the methods of miniature painters in the West.[8]

Traditional artists learned their craft as apprentices, either in the extensive royal ateliers, in the few workshops supported by great nobles, or in the bazaars, where work was carried out less painstakingly and with less costly materials. An important part of artists' training was the use of tracings (*charba*s), which enabled them to borrow earlier motifs from paintings or sketches and transfer them to works for presentation. This shortcut not only instructed fledgling painters in the elements of the Kotah style, but enriched their work with quotations from the impressive Kotah classics. Thus, a dying lion painted in 1700 by the Kotah Master might be reborn in a hunting scene of 1830.

Although many of the drawings and paintings seen here are painstakingly detailed, finished works intended for royal appreciation and collection, others — especially drawings — were made for the artists' own purposes, in many cases as steps toward the creation of a commissioned work. Varying in degree of finish, and often from life, some of the sketches were casual jottings, never intended for public view. Owing to the emphasis on line at Kotah — Rajasthan's most draftsmanly school — many Kotah pictures could be described as tinted drawings. Among the finished works, some qualify as masterpieces, for they seem to have been made from beginning to end by master artists working virtually unassisted. Others are joint creations by major masters in collaboration with their apprentices or assistants, since it was more important for pictures to meet standards of quality than to be executed entirely by a single eminent hand.

Interaction between patrons and artists at Kotah is not easy to define, owing to the unavailability (and loss) of archival material. Helpfully, several paintings were inscribed with such formulas as "This is obtained from the hand of the painter S[h]eikh Taju, given by him" (cat. 45). This suggests that it might have been an actual gift and implies cordiality between Maharao Umed Singh I (r. 1771–1819) and his leading artist. The exhilaration of many Kotah pictures, regardless of date or artist, conveys the artists' infectious pleasure in their accomplishment. This strongly argues that the relationship between artists and patrons was a happy one; when especially pleased, the latter lavished presents on the former. It should be remembered, however, that Kotah rulers were often away from Kotah, serving in the Deccan, Qandahar, or elsewhere.

It is likely, therefore, that supervision of the Kotah ateliers sometimes fell to other members of the royal family or to senior staff members. In any case, the active, appreciative guidance and support by royal connoisseurs no doubt contributed greatly to Kotah art's vital zing.

The Kotah Master's major predecessor in the Kotah style was a gifted and engaging artist whose earliest works exhibit stylistic links to paintings from the commercial workshops of Agra, the Mughal capital where Kotah princes attended imperial gatherings. Although this important artist's name is not known, his development at Kotah can be traced from several pictures assignable to him on stylistic grounds over a span of years. The key to understanding his artistic personality and identifying his work at Kotah is a group

Figure 4
Jagat Singh of Kotah in a Garden, *attributed to the Kotah Master, c. 1675–1700, Kotah. Opaque watercolor and gold on paper, 27 x 17.8 cm. Private collection in the Arthur M. Sackler Museum, Harvard University Art Museums, Cambridge, Massachusetts.*

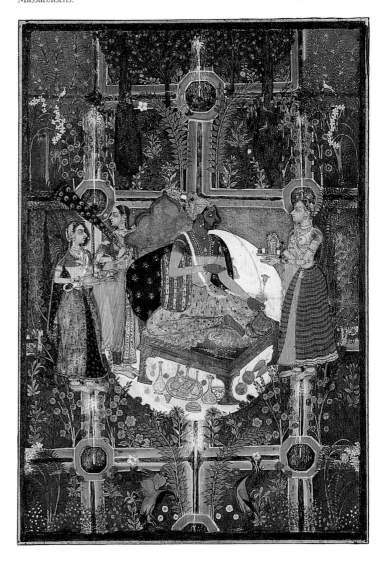

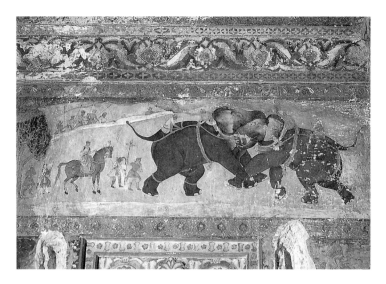

Figure 5
Elephant Combat with Figures in a Landscape, *wall painting in the Baddal Mahal, Bundi Fort, c. 1600–25, Bundi. Opaque pigments on fibrous ground prepared with lime.*

of late-seventeenth-century drawings of elephants that are clearly by a single innovative, highly idiosyncratic artist. Characteristically brilliant is his elephant combat in the Lucknow Museum, tantalizingly inscribed with a name (or more likely a nickname), "Niju," and with the year 1725. The date, however, is forty or so years later than the style of the picture, so it is possible that the inscription postdates the drawing and is therefore not as reliable as we might wish.[9]

Because the brilliantly spirited elephants are stylistically identical to several drawings in other collections, all depicting elephants, the artist's — and Kotah art's — quintessential subject, this artist may best be designated the "Master of Elephants." Prior to the arrival of the Kotah Master, he most likely served as the chief Kotah court artist, working exclusively on royal projects. Because his earth-trembling elephants recall those in the still strongly sixteenth-century-style wall and ceiling paintings of the Baddal Mahal of Bundi Fort, it would appear that he studied either them or other, now lost Bundi pictures of comparable power (fig. 5).[10] Along with Madho Singh's personal servants, cooks, and bard, this artist seems to have accompanied the ruler everywhere — including Bundi — whether on military campaigns, on hunting expeditions, to weddings, or on pleasure trips. Like today's photographers and filmmakers, he would have kept close to the royal presence in order to document noteworthy events day by day. When not on the road, he — like other leading court artists — probably lived with his family in town and worked both there and in studios within the fort.

A second wonderful elephant combat of the same date, in the collection of Sir Howard Hodgkin, amplifies our understanding

of this artist's undulating line, incisive as wire, and of his vibrant images, which hover between tangible, observed reality and the dream world of a fervent imagination (fig. 6).[11] However well this vigorous artist rendered people, trees, black bucks, or cows, only his elephants were truly visionary. Without them, his accomplishment might be overlooked. Because he flowered artistically at Kotah, a major center of elephants, he could scrutinize his archetypal subject daily. And if we compare his elephants to those of virtually any other of the world's artists, most of whom imbue them with the ponderousness of battered old sofas, it is evident that only he fully appreciated their catlike antics and the look of bones, gristle, and muscle fluidly packed into thick, flexible skins. Heightening empathy, he calculatedly exaggerated hollows and lumps, and contracted or expanded distances between anatomical parts.

Close study of the Hodgkin and Lucknow Museum drawings enables us to identify other major Kotah pictures as his. Early among them is the series of illustrations to a *Bhagavata Purana* of about 1630 or 1640, given by H.H. the late Maharao Bhim Singh II to the Government Museum of Kota (cat. 3–5). In one of these, *Krishna Slays the Elephant Kuvalayapida* (cat. 5), he concentrated on the heap of elephant debris with far more than the usual Rajput artist's concern for anatomy. Although painted decades earlier, it so closely prefigures his Lucknow drawing both in quality of line and in the analytical, scientific approach to the elephant that this painting may be attributed to him at the time of his emergence as a Kotah artist. This attractive painting, in which the personage in the "window of appearances" (*jharoka*) might be Madho Singh himself, conveys the state of pictorial art at Kotah in about 1635. Together with *Krishna Quells the Snake, Kaliya,* perhaps the most attractive illustration from this series (cat. 4), it indicates that Madho Singh was the progressive and imaginative patron of a gifted and innovative artist, and the first of a long line of Kotah ruler-patrons who put their frequently visionary stamp on Kotah art. Like many devoted

Figure 6
Elephant Combat, *attributed to the Master of Elephants, c. 1675–1700, Kotah. Black line heightened with opaque watercolor and white on paper, 34.3 x 67.4 cm. Collection of Sir Howard Hodgkin, London.*

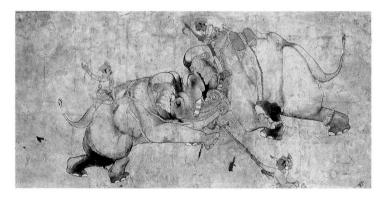

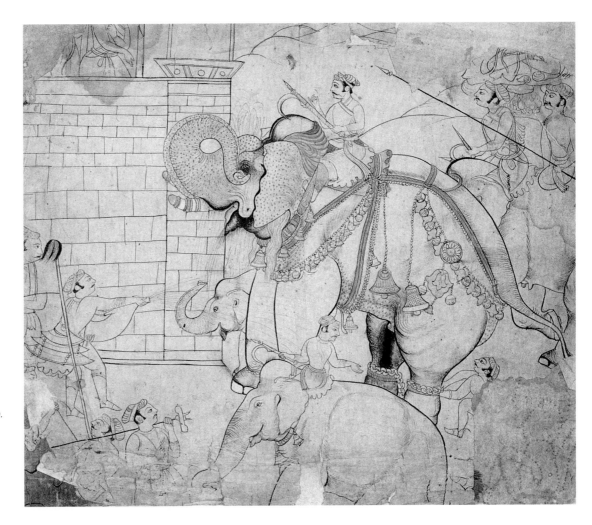

Figure 7
A Proud Elephant with Progeny
Viewed by a Prince, *attributed to the*
Master of Elephants, c. 1640–50, Kotah.
Black line heightened with opaque water-
color on paper, 24 x 28 cm. Private
collection in the Arthur M. Sackler
Museum, Harvard University Art
Museums, Cambridge, Massachusetts.

hunters, Madho Singh not only loved and sympathized with the animals he pursued, but wanted to know everything about them, inside and out. Under his patronage, Kotah painting established itself as *the* hunting, shooting, and fishing school of Rajput art.[12]

In 1631, Madho Singh earned Shah Jahan's approval by felling the despised traitor Khan Jahan Lodi, whose severed head was brought to Shah Jahan to enhance his pleasure while boating on the Tapti River, near Burhanpur. The Kotah ruler's close contacts with both Jahangir and Shah Jahan probably familiarized him with imperial Mughal art; particularly influential were its sensitive and detailed reportage and its success in representing many people and animals in space. Both are apparent in a damaged drawing attributable to the Master of Elephants showing a richly caparisoned, apparently overagitated elephant and its progeny being sprayed with water beneath the eye of a now headless prince, probably Madho Singh (fig. 7).[13] Less accurately observed than the Hodgkin and Lucknow drawings, it nevertheless shares their even, controlled line, vibrant spirit, and use of broadly brushed darks — instead of crosshatching and massed arcing lines — to deepen shadows. Above all, it brings out the Master of Elephants' sharply sensitive observation of elephant behavior and psychology. One of his stock

human characters reappears here — the same acquiline-nosed, mustached man who risks life as a mahout in the Hodgkin elephant combat. Later than the series of preparatory drawings for the Government Museum of Kota's *Bhagavata Purana* paintings, this work can be dated to the 1650s or early 1660s, between the *Bhagavata Purana* project and the Hodgkin and Lucknow drawings.[14]

The Kotah ateliers worked hard and spiritedly at varying assignments. Like many Renaissance artists in the West, artists at Kotah were called upon not only to paint both secular and religious subjects on paper but also to adorn walls. The most ambitious commission from Rao Madho Singh was a cycle of murals in the inner room of the fort's Chhattar Mahal. This complex panorama showing the fort, nearby temples, and hundreds of lively figures of men and gods was daubed over by well-intentioned late-nineteenth-century hacks, who scrupulously followed every line of the original work; although no single figure, animal, tree, or flower can be enjoyed in its present state, a few darkened but intact patches of once-splendid floral border attest to the high quality of the otherwise unattractively veiled original.

It would be hard to overemphasize the importance to Kotah art of these ill-served wall paintings. Their iconographic program

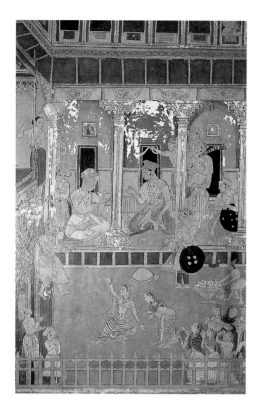

contains the entire gamut of Kotah subjects, religious and secular: episodes from the *Bhagavata Purana*, anecdotes of town and court life, gardens, river-boating, hunts, elephant and other animal combats, and more elephants, shown in Kotah service and being caught in the wild. On entering the room, one faces, at the left side, a busy celebration of the arrival at Kotah Fort of Krishna and Radha, who then enter the building and reappear upstairs, where Krishna bestows the sacred forehead mark (*tilak*) on Madho Singh. On the floor above, the busy god joins Radha on a throne platform, where

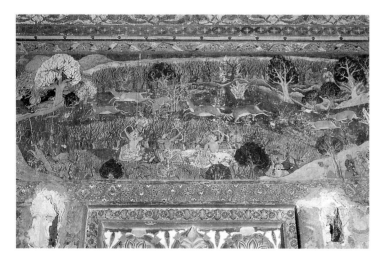

they are blessed by Brahma. To the right on the same wall, we see Madho Singh in formal audience, facing a pandit to his right (fig. 8). To his left are men of his family and courtiers, all enjoying music and dance. The entire left-hand wall is devoted to a large view of the palace and gardens during the reception of a delegation of prestigious Mughals, a few years before Kotah's enfeoffment as an independent state by the emperor in 1631. They have brought an offering of golden vessels to Madho Singh, who most casually grants them an audience while taking his ease on a platform at the center of a garden pool. Next, in the upper left, the Mughals honor the enthroned ruler in his hall of private audience. In every scene, the prestige of the Kotah ruler is raised and that of his imperial visitors lowered. Pointedly, Madho Singh's menial employees, including a gardener and water-carrier, are of Mughal ilk, with characteristic Muslim beards. Other walls of the cycle are richly painted with familiar Hindu motifs. Throughout, alas, the lively animals, gods, royals, courtiers, attendants, and townspeople (if such they are) of the original have been reduced to zombiedom.[15]

Stylistically very similar to these wall paintings are many unretouched miniatures in the Rao Madho Singh Trust Museum, Fort Kotah, illustrating the *Madhavanala Kamakandala-chaupai*. Two are included here (cat. 1 and 2). The set can be dated between 1620 and 1630, and although stylistic elements of the commercial Mughal style of Agra predominate, it contains women posed in the geometricized Chaurapanchasika style of the pre-Mughal period, while already (like the more complex, somewhat later compositions of the Chhattar Mahal murals) looking ahead to riper periods of Kotah art.[16] Vegetation and architectural detail — especially the deeply scalloped pediments and picturesquely silhouetted domes — anticipate later Kotah motifs. Moreover, the leading royal personage, facing the heroine in *A Lady Swoons* (cat. 2), strikingly resembles Madho Singh, with his lengthy, drooping mustache, as known from the bedaubed Chhattar Mahal murals. If these attractive small pictures, probably the earliest to have survived from Kotah, contained elephants or other animals to compare with those by the Master of Elephants, they might more confidently be attributed to this multifaceted pioneer of Kotah art.

The latest of the stunningly powerful drawings attributable to the Master of Elephants is an energetic study, belonging to the Rao Madho Singh Trust Museum, of a raging elephant struggling to break its chains (cat. 12). Increasing the animal's frustration, he is hemmed in by grooms (now missing) who are attempting to subdue him by brandishing terrifying spinning fireworks at the ends of poles, ignited by smoldering lengths of rope (*charki*s). In addition to being one of Indian art's most powerful depictions of an elephant, this drawing represents the Master of Elephants' accomplishment at a critical, final stage. It also constitutes evidence that he was a major influence on, if not the tutor of, the Kotah Master;

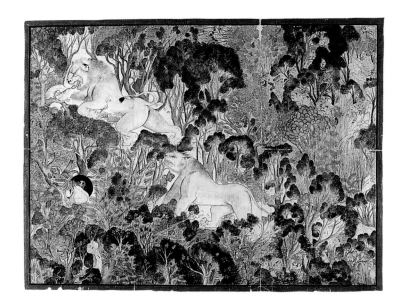

indeed, without the earlier Kotah artist's examples of elephant drawing, the later one could not have excelled so remarkably in this Kotah specialty.

Other significant works were also painted before the Kotah Master appeared in the Kotah studios. *Two Princes Shooting Deer; Dogs Hunting Down Boar*, a paradoxically lyrical hunting scene, stands alone in the Kotah collection (cat. 6). On the basis of Joachim K. Bautze's discoveries, we know that this picture was based on a wall

painting at Bundi, in the Baddal Mahal, datable to the first quarter of the seventeenth century (fig. 9). Because Bundi was the senior Hara house, from which Kotah emerged under Madho Singh, it would be surprising if the artistic connections between them were not close. The present picture, dating from about 1660 or slightly earlier, stands midway not only between Bundi and Kotah but also between secular and religious painting. The two virtually congruent figures, not quite portraits, bring to mind Rama and Lakshman, the godly brothers whose heroism enlivens the *Ramayana*, a great Hindu epic.[17]

Also unusual within the canon of Kotah art are two large sets of illustrations to the *Rukminimangala* (Tale of Rukmini), one with simple red borders, the other with borders adorned with floral arabesques. They represent Kotah religious painting in about 1660, sometime before the arrival of the Kotah Master. Everyone in these densely packed, brightly hued, busy compositions is lively and individualized. Although they are lacking in psychological depth, anecdotal incidents and bright faces abound. Unlike the earlier Kotah illustrations to the *Madhavanala Kamakandala-chaupai*, these are excellent sources of information about buildings, costume, all of the decorative arts, and human behavior, both formal and informal. The opening picture of the more sumptuous, slightly later set includes a splendidly dressed Jagat Singh standing before a sage (cat. 8). Jagat Singh's short, richly flowered robe of honor (*kaftan*)

Figure 10
Bhoj Singh of Bundi Slays a Lion, *attributed to the Kotah Master, c. 1700–25, Kotah. Opaque watercolor on paper, 47.6 x 66 cm. Stuart Cary Welch collection in the Arthur M. Sackler Museum, Harvard University Art Museums, Cambridge, Massachusetts.*

Figure 11
Detail of Bhoj Singh of Bundi Slays a Lion, *attributed to the Kotah Master, c. 1700–25, Kotah. Opaque watercolor on paper, 47.6 x 66 cm. Stuart Cary Welch collection in the Arthur M. Sackler Museum, Harvard University Art Museums, Cambridge, Massachusetts.*

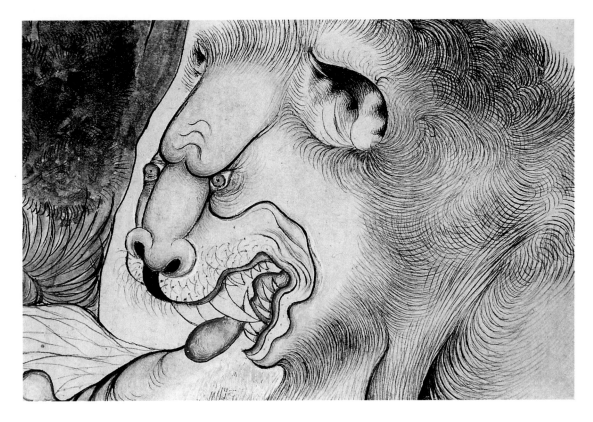

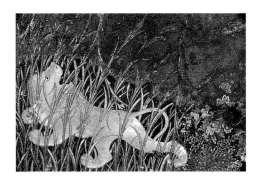

Figure 12
Detail of Faridun Crosses the River Dijleh *(fol. 33b of the* Shahnameh *of Shah Tahmasp, the "Houghton Shahnameh"), attributed to Sultan-Muhammad, c. 1525, Tabriz, Iran. Opaque watercolor, gold, silver, and mica on paper, 47 x 31.8 cm. Private collection in the Arthur M. Sackler Museum, Harvard University Art Museums, Cambridge, Massachusetts.*

is of the sort presented by the Mughals to appreciated courtiers and distinguished visitors, and most of the lesser noblemen's costumes are also of imperial cut. The artist projects life at its material and spiritual best. Everyone seems to be dressed for a wedding reception or darbar. These pictures document the increasing wealth of Kotah, whose princes had been sharing in the Deccani spoils since the days of Madho Singh. One wonders where these opulent miniatures were painted, at a time when the ruler probably spent very little time at Kotah, and for whom the Raj Mahal (Throne Room, or "throne-tent") was set up wherever he happened to be. The paintings exhibit no traces of the Master of Elephants' style or of the style of any other known Kotah artist. Perhaps the accomplished artist, who seems to have worked with an assistant, was an Aurangabadi influenced by Mughal, Rajput, and Deccani art. If his reportorial tendencies are indebted to the Mughal example, his penchant for purples and rose-violets is reminiscent of the Deccan. Whatever his place of origin and wherever he lived, he worked diligently and well on these two series, after which his style vanished from the Kotah artistic scene.

Other examples from the Kotah school's evolution provide further agreeable divergences from the artistic norm, with its emphasis on the rulers' active roles at Mughal and Deccani cultural centers. A nameless colleague of the Master of Elephants and of the Kotah Master during the last quarter of the seventeenth century is identifiable from his idiosyncratic manner. He painted an ebullient scene of ladies — one of whom is coyly pouting — celebrating the spring festival of Holi with the god Indra's vehicle, an astoundingly obliging elephant with four tusks named Airavat (cat. 13). Gently, femininely soft in design, drawing, and color, this almost rococo confection brings to mind another delightful picture, probably by the same hand: *Prince in the Zenana Garden,* from the collection of the late Kumar Sangram Singh of Nawalgarh.[18]

Lacking the linear power associated with the Master of Elephants and the Kotah Master, both of whom normally painted pictures celebrating the masculine activities of the men's quarters, they may have been commissioned especially in zenana taste for the delectation of Kotah ladies. During the formative period of the Kotah ateliers, artists' places of origin ranged widely. Although the "Master of the Zenana," as he might be known, appears to have shed most earmarks of his original style after settling at Kotah, enough traces remain to allow speculation. He seems to have emerged from the central Indian tradition, in which artists interpreted the world in rhythmic, broad, flat, brightly colored areas, rich in decorative formulas for trees, flowers, and water — elements that persist here.

The Kotah Master seems to have joined the workshops of Jagat Singh at a propitious moment. The ruler was rich with Deccani spoils and had time for the arts. The workshop of which the Kotah Master was in charge was modest, probably consisting of no more than one or two permanent senior artists and a few apprentices and helpers. (Written historical evidence for the Kotah ateliers is scarce, although information might be found in the

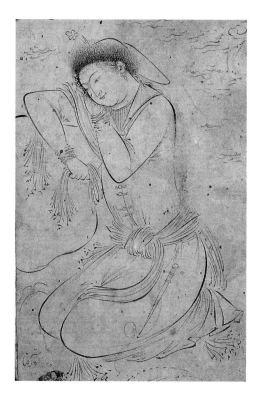

Figure 13
Daydreaming Youth, *Aqa Riza, c. 1585, Isfahan, Iran. Reed pen or brush and black ink on paper, 12 x 6.7 cm. Arthur M. Sackler Museum, Harvard University Art Museums, Cambridge, Massachusetts.*

archives stored at Bikaner. Visual evidence, based on a survey of a great many Kotah pictures, indicates that there were never more than a few master artists, assistants, and apprentices working at Kotah at any one time.) Once the Kotah Master himself entered Kotah employment, his themes were fundamentally transformed. Stock Muslim heroes such as Rustam or Bahram Gur became

Kotah warriors and hunters; dragons and simurghs metamorphosed into elephants and lions or soaring geese. Golconda palaces were transmuted into Kotah forts and pavilions. In *Bhoj Singh of Bundi Slays a Lion*, attributable to him, one of the Kotah ancestors looses a killing arrow into the heart of a striding lion (fig. 10). Close inspection of the angered beast, particularly of his mask, reveals the artist's empathy with the dying animal — and also points to his artistic sources. The stylization of the mask harks back to the noble lions of Persepolis and to those painted in Turkman, Timurid, and Safavid Iran. It scarcely seems coincidental that a striding lion in the foreground of *Faridun Crosses the River Dijleh*, painted by the great Persian artist Sultan-Muhammad in about 1525 for Shah Tahmasp Safavi's copy of the *Shahnameh* (Book of Kings), could easily be mistaken for a Kotah picture (figs. 11 and 12).[19] In the Kotah lion's mask and well-groomed mane, crescendos of calligraphic line thicken, thin, and crisscross with expressively defining elegance. They demonstrate the Kotah artist's mastery of the calligraphic style of Aqa Riza,[20] the influential later Safavid draftsman and painter, who drew in the rhythmic flourishes of Nastaliq script; for visual evidence of the spread of the Iranian's style to Kotah via Golconda and Aurangabad, we might compare the undulating sinuosities of the Kotah Master's lion mask with Aqa Riza's brilliant reed pen sketch of a youth (fig. 13).[21] Both artists delighted in metaphor: the Kotah Master lent his lion's ears the geometric grace of conch shells, and Aqa Riza's youth's hands became flowers.

The Kotah Master's interpretations of blood sports transmuted them from mundane reality to otherworldliness. If we compare earlier hunting pictures from Bundi or Kotah to his, it is evident that he brought new symbolic depth to this very Rajput activity. In *A Raja Slays a Tiger*, for example, probably painted at Bundi in about 1625, a true-to-life hunter batters a ferociously credible wounded beast with the butt of his matchlock (fig. 16).[22] Tree, rocks, starry sky, and grass are alive with rhythmic force and glowing color; but the drama — with its pathetic white cow serving as dead tethered bait, a terrified fellow huntsman, and the intent raja, balancing on a cot (*charpoi*) safely up a tree — describes a particular act of skill and bravery. It contrasts sharply with *Bhoj Singh of Bundi Slays a Lion* (fig. 10), in which the splendidly regal, jeweled, and plumed Rajput, graceful as a Safavid Bahram Gur or Rustam, draws his bow with Nijinskian verve, releasing an exquisite shaft into a lion more magnificent than those from any jungle. Although the artist has captured the determined spirits of both man and beast, he projects their drama as an emblematic, cosmic metaphor: a good ruler triumphing over an evil monster.

The Kotah Master's Iranian — specifically Turkman and Safavid — stylistic roots are even more clearly demonstrated in a partially colored drawing attributable to him (fig. 14). In it, a graceful, Rustam-like hero topples a snarlingly petulent demon (*div*). Line

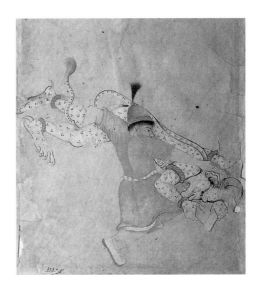

Figure 14
A Hero Topples a Demon (Div), *attributed to the Kotah Master (perhaps working after a tracing from the painting shown here as fig. 15), late seventeenth century, possibly the Deccan, Golconda or Aurangabad. Black ink and opaque watercolor on paper, 24.2 x 22.5 cm. Private collection in the Arthur M. Sackler Museum, Harvard University Art Museums, Cambridge, Massachusetts.*

for line, this was borrowed from a powerful Turkman picture in the so-called Yaqub Bek Album[23] preserved in the Topkapi Sarayi Museum Library of Istanbul (fig. 15). It is quite likely that the Kotah Master's picture was based on a version of the Turkman picture brought to Golconda by its founder, Sultan-Quli Qutbul Mulk, the erstwhile Aq-Quyunlu prince admired for his knowledge

Figure 15
A Hero Topples a Demon (Div), *showing Aq-Quyunlu Turkman style, c. 1450– 1500, Tabriz, Iran. Black and opaque watercolor and gold on paper, 19.2 x 27 cm. After Ipsiroglu 1976, pl. 32.*

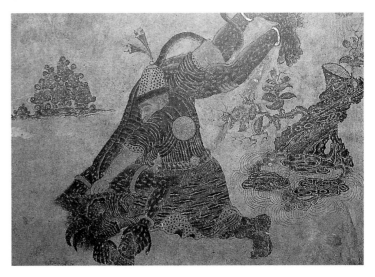

and patronage of poetry and art. Whether executed at Golconda, Aurangabad, or Kotah, this spirited picture owes its existence to a tracing or pounce, which the artist chose to reverse. While drawing it, he transformed the fifteenth-century Aq-Quyunlu line of the original into the more graceful and currently influential mode of Aqa Riza. Examined together, details of the Kotah Master's lion mask and his demon's face point strongly to a Turkman-Golconda-Kotah connection.

Works attributable to the Kotah Master show him to have been greatly prolific: he not only drew and painted on paper, but also turned his hand to painting murals, at least one of which, a ceiling in the Chhattar Mahal, has survived (fig. 17). Although crudely restored in areas damaged by monsoon rains, the swirling composition of simurghlike birds, geese, and other local plumed game, framed in characteristic Golconda arabesques, brings to mind the sharply observed sketch of Kotah geese reproduced above (fig. 2). Occupying a space that was once the portico leading into the room containing the Master of Elephants' mural cycle, the ceiling suffered considerably from lengthy exposure to intense sunlight before the wide entrance was narrowed toward the end of the nineteenth century. At that time, the new interior walls, to the right and left of the door, were decorated with awkwardly amusing pictures containing railway trains, steamboats, Victorian costumes,

and other exotic elements. These can be assigned to the same daubers who so carefully gummed over the Master of Elephants' murals.

Far more important, and calling for serious study, are the earlier, also faded and damaged, wall paintings in this erstwhile portico. Consisting of hunts, processions, darbars, animal studies, and many other standard secular Kotah topics, they appear to have been painted over several decades, from the later seventeenth century into the 1740s. Masterly and finely drawn, and colored in a style that contains Deccani, Mughal, and Kotah elements, they can be ascribed to the Kotah Master, working over several decades, later assisted by his most illustrious successor, Sheikh Taju, who is discussed below. Although they do not display the full measure of the Kotah Master's linear exuberance, many details are strikingly similar to his more familiar work, in full Kotah style. As noted above, *Rao Ram Singh of Kotah Pursuing a Rhinoceros,* for instance, appears on the wall in the restrained Deccani-Mughal mode probably representative of the Kotah Master's style before he adjusted to the more dynamically expressive Kotah ways shown him by the Master of Elephants. Similar in style are hundreds of figures, among whom are several in early-seventeenth-century Safavid dress, with the bulky, loosely tied turbans also seen in mid- to late-seventeenth-century Golconda pictures. It is tempting to posit that

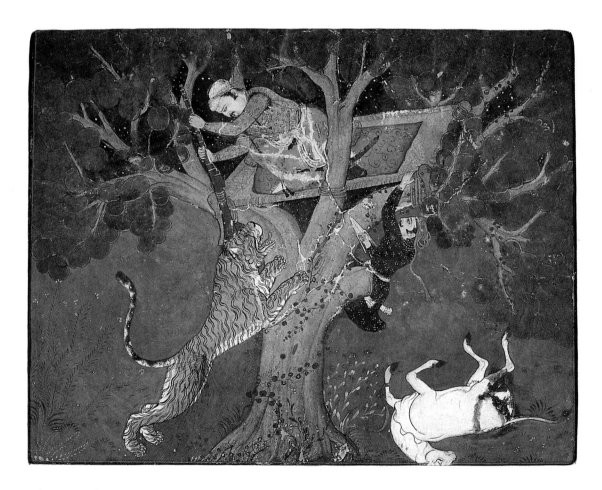

Figure 16
A Raja Slays a Tiger, *c. 1625, Bundi. Opaque watercolor on paper, 18.4 x 23.7 cm. Private collection in the Arthur M. Sackler Museum, Harvard University Art Museums, Cambridge, Massachusetts.*

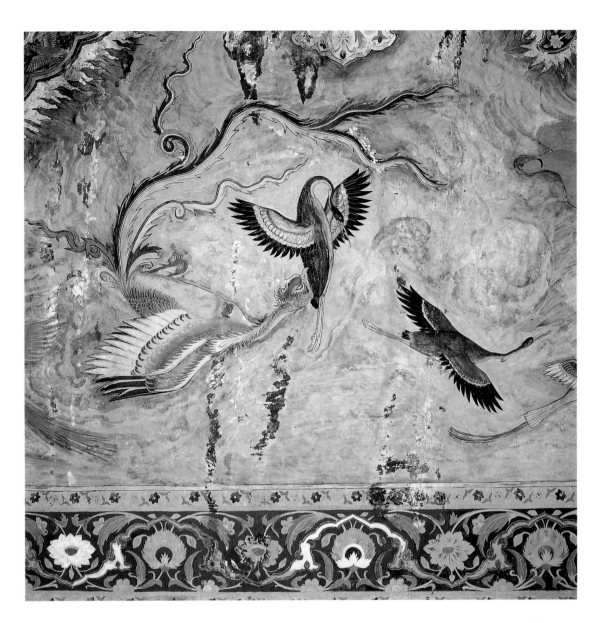

Figure 17
Worldly and Otherworldly Birds,
ceiling painting from the Chhattar Mahal,
Kotah Fort, attributed to the Kotah
Master, Kotah, c. 1680–1710. Opaque
watercolor on fibrous ground prepared
with lime, detail illustrated approx.
305 x 305 cm.

these fascinating murals were initiated by the Kotah Master, working in his disciplined Mughal-Deccani style, shortly after he had arrived in Kotah from Aurangabad, perhaps just before his painted ceiling. In any case, this mural cycle must have been carried out over many years, eventually in collaboration with Sheikh Taju, who probably finished it after the Kotah Master's death. Unfortunately, most of the rulers' portraits, which would have helped to date the pictures, have been effaced or covered over.

Few if any other Rajput artists of any period drew as brilliantly as the Kotah Master, who seems to have carried brushes, paints, and paper on his daily rounds — a constructive and sociable habit emulated by later generations of Kotah artists. His powerful yet subtle sketches provide candid glimpses of local folk in fort, palace, and town. Like other inventive artists in the Turko-Indo-Iranian tradition, he drew from life to provide models for his finished works, which almost always reveal draftsmanly bones beneath their coloring. When he sketched, most often with a brush, his line was fine and free, spirited onto the paper at lightning speed. He usually began with faint outlines in red or gray pigment, strengthening them later with deeper grays and blacks. Like his colleagues, he drew corrections over the scumbled whites employed to hide mistakes. In works intended for presentation to his patrons, backgrounds were often enriched and lent lively depth around figures and animals by networks of crosshatching. Beautiful in themselves, these are as crisply articulate as another characteristic element of his pictorial vocabulary: banks of fine, arcing brushstrokes, reminiscent of wheatfields undulating in a brisk wind. When, like other Turko-Indo-Iranian artists, the Kotah Master pointed his brush, he created richly colored abstractions, unique as handwriting in their shapes and touch. His are especially rich, dense, and emotionally charged, akin to Jackson Pollock's inspired drips or Cy Twombly's poetic scribbles.

Beyond his piercingly observant eye, or even the dynamic grace of his line, the Kotah Master's harmonious understanding of nature was his rarest gift. He may have embraced the Sufi mysticism that flourished in Muslim India. In any case, he seems to have been able easily to project himself into the movements of clouds, flowing water, or animals, and although he happily painted royalty and royal activities, nothing was too humble, trivial, or small for his attention. Every inch of his pictures rewards scrutiny, from the spontaneous rhythmic choreography danced by tiny hairs sprouting from Bhoj Singh's lion's upper lip (fig. 11) to the sensitively rendered veins, resembling river systems or charts of the human nervous system, on the back of an elephant's ear (fig. 18). His pictorial range, encompassing the entire panorama of Kotah — its people, architecture, flora, fauna, and still life — was established not only by his own inclinations, but by his patrons' requests. Without these, the Kotah Master might not have drawn and painted so many Hindu subjects, the multiplicity of which reflects the increasing interest in Vaishnava devotion, not only at Kotah, but at other Rajasthani centers, during the eighteenth century. In the past, religious subjects had usually been painted or drawn in appropriately traditional, archaic, and indigenous modes, giving form to inner visions rather than to anything observed. In this respect, they differed greatly from the comparative naturalism of hunting scenes, historical incidents, or portraits, which were often influenced by Mughal and European examples.

Although the Kotah Master was probably born a Muslim, his Golconda influences clearly included tolerance — also a Sufi value; in Golconda, the arts blended Muslim elements from Turkman and Safavid Iran and Mughal India with those from indigenous Hindu traditions of Andhra Pradesh. Equally accepting and understanding of religious and cultural differences were his Kotah patrons, whose long Mughal service in the Deccan taught them to appreciate Muslim culture. Prior to the move to Rajasthan, however, it is unlikely that he experienced life in a predominantly Hindu Rajput community. Once there, busily painting and drawing, he partook of local customs and festivals, thereby expanding his artistic repertoire. Initially, however, Hindu subjects attributable to the Kotah Master were his least characteristic pictures, and it would seem that some if not all of them were carried out with the aid of his workshop. Later, he enriched standardized compositions with motifs derived from his sketches, as can be seen in several sets of musical modes, the *Barahmasa*s, and others. Included here is his *May/June (Jeth Masa)* — the hottest month, when elephants seek shade and are so distracted that they will suffer the presence of their archenemy, the tiger (cat. 40). Also attributable to the Kotah Master and his workshop is *Krishna Hiding the Milkmaids' Clothing (Gopivashtraharana)*, the much-loved scene of youthful Krishna playfully hiding the clothes of bathing milkmaids (cat. 28).

If the Kotah Master was disinclined to paint such pictures, which at times verge on sentimentality and occasionally are explicitly amorous, there is no hint of any distaste in his work.[24]

Emperor Aurangzeb, the last militantly orthodox emperor, unintentionally sparked a Hindu renaissance. His defeat of the Deccani sultanates, achieved at the cost of overextending Mughal territories and draining imperial power, not only catalyzed and enriched northern Indian culture by bringing in talent from the Deccan but also enabled the rajas, maharajas, and raos to remain at home long enough to cultivate religion and the arts of peace. Kotah painting's themes and moods reflect this in such exciting projects as the Kotah Master's delightfully inventive *Ramayana* set, probably commissioned by Rao Ram Singh (r. 1696–1707) and left unfinished at his death. One of its lively illustrations, in the collection of Dr. Horst Metzger, depicts the battle of tyrannical Ravan and his demon army against admirable Ram and Lakshman, who triumphed with the help of toothy black bears and two sorts of scampering monkeys (fig. 19). Although small in size, this jubilantly gratifying scene of good vanquishing evil again recalls works by Sultan-Muhammad, whose comically ferocious demons and soldierly animals are rivaled in zaniness only by the Kotah Master's.[25]

Like Emperor Jahangir's favorite artist, Abul Hasan, the Kotah Master seems to have been able to paint anything and everything. Both painters stand out among Indian artists of all schools for their brilliant psychological portraits, natural-history studies, and densely complex scenes containing many human figures, buildings, and animals; both drew and painted with compelling verve and total conviction.[26] The Kotah Master's breadth is apparent in a damaged drawing laying bare the horrors and heroics of battle, probably as experienced at Dharmat in 1658, when four Kotah princes were slain and only one survived.[27] Perhaps a design for a wall painting or large picture on cloth, this venturesome composition is coherent and dramatic. The sprawling melee of compacted horsemen, elephants, and foot soldiers, charged with bloodcurdling anecdote and pinned together by a rhythmic war dance of spears, attests to the artist's intellectual capacity in its resourceful disposition of wheeling multitudes. Probably commissioned by the survivor, Kishor Singh (r. 1684–96), whose bleeding but brighteyed young body is shown being hauled from the welter, it can be seen as a tattered dress rehearsal for a later painting, dated 1720, *The Battle of Pandher*.[28] Although damaged, clumsily reworked in several areas, and apparently carried out with the help of an assistant, this surging clash of arms includes troops of elephants, horses, and bold Rajputs, presented in the Kotah Master's vigorously authoritative manner. A more evocative presentation in Indian art of the noise, chaos, bravery, and horror of hand-to-hand combat is difficult to imagine.

The Kotah Master was also a gifted portraitist. His delightful characterization of a beguilingly assiduous matchlock-maker, squatting next to his tools while shaping a stock, is evidently based on a sketch from life (cat. 26). It is one of several portraits that exemplify his knack for making psychologically penetrating likenesses of every kind of person: royalty, ladies of the zenana, soldiers, craftsmen.

Although Maharao Arjun Singh reigned only from 1720 to 1723, there are paintings that surely commemorate his effective and congenial patronage of the Kotah Master. From them, it is evident that the maharao's character was true to the Kotah pattern: a blend of religious devotion, sociability, and good humor, qualities vitally united by the Kotah Master in a pair of large compositions showing the maharao celebrating Krishna's birthday, the Janmashtami Festival (cat. 21 and 22). For Arjun Singh, in whom worldliness and spirituality met, the artist combined his religious mode — the dashing style associated with his musical modes and other Hindu subjects — with the finely finished, more naturalistic style usually reserved for secular topics. In these sparkling souvenirs of a joyous party, the merry ruler, his family, courtiers, musicians, and a battery of singing and dancing girls and youths seem to have tripped from the flashing brush at dizzying speed. We meet the artist's entire repertoire of figures and faces, many of them in profile. Eyes resembling half-opened clamshells and talkative open mouths issue from a seeming chaos of knowingly scribbled dashes, dots, and rectangles. Casual as these shorthand brushstrokes might seem, they were rendered with such utter conviction that the people they evoke ring true. These amusing yet serious pictures, painted after the death of Aurangzeb, describe the ecstatic releases of Vaishnava bhakhti practices. This movement flourished at Rajput courts during the early eighteenth century, and inasmuch as its divine message and techniques of worship — dancing, singing, and spinning — are paralleled in Sufi practices, they would probably not have been unfamiliar to the Kotah Master.

The maharao's devotions appear again, hardly less festively, in *Brijnathji and Maharao Arjun Singh aboard a Hunting Barge on the Chambal River* (cat. 19). Like the two pictures of Krishna's birthday party, this one was painted in the Kotah Master's simplified, bold style. God, maharao, and devotee share not only a barge, but the shapes of nose and beak. The shape of the maharao's is echoed in the beak of the Garuda (the mythical parrotlike godling whose plumed form is both Brijrajji's vehicle and Kotah's emblem) and in the noses of the devotee and of Brijnathji (the tutelary deity of Kotah; cat. 42). Painterly passages abound here, in the glittering configurations of the seated god, the reverent devotee, the adoring maharao, the boatloads of musicians, and the aloofly royal, dragonlike crocodile finial on the prow. Boulders and rocks along the riverbank form a worshipful chorus of grotesques.

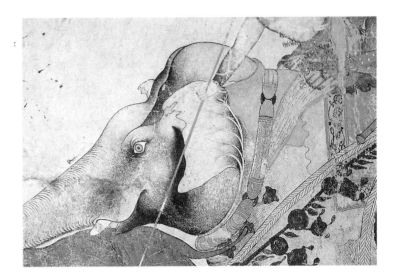

Figure 18
Detail of Rao Ram Singh of Kotah Pursuing a Rhinoceros, *attributed to the Kotah Master, Kotah, c. 1690. Opaque watercolor on paper, 32.1 x 47.6 cm. Private collection in the Arthur M. Sackler Museum, Harvard University Art Museums, Cambridge, Massachusetts.*

Yet another vigorous picture attributable to the Kotah Master at about the same time honors Maharao Arjun Singh's militaristically Rajput persona, in the role of Brijnathji on a war chariot (cat. 20). Even such minor details as ropes and bridles recall the Kotah Master's powerful line, as seen in the bell-ropes of Rao Ram Singh's hurtling elephant.[29] Slightly earlier, perhaps, is *Dancers*, a large painted pas de deux, in which natural forms are transformed into startlingly playful shapes (cat. 33).

A large hunting scene of golden-skinned Brijnathji and Maharao Durjan Sal (r. 1723–56) hunting lions seems to have been planned and largely drawn and painted by the Kotah Master himself, with the assistance of a lesser hand, perhaps Sheikh Taju (cat. 29). The visionary junglescape, with its rhythmic patterns of flowering trees, lacy grasses, and stands of bamboo harking back to the setting of *Bhoj Singh of Bundi Slays a Lion* (fig. 10), is reminiscent of the artist's strength in landscape painting.

By the later 1730s, the Kotah Master shows signs of age; his hand seems to lose its steadiness, and his eyesight some of its sharpness. Like other wise old artists, he continued to explore new ground, as can be seen in his very late, small, deeply glowing portrayal of Maharao Durjan Sal and Brijnathji hunting deer (cat. 35). The god, who resembles Arjun Singh, props his matchlock on the shoulder of an obliging bull, perhaps a good-humored reference to the artist's own need for help in stabilizing his brush. The deer and bull, painted with undiminished charm, are hesitantly outlined, and passages of crosshatching, while still vigorous, lack crispness. This humble, slightly awkward little painting is nevertheless one of the artist's most moving compositions.

The Kotah Master's evolution as an artist is traceable from the 1670s, when he might have been in his late twenties, into the 1730s, when he was eighty or older. Most of his career seems to have been spent at the Kotah court. After having been hired by Jagat Singh and brought to Rajasthan, he eased away from his Golconda-Aurangabad style — perhaps under the guidance or influence of the Master of Elephants — and adjusted fulfillingly to Rajput life. His patrons included six Kotah rulers, whose Hinduism he clearly respected. Encouraged by imaginative and supportive patrons, the Kotah Master changed the course of art at Kotah. Along with his essentially serious vision of humanity and nature, the scintillating line of his reportorial vignettes of Kotah's people, animals, and places provided a legacy that was studied, emulated, and expanded upon by generations of successors.

Sheikh Taju and Later Kotah Artists

Sheikh Taju probably entered Kotah service when the Kotah Master was well on in age. Following his dynasty's custom, the patron, probably Maharao Bhim Singh I (r. 1707–20), sought an artist of equivalent stature to assist, learn from, and eventually replace the genius from Aurangabad.[30] Sheikh Taju was prolific, industrious to a fault, and almost as talented as the Kotah Master. If his name were not known from several inscribed pictures, he could be dubbed the "Master of Elephants II," for these quintessential denizens of Kotah art were his primary subject. In the tradition of the Master of Elephants, he studied their many moods with the combined intensities of a scientist, documentary filmmaker, choreographer, and stand-up comedian.

Sheikh Taju seems rarely to have put down brush, paints, and paper; even more than his predecessor, he explored the far reaches of the kingdom of Kotah, from its forts to its towns and countryside, drawing everything that crossed his path. A major inscribed work, and a key to his style, is a finely finished studio picture, a processional double portrait showing Maharao Durjan Sal and Maharana Jagat Singh of Mewar (r. 1734–52) carried in a palanquin (cat. 36).[31] Sensibly and practically, the artist lavished time on the rulers' portraits: their faces, jewels, and costumes were built up painstakingly, with several levels of finely burnished pigment. While these minutely detailed passages show that he had mastered the nuances of Mughal and Deccani technique, he took less trouble when drawing and painting mere soldiers. The maharana and maharao are impressively characterized, worthy of close inspection; their underlings, reduced to ranks of squat, mustached ciphers, are unlikely to be examined with care, or remembered.

In such pictures, intended for presentation, Sheikh Taju's formal style is apparent in all its strengths and weaknesses. Outlines are hard-edged and firm; shading, based on the techniques of the Master of Elephants and the Kotah Master, is carried out with almost excessively fine, localized crosshatches or arcing lines. Proportions of people and animals are compact, almost squat. Always impressive, spritely, and enjoyable, the best of his presentation pictures are also expressive and moving. The least good, somewhat overwrought, become dryly, admirably academic.[32]

Resembling this double portrait is another likeness of an eminent figure in a palanquin, *The Mughal Emperor Farrukh Siyar Carried in a Palanquin* (cat. 18). Farrukh Siyar (r. 1713–19) welcomed Rajputs into his personal circle at court. Here, the artist follows the Kotah Master's formula for eyes (half-opened clamshells), carefully modeled forms, and repeated curlicues, but the senior artist's penetrating characterization is missing. Although no element of Farrukh Siyar's august countenance has been omitted, the emperor, in whose studios Sheikh Taju probably was trained — and perhaps intimidated — is little more than a clotheshorse. The characterization is far less penetrating and sympathetic than the sheikh's studies of elephants. A more compelling side of Sheikh Taju is found in a drawing inscribed with his name: *Siege of a Strong Fort*, a detailed and informative encyclopedia of military techniques (cat. 17).[33] This fanciful yet believable sketch tallies well with the sheikh's other spontaneously conceived pictures, a survey of which reveals a penchant for military topics. Forts, battles, and soldierly paraphernalia are itemized so accurately as to suggest that he, like a number of Mughal artists who were soldiers as well as painters, had experienced military life. But if he was soldierly, he was also an aesthete, and at times a visionary. This *Siege* and two other attributable works — *Great Siege* (cat. 23), a tinted, cartographic fantasy reminiscent of Brueghel's *Tower of Babel*, and the monochromatic *Bird's-Eye View of a Fort* (cat. 38) — are among his most imaginatively appealing drawings. Although both hint that his military specialties might have included topographical rendering and mapmaking, the second quite literally carried its artist and the viewer above earthliness, to heights from which fort walls resemble unmilitarily frivolous ribbons. The picture's amusing, mysterious incidents reward close inspection. Near one of the edges of this drawing, which can be approached from every direction, is a scene worthy of comic opera: two tightrope walkers inch along, to the sound of drumming, to one of the battlements.

Related to this group is the small bird's-eye projection of fort ramparts, garden, and moat, made all the more delightful, yet hauntingly nostalgic, by the total absence of people and animals

Figure 19
Ram and Lakshman, Aided by the Bears and the Monkeys, Defeat the Demon Ravan *(from a* Ramayana *series), attributed to the Kotah Master, c. 1700, Kotah. Opaque watercolor on paper, 28.2 x 36.6 cm. Collection of Dr. Horst Metzger.*

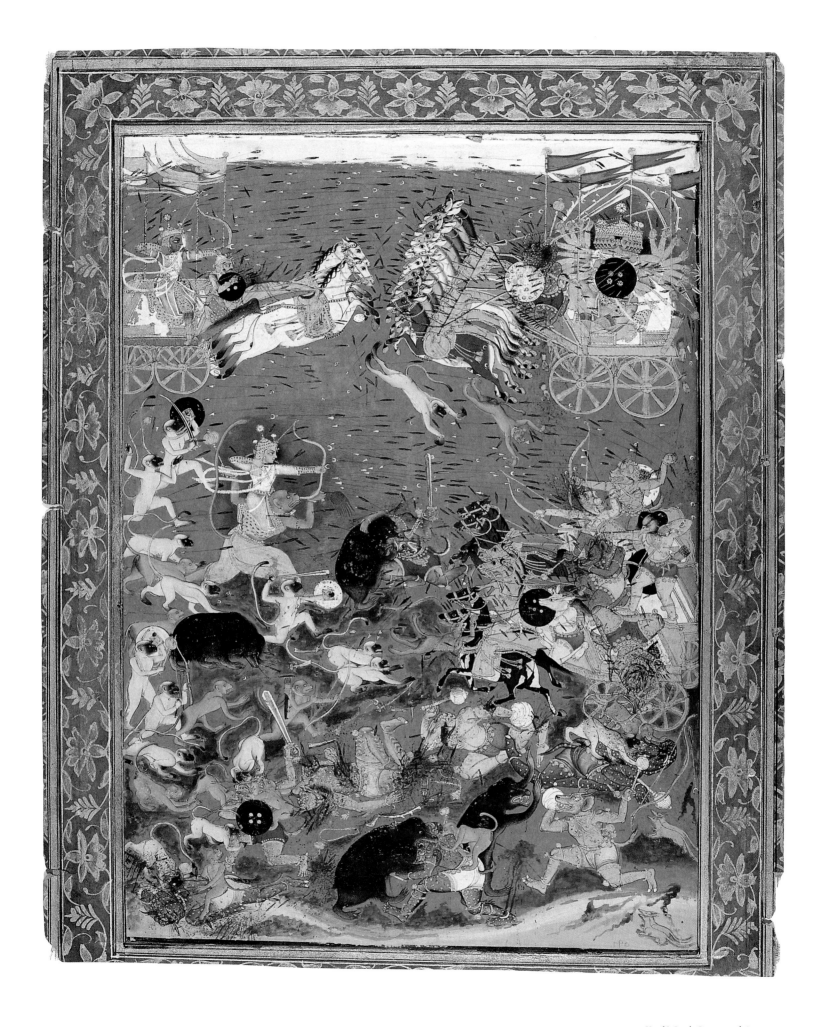

(cat. 39). The palette, the sheikh's favorite, is limited to the natural tone of the paper, white, black, and Indian yellow, to which have been added tiny accents of richly colored flowers.

Ranking high in the great tradition of paintings of elephants established by the Master of Elephants and the Kotah Master is a starkly moving tinted drawing, *A Chained Elephant*, attributable to Sheikh Taju (cat. 31). Confronted by the low protective wall between elephants during combats — the frequent lifesaver of both elephants and mahouts — this monumental champion looms silently. At once eager, pensive, and apprehensive, he is the soulful Hamlet of his breed. Though his head is held proudly and his rear legs are dug in as though to lunge against an opponent, his tail sags slightly, suggesting doubt. As in the bird's-eye view of a fort, colors were chosen with wise economy: yellows, whites, discreetly placed bright accents, and admirably scumbled greens, hinting at past battles. Starkly dramatic, this is one of Sheikh Taju's most expressive presentation pictures, one in which his excitement seems to have been fully sustained throughout the long process of making it.

Comparably praiseworthy is another splendid elephant attributable to Sheikh Taju, *Maharao Durjan Sal's Elephant, Kisanprasad* (cat. 27). In this true portrait, surely based on an actual episode, Kisanprasad lifts into the air a snarling, terrified panther, whose imminent and gory death by crushing and tusking is signaled by the mahout's blood-red saddle blanket. Blood spurts unsettlingly from the panther's eyes. Although this hunting drama ranks among Kotah art's inspiring achievements, in several ways it is outshone by the Kotah Master's animal studies. If we compare the dynamic gestures, impassioned expressions, and whipping lines of bell-ropes by the earlier artist to equivalent passages by Sheikh Taju, the latter's are slackly ponderous, less sharply observed, and considerably less animated.

A group of drawings of Mughal darbars attributable to Sheikh Taju further attests to the artist's presumed affiliation with the imperial ateliers. The earliest of these (cat. 16) resembles darbar scenes in the *Padshahnameh*, Shah Jahan's official history of his reign. In the drawing, the enthroned emperor receives three of his four sons, Princes Dara Shikoh, Shah Shuja, and Murad Baksh, who appears to be about fifteen, which dates the darbar to about 1639. Whatever the occasion, Aurangzeb is absent. Although parts of this composition closely resemble comparable passages painted for the now incomplete Windsor Castle manuscript, it is not based on any specific painting as yet uncovered. The drawing is painstakingly detailed, finely worked in lean, wiry outlines. There are no traces of Kotah idiom. Although attributable to Sheikh Taju, it must have been composed in a Mughal workshop by tracing segments of Mughal originals prior to his departure for Kotah, for only there would its especially fine and thin paper — finer than those employed at Kotah — have been available.

The second, considerably larger, drawing of a darbar scene exemplifies Sheikh Taju's work after he had joined the Kotah ateliers and learned the Kotah style. Purely Kotah in draftsmanship, characteristically zoomorphic, and comically outlandish, it shows a young tiger striding unabashedly through an imperial darbar. Although he is silhouetted against the throne platform, no one is in the least perturbed. The emperor, most formal of all, does not deign to look, and his many courtiers are resolutely unflappable (cat. 15). The third darbar, mistakenly inscribed with the name of Emperor Aurangzeb, depicts Kotah Rajputs being received at court, probably to hear their imperial assignments or to be rewarded for bravery. Demonstrating solidarity with their overlords, the Kotah courtiers are lightly bearded in Mughal style.[34]

Sheikh Taju continued to grow as an artist during his long life at Kotah, where he served under a succession of seven maharaos. His second Kotah patron probably was Maharao Bhim Singh I's heir, Maharao Arjun Singh, and he remained in service during the reign of Maharao Umed Singh I, if we are to accept the date of 1780 on an unfinished tinted sketch of a hunting scene.[35]

Sheikh Taju's fine Mughal brush drawing gradually gave way to bolder Kotah idioms, carried out with thicker brushes, often over charcoaled outlines. Artists at Kotah adjusted their styles to their patrons' wishes and needs. When a maharao commissioned a portrait, hunting scene, wall painting, or elephant study, he, or someone in charge of the painting atelier, stipulated the size, complexity of the composition, and degree of finish. Sometimes, it appears, he asked for work in the earlier manner of a particularly admired picture. Sheikh Taju, therefore, painted and drew pictures of great variety. Although he seems to have been happiest when drawing and painting boldly from nature, he occasionally was called upon to revert to his finely naturalistic Mughal mode, as in his contributions to the wall paintings initiated by the Kotah Master in the portico of the Chhattar Mahal, beneath the ceiling of simurghs, geese, and arabesques. Inasmuch as the atelier's earlier works, by whichever artist, were readily available, they could be reused at will; and many of the motifs in these murals were traced from admired older images. One of these, as previously noted, is the memorable *Rao Ram Singh of Kotah Pursuing a Rhinoceros* (fig. 1).[36] Fresh designs were also made for this complex of images, balanced across the walls like a juggler's lemons, oranges, and pineapples. One of them, a circular hunting composition in which two furious water buffalo ram their horns deeply into two horses' bellies, shows Maharao Durjan Sal (r. 1723–56) wounding one of them with an arrow.

Inasmuch as Sheikh Taju's tenure at Kotah seems to have overlapped with the Kotah Master's, it is not surprising that attributing pictures to one or the other can be difficult. *Elephants and Horses Assembled before the Image of Brijnathji, Who Is Seen Looking Down from a*

Balcony in the Palace, an excellent large drawing, probably for a wall painting, could almost be their collaborative effort (cat. 30). Although its logical treatment of space would seem to stem from Sheikh Taju's imperial training, the dashingly bold draftsmanship is reminiscent of the Kotah Master. Complex and highly finished portraits of elephants in ranks, each inscribed with its name; a mob of formally arranged soldiers and attendants; and the particularly detailed and articulate study of the main courtyard of Kotah Fort must represent several weeks of hard work. One of the elephants, animatingly redrawn over whited-out mistakes, prostrates himself before Brijnathji. Behind him stands a mysterious boxlike structure once used to house the tigers or other animals released in staged combats. The small, seated observer, almost outside the picture at the lower right, appears to be a portrait of a friend — or even a self-portrait.

Two spirited drawings are easier to attribute to Sheikh Taju working alone. The first, *An Elephant near a Palace Gate*, of about 1730 (cat. 24), retains Mughal spatial characteristics in the relationship between figures and architecture, while harking back to both the Master of Elephants and the Kotah Master in its vigor of interpretation. It suggests that the excellence of Kotah pictures of elephants — even Sheikh Taju's — depended largely on the atelier's rich archive of drawings and tracings by the major earlier artists. The second, *Camp of Maharao Shatru Sal I*, is a monumentally large, later, and bolder tinted drawing on cotton, probably conceived as a major piece of ephemera to adorn a tent wall (cat. 44). Datable to 1764, this tour de force commemorates a prestigious gathering following a battle. For Shatru Sal I (r. 1758–64) and the throngs of guests, troops, and attendants seen in the picture, it would have been a gripping forerunner of today's newsreels or televised current events. In response to the ambitious challenge, the artist thoughtfully expanded his usually far smaller slice of the world to encompass a spectacular panorama as seen by a bird in flight. Artfully, he filled the corners with forms that lure the viewer's eyes back toward the center; then he roughed in tents, enclosures for horses, elephants, and other animals; finally, he piled anecdote upon anecdote. Sheikh Taju's endearing corrections, one of which buries horses beneath an elephant, lend spontaneity to this stirring entertainment, in which every consequential personage can be found — in a few cases, several times. Shatru Sal I and his powerful chief minister, Zalim Singh Jhala, chat in a tent; courtiers babble; cooks cook; waiters wait; and grooms struggle to separate fighting stallions. For insights into Rajput life at camp, no more explicit account could be found.

Sheikh Taju was commissioned to paint religious pictures as well as portraits, hunts, and depictions of every sort of Rajput activity. *Heroine Going to Meet Her Lover (Krishna Abhisarika Nayika)*, datable to about 1750, brings a much-loved Hindu scene to a Kotah

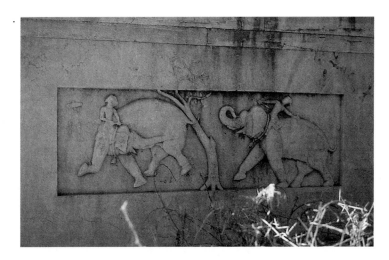

Figure 20
A Conversation of Elephants, *stone relief from one of the Kotah cenotaphs* (chatri*s*), *perhaps designed by Sheikh Taju, eighteenth century, Kotah.*

setting. The eager heroine approaches a pleasure pavilion, observed from above by Krishna, the Divine Lover (cat. 37). H.H. Maharao Brijraj Singh, in his thoughtful account of this painting, suggests that the pleasure palace is Umed Gañj, seven miles east of Kotah; he also identifies many of the trees and bushes.[37] Sheikh Taju rendered these in an ornamental counterpoint. Clusters of foliage and green fruit emerge from rhythmically composed trunks and limbs akin to those in his hunting pictures. Reminding us of the affinity between painting and music in Rajput art, these rhythms intensify the picture's sensuous spirit. Passionate anticipation is stirred by the flaming reds and oranges of the costumes, canopies, and carpets, glowing against the charged patterns of greenery beneath a broodingly dark sky.

Although his characterizations of people probe less deeply than the Kotah Master's, Sheikh Taju compensated for this by becoming Kotah art's most penetrating psychologist of elephants. In revealing nuances of mood, his portraits of them surpass those of his predecessors. Never sentimentalizing or anthropomorphizing these fascinating animals, he recorded not only the truculence that makes them dangerous and as hard to handle as live bombs but also their moments of amiability, tenderness, and even self-doubt. On grounds of style, it seems likely that Sheikh Taju's elephants were so respected that he was commissioned to design and supervise — if not cut into stone — bas-reliefs of elephants on several of the Kotah cenotaphs (*chhatris*), the memorials to the raos and maharaos constructed at the locations where their bodies were burned (fig. 20).

Kotah's major artists give every evidence of being long-lived. Nevertheless, the time came when Sheikh Taju's final patron, Maharao Umed Singh I, fearing that his studios might lose their director, sought younger talent. The search seems to have been carried out with the help of Zalim Singh Jhala, whose distaste for half measures prompted the hiring of not one promising master, as in the past, but several. On the basis of their work, it is clear that these well-trained new arrivals came from Mewar, the seniormost Rajput court, which had become ever more closely linked to Kotah under Maharaos Durjan Sal and Umed Singh I. The new artists' decoratively patterned trees and foliage, long a Mewar specialty, attest to their place of origin.[38]

Seemingly appreciative of the newcomers' gift for decorative landscape, Sheikh Taju employed such passages to enrich the hunting scenes eagerly commissioned by Maharao Umed Singh I and his chief minister, both of whom were ardent shots. At Kotah, as at Bundi, hunting pictures had been favored by a succession of patrons, but now that so many more were ordered by the maharao and his chief minister, a problem loomed. Although Sheikh Taju himself could — and did — satisfy some of the demand, it was insatiable. He needed help. Unfortunately, the new arrivals' animals were undistinguished. Although few Rajput artists could match their cheerfully bright, tapestrylike jungles and gardens, their animals are drab. At best, they are sleek but lifeless; at worst, they resemble overchewed teddy bears or Christmas stockings.

Sheikh Taju's example, and cleverness, saved the day. He devised eye-catching compositions in which both hunters and hunted — as though camouflaged — are hard to single out in lushly conceived Kotah junglescapes. Despite problems of draftsmanship, these hunting pictures stir delight, ranking high not only among Kotah pictures, but among Indian paintings of all schools. They could, indeed, be the legendary pictures occasionally supposed to have inspired the Douanier Rousseau's lushly poetic canvases of nude women in jungles.

Maharao Umed Singh and His Chief Minister, Zalim Singh Jhala, Tiger Shooting is one of the earlier examples of this greatly appealing genre (cat. 45). Fully inscribed, like most of these hunting pictures, it gives the huntsmen's names along with the time and place of the kill. It also says that it was "from the hand of the painter S[h]eikh Taju." Most of the painted surface is taken up by visually exciting jungle vegetation, within which men and animals are as difficult to spot as they would be during an actual hunt.

Although the Mewar artists never recorded animal anatomy or plumbed animal psychology to the degrees achieved by earlier Kotah artists, they soon adjusted to the Kotah style. Before he vanished from the Kotah scene, Sheikh Taju served as mentor and teacher to Joshi Hansraj, Joshi Hatuva, and Sita Ram — who are known by signed paintings — and others. Soon, and with remarkable grace, the Mewar contingent not only mastered, but further enriched the Kotah style.[39]

Kotah Painting and Drawing of the Later Eighteenth and Nineteenth Centuries

The arts at Kotah continued to flourish. Whenever a stylistic flowering seemed to have gone to seed, another sprang to life. Eventually, even Maharao Umed Singh I's thrilling cycle of hunting pictures with their tigerish heroics, royal bravery, and decorative splurges of vegetation lost their savor; the Cleveland Museum of Art's wonderful related picture, in which Vaishnava religiosity and the mysteries of field sports blend, is an exception.[40] But as before, another talented newcomer, under the patronage of another maharao, Maharao Kishor Singh (r. 1819–27), breathed fresh life into the Kotah tradition. This time, art was inspired not by a ruler's enthusiasm for festivals or hunting, but by a certain kind of Vaishnava devotion.

More than his predecessors, Maharao Kishor Singh turned his attention to the shrine at Nathadvara to Shri Nathji, an avatar of Lord Krishna. This shrine centered around a powerful naturally formed image. When it was banished from Mathura by Emperor Aurangzeb, the image was offered sanctuary at Udaipur, the capital of Rajputana's senior ruler, by the rana of Mewar. The god was carried in a sacred procession toward Udaipur, but not many miles from its destination it refused to budge. However many bullocks, camels, elephants, and men tugged at ropes attached to his chariot, Shri Nathji would go no further. The god insisted on remaining at Nathadvara, which soon became one of the holiest of Vaishnava pilgrimage places. Complex rituals, carried out by a large staff of priests, were developed to honor Shri Nathji, who received offerings and changes of costume hour by hour. The shrine expanded, and the holy town of Nathadvara prospered in the service of the deity. Its craftsmen and artists, employed to serve both visiting pilgrims and the temple, developed a new style of painting in the service of Shri Nathji, for whom painted backdrops were commissioned by the shrine's head priest (*mahant*) and staff. Easily damaged, these large pictures on cloth were frequently replaced, lest they offend the god they were made to honor. Visitors to the shrine eagerly acquired paintings of the image and offerings, of the shrine, and of the priests. As at other religious centers, such as Banaras, Puri, and Madurai, accomplished artists supplied works of art for everyone, from simple villagers who could barely afford to spend a few cents for folkloristic daubs, to Maharao Kishor Singh, who preferred highly finished works.

The Kotah collection contains several pictures by a nameless but remarkable Nathadvara artist who apparently was brought to Kotah, along with his work, by the ardent maharao. One of these paintings is a crisp and glowing depiction of Shri Nathji attended by priests (cat. 54). Challengingly, it occupies a stylistic zone midway between Kotah and Nathadvara. This vibrant style, with its crystalline outlining and subtly modulated purple-reds, blue-greens, burning red-oranges, and sulfurous yellows, would have excited Mondrian, Rothko, or Ingres. Evidently, it also excited Maharao Kishor Singh, who nevertheless prompted this remarkable painter from Nathadvara to adjust his style in honor of the Kotah tutelary gods, Brijnathji and Brijrajji. For the maharao, the artist painted two series of devotional pictures, in which the Kotah gods are rendered as Shri Nathji had been, but in a style enriched by the example of earlier Kotah art. As Woodman Taylor has pointed out, Maharao Kishor Singh himself appears as a royal worshiper in many of these brilliant small paintings.[41]

Several of the small devotional pictures commissioned by Maharao Kishor Singh rank high among Kotah paintings. Most impressive, perhaps, is the one in which the household image is backed by two lashed-together palm trees, silhouetted against a vivid red-orange. Although trained as a painter of Shri Nathji and the Nathadvara priesthood, this artist became a remarkable portraitist and still-life painter. His greatest contribution, however, was his extraordinarily original handling of color, which achieved new heights following the move from Nathadvara to Kotah.

The Nathadvara master was a worthy successor to his Kotah predecessors. He perpetuated Kotah's draftsmanly tradition by sketching everything that crossed his path, animals included. For Maharao Kishor Singh — a seeker not of game but of the divine — he probably painted the magnificent devotional hunting scene at Cleveland mentioned above, India's equivalent to Dürer's vision of St. Eustace, in which a gentle, godlike deer, blue as Krishna, transmutes the gory chase.

This last great Kotah artist continued to paint during the reign of Maharao Ram Singh (r. 1827–66), who was one of Kotah's most vigorous and jovially eccentric patrons. Like earlier Kotah rulers enamored of art, he encouraged his painters to note every aspect of Kotah life. And, like Emperor Jahangir, Balwant Singh of Jammu, and other Indian patrons fascinated by people, Maharao Ram Singh urged his artists particularly to fathom and record the personality and activities of his kingdom's preeminent figure, himself. Sometimes, this task was carried out with unanticipated candor. A drawing in a private collection, blessed with the linear elegances associated with ancient Greek oil-jug (lekythos) painting, portrays the spirited ruler sportively adoring five ladies at once. In another picture, he mans an elephant, shoots a tiger, and, without pausing for breath, celebrates the art of love. Apparently given to robust pranks, he — if we are to believe a painting mounted in the Bada Mahal — coaxed an elephant to ascend to the upper floor of a building and walk death-defyingly around its seemingly far too flimsy sandstone skirting. The aftermath was not recorded.

It is a loss to travel art that Maharao Ram Singh was born too early for steam vessels; had he and his artists visited London, Paris, Rome, and the Egyptian pyramids, their fascinatingly quirky paintings and sketches would have revealed new facets of the world. In compensation for these uncreated masterpieces, Maharao Ram Singh's artists left us such delightful pictures as *Maharao Ram Singh Playing Polo near Gagraon* (cat. 63). Soaring at the center of the picture is a large red ball, bracketed by the players and set against a telling if schematic view of Gagraon Fort, protector of the state's southern districts. By now, Mughal-inspired spatial logic and naturalism had given way to older Rajput traditons, in which people, animals, and architecture were assigned amounts of space appropriate to their importance within the royal scheme. Maharao Ram Singh himself and a few admired noblemen loom larger than their underlings, who have been further reduced to unindividualized geometric formulas. Nevertheless, the artist conveys the mood of a friendly game on a sunny day at a particular place, about which we are shown everything Maharao Ram Singh thought we should know. The royal traveler's artists also accompanied him to Jaisalmer, where he was depicted as a bridegroom at the entrance to his bride's palace (cat. 66). He is faced by his new father-in-law, Maharawal Gaj Singh, whose features are as craggily and invitingly caricaturable as Maharao Ram Singh's own.

The gigantic painting commemorating Maharao Ram Singh's visit to Delhi in 1842 (cat. 65) is his penultimate Kotah masterpiece. Crammed with humorous incident, anecdote, and imponderables, it weaves a spell dedicated to its two principals: the last Mughal emperor, Bahadur Shah II (r. 1837–58), and Maharao Ram Singh. Together, they could recall two and a half centuries of close dynastic connections. Sharers of history and legend, the thirty-four-year-old maharao and the sixty-seven-year-old emperor must have been greatly curious about one another, and eager for conversation. Both suffered from a single serious problem: the British. The emperor had lost virtually every vestige of power to them and now held sway over no more than a once-proud palace (the Red Fort of Delhi, or Shah Jahanabad) inhabited by vast numbers of needy retainers and a mob of indigent relatives. But if the Mughal state was enfeebled, Mughal culture continued to thrive. The emperor's intelligence and energy were narrowly channeled by circumstances into writing poetry, which was good, and to encouraging the verse of others, such as Ghalib, which was far better. Maharao Ram Singh had lost less. Although also dominated by the British, life in distant, airy Kotah, with its hunting grounds, agricultural wealth, and supportive court, was less trying. Still, a major mutual complaint must have been the grinding, constant presences of British government residents, nannyish busybodies as unbearable at Kotah as in Shah Jahanabad.

To document this visit, Maharao Ram Singh's artists accompanied him. They sketched diligently from life, noting everything necessary to vivify a picture even larger than Sheikh Taju's sketch of Maharao Shatru Sal I's camp (cat. 44). Maharao Ram Singh is shown twice: once in an outer court of the fort, resplendent on a richly caparisoned elephant, and at the far left, near a comically dressed monkey. From the Shah Burj (Imperial Tower), Bahadur Shah II peeps at the Kotah visitor through a newfangled gilt-brass telescope. From a balcony, the emperor's stout senior wife gazes upon the busy scene. Given the nature of Kotah art, it is not unexpected that this painting is the most detailed, explicit, and lively view of the imperial fort and its surroundings. These include every building, garden, and wall as well as Chandni Chowk (the market) and Shah Jahan's Friday mosque, in which a rude English couple amorously hold hands. Other picturesque topics range from dancing goats to skittish camels, rows of shops and shopkeepers, someone having his armpit shaved by a barber, and — of course — elephants. Who, one wonders, is the fashionable, stout Delhi citizen trotting along in his British carriage? Could he be Hindu Rao, a social force in Delhi prior to the Indian Mutiny?

This huge work, however, was not painted — and then repeated at Kotah as a mural — merely as a diverting account of Maharao Ram Singh's doings in Shah Jahanabad. Despite all of Maharao Ram Singh's efforts, despite his and the emperor's curiosity, and despite his artists' detailed reportage, we are not shown the anticipated fulfilling encounter. Based on the evidence presented by this mural-size painting, we can only conclude that the emperor and the maharao in fact never met. Had they done so, surely the artist would have shown them together. The reason for this frustrating nonevent is easy to guess: neither the Mughal nor the Rajput was permitted to meet the other because their British residents both feared the consequences.

Maharao Ram Singh's visit to Shah Jahanabad took place in 1842, only fifteen years before the Indian Mutiny of 1857, of which Bahadur Shah became the nominal leader. Already rankled in 1842, both the Mughal and the Rajput must have harbored anti-British sentiments, and so the latter's visit was more likely intended for the delivery and discussion of messages from an alliance of his fellows than for sightseeing. This picture, therefore, can be interpreted as a particularly subtle allusion to a Kotah hunting trope. Although Maharao Ram Singh failed to enter the "hunting blind" (machan) — that is, the Red Fort — or even to meet his imperial fellow-huntsman, and although the actual hunt was delayed until 1857, it is hardly coincidental that during the Mutiny Major Burton, the resident, and two of his sons were slain at Kotah. For this crime, and for what was deemed less than full support of the British cause, the maharao's salute was lowered by several guns. Emperor Bahadur Shah was tried in 1858 and exiled to Rangoon, where he died.

Maharao Ram Singh's son and successor, Shatru Sal II (r. 1866–89), maintained his father's studios. Early in his reign, artistic standards were high, sustained by Maharao Ram Singh's surviving painters, who provided fine portraits and genre pictures of an increasingly Westernized world. Kotah artists broadened their repertoires by studying and copying illustrations from imported books and magazines: fashion plates of English ladies and gentlemen, steel engravings of such topics as Napoleon and of Phrygian-capped French revolutionists, and mythological subjects. Studies for architectural decoration — stained-glass windows, stucco ceilings, and tile revetments — were also commissioned, and, as in the past, artists explored fort, palace, and town, sketching everything picturesque. Kotah zest survives in *Thunderous Tryst*, the latest painting included in this exhibition (cat. 67). As passionately erotic as its dragonish golden lightning, this determinedly awkward spoof describes the perils of a disjointed Rajput lover: in hot pursuit of his beloved, he ascends a rope wobbly as overcooked spaghetti.

The royal Kotah ateliers dwindled after the death of Shatru Sal II; photographs replaced miniatures. Maharao Umed Singh II (r. 1889–1940), the next ruler, perfectly exemplified the "age of the Maharajas." Born toward the end of the nineteenth century, he escaped the hostile bitterness of the British following the Indian Mutiny, and his death in 1940 spared him both the rigors of World War II and the dramatic disruption of royal Indian life that marked the end of the Raj in 1947. He was educated when it was the policy of the Queen Empress's goverment to control India's Native States through their traditional princes. As a Rajput of high degree, he could rule — provided he conformed to a deceptively flexible behavioral code. He was assigned a British resident, but one of a new sort — more courteous, subtler, and seemingly less demanding than the likes of Major Burton. Because Umed Singh II's behavior was most gentlemanly, his life was tranquil. As a youth, the maharao was among the first students to attend an institution modeled on Eton College: Chiefs' College, Rajputana, which survives, at Ajmer, as Mayo College (cat. 75). Albeit insulated by servants and attendants, he followed a curriculum that combined traditional Indian and English subjects, emphasizing Shakespeare and Browning more than the *Bhagavad Gita* or Kalidasa, the renowned Sanskrit dramatist. Cricket, polo, tennis, and other acceptably upper-class sports were leavened by tiger shooting and pig-sticking.

As a virtually ducal Rajput, the maharao was strongly encouraged to forsake the militaristic independence of his family fort and to build a palace comparable to a great English country house. In time to receive King George and Princess Alexandra on the occasion of the darbar of 1911, he commissioned Sir Swinton Jacobs to design the Umed Bhavan. Work began in 1906 on this huge Indo-Saracenic edifice, which includes darbar and banquet halls, men's quarters and zenana, vast inner courtyards, and a billiards room. Sir Swinton was artistic but practical. Historical expertise that blossomed in Rajput-Mughal archways and pierced stone windows was matched by his grasp of such practicalities as plumbing and air-cooling. An impressive network of lengthy, thickly walled stone passageways maintains coolness even on sweltering June nights. Although Rajput darbars and festivals were still held, the Umed Bhavan was also suited to receptions, garden parties, teas, and balls. Like equivalent palaces at Bikaner, Mysore, and elsewhere, the Umed Bhavan was plumbed, electrified, and outfitted with the finest British goods. Its carpets, draperies, furniture, pictures, and objets d'art were all imported from England. And inasmuch as living in such surroundings under the encouraging eye of the resident demanded a certain way of life, there was a never-ending list of needs to be supplied. Horse-drawn carriages — and, later, Rolls Royces and Bentleys — shotguns, shooting-sticks, plate,

jewels, and more were chosen, with the discerning advice of the resident, and imported from England.

Although after the death of Shatru Sal II the traditional arts ceased to flourish at court, a few families of painters live on at Kotah, kept busy and modestly prosperous. When a commission comes from H.H. Maharao Brijraj Singh, a painter bicycles to the Brijraj Bhavan to discuss subject matter, color, size, and other traditional concerns. Artists at Kota recreate eighteenth-century Kotah miniatures to supply the new patronage of international tourism. Before long, variants of Maharao Umed Singh I's tiger hunts, the Master of Elephants' pachydermal fantasies, and Sheikh Taju's *Barahmasa* series will brighten bedroom walls in the Umed Bhavan, parts of which have been remodeled as a comfortable, supremely spacious four-star hotel.

NOTES

1 Lee and Montgomery 1960, no. 36. A traced drawing of this miniature was apparently made in order to reemploy it for a mural in the outer chamber of the Chhattar Mahal of Kotah Fort, which is discussed below. The drawing, made before the painting was damaged, is in a private collection. Both are published in Beach 1974, figs. 74 and 73. Other publications of this painting include Welch 1983, 79–80, fig. 4, and Welch 1985, 359–60, no. 242.

2 Although the Kotah artist's fighting dragons, knotted together like pretzels, are more wiggly and "noisy" than those in an otherwise comparable Turkman drawing in Istanbul, the latter appears to be an influential ancestor from the Kotah creature's family tree. It is in the so-called Yaqub Bek Album (H. 2160), the richest of several containing Turkman material in the Topkapi Sarayi Museum Library, Istanbul.

3 Sherwani 1974, 3–15. For the Turkmans, see Woods 1976. For Turkman drawing and painting, see Dickson and Welch 1981, 1:15–26.

4 For further discussions of this drawing, see Welch 1976, 67, no. 28, and Welch 1983, 78–93.

5 Dr. John Fryer wrote in the 1670s that "the Mogul hath made no farther Progress of late Years, satisfying himself to keep these Kingdoms in the nature of Vassals, though never absolutely Conquered; frustrated by the great Omrahs [nobles] who live Lazily and in pay, whereupon they term Deccan, The Bread of the Military Men." In the preceding paragraph, he refers to the Deccanis "stopping the Mogul's Mouth with a Tribute, as also his Generals with large Presents." See Roe and Fryer 1873, 402.

6 For an account of a great Aurangabad artist hired by a Rajput from Kishangarh, see Welch 1994.

This topic will be amplified in a forthcoming publication by Dr. Navina Najat Haidar.

7 For other portraits in the collections of Gopi Krishna Kanoria and Ralph Benkaim, see Beach 1974, figs. 68 and 69. Both might be by the Kotah Master.

8 See Craigen W. Bowen's essay, below, for a discussion of pigments, papers, brushes, binding medium, etc.

9 For the Lucknow drawing, see Beach 1974, fig. 126. I am grateful to Pramod Chandra for telling me that "Niju" is a nickname offering no hints as to the artist's religion, caste, or place of origin. The date probably refers to the year when one royal personage presented the drawing to another. This idea is supported by Joachim K. Bautze's statement to the author that the inscription is probably in a Mewar hand. It might have been presented to the rana of Mewar by Maharao Durjan Sal (r. 1723–56), who was strongly connected with the Mewar house.

10 For these magnificent pictures, see Bautze 1989b. The Master of Elephants' career may have included a stint at Bundi, between his Agra and Kotah periods.

11 For the Hodgkin drawing, see Welch 1976, 89, no. 44; Ashton 1950, no. 484; and Hodgkin and McInerney 1983, no. 20.

12 For another instance of Indian scientific concern with anatomy during the early seventeenth century, consider Jahangir's order to dissect a lion in 1616:

On the 16th [January 25], we decamped. After marching four and an eighth kos we stopped in the vicinity of the village of Ghiri. Along the way the scouts brought word of a lion in the area. I set out, intending to hunt it down, and polished it off with

one shot. Inasmuch as the bravery and valor of lions and tigers are established facts, I wanted to open it up and have a look. After it was cut open it was apparent that, unlike other animals, whose gall bladders are outside the liver, lions' and tigers' gall bladders are located inside their livers. It occurs to me that lions' and tigers' courage is due to this fact.

I am grateful to Wheeler M. Thackston for permitting me to quote from his translation of Jahangir's memoirs (Jahangir, forthcoming ed.).

13 Private collection; published in Beach 1974, fig. 81, and Hodgkin and McInerney 1983, no. 25. The latter publication illustrates two other drawings attributable to this artist in about 1670–80, *Elephant Being Excited by Fireworks*, no. 23, and a large, ambitiously conceived *Royal Elephant Hunt*, no. 38.

14 Several preparatory drawings for the *Bhagavata Purana* series, attributable to the Master of Elephants, are in the National Museum of India, New Delhi, and in a private collection.

15 It is hoped that conservators will be able to remove the dismaying overpaint from this important early monument of Rajput art at Kotah. Although at present outshone by the extraordinary, comparatively well-preserved wall and ceiling pictures in the Baddal Mahal of the fort at Bundi (see Bautze 1989b), they deserve serious attention.

16 For the Chaurapanchasika style, see Khadalavala and Chandra 1974.

17 For early Bundi painting, see Bautze 1987a.

18 Published in Beach 1974, fig. 70.

19 See Dickson and Welch 1981, 1: pl. 10.

20 More accurately known as Riza-yi Abbasi of Isfahan; see Canby 1996.

21 Harvard University Art Museums, Alpheus Hyatt

Fund, 1952.7. Published in Simpson and Welch 1980, no. 30.

22 This powerful painting is closely related to inscribed works by Fazl, who was employed at Burhanpur by Abdur-Rahim, the Khan Khanan, a poet, statesman, and soldier in the service of both Akbar and Jahangir, for whom see Schimmel 1987. The hunting scene is published in Welch and Beach 1965, no. 11, with the suggested identification of Gopinath Singh of Bundi. It seems most likely that the Burhanpur style was transmitted to Bundi and Kotah by Rajputs who had served there under the Rajput-inclined Mughal. The Khan Khanan maintained his own ateliers and commissioned subimperial illustrated manuscripts of Hindu epics as well as of Persian classics. Fazl, whose influence can be seen in the so-called Laud *Ragamala* series at Oxford (see Stooke and Khandalavala 1953), must have painted this hunting scene at Bundi, or even Kotah, during the 1620s. His unmistakable hand is evident in the shapes and peculiarly glowing colors of rocks and in his characteristic treatment of grasses and trees. The Khan Khanan's manuscripts are listed and described in Beach 1982, no. 15; see also Beach 1983.

23 H. 2153, fol. 64b.

24 Several erotic pictures can be attributed to him. Most bring together "this world" and "the other," as in depictions of Maharao Durjan Sal envisioned as Brijrajji in flagrante delicto.

25 For a preparatory drawing for this series, see Welch 1976, 47, 92–93. For demons attributable to Sultan-Muhammad, see Dickson and Welch 1981, 1: pl. 4, fig. 92, and 2: pl. 8; and Zettersteen and Lamm 1948, pl. 16. Other illustrations from this *Ramayana* are in the collection of the Bharat Kala Bhavan, Banaras, and the Museum of Fine Arts, Boston.

26 Many works by Abul Hasan will be included in Akimushkin, Ivanov, and Welch, forthcoming.

27 Beach 1974, dustjacket and figs. 78 and 79; Welch 1976, 90–91, no. 45.

28 See Joachim K. Bautze's historical remarks, below. For a comparable hunting scene of Maharao Durjan Sal, also on cloth and by the Kotah Master, see Topsfield and Beach 1991, no. 37; other fragments of this painting are in a private collection.

29 Another picture in this mode shows Durjan Sal inspecting a white horse; see Beach 1974, fig. 84.

30 An impressive, life-size portrait on cloth of Maharao Bhim Singh 1 hangs in the armory of Kotah Fort. Although the face appears to have been touched up, it would seem to have been painted by Sheikh Taju.

31 For three closely related paintings, see Beach 1974, figs. 82 (Severence Milliken Collection) and 128 (Jagdish and Kamla Mittal Museum of Indian Art, Hyderabad); and Noey and Temos 1994, 61, no. 31.

32 See Leach 1995, 2: 996–1003, no. 10.41, pl. 13.

33 A related drawing, perhaps a fragment of this one, is in the Red Fort Museum, Delhi.

34 At Kotah, princes sometimes adopted this imperial mode. Note the beard worn by a Kotah prince in the Zenana Master's rendering of a gathering in a zenana (Beach 1974, fig. 70).

35 The lower half of this signed and dated picture is in the Jagdish and Kamla Mittal Museum of Indian Art, Hyderabad; for the upper section, see Hodgkin and McInerney 1983, cover and no. 35.

Although I do not question the attribution of this sketch, which could have been done by Sheikh Taju at the age of eighty or so, the identification of the faintly outlined ruler, who resembles Maharao Guman Singh (r. 1764–71), and the inscription, which might have been added in 1780 to a somewhat earlier work, are puzzling.

36 Sheikh Taju's drawing is in a private collection.

37 M. B. Singh 1985, 36, pl. 6.

38 See Topsfield 1980, especially nos. 12, 62, 66, and 84. For a typical mid-eighteenth-century Mewar painting, see Sotheby's, Inc., 1996, lot 34, *Maharana Jagat Singh (1734–1751) Shooting Tiger from a Shooting Box at the Corner of an Enclosure*. Although lacking the magic of Maharao Umed Singh 1's zestfully composed hunting pictures, Mewar paintings of this sort contain most of their ingredients, particularly in their finely — too finely — detailed vegetation.

39 Such adjustments by "foreign" artists were frequent in Rajasthan and in the Hills, where artists from Mughal, Deccani, or other outside traditions not only learned to paint in the manners of Kishangarh, Bikaner, or Basohli with astonishing speed and skill, but became leading, often innovative figures at their new courts.

40 See Leach 1986, 197–203, no. 77, as *Ladies Shooting from a Pavilion*, pl. 8, and dustjacket.

41 Woodman Taylor's identification is based on many surviving likenesses of Kishor Singh that feature his aquiline nose and firm jaw, including a fine large portrait in the Bada Mahal of Kotah Fort. It can be ascribed to the artist from Nathadvara.

JOACHIM K. BAUTZE

The History of Kotah in an Art-Historical Context

Kotah was a princely state of "Rajpootana," an area that nowadays corresponds more or less to Rajasthan, a state in northwest India. Before it merged with other states following independence in 1947 to form the India of today, Kotah measured about ninety miles in length from north to south and eighty in breadth. Kota (the spelling "Kotah" is historical) now forms the southeastern district of Rajasthan, which is the third-largest state of India.

Each of the princely states in northwest India was founded and ruled by a Rajput clan. The provenance of the altogether thirty-six Rajput clans is obscured by innumerable myths explaining their origin. No historical source seems to be older than the seventh century, when the Rajputs made their first entrance on the stage of Indian history; very few dates are available before the beginning of the thirteenth century. In the mid seventeenth century, a Rajput was considered equal to a member of the Kshatriya, or second class, of the Indian caste system.[1] Toward the nineteenth century, the term *Rajput* began to denote a caste in Rajasthan, often suggesting the aristocratic origin of its member.[2] Rajputs were known for their brave conduct on the battlefield. Several impoverished Rajputs became highway robbers and as such figure greatly in seventeenth-century European accounts of India; the Rajputs were too proud to change what they must have considered their primary profession: the art of warfare. In the early seventeenth century, the traveler Peter Mundy, passing through the territory of Raja Gaj Singh of Marwar on his way from Agra to Surat, noted, "Theis Inhabitants are Rashpootes which goe after a more free and Souldier like manner then other Hindooes, rather like Masters then Subjects."[3]

The Early History of Kotah and the Haras of Bundi

Kotah history as such starts only in 1631, by imperial — in this case Mughal — decree, which guaranteed Kotah's quasi independence from the parental state of Bundi. The early history of Kotah is hence closely linked to that of the older Hara state.

Bundi, like Kotah, is a state with a capital of the same name; it is situated to the north of Kotah. This state was also called Haravati (or Hadauti or Haraoti), due to the fact that a subclan of the Chauhans known as the Haras predominantly ruled that part of

the country. Most probably, the name of the subclan derives from Har Raj, the name of an important Chauhan ruler.[4]

The Chauhan dynasty of Bundi is first mentioned in an inscription dated 1247 C.E. (V.S. 1304) and found in the Bundi district.[5] However, it was only around 1341 that Bundi was wrested from the original population, the Minas, by Rao Deva, who enlarged the territory around Bundi through military campaigns. Kotah became part of Bundi territory when Rao Deva's grandson Jaitra Singh attacked the Bhils of Kotah and defeated them. From this time on, Kotah belonged to the kingdom of the Haras.

From the mid fourteenth century through the late sixteenth century, the history of Kotah is inextricably linked not only with that of Bundi but also with political and social developments in north and central India, where the major players included the Sisodia rulers (one of the preeminent Rajput clans) of Mewar, the Muslim rulers of Malwa, and, later on, the Mughal rulers, whose capital was in Agra and Fatehpur Sikri and then Delhi. If the connection with Muslim rulers was primarily in the form of attacks and military alliances, the relationship with Mewar was both political and matrimonial: members of the ruling families of Bundi and Mewar (and, later, Kotah and Mewar) often intermarried.

With the arrival of the Mughals — led by Babur, the former ruler of a petty fiefdom in Farghana, in Central Asia — in 1526, the political landscape of northern India changed dramatically. Initially, the Rajputs banded together to fight yet another Muslim invader, but in the end, the Mughals established one of the most powerful dynasties of India since the Muslim conquest.

When Akbar, the third Mughal emperor (r. 1556–1605), ascended the throne, the relationship between various Rajput courts and the seat of empire in Agra and Fatehpur Sikri became more complex. If the rulers of courts such as Mewar refused to surrender, others, such as Raja Bagwan Das of Amer, chose to surrender and negotiate, and became important leaders at the Mughal court.

Rao Surjan, who became the ruler of Bundi in 1554, was one of those who began by fighting the Mughal army, like his erstwhile protector and maternal uncle Rana Udai Singh of Mewar. In 1569, a year after conquering the Mewar city of Chittaurgarh, Akbar besieged the strategic fort Ranthambhor, which was in Mewar territory but under the protection of the Bundi royal family. This was the last battle between the Hara ruler and the Mughal army. After more than two months of shelling, Rao Surjan surrendered the fortress to Akbar on very favorable terms.[6] The first condition of surrender was that the Haras were to be exempt from giving any of their princesses to the Mughal harem: unlike many other Rajput clans, the Haras in fact never intermarried with the Mughals.[7]

As a sign of respect, Surjan sent his sons, Duda[8] and Bhoj, to Akbar as hostages before he himself greeted the emperor on March 22, 1569. This event was painted by the Mughal artists Mukund and Shankar at a later stage of Akbar's life; the painting shows the first near-contemporary portrait of a Hara ruler.[9] From that day, the Haras were allied to the Mughal imperial cause and continued to be the most faithful ally the Mughals ever had; Rao Surjan became a great military commander in Akbar's army.

Following Akbar's command, Rao Surjan left the administration of Bundi to his eldest son, Duda. Duda was loyal to the Haras' former ally, the rana of Mewar — who had still not yielded to the Mughals' power — and must have thought of his father as a traitor to the Rajput cause. In June 1576, Rana Pratap, the son of Rana Udai Singh, challenged the imperial army in the field of Haldighati — a battle that evokes national Rajput feelings like no other military action to date.[10] The Rajputs lost the battle but not their pride. Rana Pratap continued to offer resistance from Kumbhalgarh and other places, employing guerilla warfare; as for Duda, according to the chronicler Abul Fazl, "that evil-disposed one went off without leave to his native country of Bundi and opened the hand of oppression."[11] A punitive expedition sent to Bundi by Akbar probably met a disastrous defeat, since Akbar's chronicler preferred not to report on it in detail.[12] On March 30, 1577, Akbar sent another army, led by Rao Surjan and his second son, Bhoj, along with other Rajputs, against Duda. Bundi was taken by the Rajputs under imperial command; to Akbar, this event was of such importance that he had it painted for his biography.[13] Duda escaped, but was never again able to present a serious threat to the empire.

Throughout the period of strong Mughal sway over the northern parts of India, the Rajput chieftains, and the Haras in particular, were sent to different areas of the subcontinent in order to lead military campaigns vital to the upkeep of the Mughal empire. They were also used to escort members of the royal family. As a reward for these services, the Mughal emperors granted lands — but only for a certain amount of time, never forever:

> The Mughal polity, so long as it functioned with any effectiveness, say, until the early years of the eighteenth century, continued basically with the organizational forms that Akbar instituted. The most striking aspect of the systematization was the *mansab* ("rank"), the result of an attempt to coalesce into a pair of numbers exact indications of rank, payment, military and other obligations of the holder of the *mansab*. Every officer serving in the army and every official in the bureaucracy . . . was given a *mansab* or pair of *mansab*s (*zat* and *sawar*) upon appointment; any promotion in rank and emoluments was indicated by additions to the numbers; conversely, demotions took the form of diminutions of *mansab*s.[14]

Basically, the number or numbers indicated how many troopers were commanded by the holder of the rank (*mansab*): the first number indicated infantry, the second cavalry. In later years, these were only nominal figures, but still indicated social rank within Mughal society.

The Haras Enter onto the Stage of Indian Painting

Rao Surjan fought extensively for the Mughal emperor and was responsible for crushing revolts in the far reaches of eastern and northeastern regions. When he died in 1585 in Banaras, where he had been sent by the emperor, his highest *mansab* was two thousand.[15]

Bhoj, Surjan's second son, succeeded his father in about 1585, when he was thirty-four years old.[16] He fought bravely in Orissa in 1591 and 1592 and distinguished himself in Akbar's Deccan campaigns in the early seventeenth century. He died in 1607.[17] He had started out with a *mansab* of one thousand in 1593–94, had nine hundred in 1595–96, and kept this rank to the end of his life.[18] He is said to have built the Baddal Mahal and the Phulla Mahal, presumably in Bundi Fort and still existing today.[19]

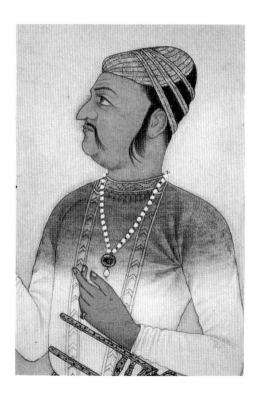

Figure 1
Detail of a portrait of Rao Bhoj Hara of Bundi, c. 1680, Bikaner. Opaque watercolor, silver, and gold on paper with inscription, 29.8 x 19.9 cm. Private collection.

In late 1590 and early 1591, Bhoj must have been posted at Chunar-Banaras, where his father had been. There, disciples of the founders of the Mughal painting atelier (Mir Sayyid Ali and Abd al-Samad) completed a *Ragamala* of thirty-six paintings[20] which became the standard painting theme of almost all subsequent Hara chieftains.[21] This set of paintings, with its Devanagari inscriptions in the text panel, constitutes the oldest dated *Ragamala* and the earliest dated proof of paintings done for a Rajput ruler. That they were commissioned by a Hara is indicated by the fact that numerous copies of them became more and more Rajput and less and less Mughal in style over time.

Figure 1, a portrait of "Hara Rao Bhoj" according to the Devanagari inscription on the back, belongs to a set of Bikaner portraits of the rulers of Bundi. It is a later version of an often-published painting from 1606 by Nur Muhammad, which reportedly represents Rao Bhoj Rathor, an uncle of Raja Rai Singh of Bikaner.[22] Historical evidence, however, suggests strongly that the subject is a Hara.[23]

Rao Ratan, the eldest son of Rao Bhoj, became the ruler of Bundi in 1608,[24] after his father's death.[25] Hriday Narayan, Rao Bhoj's second son, was to administer Kotah.[26] In early 1608, the Mughal emperor Jahangir (r. 1605–27) noted a visit from Rao Ratan, during which the latter presented the former with three elephants, one of which "was much approved."[27] A contemporary Mughal portrait of that elephant has survived;[28] this authentic reference to elephants in the possession of one of the Hara rulers shows their predilection for this animal, which is otherwise testified to by numerous paintings.

Rao Ratan, like his predecessors, was sent to diverse places. In 1614, he fought against Rana Amar Singh of Mewar, Bundi's former suzerain. A year later, his son Hriday Narayan was sent to Kangra in the north, where he fought until 1620. In 1617, Rao Ratan moved to Burhanpur in the Deccan; he was recalled from there to the court in 1623 and received "a special jewelled dagger."[29] From Agra he went to the Deccan again, to pursue the army of the rebellious prince Khurram, the future Shah Jahan (r. 1628–58). In the course of time, Rao Ratan became "chargé d'affaires" of the Deccan[30] and was rightly called the "incarnation of loyalty and chivalry."[31] He is described as fighting from the back of an elephant called "Light of the World" (Jagajot),[32] and so gallantly defended Burhanpur from the attacks of the united armies of Malik Ambar and Prince Khurram that he received the title of Ram Raj, "than which there is no higher title in the Dakhin."[33] He was also awarded the rank of five thousand, a rank he held from 1624[34] until his death in 1631.[35]

In Agra, Rao Ratan took over his father's palace and there saw the murals in the Bagh-i Nur Afshan, commonly called Ram Bagh.[36] This probably led him to have the Baddal Mahal in Bundi, also

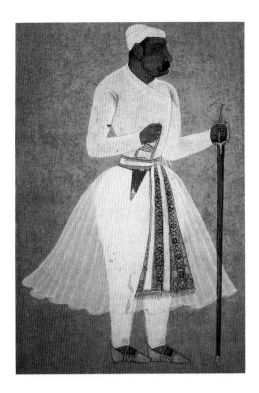

Figure 2
Rao Ratan Hara of Bundi, *c. 1630, India. Opaque watercolor and gold on paper with inscription, 19.7 x 12.2 cm. Private collection.*

built by his father, decorated with frescoes, which are stylistically still very Mughal but which betray a Rajput influence more than any other paintings done thus far for a Hara ruler.[37] In the Deccan, where he spent the greater part of the rest of his life, he founded Ratanpur near Burhanpur.[38] In Burhanpur, Rao Ratan apparently met a European merchant, Mr. Willoughby, from whom he purchased "some tapestry," presumably from Arras.[39] Echoes of these tapestries can still be seen in the frescoes of the Baddal Mahal in Bundi.

No other Hara of the seventeenth century was portrayed more often than Rao Ratan, and it is not surprising that he is depicted inspecting a painting of an elephant amid his nobles in a large mural in his own palace in Bundi.[40] Equally unsurprising are certain Deccani influences, such as the long sword or the Deccani shawl as signs of honor and rank.[41] Figure 2, an inscribed portrait in a subimperial Mughal style, shows him at an advanced age.[42]

In the absence of Rao Ratan, Bundi was ruled by his eldest son, Gopinath,[43] who died during his father's lifetime under circumstances that are not entirely clear.[44] Gopinath's eldest son, Shatru Sal, succeeded to the throne of Bundi with the rank of two thousand/three thousand.[45]

Kotah Becomes Formally Independent under Madho Singh

Madho Singh, the second son of Rao Ratan, was born in Bundi on May 18, 1599.[46] He was granted the rank of one thousand/six hundred in 1627–28,[47] and was awarded an increase to twenty-five hundred/fifteen hundred a few years later when his father died.[48] Madho Singh was favored by Shah Jahan because he overpowered the rebel Khan Jahan Lodi on February 3, 1631.[49] Later in 1631, after the death of Rao Ratan, Shah Jahan granted the fiefdoms (*parganas*) of Kotah and Palaitha to Madho Singh.[50] Kotah was thus separated from Bundi by imperial decree, becoming an independent state. The result of the separation of the Hara state has been summarized as follows:

> The action of Shahjahan to bifurcate the Hara state had a far reaching consequence. The Haras who had been serving the Mughals as a single force were divided into two branches known as Haras of Bundi and Haras of Kotah and they were to render service for the Mughals under their respective Chiefs. The Chiefs of these two states —

Bundi and Kotah — were sometimes appointed in different campaigns and sometimes in the same campaign. The result was that gradually they became competitors among themselves so as to earn honour and position in rank more than the other. Sometimes the competition converted into a tussle between these two branches. During the later period we find that they became hostile to each other and the enmity between the two developed to the extent that each branch tried to snatch the territory of the other with the consent of the Emperor.[51]

This enmity can still be felt today, when the Haras of Bundi claim descent from the sun and the Haras of Kotah claim descent from the fire, even though this distinction is impossible to make.[52]

In August 1633, Madho Singh was sent to the Deccan, where he was appointed governor of Burhanpur, a post formerly held by his father.[53] Madho Singh was a brave warrior, as a description by Shah Jahan's own chronicler of an event during late 1635 in the Deccan illustrates: "Just then Madho Singh, son of Rao Ratan, made a charge from Neknam's right flank, and with the edge of the sword, dispatched a host of the enemy into the flames of hell and routed and chased the remainder."[54] Starting in 1645, he was in charge of Balkh for two years, during which he had to fight the attacking Uzbeks in the north.[55] In 1648, Madho Singh received permission to leave for Kotah, where he died.[56] At the time of his death, his rank was equal to that of the rao of Bundi, Shatru Sal — three thousand/three thousand.[57]

Madho Singh is said to have constructed the lake in front of the Raj Mahal, visible in catalogue numbers 21 and 22; the Nakkarkhana Darwaza (Drumhouse Gate) of the Kotah palace; and several other buildings.[58] The only known contemporary portrait of Madho Singh is a detail of a mural in the Baddal Mahal of the palace of Bundi,[59] a later version of which is catalogue number 32. Figure 3 shows the founder of the Kotah state as portrayed posthumously by a Bundi artist in about 1670. The turban is flat, as in the early fashion, and the sword shows the long blade typical of Deccani straight-bladed swords (*khandas*).

Mukund Singh

Madho Singh had seven daughters[60] and seven sons.[61] Mukund Singh, the eldest son of Madho Singh, succeeded to the throne of Kotah in 1648. His succession was confirmed in May 1648 by Shah Jahan,[62] who granted him the rank of two thousand/fifteen hundred — lower than his father's.[63] He fought Mughal battles in far-flung places such as Qandahar, Lahore,[64] and Malwa[65] and was ultimately killed in the battle of Dharmat, where he fought the rebellious Aurangzeb (r. 1658–1707).[66] Mukund Singh's rank at the time was three thousand/two thousand.[67] His younger brothers Mohan, Kanhiram, and Jujhar Singh were also killed in the battle

Figure 3
Detail of a portrait of Madho Singh, the first official ruler of Kotah, c. 1675–1700, Bundi. Opaque watercolor, silver, and gold on paper with inscription, 21.5 x 15.4 cm. Collection of Vinod Krishna Kanoria.

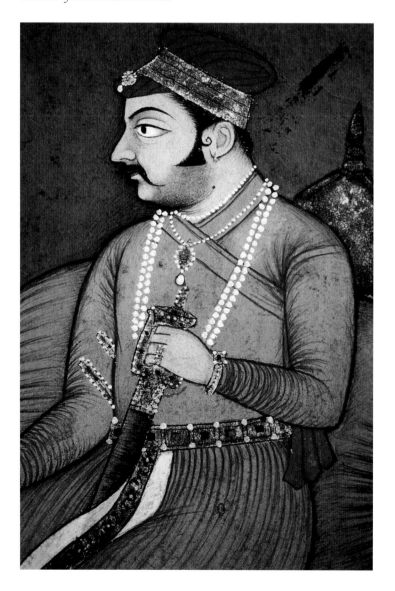

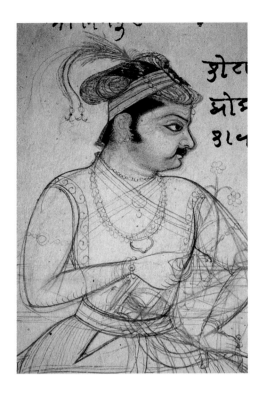

Figure 4
Detail of a portrait
of Mukund Singh,
c. 1650–1700, Kotah.
Ink and watercolor on
paper with inscription,
19.3 x 12.5 cm. Private
collection in the Fogg Art
Museum, Cambridge,
Massachusetts.

of Dharmat;[68] his youngest brother, Kishor Singh, was severely wounded, but survived.

Only a very few portraits of Mukund Singh have come down to us. Probably the best, and most nearly contemporary, likeness is shown here (fig. 4). The inscriptions say that this is "Ap Mukund Singh [son of] Madho Singh" and "eldest son of Madho Singhji of Kotah."

Jagat Singh

When Jagat Singh succeeded his father in July 1658,[69] he was about fourteen years old.[70] In July/August, he went to Delhi, where Aurangzeb confirmed him, along with Rao Shatru Sal's son Rao Bhao Singh, as the rulers of Kotah and Bundi, respectively. While Rao Bhao Singh was given the rank of three thousand/two thousand, the title of Rao and other signs of honor,[71] Jagat Singh's rank was set at fifteen hundred/one thousand. In 1660, he was appointed to Allahabad, and thereafter he was involved in numerous campaigns, especially in the Deccan. Bhimsen Saksena, the author of the *Tarikh-i-Dilkasha*, recalled meeting Jagat Singh in 1680–81: "I happened to meet him in Bahadurgarh.[72] He became very friendly with me. In fact he is a staunch drunkard and loves wine very much and drinks that heavily."[73] Jagat Singh died in October/ November 1683.[74]

A number of contemporary portraits of Jagat Singh are known. Not surprisingly, some of them show drinks being offered to him by women in a luxurious garden[75] or a palace.[76] More formal portraits in the Mughal fashion,[77] or in the Rajput fashion in a some-

what Mughalized style, also exist.[78] Figure 5 is a detail of a portrait that shows Jagat Singh driving an elephant with an enormous elephant hook (*ankusha*); it is strongly reminiscent of contemporary Mughal painting[79] as well as of Bundi-Rajput prototypes.[80] In all these paintings, Jagat Singh appears as a slightly dark-complexioned man in his early to mid thirties. He sports a mustache and has narrow sideburns. With his comparatively slender figure, he has a handsome appearance.

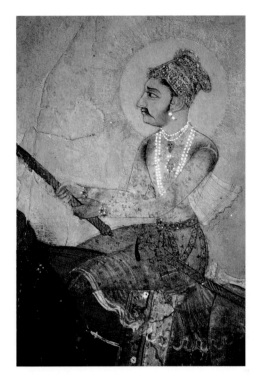

Figure 5
Detail of a portrait of
Jagat Singh driving an
elephant, c. 1670, Kotah.
Opaque watercolor and
gold on paper, 28.7 x
40.4 cm. Collection of
Vinod Krishna Kanoria.

Kishor Singh

Since Jagat Singh left no male issue, a council of chiefs selected Prem Singh, a son of Kanhiram (the fourth son of Madho Singh, who died in the battle of Dharmat), as the successor of Jagat Singh. Prem Singh, however, was apparently not capable of managing the affairs of state properly. His rule was in fact so short that his nomination was not confirmed by the Mughal emperor, and all relevant historical sources mention Kishor Singh as the direct successor to Jagat Singh instead.[81]

Kishor Singh was one of the younger sons of Madho Singh, and it was he who received, but recovered from, multiple wounds in the battle of Dharmat.[82] His coronation ceremony (*rajtilak*) occurred in October/November 1684.[83] His date of birth is not mentioned by any of the sources, but by the time of his accession, his age must have been considerable; he had served Shah Jahan since 1654–55.[84]

After his accession, Kishor Singh was sent to the Deccan by Aurangzeb. He took part in the siege of Bijapur, which started on April 1, 1685;[85] Bijapur was eventually conquered, on September 12, 1686.[86] Again, Kishor Singh sustained injuries.[87] At the end of January 1687, he successfully fought the cavalry under Sheikh Nizam Hyderabadi.[88] Apparently mortally wounded, he fell from his horse,[89] but once again recovered. In July 1688, Kishor Singh helped rout the army of the rebellious Raja Ram in Malwa. During the fight, he suffered fresh injuries and was allowed to return to Kotah in order to have them treated;[90] he had hardly regained his health when he was called to the Deccan again. He took part in many campaigns, and in December 1695, near Vellore, served Zulfiqar Khan (the Mughal army commander who held high office under Aurangzeb in the Deccan)[91] so well that he was granted kettledrums.[92] His rank was then twenty-five hundred/three thousand,[93] while that of his contemporary Rao Aniruddh Singh of Bundi was thirty-five hundred/three thousand.[94] In April 1696, Kishor Singh died.[95]

In all portraits of him, Kishor Singh appears in an advanced stage of life: his mustache and sideburns are white, but his bearing is still full of dignity.[96] Figure 6, possibly a contemporary likeness, shows him out hawking on horseback; an inscription on the back of this painting ("Ap Shri Kishor Singhji") confirms its identification. That Kishor Singh must have been fond of hawking is proved by an unpublished portrait from the 1730s, which shows him standing with a hawk.

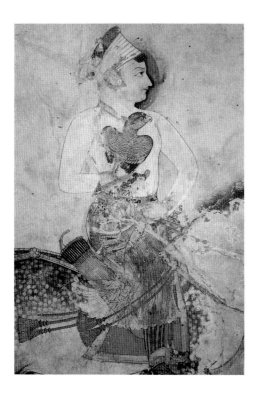

Figure 6
Detail of a portrait of Kishor Singh on horseback holding a hawk, late seventeenth century, Kotah. Opaque watercolor and gold on paper with inscription, 21.2 x 24.3 cm. Rao Madho Singh Trust Museum, Fort Kotah.

Rao Ram Singh

Kishor Singh had four sons: Bishan Singh, Ram Singh, Arjun Singh, and Harnath Singh. He had excluded his eldest son from the succesion, for disobeying orders.[97] In a letter to Aurangzeb, Zulfiqar Khan pleaded for Ram Singh to be made successor to Kishor Singh;[98] by that time Ram Singh was at Kotah, and he had to fight his elder brother, who still wanted to become the ruler there. This conflict was solved on the battlefield. Harnath Singh, who sided with Ram Singh, was killed; Bishan Singh was wounded and died three years later.[99]

At the further request of Zulfiqar Khan, Ram Singh was granted his ancestral estate in 1696–97.[100] By that time, he had already joined the army of Zulfiqar Khan in the Deccan. He distinguished himself at the battle of Jinji in November 1697.[101] In connection with campaigns against the Maratha leader Dhanaji Jadav, he received "praise, robes, jewels and promotion."[102] Kettledrums were granted to him on the request of Zulfiqar Khan after the taking of the fort of Panhala in March 1701.[103] By that time, Ram Singh's rank amounted to three thousand/fifteen hundred.[104]

The following year was again full of military action for Ram Singh. For four successive days, he was severally attacked by the Marathas near Kularasgarh, but was able to repulse each onslaught.[105]

Together with Raja Jai Singh of Amer and Rao Dalpat of Bundela, Rao Ram Singh was by this time one of the key figures of the Mughal force in the Deccan.[106] Ram Singh's activities in the Deccan on the whole are summarized as follows:

> Zulifiqar Khan Bahadur in consultation with Rao Dalpat and Ram Singh and his comrades, with his small force, attacked the vast numbers of the enemy, in six months, fought nineteen big battles and severely punished the enemy. He gained remarkable victories. During this time he covered nearly three thousand *kos* in pursuit of the enemy.[107]

Ram Singh returned to Aurangabad in 1704 after attacking the enemy near Bijapur.[108] For his bravery at Wagingera, he was rewarded with an increment of five hundred in his rank.[109]

In 1706, the confrontation between the houses of Bundi and Kotah became more apparent, after Mau Maidana, then an estate of Bundi, was taken from Rao Budh Singh of Bundi and given to Rao Ram Singh at the urging of Zulfiqar Khan.[110]

Aurangzeb died at Ahmadnagar in 1707.[111] A war of succession followed. Rao Budh Singh of Bundi sided with the second of the three surviving sons of Aurangzeb (and the ultimate victor), Prince Muazzam. Ram Singh supported Muhammad Azam, Aurangzeb's third son. Both rivals crowned themselves emperors; Prince Muazzam assumed the title of Bahadur Shah in Kabul and moved

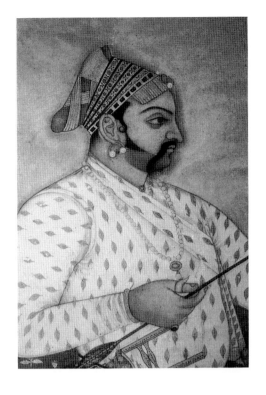

Figure 7
Detail of a portrait
showing Rao Ram Singh
seated on a terrace,
Gobind Ram, mid-eigh-
teenth century, possibly
Kishangarh. Opaque
watercolor and gold
on paper with inscription,
18.3 x 24.1 cm. From
the collection of Mr. and
Mrs. Clark Blaise.

toward Delhi, while Muhammad Azam hastened from the Deccan in that direction. The armies met on June 18, 1707, at Jajau, near Agra; according to the British historian James Tod, "A more desperate conflict was never recorded in the many bloody pages of the history of India."[112] During the battle, of which several detailed descriptions exist,[113] Rao Ram Singh was killed by a cannonball[114] — and so was Rao Dalpat of Bundela, behind whom sat the historian Bhimsen.[115]

The title of Rao must have formed one of the numerous awards that Ram Singh received, according to one historian;[116] his title is sometimes given as "Raja."[117] A near contemporary equestrian portrait of Ram Singh from Kotah is inscribed with the title "Maharao Sahib," which indicates that the inscription was added later. Another portrait of this important ruler (fig. 7) is by the artist Gobind Ram, who probably worked for a ruler of Kishangarh.[118] It is also inscribed with the title of Maharao and the additional information that Ram Singh was the son of Kishor Singh and hailed from Kotah in Rajasthan. Both these portraits show Ram Singh of stout body, comparatively light complexion, narrow sideburns that run out into a pronounced triangle, and a long mustache that frames a round little chin. This physiognomy appears on other inscribed portraits of him as well.[119]

Maharao Bhim Singh 1

Bhim Singh 1, the only son of Rao Ram Singh, became the ruler of Kotah in June/July 1707.[120] He was then about twenty-five years of age.[121] Rao Budh Singh of Bundi, who had fought for the victor of the Mughal war of succession, received the title of Maharao Raja[122] in addition to fifty-four districts[123] including Kotah.[124]

Bhim Singh, however, did not wish to give up Kotah so easily. Maharao Raja Budh Singh was busy in the Deccan[125] and sent his trusted general Jogi Ram[126] to Kotah to negotiate the surrender of the Kotah fort with Bhim Singh's emissaries.[127] These negotiations led to nothing but two battles, both of which the army of Bundi lost.[128]

Bahadur Shah died on February 27, 1712,[129] and another war of succession started; it culminated on January 10, 1713, in the battle of Agra between Jahandar Shah, for some time the successor of Bahadur Shah, and Farrukh Siyar.[130] This battle was won by Farrukh Siyar, who became the new Mughal emperor; Jahandar Shah died on February 11, 1713.[131]

Bhim Singh arrived in Delhi on August 28, 1713,[132] greeted the newly installed emperor on September 8,[133] and on September 12 was granted the title of Maharao, a rank of thirty-five hundred, and the fort of Mau Maidana, formerly granted to the ruler of Bundi[134] — probably because of Maharao Raja Budh Singh's nonappearance at the Delhi court for the installation formalities. This provoked Maharao Raja Budh Singh, who made preparations to attack Kotah. On November 22, Farrukh Siyar asked Maharao Raja Budh Singh to withdraw his troops from Kotah, an order the Bundi ruler ignored. The Mughal emperor, in return, withdrew Budh Singh's rank and granted Bundi to Maharao Bhim Singh, who by then had already successfully repulsed an attack by Budh Singh.[135] Maharao Bhim Singh defeated the army of Bundi sometime in early February 1714;[136] following the defeat of the Bundi army, Maharao Bhim Singh stripped Bundi of its treasures.[137] A Rajasthani agent (vakil) report dated February 17, 1714, notes that Bhim Singh had conquered Bundi and submitted it to the emperor, who changed its name to Farrukhabad.[138] Maharao Bhim Singh's rank was then raised to five thousand/four thousand.[139]

In September 1715, Farrukh Siyar sent an official order (farman) to Maharao Raja Budh Singh's brother-in-law Sawai Jai Singh of Amer, with the request that he come to the court with Budh Singh, to whom the state of Bundi would be returned.[140] After Jai Singh pleaded for his brother-in-law, an official order dated December 20, 1715, was issued by the emperor to the effect that Bundi should be returned to Maharao Raja Budh Singh.[141] In May/June 1716, Maharao Raja Budh Singh, by arrangement of Sawai Jai Singh, personally met the emperor, and after this audience all rights to his state were returned to him.[142] On August 6, 1716, orders were given that Maharao Bhim Singh should be expelled from Bundi.[143] It seems Maharao Bhim Singh complied with these orders.[144]

Maharao Bhim Singh now sided, together with Ajit Singh Rathor, with the "kingmakers" — the Barha Sayyids, who opposed the emperor, Farrukh Siyar.[145] Maharao Raja Budh Singh of Bundi and Raja Sawai Jai Singh of Amer, then also in Delhi, supported the emperor. The Sayyid brothers, who wanted to get rid of the emperor's supporters, succeeded in arranging matters so that Farrukh Siyar asked Maharao Raja Budh Singh to leave Delhi for Bundi and Sawai Jai Singh to leave Delhi for his home in Amer, which the latter did on February 22, 1719.[146] The tension that prevailed between the two Haras became obvious that day: Maharao Bhim Singh attacked Maharao Raja Budh Singh at Delhi "while exercising his horse."[147] One of the Bundi ruler's followers, Jait

Figure 8
Detail of Maharao Bhim Singh I fighting Nizam-ul-Mulk, c. 1720, Kotah. Opaque watercolor and gold on paper with inscription, 18.3 x 24.1 cm. Private collection.

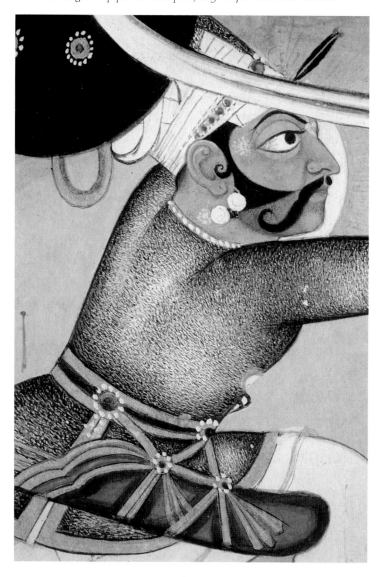

Singh Hara, sacrificed his life to save Budh Singh,[148] who "had to cut his way through the troops of Bhim Singh,"[149] but who managed to escape and, with a small following, join the troops of his brother-in-law about sixteen miles southwest of Delhi.[150]

Maharao Bhim Singh, together with Maharaja Ajit Singh Rathor and Raja Gaj Singh of Narwar, actively supported the "kingmakers" on February 27, 1719, when Farrukh Siyar was searched for in the palace, spotted in his harem, dragged out from there, blinded, and thrown into a prisonlike chamber.[151] He was killed two months later.[152] Rafi-ad-Darjat was made the new Mughal emperor on February 28. At his first audience, Maharao Bhim Singh, Maharaja Ajit Singh, and Raja Ratan Chand appealed to him to abolish the poll tax (*jazya*) on Hindus, and this appeal was granted.[153]

Meanwhile, Sawai Jai Singh and others proclaimed Nekusiyar, the eldest surviving son of prince Muhammad Akbar, who was the fourth son of Emperor Alamgir, as the new Mughal emperor at Agra.[154] When this news reached Delhi in May 1719, Maharao Bhim Singh and others were sent to Agra to assist the provincial administrator (*nazim*) there.[155]

Rafi-ad-Darjat, the Mughal emperor at Delhi, had severe tuberculosis; on June 6, he was replaced by his elder brother, Rafi-ad-Daula.[156] Rafi-ad-Daula did not live much longer than his predecessor: addicted to opium, he died on September 17 or 18, 1719, in a camp near Fatehpur Sikri.[157] On September 28, Roshan Akhtar, a grandson of the emperor Bahadur Shah, was made the new Mughal emperor; he subsequently became known by his title, Muhammad Shah.[158] All these emperors, however, were mere puppets in the hands of the Sayyids, who actually ruled Mughal India.

Maharao Raja Budh Singh of Bundi assisted Girdhar Bahadur, the rebellious governor of Allahabad, and thus infuriated the Sayyids, who asked Maharao Bhim Singh to march against Bundi on November 17, 1719.[159] In this campaign, he was accompanied by a number of Sayyid-Mughal leaders.[160] When he reached Mathura, Maharao Bhim Singh went to Brindaban, where he distributed silver coins in charity equal to his own weight and, following initiation through a religious leader (*gusain*), became a follower of the Vallabha Sampraday, a religious community.[161] From this point, he regarded the image of Brijnathji as the tutelary deity of the Kotah state, and Kotah was thus named Nandgaon, after the village near Mathura in which Krishna passed part of his youth. Maharao Bhim Singh henceforth considered himself "minister" to Brijnathji and called himself Krishnadas, "the servant of Krishna."[162]

Disturbances at Kotah, caused by the army of Bundi following a rumor that Maharao Bhim Singh had died, interrupted the maharao's stay at Mathura; he rushed to Bundi with contingents of the imperial army amounting to fifteen thousand horsemen,[163] six thousand of whom were "veteran troops and all Seids [Sayyids] of Barha," which means they were selected by the Barha Sayyids, or "kingmakers," themselves.[164]

Maharao Bhim Singh was promised the rank of seven thousand in addition to the "insignia of the fish," the "highest military decoration that can be conferred,"[165] if his expedition against Bundi and Nizam-ul-Mulk in Malwa was successful.[166] Salim Singh, a relative of Nizam-ul-Mulk, was defeated at Kotah, and in early February 1720, the defender of Bundi, an uncle of Maharao Raja Budh Singh, died fighting, together with five to six thousand Haras, against the imperial army led by Maharao Bhim Singh.[167] Loot taken by Maharao Bhim Singh from Bundi included the kettledrums and, reportedly, even the elephants that decorated the "Raj Mahal."[168]

After the battle at Bundi, in June 1720, Dilaver Ali Khan (the paymaster [bakshi] of the Mughal army), Maharao Bhim Singh, and Raja Gaj Singh of Narwar engaged the armies of Nizam-ul-Mulk in battle near the western border of Malwa, in the vicinity of Ratanpur.[169] The battle began on the afternoon of June 19 and continued the following day. Maharao Bhim Singh, one of the "mail-clad Rajputs,"[170] sat in the howdah of his elephant, where the image of Brijnathji was hidden.[171] What happened is described even by Islamic historians in the following words:

> Dilaver Ali Khan, mounted on an elephant, fought resolutely, but he was struck by a musket ball and killed. The army of the Barhas [Sayyids] then turned to flee; but the Rajputs, Raja Bhim, and Raja Gaj Singh, disdained to escape, and fought with great valour. They and three or four hundred other Rajputs ... were killed.[172]

There are a number of descriptions of this battle and the death of the Kotah maharao, which are mostly based on Khafi Khan's account.[173] The hidden artillery that annihilated a great part of Dilaver Ali Khan's army and the maharao's contingent is mentioned in most of these descriptions; it is also shown in a large painting on cloth now in the Rao Madho Singh Trust Museum.

Maharao Bhim Singh I had arranged for a number of temples to be constructed and renovated.[174] Furthermore, he introduced the emblem of the Kotah state, the Garuda standard (garudadhvaja).[175] In all known inscribed portraits of him, he appears to have been of dark complexion and somewhat short-necked.[176] His broad sideburns and long mustache terminating in a curl were probably meant to hide his numerous scars, mentioned by the historian James Tod.[177] Figure 8, a hitherto unpublished version on paper of the central scene of the large cloth painting of Maharao Bhim Singh's final battle, in which he beheads Nizam-ul-Mulk in the artist's fantasy, is inscribed on the back "portrait of Bhim Singh Hara" (Hara Bhim Singhji ri surat).[178] A number of paintings show Bhim Singh as a servant (sevaka) or devotee (bhakta) to Brijnathji,[179]

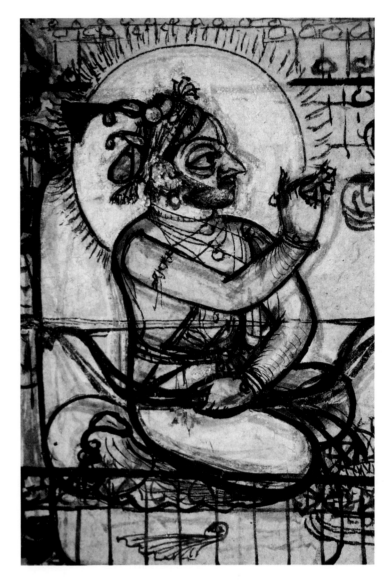

Figure 9
Detail of Maharao Arjun Singh during the celebration of Krishna's birthday at the Kotah palace, c. 1720–23, Kotah. Ink and watercolor on paper, 11.1 x 10.5 cm. Private collection.

and he even arranged for certain areas of the early murals of the Chhattar Mahal within the Kotah palace to be repainted, in order to have his own portrait, together with that of Brijnathji, inserted.[180] Nowadays, a life-size portrait of Maharao Bhim Singh I on cloth[181] forms part of the royal Dashahra celebrations in the old palace.

Maharao Arjun Singh

Maharao Bhim Singh had four sons: Arjun Singh, Shyam Singh, Durjan Sal, and Kishan Singh.[182] The eldest, Arjun Singh — whose mother was a daughter of Maharana Amar Singh of Mewar[183] —

ascended to the throne of Kotah after his father's death.[184] His reign, however, was brief: he died in October 1723.[185]

During the short reign of Arjun Singh, the Arjun Mahal and the Moti Mahal of the Kotah fort were built.[186] A few contemporary and near-contemporary portraits are known,[187] in which he is often associated with Brijnathji, the idol that was lost during Maharao Bhim Singh's last battle.[188] In all these paintings, Arjun Singh's characteristic facial features are apparent. His complexion was as dark as that of his younger brother Shyam Singh,[189] and he had the broad sideburns of his father; figure 9, a preparatory drawing for catalogue number 21 or 22, reveals the thin mustache, the pointed, beaklike nose, and the large eyes with heavy lids, in addition to the short neck, that make him the most unmistakable of all Kotah rulers.

Maharao Durjan Sal

Maharao Arjun Singh died without leaving an heir. Maharao Durjan Sal, the third son of Maharao Bhim Singh, became the ruler of Kotah on November 18, 1723.[190] His elder brother, Shyam Singh, contested his succession to the throne, and on December 12, 1723, at the border between the states of Kotah and Bundi (at Udaipuriya), a battle between the two and their supporters was fought, during which Shyam Singh and several other noted Haras were killed.[191] Durjan Sal became the ruler of Kotah.

By this time, the power of the Mughals was declining rapidly, while the power of the Marathas was increasing; the Rajput courts were busy fighting among themselves, and their feuds brought the Marathas into the Rajput territories in unexpected ways. For example, in April 1730, Kotah welcomed Maharao Raja Budh Singh, who was trying to reconquer the capital of Bundi, which had been taken from him by his brother-in-law Sawai Jai Singh of Jaipur following a family dispute.[192] The following month, Sawai Jai Singh arrived in Kotah, accompanied by Dalel Singh Hara of Karwar, son of Salim Singh of Karwar (an estate in Bundi). On May 19, 1730, Sawai Jai Singh crowned Dalel Singh, "the Kotah ruler first applying the *tika* [forehead mark] on Dalel Singh's brow, followed by Jai Singh, who, waving the *chamvar* [flywhisk, a symbol of royalty] over the head of the young Hara, proclaimed him as the new Rao Raja of Bundi."[193]

At this point, Amar Kumari, sister of Sawai Jai Singh and wife of Maharao Raja Budh Singh of Bundi, called on the Marathas to interfere; for a sum of six hundred thousand rupees, she hired them to fight against her brother and the ruler of Bundi at that time, Dalel Singh. The Marathas, supported by Dalel Singh's elder brother, conquered Bundi for Amar Kumari on April 22, 1734, and reinstalled Maharao Raja Budh Singh as rightful ruler.[194] Soon after, a large Jaipur army arrived and restored Dalel Singh in Bundi.

The intrusion of the Marathas into Rajput affairs was a serious enough threat for the Rajputs to unite and convene the famous Hurda conference. Meeting at Hurda, a village about thirty-six miles from Ajmer, the more important rulers of Rajasthan officially formed a league against the Marathas, on July 16, 1734.[195] It was probably in connection with this conference that Maharao Durjan Sal married Brajkunwar, a daughter of Maharana Sangram Singh II.[196] Durjan Sal, Sawai Jai Singh, and other participants in the conference supported the Mughal imperial army under Khan-i-Dauran in a campaign against the Marathas, but a battle was not fought. Instead, peace was negotiated.[197]

On November 27, 1741, Maharao Durjan Sal organized a special religious function in honor of his father at Nathadvara, to which he invited various Rajput rulers. It is possible that talks about the organization of resistance against the Marathas were held during that function.[198] In February 1742, it was planned that Maharao Durjan Sal and other major Rajput rulers should reassemble at Hurda and prepare to attack the Marathas to bring parts of Malwa under Rajasthani rule, but nothing came of this.[199]

The Armies of Bundi and Kotah Unite against Jaipur, and Hostilities between the Two Hara States Come to an End

Maharao Raja Umed Singh, son and successor of Budh Singh of Bundi, carried on his father's attempts to reconquer Bundi. In this, he was actively assisted by Maharao Durjan Sal of Kotah. Durjan Sal also sided with the maharana of Mewar against Ishvari Singh of Jaipur,[200] and Raja Aya Mal Khatri, the agent of Maharaja Ishvari Singh of Jaipur, bombarded and raided Kotah because of this.[201] Raja Aya Mal also secured Maratha help and successfully attacked another ally of Bundi and Kotah, the maharana of Mewar. Bundi changed hands several times over the next several years before an alliance of the forces of Kotah, Mewar, and the Marathas defeated Ishvari Singh in August 1748, in a battle that raged for six days. Ishvari Singh was required to cede five districts of the Jaipur state to Madho Singh and to restore Bundi to Umed Singh.[202]

Before long, however, the Marathas were once more enemies of the Rajputs. In early 1751, Maharao Durjan Sal went to Nathadvara and there met envoys of Sawai Madho Singh (who had inherited the throne of Jaipur after the suicide of Ishvari Singh, his elder brother)[203] to talk about checking the marauding Marathas in Rajasthan. Durjan Sal also sent a message to Maharana Jagat Singh saying that he would meet him for further talks on the Maratha problem on the occasion of Phuldol (the flower swing festival), the "ritual decoration" (*singar*) of which is illustrated in this catalogue (cat. 55).[204]

Durjan Sal had two sons, both of whom predeceased him.[205] While visiting Anta in 1755, he decided to adopt Ajit Singh,[206] a grandson of Bishan Singh, who was the elder brother of Rao Ram Singh and the eldest son of Kishor Singh.[207]

Durjan Sal enjoyed hunting in the company of his queens; his preferred game was the lion.[208] In 1740, he arranged for the construction of the Jagmandir in the center of the Kishor Sagar (an artificial lake named after Kishor Singh) for Brajkunwar, his queen from the Sisodia clan of Mewar.[209] This artificial island caught the attention of James Tod, who published an engraving of it in the second volume of the first edition of his *Annals*.[210] Durjan Sal was a learned man, well versed in Sanskrit, and a devotee of the Vallabha Sampraday. He undertook yearly pilgrimages to several holy places, saw seven of Shri Nathji's "divine manifestations" (*svarups*) in 1740,[211] distributed thousands of rupees in charity, and generously rewarded the chief priests of Shri Nathji in Nathadvara. In 1744, he

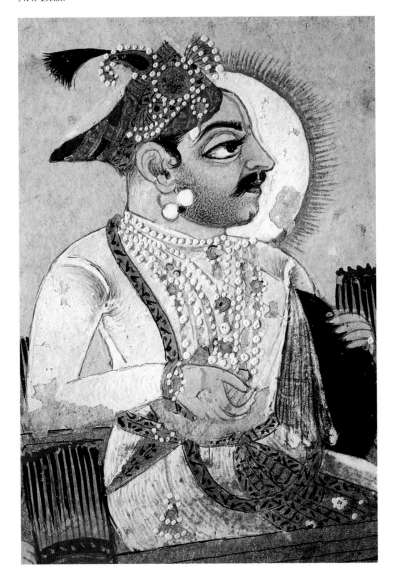

Figure 10
Detail of a portrait of Maharao Durjan Sal on the state elephant, c. 1730–40, Kotah. Opaque watercolor and gold on paper with inscription, 26 x 33.8 cm. National Museum, New Delhi.

brought the image of Mathuradhish or Mathuranath from Bundi to Kotah, where it is still venerated.[212] Also during his reign, Brijnathji, the idol of the tutelary deity of Kotah that was lost during the last battle of Maharao Bhim Singh, found its way back to Kotah. His last and probably longest pilgrimage took Durjan Sal to Dwarka in 1755.[213] He died on August 1, 1756.[214]

A fairly large number of contemporary portraits of Maharao Durjan Sal exists.[215] Hunting expeditions, including those on which he was accompanied by his three queens and concubines, are shown in several contemporary paintings.[216] Figure 10, an inscribed painting in the National Museum, New Delhi,[217] is a detail of a painting showing the ruler in the howdah of his elephant. His light complexion clearly distinguishes him from his father and elder brothers. He sports a comparatively short mustache and has no sideburns. Compared to that of his elder brother Arjun Singh, his nose is inconspicuous, but the dimple on his chin is remarkable. A Vaishnava mark adorns his forehead. Due to his connection with Mewar through Brajkunwar, his Sisodia queen, a number of his portraits were also painted by artists from there.[218] A posthumous but important portrait, which also includes a portrait of his religious adviser, is dated August/September 1778; this often-reproduced hunting scene is in the Victoria and Albert Museum, London.[219]

Maharao Ajit Singh

At the time of Durjan Sal's death, Maharao Ajit Singh was approximately eighty years of age and "very weak and infirm."[220] Durjan Sal's dowager queen was less than fifty and refused to adopt a man who could have been her father.[221] She was more in favor of the adoption of Ajit Singh's eldest son, Shatru Sal, who was then over forty. Nevertheless, Himat Singh Jhala, the military commander (*faujdar*) of Kotah, managed to have Ajit Singh installed on the throne of Kotah. His reign, however, as might have been expected, was extremely brief; he died in March 1757.[222]

Not surprisingly, only a few contemporary and near-contemporary portraits of Maharao Ajit Singh have survived. Figure 11, an inscribed sketch, reveals his heavy chin and long, pointed nose — which is, however, not as prominent as that of Maharao Arjun Singh. Other portraits of Maharao Ajit Singh emphasize the heaviness of his body.[223]

Maharao Shatru Sal I and the Rise of Zalim Singh Jhala

Ajit Singh left three sons: Shatru Sal, Guman Singh, and Raj Singh.[224] His eldest son, Shatru Sal, ascended to the throne of Kotah on September 15, 1758.[225]

In 1761, eight Hara principalities (*kotris*) — Pipalda, Gainta, Karwar, Pusod, Indargarh, Khatoli, Balban, and Antarda — were

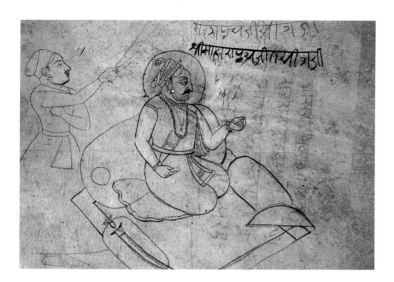

Figure 11
Portrait of Maharao Ajit Singh on a throne, c. 1757, Kotah. Ink and watercolor on paper with inscription, 14.2 x 20.5 cm. Collection of the late Sangram Singh of Nawalgarh, Jaipur.

under the protection of the rule of governance (*sarkar*) of the fortress of Ranthambhor. These principalities always paid some sort of tribute to the commander of Ranthambhor and served him. The fortress was handed over to Sawai Madho Singh of Jaipur in 1753;[226] after this, Himat Singh Jhala, the commander of Kotah, offered political protection to the principalities if they would transfer their allegiance to the maharao of Kotah.[227] The chiefs of the principalities signed an agreement to this effect, but the childless Himat Singh died suddenly in 1758; before he died, however, he adopted Zalim Singh Jhala, a grandson of his elder brother Madan Singh, himself a former commander of Kotah.

Madho Singh of Jaipur learned about the alliance between the chiefs of the eight Hara principalities and the maharao of Kotah and decided to challenge it. Jaipur troops entered Kotah by crossing the Chambal River in the territory of Indargarh. The chieftain (*jagirdar*) of Sultanpur of the Kotah state gallantly defended this fort against the Jaipur army and was slain; the Jaipur army marched on until it reached the neighborhood of the village of Bhatwara, four miles from the district (*tahsil*) headquarters of Mangrol. Here they came in touch with the Kotah army, commanded by Zalim Singh Jhala, assisted by the chief minister of the state, Akhai Ram Pancholi, and the maharao's foster brother, Jaskaran.

The Maratha army, under the leadership of Malhar Rao Holkar, was also poised to attack the Kotah state at this point.[228] At this time, Malhar Rao Holkar was encamped near Mukundarra. He was visited by Akhai Ram Pancholi, who tried to win over the Maratha army against the troops of Jaipur. Though it is not known on what terms Holkar agreed to support the Kotah army, he and

his troops accompanied it in the direction of Bhatwara, where the Maratha army finally encamped. The mere presence of the Maratha army near Bhatwara must have created the idea in the mind of the leaders of the Jaipur army that Kotah and the Marathas were in a military alliance. The Jaipur army numbered between ten and twenty-five thousand[229] and thus outnumbered the army of Kotah, which, even with the support of all the major chieftains with their contingents, in addition to some chieftains from the eight principalities, numbered only three thousand men.[230]

The young Zalim Singh Jhala prepared the battlefield well for this action in order to secure a fast retreat to the fortress of Kotah should this be needed. The battle started on November 29, 1761,[231] and raged for three days.[232] Although the Jaipur artillery played havoc among the Kotah troops and instantly killed seven hundred men,[233] at the end of the battle the army of Jaipur was completely routed.

The Kotah camp is illustrated in this catalogue (cat. 44). The Jaipur camp was plundered by the Marathas under Malhar Rao Holkar, but it is not clear whether they actively supported the Kotah army,[234] which also suffered heavy losses.[235] Seventeen elephants, eighteen hundred horses, seventy-three cannons, and a state flag of Jaipur (*panchranga*) fell into the hands of the victorious Kotah army.[236] From a sentimental point of view, the flag was the richest booty, and from that day on it was exhibited on the head of the effigy of Ravan on the occasion of the Dashahra Festival.[237] The Marathas were amply rewarded,[238] and Zalim Singh, together with Malhar Rao Holkar, was received in darbar by Maharao Shatru Sal.

Figure 12
Detail of Maharao Shatru Sal I and Zalim Singh Jhala, chief minister of the Kotah state, watching an elephant fight, c. 1764, Kotah. Ink and watercolor on paper, 20.8 x 25.6 cm. Private collection.

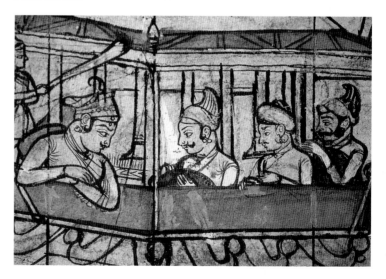

In 1762–63, the Kotah army was required to join the Marathas against Maharao Raja Umed Singh of Bundi, who was in arrears with the tribute he was supposed to pay to the Marathas. Maharao Shatru Sal accompanied the Marathas for forty days on this campaign. He died on December 17, 1764.[239]

Quite a number of portraits of this ruler exist. In four large, partly dated paintings, he rides a prancing horse.[240] Often he appears together with Zalim Singh Jhala, owing to the fact that most of these paintings were commissioned and donated by the commander to his overlord.[241] Figure 12, a fragment of a larger drawing, shows Maharao Shatru Sal watching an elephant fight from the Kotah palace. His arms rest on the balustrade while a servant behind him waves a royal emblem made of peacock feathers (*morchal*). Next to him sits Zalim Singh Jhala, recognizable by his Bundi turban (*khadgar pagri*), the shape of which somewhat resembles a shark fin. He looks at the maharao, while his hands hold a shield on his knees.[242] Similarly, he appears next to Shatru Sal in catalogue number 44, next to the large tent called the "carpet house" (*darikhana*) in the right half of the drawing. Behind the commander sits a Maratha chieftain (*sardar*), recognizable by his turban and large earrings.

Maharao Guman Singh

Maharao Guman Singh was a younger brother of Maharao Shatru Sal I, who died issueless. Guman Singh was about forty years of age[243] when he ascended the throne of Kotah on December 28, 1764.[244] On the very same day, Zalim Singh Jhala was appointed prime minister or chief minister (*musahib-i-ala* or *divan*) of the state.[245] Soon after, however, he was expelled from Kotah by Maharao Guman Singh.[246] In the middle of 1765, Zalim Singh left his estate in Kotah for Mewar, where Maharana Ari Singh welcomed him and where he received the title of Rajrana and a small estate.[247]

Maharao Guman Singh was unable to find a competent replacement for Zalim Singh. In the end, he had no choice and had to ask Zalim Singh to return to Kotah. After some hesitation, Zalim Singh accepted and returned to Kotah, where he was reinstalled as commander, in 1770. In addition, a part of the palace was made over to him for his residence; this palace, a kind of small fortress within Kotah Fort, is the Jhala-ki-Haveli, which today is almost completely in ruins.[248]

Maharao Guman Singh suffered from ulcers; the historian of Bundi, Suryamalla Mishran, claims that Zalim Singh managed to have poisoned bandages applied to the wounds.[249] Be that as it may, Guman Singh, while on his deathbed, entrusted his eldest son, Umed, to Zalim Singh's care before he died, on January 17, 1771.[250]

The only apparently contemporary portrait of Guman Singh is a drawing dated July/August 1757. This drawing is closely related

to a painting in the Williams College Museum of Art,[251] but includes additional sketches of both of Maharao Ajit Singh's sons, Shatru Sal (here written as "Chhatra Sal"), and, behind him, Guman Singh, when still a prince. Guman Singh's face is still without the customary mustache. Posthumous portraits of Guman Singh are abundant, but only a very few are published.[252] One of the most important artistic documents of Guman Singh's reign is a *Ragamala* of 251 folios, the greatest illustrated *Ragamala* ever produced.[253]

Maharao Umed Singh I

Maharao Guman Singh had three sons,[254] of whom Umed Singh was the eldest. When Umed Singh succeeded his father as maharao of Kotah on January 28, 1771,[255] he was about ten years old.[256] By this time, the maharao of Kotah had become a mere titular head of the state, which was completely under the control of Rajrana Zalim Singh, whose strategy is described in the following terms:

> There was no one who could share with Zalim Singh the power of administration, or who could be considered even socially his equal. Zalim Singh could not be contented with anything less than an unchallenged supreme position. He had nothing but hostility for those who claimed equality with him. He always found something to denounce in every man. If a man was intellectually superior, he would condemn him as socially inferior, and if a man were socially superior, he would run him down as intellectually inferior.[257]

Under Zalim Singh, Kotah prospered, whereas the neighboring states fell victim to marauding Marathas, Jats, and Pindaris. Zalim Singh always appeared to be subservient, but it was he who in fact pulled the strings.[258] He knew exactly how to entertain friend and foe, and distributed large numbers of gifts, often well-chosen art objects, turban ornaments, precious Kashmir shawls, paintings, and the like.[259]

According to the historian R. P. Shastri, Maharao Umed Singh I "was by temperament a non-assertive and submissive sort of man. From boyhood till his death he stood in awe of Zalim Singh and, therefore, there never occurred a chance of any conflict with him."[260] Shastri's estimation of Maharao Umed Singh's character is supported by a French eyewitness, the Comte de Modave, who visited Kotah during the monsoon season of 1776 and who wrote what is probably the earliest published non-Indian firsthand report of that city and its maharao. Modave, who noted that "Kotah offers one of the most magnificent courts of India,"[261] actually met Umed Singh I at Mukundarra and described him as "weak and cowardish to the extreme."[262] The history of Umed Singh is in fact best told by paintings, which were commissioned either by Zalim Singh or by himself, rather than by history books, which, as a rule, focus exclusively on the activities of Zalim Singh Jhala.

The earliest communication that the British had with Kotah took place in July 1803, when, during the British campaigns against the Marathas, Colonel Monson's detachment passed through the territory of that state and was given aid to facilitate its progress toward Gujarat.[263] Brigadier General Monson had to pass through Kotah again the following year, this time greatly harassed by the Marathas under Holkar, on July 12.[264] Monson had his retreat cut off by Holkar and tried to take shelter in the fort of Kotah; the official British historian William Thorn remarked that "the Rajah of Kottah was unwilling to admit our troops into the town, on the plea that he could not furnish them with provisions."[265] In fact, "the Raj Rana of Kotah, when the British troops arrived as fugitives, would neither admit them into the town nor supply them with food."[266] Zalim Singh was very careful. Had he assisted the weak British contingent, he would have provoked an attack by the then-successful Marathas on Kotah. The regent had no choice but to keep the British army out. Indeed, for the help rendered to the British the previous year, Zalim Singh had been fined one million rupees by the Maratha leader Holkar, while the latter camped in the neighborhood of Kotah.[267]

Thus were British officials made aware of Kotah. But whenever they turned their attention in that direction, it was exclusively with regard to Kotah's regent, never together with the rightful ruler, Maharao Umed Singh I, "who had been all his life a nonentity."[268] A letter written by a Western writer, dated January 31, 1809, remarks:

> The legitimate Raja of Kota is, with his family, kept in close confinement by a person named Zalim Singh, who has long usurped the entire management of public affairs; and is indeed recognized as ruler by all the states of Hindoostan. He is a man of very considerable talents; and, though not governing a very extensive territory, has yet contrived to render himself feared and respected by all his neighbours.[269]

A letter addressed to the Marquess of Hastings, dated July 7, 1817, says that

> Zalim Singh, Rajah of Kottah, has attained a power, through the influence of his personal character, far exceeding either his military means or the limits of his possessions: wise, consistent, and politic, he manages his own affairs and interferes with those of others with equal prudence: he pays tribute when protection is necessary, but his character causes him to be treated with comparative moderation. His territories are an asylum to distressed princes and offending subjects; he is a general arbitrator of disputes, and all concur in granting him a respect and confidence which they refuse to each other. His country, though situated in the vortex of anarchy and confusion, is usually exempt from the misery of surrounding districts.[270]

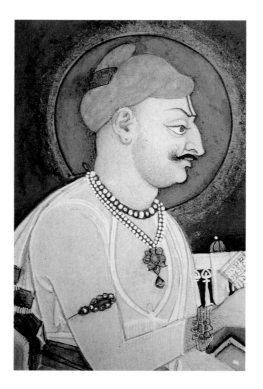

Figure 13
Detail of a portrait of Maharao Kishor Singh reading a letter on a terrace, c. 1820, Kotah. Opaque watercolor, silver, and gold on paper, approx. 21 x 14 cm. Collection of R. K. Tandan, Secunderabad.

Beale's *Oriental Biographical Dictionary*, even in its new edition, listed Zalim Singh as "the present Raja of Kota."[271]

On December 26, 1817, a treaty between the "Honourable English East India Company" and "Maha Rao Omeid Sing Bahadoor, the Rajah of Kotah … through Raj Rana Zalim Singh Bahadoor" was drawn up at Delhi. Kotah was taken under British protection and now had to pay to the British the tribute that had been due to the Marathas. Kotah was also to furnish troops to the British.[272] Of great historical consequence was the "Supplementary Article," according to which "the principality" was guaranteed to Umed Singh and his heirs "in perpetuity." The "principality," however, was separated in that article from the administration of the state, the passage concerning which reads: "The entire administration of the affairs of the principality shall be vested in Rajrana Zalim Sing, and after him in his eldest son, Koowar Madho Singh and his heirs, in regular succession and perpetuity."[273] Maharao Umed Singh I was thus officially without any political power. This article became known as the "secret clause."[274] It was signed at Delhi on February 20, 1818, and ratified by the governor general at Lucknow on March 7, 1818.[275]

Near-contemporary sources claim that Umed Singh was unaware of the "secret clause."[276] Zalim Singh continued to rule Kotah in the name of the maharao, and Umed Singh offered but little resistance to the Raj Rana.[277] He died on November 19, 1819,[278] a few hours after a viewing session (*darshan*) of Shri Brijnathji.

Politically, Maharao Umed Singh's rule is of little importance. Art historically, however, he was either one of the greatest Kotah patrons or one of the greatest connoisseurs of painting, or both.

Numerous hunting scenes showing him next to the regent attest to a high level of artistic activity, which was certainly also enjoyed by Zalim Singh.[279] Umed Singh, though a puppet in the hands of the regent, was one of the few Kotah rulers whose life was not endangered by his nearest relatives or rulers of neighboring states; he could enjoy life during a period of comparable prosperity. According to one Western observer, "Kota being in a central position, and the rajah a man of good character, is a place of great trade, and serves as a general deposit for merchandize."[280]

Portraits of Maharao Umed Singh are numerous and may be roughly divided into three categories: those showing him as a young lad without any trace of mustache; those in which he appears as a man, with mustache and sideburns; and those that show him in old age, with a white mustache brushed upwards as if to replace the shaved sideburns. The first category is best exemplified by a dated painting showing the young maharao on horseback at pigsticking. The date on the back of this published picture corresponds to May/June 1771,[281] and confirms the Comte de Modave's observation of the maharao's then-favorite sport.[282] Umed Singh appears to be of a similar young age in a painting that documents his early worship of Shri Brijnathji.[283] The second category of portraits represents the maharao mostly in hunting scenes, as is demonstrated by catalogue numbers 45, 46, and 48–51, as well as by equestrian portraits.[284] A religious scene dated 1803 introduces a portrait of the third category,[285] among which hunting scenes can also be found.[286]

Maharao Kishor Singh

Maharao Umed Singh had three sons: Kishor Singh, Vishnu Singh, and Prithvi Singh.[287] The eldest, Kishor Singh, was probably born in 1781,[288] but this date is not certain.[289] He ascended to the throne of Kotah on November 30, 1819.[290]

By this time, Zalim Singh Jhala had lost his eyesight. His eldest son, Madho Singh, was either forty or forty-six years of age, and his second son, Gordhan Das — whose mother was Zalim Singh's unofficial Muslim wife, Mannibai — was about twenty-seven.[291] The regent, thinking that his end was near, invested his eldest son with the power of commander.[292]

Unlike his father, Maharao Kishor Singh could not tolerate having no political power; Madho Singh did not possess the diplomatic virtues of his father. Prithvi Singh was loyal to his elder brother, but Gordhan Das, jealous of his elder half-brother, supported Kishor Singh and hence tried to remove his own father — who was not unaware of these developments. Zalim Singh ordered the siege of the palace in order to capture Prithvi Singh and Gordhan Das; after a few days in the beginning of May, Kishor Singh, with the tutelary deity at his saddlebow and about five hundred

horsemen, broke the siege and moved to Rangbari, some four to six miles south of Kotah.[293]

The British political agent, James Tod, rushed to the camp of the regent and then, after some consultation, went to the camp of the maharao. Tod effected a reconciliation of Kishor Singh with Zalim Singh and led the former back to the palace. Kishor Singh was formally reinstalled on August 17, 1820; Tod himself took part in the celebrations.[294] A robe of honor (khilat) was presented to the regent in the name of the governor-general of India. Madho Singh acted as commander and exchanged ceremonial gifts with the maharao. Gordhan Das was expelled from Kotah and chose to stay at Delhi, receiving thirty thousand rupees in cash from the court.[295] All seemed fine.

By the end of 1820, Gordhan Das had received permission to travel to Jhabua, a place in central India some 125 miles from Kotah,

Figure 14
Detail of a portrait of Maharao Ram Singh riding with retainers on foot, c. 1833, Kotah. Opaque watercolor, silver, and gold on paper, approx. 30 x 26.5 cm. San Diego Museum of Art.

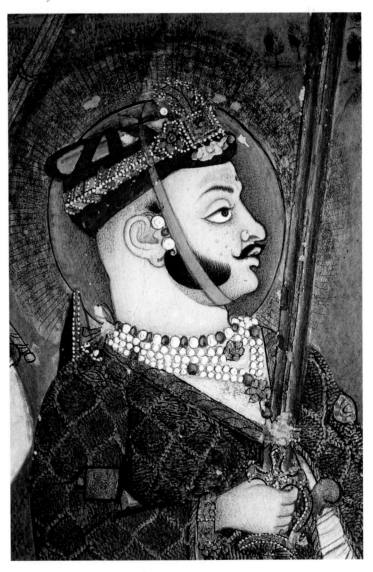

in order to fulfill a marriage contract. When he arrived there, a secret correspondence between him and Maharao Kishor Singh began. Zalim Singh, being aware of it, closed the city gates of Kotah in order to prevent outside help from entering. To make things worse, he ordered two twenty-four-pounders to shell the palace. Zaif Ali, a Muslim commander of Zalim Singh's army, deserted to Kishor Singh, who left the palace at night and reached Bundi territory by crossing the Chambal by boat. He was accompanied by his brother Prithvi Singh and Prithvi Singh's son, Ram Singh.[296]

Maharao Raja Bishan Singh of Bundi welcomed Maharao Kishor Singh, receiving him two miles from the city of Bundi.[297] The British tried to "capture Gordhandas, dead or alive, if he attempted to join the Maharao,"[298] but failed to do so. Gordhan Das escaped British surveillance, but could not achieve his purpose and returned to Delhi. Kishor Singh left Bundi for a pilgrimage to Brindaban near Mathura, where Tod hoped "that the tranquility and repose he would find amidst the fanes of the tutelary deity, Brijnathji, might tempt a mind prone to religious seclusion, to pass his days there."[299] By the middle of April, Kishor Singh had reached Mathura on his return from Brindaban to Kotah; crossing the Chambal, he entered Kotah State about forty miles north-northeast of Kotah City, with about three thousand followers. A letter dated September 16 was sent to James Tod; in this letter, Kishor Singh requested from the "English Government" the abolition of the "secret clause."[300] The regent, however, did not give in, and Kishor Singh is reported to have exclaimed, "What was life without honour; what was a sovereign without authority? Death, or the full sovereignty of his ancestors!"[301]

An armed conflict was inevitable:

> At daybreak on the 1st October 1821 the opposing forces took up their positions near Mangrol. The Regent's army consisted of 8 bataillons with 14 guns and 14 paigas [units] of cavalry…. The British troops consisting of 2 bataillons of infantry and 6 squadrons of cavalry with a Horse Artillery Battery formed on the right of the Regent's line.[302]

Maharao Kishor Singh commanded five hundred horsemen, the elite of the Hara army, as Tod himself, who was not only an eyewitness but also gave the signal for attack, acknowledged.[303] Kishor Singh had no artillery at his disposal, but kept charging the British army and that of the regent: "With all the gallantry that has ever distinguished the Haras, they … charged the regent's line, when several were killed at the very muzzle of the guns, and but for the advance of three squadrons of British cavalry, would have turned his left flank, and probably penetrated to the reserve, where the regent was in person."[304] Lieutenant and Adjutant John Clerk and Lieutenant Reade of the Fourth Regiment Bengal Light Cavalry died in action.[305] Their commander, Major Ridge, was seriously

wounded and only saved by his orderly. Prithvi Singh was found wounded by a trooper of the cavalry regiment Skinner's Horse and died the following day.[306] Maharao Kishor Singh had to retreat; he crossed the Parbati River and reached Baroda in western India (Gwalior State), where he took leave of his comrades in order to depart to Nathadvara, accompanied by Ram Singh, son of the gallant Prithvi. (Kishor Singh was married five times, but had only one son, who died at the age of four. After this, he lavished parental affection on Ram Singh, who was to become his successor.[307]) In the meantime, the regent was asked to grant a complete amnesty to those who participated in the battle against him.

Maharana Bhim Singh of Mewar welcomed Maharao Kishor Singh: strong matrimonial relations existed between these two states.[308] Bhim Singh also acted as mediator, and an engagement addressed to Captain James Tod was signed by Kishor Singh on November 22, 1821, at Nathadvara. In this engagement, Kishor Singh ceded all power to the British government and acknowledged the position of "Nanahjee Zalim Sing."[309]

Maharao Kishor Singh was escorted back to Kotah, which he reached on the last day of 1821.[310] He was warmly received by the regent, who waited on him four miles from the city. After a hearty welcome was rendered to Kishor Singh by the city of Kotah, he was again formally installed on the ancestral throne. On January 8, 1822, Madho Singh Jhala agreed to an annual allowance of 164,877 rupees for the maintenance of Maharao Kishor Singh and his household and establishments. Out of this amount, forty-eight hundred rupees were spent annually on the temple of Brijrajji, Kishor Singh's personal deity. Another contract was drawn up that secured eighteen thousand rupees annually for "Baapoo Lall" — Madan Singh, the grandson of Zalim Singh.[311] A day earlier, another cluster of articles had been drawn up by Tod "for the observance and provision of the Maha Rao Kishore Sing and successors, and signed by Kunwar Madhoo Sing."[312] These articles regulated the possession of the maharao's lands and limited the "personal guards" of the maharao to "one hundred horse and 200 foot."

Rajrana Zalim Singh Jhala died on June 15, 1824,[313] and Maharao Kishor Singh on July 2, 1827.[314]

Maharao Kishor Singh figures prominently in a number of wall paintings within the Bada Mahal of Kotah Fort. He appears as the major figure in two darbars, facing the regent, Madho Singh, in one, and Prithvi Singh in another. In other murals, he is seen worshiping Shri Mathureshji or other divinities of the Vallabha Sampraday.[315] Like his father, he is shown shooting at game from tree-blinds, but none of the hunting scenes showing Kishor Singh in action seems to have been published. The great majority of his portraits show him as a pious man; from these, it is difficult to believe that Kishor Singh dared to fight against the regent of the state and the British army with so much vigor. Figure 13 introduces him as he appears in most of his portraits: light-complexioned, with a yellow turban showing a short cone on top, and a thin but long mustache, the ends of which are gray; his face is otherwise clean-shaven. His nose is slightly curved in sharp outline, and his chin is comparatively round and small. In this illustration, he holds a book the text of which begins: "Reverence to Shri Krishna! Reverence to Gopijanavallabha!"

Maharao Ram Singh

Maharao Ram Singh was the son of Maharao Kishor Singh's youngest brother, Prithvi Singh. When he ascended to the throne of Kotah in 1827,[316] he was nineteen years old.[317]

Starting on January 17, 1832, Maharao Ram Singh and Madho Singh Jhala attended the great darbar held by Lord William Bentinck, the governor-general of India, near Ajmer. Five other chiefs from Rajasthan were also invited. This darbar was held with great ceremony, recorded by both historians and the court painters of Kotah.[318] Its main purpose was to suppress the anti-British feelings that prevailed in Rajasthan at the time.[319]

The "Kotah contingent," commanded by British officers and financed by the state of Kotah, was created in 1836.[320] Maharao Ram Singh wanted to exercise political power and hence could not get along with Madan Singh Jhala, who had become regent on the death of his father, Madho Singh Jhala. In order to avoid another battle of Mangrol, a treaty was signed with the officiating British political agent at Kotah on April 10, 1838. This treaty canceled the "secret clause" and ceded a certain portion of Kotah territory to Madan Singh. Maharao Ram Singh agreed to finance the "Kotah contingent" and thus regained full political power over his territory as long as he fulfilled "the pecuniary obligations arising out of the present arrangements of separation and transfer agreeable to the appended Schedule."[321]

During the Indian Mutiny of 1857, Major Burton, the British resident at Kotah, left his wife and four of his children under the safeguard of the British troops at Nimach, an important military station. Accompanied by two of his sons, he reached Kotah on October 12, 1857. Burton must have told the maharao which soldiers of the "auxiliary force" he did not trust; according to a British account,

Officers and men were, in very truth, alike disaffected, and, being so, the communication made to them by order of the maharao determined them to take the law into their own hands. Accordingly, they assembled the following morning, killed Mr. Salder, the Residency surgeon, and Mr. Saviell, the doctor of the dispensary in the city, who resided in a house in the Residency grounds, and then attacked the Residency itself.[322]

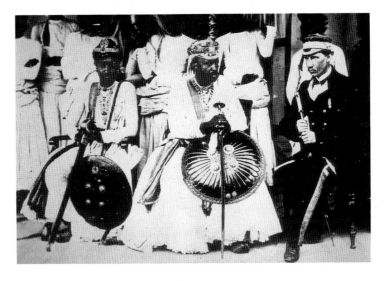

Figure 15
Maharao Ram Singh (center) with his son and the British resident, c. 1863–64, India. Albumen print from a collodion negative on paper with inscription, approx. 13 x 17 cm. Collection Sven Gahlin, London.

Burton and both of his sons were killed.[323] The former residence of the political agent now serves as the residence of the maharao of Kotah.

It was not until March 30, 1858, that Kotah was attacked by a British force, fifty-five hundred strong, under Major General Roberts. Kotah was taken on April 1. "Between 400 and 500 rebels were killed and numbers of prisoners were taken. Of the British force 14 were killed and 46 wounded."[324] Maharao Ram Singh was subsequently punished for his inactivity during the revolt: his salute was reduced by four guns.[325] He died on the evening of March 27, 1866.[326]

No other Kotah ruler was portrayed more often than Maharao Ram Singh, who appears prominently in hunting scenes, darbars, and official meetings with various Rajput rulers and British officers. He figures no less prominently in all sorts of festivities, such as the slaughter of the buffalo during the Dashahra celebrations, the procession to the temple of Ashapura Devi in the fort, the procession to the burning of Ravan, and the spring festival of Holi. Routine daily activities like the worship of the tutelary deity or horse exercises were also immortalized by his artists. In addition to such genre scenes, events demonstrating the maharao's wit were also painted. Once, for example, he brought his horse onto the top of the palace roof, and he demonstrated that he could ride an elephant on the fragile roof of a pavilion that still stands. Most of these paintings either contain dates or are datable on the basis of the events shown in them.[327]

Figure 14 is a detail of a portrait of the young Maharao Ram Singh on horseback in a painting of about 1833. His sideburns grew

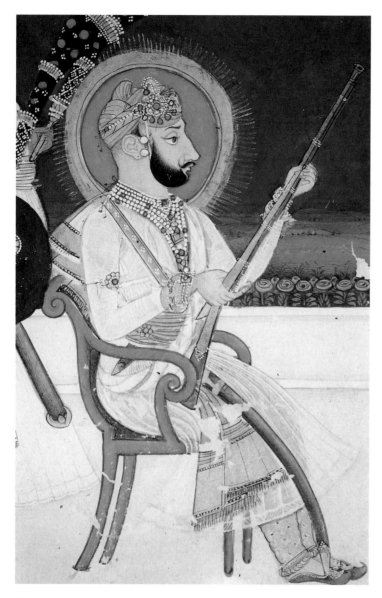

Figure 16
Detail of a portrait of Maharao Shatru Sal II seated on a terrace, c. 1868–70, Kotah.
Opaque watercolor and gold on paper, 25.5 x 17.6 cm. Rao Madho Singh Trust Museum,
Fort Kotah.

longer in the course of time, and he never shaved his mustache. His young face was marked by smallpox, his eyelids were heavy, his lips were pursed, and the tip of his nose was marked by a small round boss. His hair was shaved, except for a small area above the back of the head, mostly concealed by a turban.[328] In figure 14, his halo has a rim of radiant gold and closely resembles that of his predecessor. Figure 15, a "startling discovery,"[329] is the only known photograph of Maharao Ram Singh and shows a new kind of headgear introduced by him: a coneless, flat turban with a peak above the forehead, resembling the cap of a contemporary Britisher. The contemporary caption below the photograph reads *H.H. the Maha Row of Kotah & Son*. The print was found in an album with a number of Eugene Impey's photographs; Impey was present at the siege of

Kotah in 1858,[330] but it is more likely that he took this photograph while posted at Jodhpur as British political agent for the Marwar State between 1865 and 1868.[331]

Maharao Shatru Sal II

Maharao Shatru Sal II[332] was the eldest son of Maharao Ram Singh and the latter's first wife, the daughter of Bairisal Rathor.[333] His birth name, Bhim Singh,[334] was changed to Shatru Sal after the coronation ceremony, which took place on March 28, 1866.[335] "The Viceroy took the opportunity of [Shatru Sal's] accession to restore to him the salute of seventeen guns enjoyed by his father prior to 1857."[336]

Art historically, the most important event of Shatru Sal II's reign was his participation in the darbar of the third viceroy, Sir John Laird Mair Lawrence, later Lord Lawrence, at Agra, on November 19, 1866. A large wall painting near the Kanwarpada ka Mahal depicts the event, in which the young maharao appears three times. The seating order as observed by the Kotah artist is accurate but for the position of the begum of Bhopal, who is apparently only shown in her chariot. The accuracy of the artist's rendering was confirmed by a French eyewitness, Louis Rousselet, who published a lengthy account of the event.[337]

During Shatru Sal II's reign, a number of reforms, often based on European models, were introduced. They had no art-historical effect, however. Even the steam launch brought from England in March 1879, though "apparently much appreciated by the Durbar,"[338] does not figure in any painting done during the maharao's reign.

Another major event of Shatru Sal II's period was the imperial darbar at Delhi on January 1, 1877. During this darbar, any ruler entitled to a gun salute was given a banner, richly blazoned with what the designer, Lord Lytton, believed to be the armorial bearings of the state. The Kotah banner, which still exists,[339] bears the figure of Garuda — the Kotah emblem — in its center, held by dragons.

Shatru Sal II's health was poor;[340] around the time of the imperial darbar he became quite ill, and never really recovered.[341] He died on June 11, 1889, after having adopted Uday Singh, who was the second son of Maharaja Chagan Singh of Kotra and who succeeded Shatru Sal II under the name Maharao Umed Singh II.[342]

Maharao Shatru Sal II was portrayed in virtually the same situations as his father, but only a few good portraits of him have been published. Quite a number of paintings show him as a young prince, without sideburns;[343] after his coronation, he appears with sideburns that almost completely surround his chin.[344] Figure 16 shows the young ruler seated in a European chair, wearing a turban which, with its small cone, resembles that of Maharao Kishor

Singh. His hair is shaved, like his father's. His eyelids are less heavy, and his nose is longer, not straight, but slightly pointed.

Quite a few of Shatru Sal II's drawings and paintings are dated.[345] He was the last great patron of Kotah painting. Though during the first years of Maharao Umed Singh II's reign paintings were still commissioned, they show clear marks of decadence. It is hence not surprising that Umed Singh II succumbed to the prevailing taste; all of his later portraits are either photographs or painted after photographs.

NOTES

1 Fryer, 2:100 and 106.

2 Marwar Census 1894.

3 Mundy 1914, 2:245.

4 For a more recent discussion of this term, see Mathur 1986, 1–5.

5 Bapna, 1976, 23.

6 Tod 1920 ed., 1:482; Mishran c. 1899, 5:2265, verses 27ff; and Shyamaldas 1886, 2:84–85. The siege is reported in detail by all Islamic historians, including Akbar's biographer, Abul Fazl (Abul Fazl 1973 ed., 2:489), and is even mentioned by the Dutch chronicler Joannes De Laet in his Latin history of India from 1631 (De Laet 1928 ed., 152); it is also detailed in the often-published, near-contemporary illustrations of the *Akbar Nama* in the Victoria and Albert Museum, London (I.S., nos. 72/117–76/117). A near-contemporary Rajput account, the "great poem on Surjan's life," also describes the armies and the battle in great detail (Surjanacharitamahakavyam 1952 ed., *sargas* 16–17 and 18 and *shlokas* 1–23).

7 Abul Fazl 1977 ed., 1:510, and N. S. Khan and Hayy 1979 ed., 409.

8 The Daud or Doda of the Islamic sources.

9 Sen 1984, pl. 55, and Patnaik and Welch 1985, frontispiece and fig. 1.

10 G. N. Sharma 1962, 73–107.

11 Abul Fazl 1973 ed., 3:258.

12 See Abul Fazl 1977 ed., 3:284.

13 London, Victoria and Albert Museum, I.S. 2–1896 (103/117), published in *Petals from a Lotus* 1982, pl. 11.

14 Athar Ali 1985, xi; see also Moreland 1936.

15 Athar Ali 1985, 15.

16 Shyamaldas 1886, 2:111; for the birth date of Bhoj, see Mishran c. 1899 ed., 2434, verse 85.

17 N. S. Khan and Hayy 1979 ed., 409, and Abul Fazl 1977 ed., 1:510; on the fourth day of the bright half of [the month] Jyeshtha in v.s. 1664, according to the Bundi chronicle *Vansh Bhaskar* (Mishran c. 1899 ed., 2434, verse 87) and the (unpublished) inscription on his cenotaph (*chhatri*) near Bundi. Shyamal

das 1886, 2:111, says it was the fourth of the bright half of Asadha in v.s. 1664 — one month later, corresponding to June 26, 1607.

18 Athar Ali 1985, index under "Rai Bhuj."

19 Mishran c. 1899 ed., 2433, verse 79.

20 Bautze 1987a, 58–61.

21 This *Ragamala* "was ready on the day of Wednesday at the time of the mid-day prayer in the place Chunar … on the date of the 29th of the month Rabial-Akhir, year 999 [February 25, 1591 C.E.]" (Skelton 1981, 124).

22 Gray 1949, frontispiece; Goetz 1950, pl. x; and Gray 1955, pl. IV, just to mention a few.

23 Ojha 1939 1:186f. and 188.

24 Mishran c. 1899 ed., 1548, verse 59.

25 Shyamaldas 1886, 2:111.

26 Mishran c. 1899 ed., 2432, verse 71.

27 Jahangir 1978 ed., 1:140.

28 Ray 1975, pl. x.

29 Jahangir 1978 ed., 2:257.

30 Prasad 1973, 357, and Elliot and Dowson 1875, 412.

31 Prasad 1973, 357.

32 See N. S. Khan and Hayy 1952 ed., 604.

33 Elliot and Dowson 1875, 396.

34 Athar Ali 1985, 87, J1477.

35 Following Mishran c. 1899 ed., 2548, verse 60; the inscription on his cenotaph at Banganga near Bundi; and Athar Ali 1985, 115 and S643.

36 Koch 1986.

37 Bautze 1986b, 1986c, 1986d, 1987b, and 1989b.

38 Gahlot 1960, 89.

39 Mundy 1914, 24f.

40 Bautze 1986e, fig. 5.

41 Ibid., figs. 5, 7, 13, and 20.

42 Ibid., fig. 9.

43 Mishran c. 1899 ed., 2448, verse 204; he was born in 1589.

44 N. S. Khan and Hayy 1952 ed., 722, and Lahori's *Badshahnameh* quoted after Shyamaldas 1886, 2:112, n. 2.

45 N. S. Khan and Hayy 1952 ed., 722.

46 Gahlot 1960, kota, 9, and M. L. Sharma 1939, 1:41.

47 Athar Ali 1985, 101, S191.

48 Ibid., 115, S645.

49 Khan Jahan Lodi was decapitated — a painted event that may include a portrait of Madho Singh ('Inayat Khan 1990 ed., pl. 15; see also Bautze 1993a, 268).

50 N. S. Khan and Hayy 1952 ed., 1; Kewal Ram 1985 ed., 302; and *Padshahnameh* of Lahori, quoted after Sarkar 1984, 203, n. 4.

51 Mathur 1985, 108.

52 See Nath and Singh Jodha 1994, chart, 210.

53 N. S. Khan and Hayy 1952 ed., 1.

54 'Inayat Khan 1990 ed., 163.

55 Syed 1977, 34.

56 M. L. Sharma 1939, 1:126f.; according to sources quoted by Athar Ali, he lived ten years longer (Athar Ali 1985, 304, S6718, and 325, S7418).

57 Athar Ali 1985, 213, S3846 and S3845.

58 For which see M. L. Sharma 1939, 1:138f.

59 Bautze 1986e, fig. 12.

60 Named and numbered 194/1–194/7 in Mishran c. 1899 ed., 2455, verses 49ff.

61 Mishran c. 1899 ed., 2454, verses 48f.

62 N. S. Khan and Hayy 1952 ed., 241.

63 Athar Ali 1985, 232, S4432.

64 N. S. Khan and Hayy 1952 ed., 242.

65 Sarkar 1912, 2:12 and 14, and Syed 1977, 86.

66 Sarkar 1912, 2:18, and Kewal Ram 1985 ed., 303.

67 Athar Ali 1985, 325, S7426.

68 Syed 1977, 88; N. S. Khan and Hayy 1952 ed., 242; Mishran c. 1899 ed., 2667, lines 2–23; and M. L. Sharma 1939, 1:168.

69 M. L. Sharma 1939, 1:174.

70 Ibid., 1:172, following Lakshmandan n.d., 12, 3rd line; and Gahlot 1960, kota, 49.

71 N. S. Khan and Hayy 1979 ed., 405.

72 Probably Bahadurpura, three miles from Burhanpur; see Sarkar 1919, 4:245.

73 Bhimsen 1972 ed., 134.

74 According to Gahlot 1960, 49. It seems, however,

that this is not fully correct, since contemporary and other sources state that Jagat Singh died while defending one of the Mughal camps north of Bijapur against the Marathas in 1682, and that nine hundred other Hara soldiers died with him (Sarkar 1937, 282, and Bhimsen 1972 ed., 140).

75 Patnaik and Welch 1985, 88.

76 Beach 1974, fig. 68.

77 Ibid., fig. 69.

78 Bautze 1986a, fig. 2.

79 Kühnel 1937, pl. 8; for a more recent reproduction of this painting as a full-color facsimile, see Enderlein and Hickmann 1995, pl. 2.

80 Bautze 1986a, fig. 3.

81 N. S. Khan and Hayy 1952 ed., 242 and 593, and Bhimsen 1972 ed., 140.

82 M. L. Sharma 1939, 1:198f.

83 Ibid., 1:197.

84 Athar Ali 1985, 287.

85 Sarkar 1919, 311.

86 Ibid., 322f.

87 Bhimsen 1972 ed., 152.

88 Ibid., 160.

89 Syed 1977, 346, and Sarkar 1919, 368.

90 M. L. Sharma 1939, 1:207f.

91 For Zulfiqar Khan's biography, see N. S. Khan and Hayy 1952 ed., 1033–44.

92 Bhimsen 1972 ed., 200, and N. S. Khan and Hayy, 1952 ed., 593.

93 Athar Ali 1966, 238.

94 Ibid., 229.

95 Bhimsen 1972 ed., 201; M. L. Sharma 1939, 1:213; and Sarkar 1924, 104.

96 Hendley 1897, no. 4, pl. 11; Pal 1976, no. 41; and further posthumous unpublished portraits.

97 M. L. Sharma 1939, 1:202.

98 Bhimsen 1972 ed., 201, and N. S. Khan and Hayy 1952 ed., 2:593.

99 Shyamaldas 1886, 2:1412, and M. L. Sharma 1939, 1:222f.

100 Bhimsen 1972 ed., 205.

101 Ibid., 207–9, and Sarkar 1924, 105–8.

102 S. M. Khan 1947 ed., 260.

103 Bhimsen 1972 ed., 227.

104 Athar Ali 1966, 234.

105 Bhimsen 1972 ed., 228.

106 Ibid., 232, and S. Chandra 1979, 5.

107 Bhimsen 1972 ed., 233.

108 Ibid., 243.

109 S. M. Khan 1947 ed., 300, and Bhimsen 1972 ed., 250; it is, however, not clear how much Ram Singh's rank totaled around that time. Bhimsen mentions twenty-five hundred.

110 S. M. Khan 1947 ed., 305; Kewal Ram 1985 ed., 263; and N. S. Khan and Hayy 1952 ed., 594.

111 Sarkar 1924, 257, and Sarkar 1937, 302.

112 Tod 1920 ed., 1495.

113 Mishran c. 1899 ed., 2967–93; Irvine 1971 ed., 2:22–30.

114 M. L. Sharma 1939, 1:248; Irvine 1971 ed., 1:30; N. S. Khan and Hayy 1952 ed., 594; and Hussein-Khan 1832, 14.

115 Irvine 1971 ed., 30, and Hussein-Khan 1832, 14.

116 Kewal Ram 1985 ed., 263.

117 S. M. Khan 1947, 305, and Hussein-Khan 1832, 14.

118 See Ehnbom 1985, no. 42; Sotheby's, Inc., 1989, no. 125; and Hotel Drouot 1983, no. 82.

119 Falk 1978, pl. on 61, no. 69 (I have not seen the inscription).

120 Lakshmandan n.d., 19.

121 Ibid., 19, and Shyamaldas 1886, 2:1414.

122 Mishran c. 1899 ed., 2999, verse 29, and Shyamaldas 1886, 2:115.

123 S. Chandra 1979, 121, and Sarkar 1984, 190.

124 For a complete list, see Mishran c. 1899 ed., 2999.

125 Shyamaladas 1886, 2:1414.

126 Styled "Maharaja" by Lakshmandan n.d., 19.

127 Lakshmandan n.d., 19, and Mishran c. 1899 ed., 3008ff.

128 Mishran c. 1899 ed., 3022f, and Lakshmandan n.d., 19f.

129 Irvine 1971 ed., 1:135.

130 Ibid., 1:229ff.

131 Ibid., 1:240.

132 Bhatnagar 1974, 120.

133 S. Chandra 1979, 122, n. 21.

134 Bhatnagar 1974, 120, and S. Chandra 1979, 122, n. 21.

135 Bhatnagar 1974, 120, and S. Chandra 1979, 121f.

136 M. L. Sharma 1939, 1:249.

137 For details, see M. L. Sharma 1939, 1:262.

138 Descriptive List 1974, 50, serial no. 213.

139 S. Chandra 1979, 122, n. 21.

140 Ibid., 123.

141 Bhatnagar 1974, 121. Other official sources claim that Maharao Raja Budh Singh had already regained Bundi on June 12 or July 30; see Descriptive List 1974, 57, serial no. 279, and 58, serial no. 281.

142 Bhatnagar 1974, 121; Bhargava 1979, 161; S. Chandra 1979, 124; and Irvine 1971 ed., 1:333. Mau Maidana had already been returned to Budh Singh earlier (S. Chandra 1979, 124, n. 29).

143 S. Chandra 1979, 124.

144 M. L. Sharma 1939, 1:264f.

145 Irvine 1971 ed., 1:374, and S. Chandra 1979, 139.

146 Irvine 1971 ed., 1:376; S. Chandra 1979, 140; and Elliot and Dowson 1877, 475.

147 Tod 1920 ed., 1496.

148 N. Singh 1939, 83.

149 Sarkar 1984, 191.

150 Mishran c. 1899 ed. 3065, verses 116ff; Irvine 1971 ed., 1:376; Bhatnagar 1974, 135; and S. Chandra 1979, 140.

151 Irvine 1971 ed., 1:379ff, and Elliot and Dowson 1877, 478.

152 Irvine 1971 ed., 1:391–93.

153 Ibid., 1:198.

154 Ibid., 1:408ff.

155 Ibid., 1:413.

156 Ibid., 1:418.

157 Ibid., 1:431, and 2:1.

158 Ibid., 2:1f.

159 Ibid., 2:5.

160 Ibid., 2:6.

161 For which see Barz 1992 and the essay by Norbert Peabody, below.

162 Mishran c. 1899 ed., 3071; Lakshmandan n.d., 31; and M. L. Sharma 1939, 1:269f.

163 Irvine 1971 ed., 2:5.

164 Hussein-Khan 1832, 201.

165 Ibid., 277.

166 Elliot and Dowson 1877, 489. For a quotation of this passage, see cat. 68; for a biography of Nizam-ul-Mulk or Asaf Jah 1, see Husain 1963.

167 Bhatnagar 1974, 149, and Irvine 1971 ed., 2:6.

168 Tod 1920 ed., 1527; Lakshmandan n.d., 22, and M. L. Sharma 1939, 1:299f.; on the latter issue, see Bautze 1992a, 82.

169 Elliot and Dowson 1877, 490 and 492, and Irvine 1971 ed., 2:19, 23, and 27.

170 Irvine 1971 ed., 2:28.

171 M. L. Sharma 1939, 1:297; for the actual idol, see M. B. Singh 1985, fig. 25.

172 Elliot and Dowson 1877, 496. See also Hussein-Khan 1832, 222f., and Hussein [Hossein]-Khan 1986 ed., 1:162f.

173 Husain 1963, 101–3; Irvine 1971 ed., 2:29–31; M. L. Sharma 1939, 1:295–98; Shyamaldas 1886, 2:1414–16; Lakshmandan n.d., 2631; Tod 1920 ed., 1525–26; and Gahlot 1960, kota, 58–59.

174 For which see Lakshmandan n.d. 31, and M. L. Sharma 1939, 1:309.

175 Bautze 1986d; Bautze 1995b, pl. 134, fig. 196; and M. B. Singh 1985, 14.

176 Bautze 1989, pl. 71; Bautze 1992, figs. 37.1–2; and Hendley 1897, no. 6, pl. 11; compare Hatanaka 1994, pl. 99.

177 Tod 1920 ed., 1528.

178 The red Devanagari numerals "15/282" indicate that the painting once formed part of the royal Mewar collection: portraits of non-Mewar rulers were filed under this inventory number (see Topsfield 1995, 192).

179 Bautze 1989a, pl. 67; Sotheby's, Inc., 1972, no. 112; and an unpublished painting in a private collection.

180 Bautze 1989a, pls. 64 and 65.

181 For which see M. B. Singh 1985, fig. 4.

182 M. L. Sharma 1939, 1:310; a fifth son, Maha Singh, is also mentioned in the Jaipur records (Descriptive List 1974, 72, serial no. 332).

183 Lakshmandan n.d., 21.

184 M. L. Sharma 1939, 1:310.

185 Ibid., 1:316; Bhatnagar 1974, 169.

186 M. L. Sharma 1939, 1:319.

187 Desai and Leidy 1989, pl. v (inscribed "picture of Maharao Arjun Singhji").

188 Sotheby's, Inc., 1973, no. 175; Christie's Inc., 1980, no. 46; and cat. 19 and 20.

189 Bautze 1992b, fig. 37.5; Shyam is "the dark one," Krishna.

190 Shyamaldas 1886, 2:1416, and Gahlot 1960, kota, 60.

191 Descriptive List 1978, document no. 459, dated December 14, 1723; and Bhatnagar 1974, 169f.

192 Bhatnagar 1974, 218; for details, see Bautze 1987a, 313–22.

193 Bhatnagar 1974, 219; for Dalel Singh's portraits, see Bautze 1988, 91.

194 Bhatnagar 1974, 221; Sarkar 1932, 251f; and Sarkar 1984, 194.

195 K. S. Gupta 1971, 39–42; Bhatnagar 1974, 222–25; and M. L. Sharma 1939, 2:375–77.

196 See M. L. Sharma 1939, 1:347; Shyamaldas 1886, 2:1416, according to whom she was the daughter (kanya) of Maharana Jagat Singh; and Gahlot 1960, kota, 63, who calls her the sister (bahin) of Jagat Singh.

197 Bhatnagar 1974, 225–27.

198 M. L. Sharma 1939, 2:378f.

199 K. S. Gupta 1971, 54.

200 Ibid., 55f.

201 Sarkar 1932, 323.

202 Ibid., 293f.; K. S. Gupta 1971, 63; Sarkar 1984, 236–38; and N. Singh 134–40, based mainly on Mishran's *Vansh Bhaskar.*

203 H. Singh 1965, sheet no. 2, serial no. 32; and Sarkar 1984, 240.

204 K. S. Gupta 1971, 66.

205 M. L. Sharma 1939, 2:401.

206 R. P. Shastri 1971, 29, and M. L. Sharma 1939, 2:412.

207 Shyamaldas 1886, 2:1417f.

208 M. L. Sharma 1939, 2:403f.

209 Ibid., 2:405f. and 467 and M. B. Singh 1991, 248f.

210 See Bautze 1989c, 390, n. 42.

211 These were Vitthalnathji, Navanitapriyaji, Dvarkanathji, Gokulchandramaji, Mathuranathji, Gokulnath, and Madanmohanji; see Gahlot 1960, kota, 63.

212 M. L. Sharma 1939, 2:403–5 and 409.

213 Ibid., 2:409–11.

214 Shyamaldas 1886, 2:1417, and Gahlot 1960, kota, 63.

215 Bautze 1995b, 135; Bautze 1985b, 96f, nn. 49–54, figs. 3 and 4; Bautze 1992a, fig. 44; and Sotheby's, Inc., 1973, no. 179 (inscribed; now in the San Diego Museum of Art, Binney Collection).

216 Devkar 1957, 21, pl. XIX, and Chaitanya 1982, pl. XI.

217 56.35/2, inscribed "Maharao Durjan Salji."

218 Bautze 1995b, 136, and Sotheby's, Inc., 1994, no. 39.

219 Recent publications include Guy and Swallow 1990, 142, pl. 122.

220 R. P. Shastri 1971, 30.

221 Ibid., 31.

222 Shyamaldas 1886, 2:1418. For sources on the contention over the succession, see R. P. Shastri 1971, 32, and Gahlot 1960, kota, 64.

223 The first identified portrait of Ajit Singh is in the Linden-Museum, Stuttgart; see Bautze 1985b, pl. on 32; for further portraits see Bautze 1985b, 102f, and Noey and Temos 1994, frontispiece and no. 31.

224 M. L. Sharma 1939, 2:416, and Gahlot 1960, kota, 65.

225 Shyamaldas 1886, 2:1418, and Lakshmandan n.d., 51.

226 M. L. Sharma 1939, 2:424.

227 R. P. Shastri 1971, 38, and N. Singh 1930, 195f.

228 For details, see M. L. Sharma 1939, 2:448f, and R. P. Shastri 1971, 39f.

229 R. P. Shastri 1971, 45; Sarkar 1934, 2:506; Sarkar 1984, 250; and Bhatt 1971, 199; Gahlot 1960, kota, 67, says the Jaipur army was sixty thousand strong.

230 Sarkar 1984, 251.

231 Sarkar 1934, 506.

232 R. P. Shastri 1971, 42.

233 M. L. Sharma 1939, 2:444.

234 Compare Gahlot 1960, kota, 68; Bhatt 1971, 199f.; and R. P. Shastri 1971, 46–48.

235 For details, see M. L. Sharma 1939, 2:445f.

236 Shyamaldas 1886, 2:1418f, and R. P. Shastri 1971, 43.

237 R. P. Shastri 1971, 44.

238 For details, see R. P. Shastri 1971, 45.

239 Shyamaldas 1886, 2:1419, and Gahlot 1960, kota, 68.

240 Bautze 1988, figs. 5–8, and Bautze 1995b, pl. on 153.

241 Beach 1974, fig. 89; Bautze 1992a, figs. 45 and 84; and Sotheby's Inc., 1992, no. 155.

242 See Beach 1974, fig. 89.

243 R. P. Shastri 1971, 51.

244 Shyamaldas 1886, 2:1419, and Gahlot 1960, kota, 66.

245 R. P. Shastri 1971, 50.

246 It is not known exactly why Zalim Singh had to leave Kotah; James Tod wrote that he "dared to cross his master's path in love" (Tod 1920 ed., 1537), whereas R. P. Shastri argued that Zalim Singh left on the advice of Guman Singh's counselors. Shastri estimated that Guman Singh was about fifty years old at the time of his accession and concluded that "a man of fifty is not usually capable of any impetuous or uncontrollable passion for a girl" (R. P. Shastri 1971, 52).

247 K. S. Gupta 1971, 85, and Tod 1920 ed., 1538.

248 R. P. Shastri 1971, 58–60.

249 Ibid., 60.

250 Shyamaldas 1886, 1419; Gahlot 1960, kota, 71; Tod 1920 ed., 1539f; R. P. Shastri 1971, 60f; and M. L. Sharma 1939, 2:470.

251 Noey and Temos 1994, frontispiece.

252 See Bautze 1985a, 443, pl. 3.

253 Folio 249 gives the information that it was completed on Tuesday, the second of the bright half of the month Jyeshtha, v.s. 1825 [May/June 1768 C.E.] at Nandgrama in Kotah in the reign of Maharajadhiraja Raja Raja Shri Shri Shri Shri Shri Guman Singh for Maharani Ranawatji (Ebeling 1973, 219, fig. 131). Ebeling's interpretation of that colophon is incorrect; he identified Nandgrama with Nanta, Zalim Singh's estate. I am indebted to Robert Skelton for supplying me with a clear photograph of this important folio.

254 R. P. Shastri 1971, 58.

255 Shyamaldas 1886, 2:1420, and Gahlot 1960, kota, 71.

256 M. L. Sharma 1939, 2:471.

257 R. P. Shastri 1971, 61f.

258 Bautze 1994, 105f.

259 Ibid., 109ff.

260 R. P. Shastri 1971, 73.

261 Modave 1971 ed., 480 (*La Cour du raja de Cota passe pour une des plus magnifiques de l'Indoustan*).

262 Ibid., 488 (*C'est un prince foible et lâche ce qu'il est possible*).

263 Clunes 1833, 154.

264 Grant Duff 1863, 3:198, and Clunes 1833, 154.

265 Thorn 1818, 360.

266 Grant Duff 1863, 3:198f.

267 Ibid., 3:199; Clunes 1833, 154; and R. P. Shastri 1971, 219–25.

268 Malleson 1875, 73.

269 Broughton 1892, 28.

270 Malcolm 1826, 2:cxlviii.

271 Beale 1894, 427.

272 For the complete text, see Aitchison 1909, 368–71; for a shorter version, see Tod 1920 ed., 1833f.

273 Aitchison 1909, 372.

274 R. P. Shastri 1971, 73.

275 Aitchison 1909, 372.

276 Clunes 1833, 155.

277 R. P. Shastri 1971, 79 and 80–82.

278 Following Shyamaldas 1886, 2:1421; November 21 of that year, following Gahlot 1960, kota, 82, and M. L. Sharma 1939, 2:553.

279 Bautze 1994; see cat. 45, 46, and 48–51.

280 Francklin 1805, 348f.

281 W. G. Archer 1959, pl. 36.

282 Modave 1971 ed., 488.

283 Bautze 1987b, fig. 13.

284 Bautze 1995a, figs. 4, 5, and 9.

285 Bautze 1987b, fig. 11.

286 Henchy n.d., pl. on 13.

287 Shyamaldas 1886, 2:1421; Tod 1920 ed., 1583; and M. L. Sharma 1939, 2:554.

288 Gahlot 1960, kota, 83.

289 According to R. P. Shastri 1971, 82, Kishor Singh was only thirty-eight years old when his father died, and not forty, as stated by most other historians, such as Gahlot 1960, kota, 83; M. L. Sharma 1939, 2:555; or Tod 1920 ed., 1583.

290 Shyamaldas 1886, 2:1421; M. L. Sharma 1939, 2:554; and Gahlot 1960, kota, 83.

291 M. L. Sharma 1939, 2:555 and 563; R. P. Shastri 1971, 84; and Tod 1920 ed., 1583f.

292 R. P. Shastri 1971, 84, and Tod 1920 ed., 1584.

293 Tod 1920 ed., 1590f.; M. L. Sharma 1939, 2:460–62; and R. P. Shastri 1971, 36.

294 Ibid., 1592–93.

295 Ibid., 1595, and R. P. Shastri 1971, 37.

296 R. P. Shastri 1971, 37f, and Tod 1920 ed., 1596.

297 M. L. Sharma 1939, 2:566.

298 Tod 1920 ed., 1597.

299 Ibid.

300 Ibid., 1599.

301 Ibid., 1601.

302 Crofton 1934, 76.

303 Tod 1920 ed., 1602.

304 Ibid., 1603.

305 For their biographies, see Crofton 1934, 76f.

306 Tod 1920 ed., 1604.

307 M. L. Sharma 1939, 2:576.

308 Ibid., 2:577.

309 Aitchison 1909, 373.

310 M. L. Sharma 1939, 2:579f, and Tod 1920 ed., 1610.

311 Aitchison 1909, 374.

312 Ibid., 375f.

313 Malleson 1875, 74; for diverging dates, see R. P. Shastri 1971, 93 and 254.

314 Sharma 1939, 2:581, following Shyamaldas 1886, 2:1425; following Gahlot 1960, kota, 89, the date was August 22, 1828, but this date was wrongly converted.

315 See Varma 1989, pl. 2.

316 M. L. Sharma 1939, 2:487.

317 Gahlot 1960, kota, 90.

318 Bautze 1990.

319 Somani 1985, 183.

320 M. L. Sharma 1939, 2:593.

321 See Aitchison 1909, 376–79, for the full text.

322 Malleson 1889, 398.

323 An account of their murder was found on the tablet that once decorated Major Burton's tomb in the Kotah cemetery; see Crofton 1934, 73.

324 Crofton 1934, 75.

325 Malleson 1875, 75, and M. L. Sharma 1939, 2:629; for a fuller account of these events, see M. L. Sharma 1939, 2:604–29.

326 Malleson 1875, 75; Shyamaldas 1886, 2:1427; and Gahlot 1960, kota, 93; according to M. L. Sharma, he died almost a year earlier (M. L. Sharma 1939, 2:638), at the age of sixty-four.

327 They are enumerated in Bautze 1988–89.

328 See Bautze 1987b, fig. 6.

329 Beach 1992, 243.

330 Topsfield 1990, 257.

331 Ibid., 268.

332 Also called Chatra Sal in inscriptions, and Chhattar Sal or Chutter Singh in English literature.

333 M. L. Sharma 1939, 2:588.

334 Gahlot 1960, kota, 94.

335 Shyamaldas 1886, 2:1428, and Gahlot 1960, kota, 94 (the "1" given here for the day is a misprint for "12," since it is unlikely that Shatru Sal II was crowned king prior to his father's death); according to the historian M. L. Sharma, Maharao Ram Singh died earlier, and his son accordingly succeeded him in April/May 1865 (M. L. Sharma 1939, 2:640).

336 Malleson 1875, 76.

337 Rousselet 1877, 329, and Rousselet 1878, 277.

338 Powlett 1880, 107.

339 Bautze 1986d, fig. 11.

340 M. L. Sharma 1939, 2:697.

341 See Powlett 1880, 85.

342 Gahlot 1960, kota, 99; Chiefs and Leading Families 1903, 46; Chiefs and Leading Families 1916, 54; and Jagatnarayan 1983, 12ff.

343 See Bautze 1995c, 86.

344 Ibid.

345 For a list, see Bautze 1988–89, 343–44, and Bautze 1995c, 90.

WOODMAN TAYLOR

Picture Practice: Painting Programs, Manuscript Production, and Liturgical Performances at the Kotah Royal Palace

Visual culture at Kotah was unique in the status it accorded paintings. In sharp contrast to their role at other medieval Indian courts, paintings at Kotah not only served as visual representations but also had pivotal roles in important royal and religious rituals in which they often were (and still are) considered to be invested with life. As live gods or the living presence of a royal ancestor, the paintings took on roles and functions normally reserved in Hinduism for sculpted images. This unusual capacity of paintings created a "picture turn" at Kotah, which gave paintings an enhanced status that led to their incorporation as essential parts in all important royal rituals and as defining elements in both public and private spaces within the Kotah royal palace.[1] Viewed in these performative and architectural contexts, paintings generated a variety of meanings for Kotah viewers that extended well beyond their striking visual appeal.

Paintings from Kotah have historically had many different functions and formats that directly determined the meanings they could generate for a variety of viewers during their post-production life.[2] What happened to a Kotah painting after an artist finished transcribing his own and/or his patron's intentions into colored forms and figures, after the pigments dried, and after the painting's surface was burnished, ready for viewing? Where, by whom, and in what contexts were these paintings viewed? What system of meanings did paintings operate within, and what specific functions did they have in Kotah's court life?

To explicate these meanings that Kotah paintings generated for their intended viewers, this essay focuses on what I will call "picture practice." At Kotah, picture practice included the performative uses of paintings as well as the artistic practices of producing paintings in many formats within varying physical spaces, from manuscript pages to palace walls. Viewed within performative contexts that included religious ritual, court ceremonial, the singing of poetry, or the recitation of political narratives, Kotah paintings often had functions that transcended those of aesthetically pleasing art objects. Additional aspects of picture practice that extended possible meanings for paintings included the religious, aesthetic, and ontological systems within which the paintings operated; the relationship between paintings and poetic memory, when paintings visually cued poetic verse; explanatory relationships between texts and images found in individual paintings or within illustrated manuscripts and between adjacent paintings in wall-painting programs; the dynamics of narrative framings in paintings; the uses of paintings as historic documents and as objects of exchange value in marriage contracts; and the politics of paintings and wall-painting programs that used a visual rhetoric to communicate political messages.[3]

The size and format of Kotah paintings, which range from true miniatures with dimensions of a few inches illustrating religious texts to monumental paintings on cloth and related wall paintings on palace walls that extend up to fourteen feet in height, constitute physical variations in picture practice at Kotah. These varying dimensions, as well as the spatial contexts of paintings' placements, whether within manuscripts to be viewed while reading or singing text or on walls to be seen within specific architectural spaces, directly affected the viewing experience, and consequently the meanings, that Kotah paintings could generate for their audiences.

The strategies employed for recovering some of these picture practices at Kotah are ontological, anthropological, and archaeological. Considering the place of paintings within the specific ontology advocated by Kotah's major religious community helps explicate the unique religious and ritual roles given to paintings at Kotah. Through an anthropology of viewing and devotional practices that continue at Kotah today, the attitude toward paintings, their poetics, and performative uses specific to Kotah can be recovered.[4]

*Representation as Reality: The Ontology of Paintings
in the Vallabha Sampraday*

The fundamental logic underlying an unusual variety of functions that paintings have in Kotah is the status allowed paintings within the new ontology established by the Vallabha Sampraday religious community, to which the royal family and a majority of Kotah's Hindu population have belonged since the early eighteenth century.[5] Ontologies, as constructions of the world, define relationships between viewers and the objects they view — whether the objects viewed are real or merely creations of viewers' minds — as well as the relation of this reality perceived through sight and the other

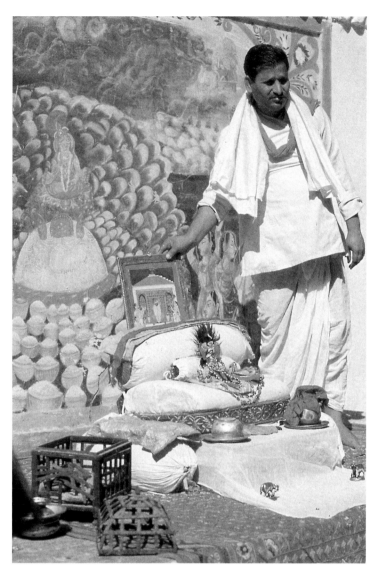

Figure 1
Wall and framed paintings (nineteenth and twentieth centuries) as visual supports for an outdoor public viewing session of Shri Brijnathji during an annual festival celebrated at Kotah palace, 1993.

The ontology of purified nondualism also undermined distinctions made within visual culture by traditional Indian classifications of the arts, in which three-dimensional sculptures are given a higher status than painting. According to these classifications, painting is normally assigned a very low status, where its representational capability is considered derivative and, as mere mimesis, of little intrinsic value. Of the visual arts, sculpture has traditionally held a privileged position because sculpted images used in religious contexts could be brought to life with the real presence of gods. But within the purified nondualist ontology advocated by Vallabhacharya, paintings could equally be endowed with divine life, as is evident in devotional practices at Kotah, where both framed and wall paintings are visual homologies of the sculptural image of Shri Brijnathji, who is himself considered the living ruler of Kotah (fig. 1). Here, paintings, particularly those viewed in devotional practice, can move beyond mimetic representation to become reality itself.

This erasing of strict distinctions between representational realms and reality in purified nondualism also explains a number of seemingly anomalous painting practices unique to Kotah. It supplies the logic for the way in which the royal deity, Shri Brijnathji, can inhabit paintings, as well as the manner in which he can move in and out of different representational realms, from a static gold statue a few inches high to an active blue painted form depicted at human scale, from three dimensions within architectural spaces to the flat surfaces of painted walls, portable paintings on cloth, and even the painted page.[7] It also explains why so many paintings from Kotah show Shri Brijnathji not only as Krishna frolicking with the milkmaids (*gopis*) but also in his role as the living ruler of Kotah, where he presides over court ceremony, leads Kotah forces into battle (cat. 20), and even engages in royal sports not normally associated with Krishna, as when he is shown with the maharao hunting lions or deer (cat. 29 and 35).[8]

Other ambiguities displayed in the realities pictured in Kotah paintings that include Shri Brijnathji are precisely those of purified nondualism, where every being and even objects are a part (*amsa*) of divinity, and where this divinity can be manifested visually in a set of homologies — as Krishna, as Shri Brijnathji, or even as the Kotah ruler. These ambiguous identities of divinity are particularly striking in paintings depicting Maharao Arjun Singh, where shared physiognomies allow for conflating the maharao with Shri Brijnathji, facilitating a doubled vision of ruler as god or god as ruler (cat. 19 and 20).[9]

Additional Kotah paintings picture the ontological blurring of time and space, where historical time is compressed or Kotah royalty inhabit mythological space. In a chronological compression, maharaos from different periods are pictured together, sharing the same devotional viewing at Nathadvara when the community's

senses to any greater divine realities. Vallabhacharya (1479? – 1531), the community's founder, advocated a new ontology called purified nondualism (*shuddhadvaita*), which collapsed previous distinctions made in Hindu and Buddhist philosophical systems between the human and divine worlds. In debates against followers of the philosopher Shankara, who claimed that the world was maya, or illusion, Vallabhacharya established a logic that insisted not only on the reality of the world but also on the location of divinity within this reality.[6] Vallabhacharya's claims had profound consequences for the ways in which an individual was to perceive and interact with the world, as well as for the status of objects and valences given to the visual.

main deities came together in a convocation of images that historically took place only twice, in 1740 and 1822.[10] Some paintings also blur distinctions between historic and mythological space. A wall painting in the Bada Mahal pictures Maharao Kishor Singh entering the mythological space where Shri Brijnathji cavorts with milkmaids in a forest bower, reflecting the Vallabha Sampraday belief that at death devout beings join Krishna in his amorous sports. In a folio painting (cat. 20), Maharao Arjun Singh as Shri Brijnathji enters the other major Hindu mythological space of Krishna's action, when Krishna as charioteer counsels Arjun on the meaning of life — the central episode in the *Bhagavad Gita* section of the epic *Mahabharata*.[11]

A final and profound effect of Vallabhacharya's new ontology on picture practice at Kotah was his appropriation of the classical Indian theory of aesthetics (*rasa*) to explain the affective experience of viewing in religious contexts.[12] When paintings are central to the religious tableaux being viewed, and divinely enlivened paintings with their own needs and desires are devoutly taken care of, the classical aesthetic theory as an aesthetics of viewing explains the ability of paintings to elicit responses from viewers.[13] This aesthetic move by Vallabhacharya makes it possible to place paintings at Kotah within the operations of classical aesthetic theory, where aesthetic enjoyment is located within viewers and meaning resides in a viewer's response, and even bodily reaction, to paintings.[14]

Paintings in Liturgical Performances and as Icons

Religious practices developed by the Vallabha Sampraday community enacted the hyperreality of Vallabhacharya's purified non-dualism ontology, where the god Krishna could reside not only in revealed metal or stone sculpture but also in paintings (honorifically referred to as *chitraji*).[15] This ability of divinity to reside in paintings, where paintings as icons can be live gods, was a radical shift from earlier representational practices in Hinduism in which divinity, when present in the reality of the perceptible world, most often resided in sculpted or other three-dimensional forms.

Although the first use of paintings as a divine being's image (*svarup*) is not documented, the extent of this picture practice within the community is vividly recounted in the hagiography of Rasakhan, an early Muslim disciple of Vallabhacharya's son and spiritual successor, Vittalnath. In the *Do Sau Bavan Vaishnavan ki Varta* of Gokulnath (c. 1551–1647), compiling accounts of the 252 earliest disciples, the story of Rasakhan is striking because his interest in the Vallabha Sampraday was sparked by being physically attracted to a painting of the community's main deity, Shri Nathji.[16] The painting of Shri Nathji that so affected Rasakhan was worshiped by a Delhi merchant as his personal deity. Rasakhan's story not only attests to a belief in the affective power of paintings; it also

documents the community practice of using paintings as the focus for daily religious viewing sessions called *darshan*, when devotees could participate in the life of their personal deity through the activity of viewing a painting.[17]

The religious practice of worshiping and lovingly caring for "live" paintings (*chitra seva*) continues at Kotah today (fig. 2), signaling a history of this picture practice within the royal household.[18] To become a revered object of devotion, a painting is normally held and subjected to the gaze of a community priest, who then initiates its feeding by giving the painting a portion of consecrated food taken from an already enlivened divine image. Once "live," the painting is given the same daily and seasonal care as a sculptural image, being fed at specific times of the day, put to bed at night, tenderly awakened with sung poetry in the morning, "bathed" with a cleaning of the painting's frame, and "dressed" in a seasonally appropriate cloth frame covering. The sacred paintings that are still cared for in the temple within the zenana of the palace were probably initially the personal deities of Kotah queens and were most likely given to them on their formal initiation into the Vallabha Sampraday.[19]

The Vallabha Sampraday tradition of viewing sessions, which were developed by Vallabhacharya's son Vittalnath into extremely elaborate visual tableaux (*shringar*) that vary by liturgical season, at times incorporated paintings as simulating the staging of activities undertaken by the main divine image. Here, cloth backdrop paintings (*pichhavai*s, which, as their name indicates, "hang behind" the

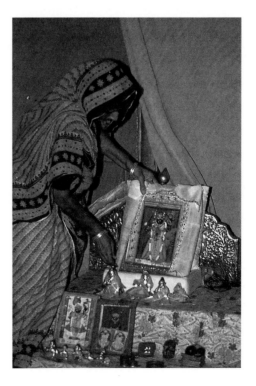

Figure 2
Painting of Krishna as Shri Nathji (nineteenth century) being "dressed" for worship at the temple within the zenana of the Kotah palace, 1993.

main divine image), as well as painted cloth coverings (*siris*) for the stairs and throne on which the divine image is seated, create virtual realities by supplying additional characters, usually milkmaids, and appropriate environmental settings for the specific narratives of Krishna's playful pastimes.[20] These representational backdrop paintings are not normally considered enlivened with a divine presence; nevertheless, consistent with a purified nondualism ontology, the characters painted in them are considered live and their depicted settings real.

Although backdrop paintings are not mentioned specifically in community literature until 1739, in his *Subodhini* Vallabhacharya comments on the possible status of paintings and the relationship between them and reality by equating Krishna's sporting activities to those "pictured in a painting." Vallabhacharya then pushes the question of the status of figures in the paintings by saying that Krishna asked both gods and their wives to "form part of the picture," thereby implying that real gods and their wives are what viewers see in paintings.[21]

A monumental painted backdrop belonging to the temple of Shri Brijnathji within the Kotah palace supplies an encyclopedic array of events, both from the story of Krishna and from Vallabhacharya's life, as well as depictions of the community's main divine images. Scaled to the three-and-a-half-inch size of Shri Brijnathji's gold image, this unique backdrop offers painted scenes for a whole liturgical year's reenactment of Krishna's life.[22] Seen during public viewing sessions reenacting Krishna's great circle (*maharas*) dance with his milkmaids during the autumnal full-moon night of Sharad Purnima, the backdrop offers devotees looking from the vantage point of the palace's large public square the characters and settings within which to picture the activity of Shri Brijnathji's love games.

For creating a tableau reality to be viewed from a closer range, a painted cloth step and throne covering from the palace temple supplies Shri Brijnathji with a golden canopy, banana trees appropriate for a bower setting, and two attending milkmaids. Additional painted registers offer scenes of a blue Krishna dancing with milkmaids, visual cues as to how devotees are to picture Shri Brijnathji enthroned above. A painting as a metapainting visually comments on these picture practices as part of a specific Vallabha Sampraday liturgy performed at the Kotah palace. Here, the very stair and throne covering still in liturgical use at Kotah is shown during the first quarter of the nineteenth century, possibly soon after its completion, when Maharao Kishor Singh used it and a related backdrop picturing Shri Nathji with milkmaids to create a visually resonant virtual reality for his personal deity, Brijrajji, appropriate for celebrating the Pavitra Festival.[23]

Ritual Uses of Paintings: At Dashahra, in Lakshmi Puja, and for Ancestor Reverence

The agency allowed paintings in the ontology of purified nondualism created a new ritual status for paintings at Kotah. Even within rituals not associated with the Vallabha Sampraday, paintings were given active roles, leading to new picture practices in a variety of different ritual realms. For the worship of royal ancestors, in devotion to Lakshmi — the goddess of wealth — and as various actors in the annual Dashahra reenactment of Ram's story, individual paintings on paper and cloth become live gods and active agents within performative ritual.

The yearly cycle of ritual traditions that continue to be performed by the Kotah maharao incorporate a number of different picture practices that signal possible historic uses and meanings associated with certain Kotah paintings.[24] The worship of a large cloth painting of royal ancestor Maharao Bhim Singh I located in the palace armory is included as an integral part of ritual sequences conducted by the ruling maharao on a number of important Hindu holy days (fig. 3). Bhim Singh's painting is worshiped during ritual sequences undertaken at Dashahra, at the Dipavali Festival of Lights, and as part of rituals marking the ruling maharao's birthday. Considered to be the live presence of Maharao Bhim Singh I, the painting is offered a freshly cracked coconut when worshiped on these ritual occasions. The painting presides over the historic warehouse of Kotah's arms, many of which are the very lances, swords, maces, and guns used by Bhim Singh's forces when

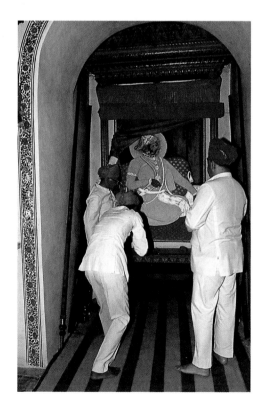

Figure 3
Maharao Brijraj Singh worshiping the large cloth painting of Maharao Bhim Singh I (c. 1800) located in the palace armory during royal rituals undertaken at the annual Dashahra Festival, 1993.

he expanded the state's borders. Placed next to Bhim Singh's painting are objects indicative of the painting's "live" status: a bow with a quiver of arrows to arm the painting and a whisk of peacock feathers for those wanting to take the role of attendant to Bhim Singh's painted presence.

In addition to expanding the physical domain of Kotah, Bhim Singh 1 secured the title of Maharao from the Mughal emperor and, through his own initiation into the Vallabha Sampraday, was responsible for refiguring Kotah rule within a purified nondualism ontology, in which Kotah was transformed into Nandgaon, the village of Krishna's youth, and the position of Kotah's ruler was given to the titular deity Shri Brijnathji.[25] It was precisely Bhim Singh 1's introduction of this new ontology that allows his own presence to remain within the Kotah palace in the form of a painting.

This unusual reverence toward a royal portrait calls for an examination of the contexts within which other Kotah portraits of royalty were viewed. The practice of a maharao distributing royal portraits to nobility seems to indicate that within court circles at Kotah other royal portraits were also the object of this reverential picture practice.[26]

The intense royal ritual activity during the ten days of Dashahra includes the use of a number of paintings created specifically for certain episodes of the ritual sequence that culminates in destroying the colossal effigy of the ten-headed demon-king Ravan. At Dashahra, paintings not only are worshiped as live gods or characters in the reenacted narrative but also become active agents in the unfolding drama, being carried in procession between sites of royal ritual action and dramatic public reenactment. As part of the royal worship of Kotah arms and regal standards (*shastra puja*), a painting of the Vallabha Sampraday deity Shri Nathji is ritually worshiped with appropriately sized weapons, which he will use to kill the demon Ravan on the last day of Dashahra.

During the culminating procession from the Kotah royal palace to the Ram-Lila grounds outside the city walls, where Ravan and his two demon (*raksha*) accomplices await the final attack, a number of paintings are used as live agents. A cloth painting (*pata*) of Hanuman and Sita is carried in procession with the paired deities of Lakshmi and Narayan, ready for use by royal priests to reenact the monkey-god Hanuman arriving within Ravan's palace to find Sita and tell her of her imminent rescue.[27] To enact the final episode, a painting showing Shri Brijnathji armed with bow and arrow and accompanied by his consort on the back of Garuda (the eagle-man who is Vishnu's mount and who also serves as Kotah's emblem) is used to shoot the arrow by which Shri Brijnathji downs Ravan (cat. 42).[28]

For the worship of Lakshmi, the goddess of wealth, during the Dipavali Festival, paintings again take a central role. At royal rituals conducted in the Lakshmi Bhandar (Treasury), located within the royal palace, a painted diptych of Lakshmi paired with Shri Nathji becomes the focus of devotion. This specific pairing of paintings — Lakshmi with Shri Nathji or Shri Nathji in the company of the other main divine images — became a devotional picture practice used in Vallabha Sampraday homes and shops throughout Kotah on a daily basis.[29]

Painting Programs: Creating Spaces of Religious and Political Rhetoric in the Royal Palace

Extensive wall-painting programs found throughout the Kotah royal palace, as well as in the family homes of many Kotah nobles and merchants, are evidence of another extensive picture practice at Kotah, in which wall paintings define certain spaces, communicate religious and political messages to viewers, or even form integral parts of visual tableaux that create personal temples. This tradition of wall painting at Kotah has a long history, as is evidenced by a poem celebrating the creation of a special room in the old Kamvar-pad section of the palace, which not only mentions paintings as a major feature but also describes a specific painting of the deity Shri Nathji as a divine image.[30] These programs are extremely elaborate and can be structured as visual theology, while at the same time proclaiming political legitimacy, often in association with deities that justify claims of divinely ordained kingship.

Of the many rooms in the royal palace where every wall and even ceilings are painted, the Bada Mahal stands out as having the most dense and significant painting program. Even framed paintings on paper were incorporated into a dense wall-painting program, thus providing a unique opportunity to consider how paintings were traditionally displayed, how their placement next to each other or with wall paintings creates specific meanings, and how the interweaving of religious and political narratives displays the politics of religion and even the resistance to colonial control of Maharao Kishor Singh. Wall paintings in the exterior room of the Bada Mahal display the religious allegiances of Maharao Kishor Singh; he is sensitively shown taking initiation into the Vallabha Sampraday from the head priest of the community, Til-kayat Damodarji 11 (also known as Dauji 11), with whom he had an extremely close devotional relationship.[31]

In the Bada Mahal's interior rooms, many wall paintings recount the politics of Maharao Kishor Singh's resistance to colonial policies that backed the regent Zalim Singh Jhala. Through a variety of maneuvers conducted from 1819 to 1821, Kishor Singh ultimately won out against this alliance, thereby securing the power of Kotah maharaos, as well as their financial resources.[32] Prithvi Singh, Maharao Kishor Singh's youngest brother and Maharao Ram Singh's father, was instrumental in assisting Maharao Kishor

Singh's efforts. Kishor Singh's indebtedness to Prithvi Singh is visually expressed in a wall painting framed within a niche, showing Maharao Kishor Singh discussing arrangements with Prithvi Singh.[33] In 1821, during military action against the combined forces of the British and Zalim Singh at Mangrol, Prithvi Singh was the main Kotah noble killed.

A large horizontal wall painting in an upper register pictures another episode of this political struggle, in which Maharao Kishor Singh and his forces are joined by his religious mentor, the head priest Dauji II.[34] With Maharao Kishor Singh taking a religiously appropriate role serving Dauji as an attending whisk bearer, they proceed on a caparisoned elephant toward the presence of an axially sited painting of Shri Nathji, shown with the seven other main divine images of the community.[35] These paintings are visual references to what occurred after the battle of Mangrol: Maharao Kishor Singh secured political asylum with Dauji II in Nathadvara, and from there negotiated an acceptable settlement with the British.[36] The central painting of Shri Nathji with the seven divine images flanked by chronological arrangements of worshiping rulers, Kotah maharaos on one side, Mewar maharanas on the other, projects the affiliation of both royal families with the religious polity of the Vallabha Sampraday. The painting program culminates chronologically with a processional scene from the coronation of Maharao Ram Singh, dating the conception and execution of this visual rhetoric to after 1828.[37]

Wall-painting programs also reflect the activities that took place in many palace spaces and are directly related to these activities. Various rooms throughout the palace complex were intended

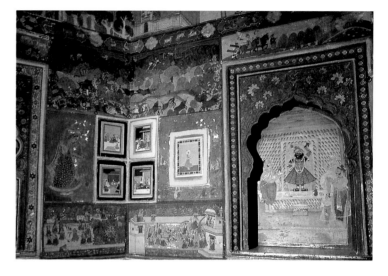

Figure 5
Wall-painting commentary showing milkmaids throwing colors at Krishna during the Holi Festival, supplying an interpretation of an adjacent wall painting in which Tilkayat Damodarji II throws color at Shri Nathji, while Maharao Umed Singh I, along with his son Kishor and grandson Ram, looks on, c. 1830, Bada Mahal, Kotah Fort. Opaque watercolor on plaster.

to be used exclusively as temples for royal household gods. Here, wall paintings, particularly those surrounding a main sculptural image, have indispensable functions in establishing a specific Vallabha Sampraday reality for Krishna's presence. Within the Kamvarpad apartments, wall paintings from a personal royal shrine supply the appropriate visual surround for a stone image, possibly of Garhu Mathureshji, which has since been removed from this space (fig. 4).[38] The painting even includes, within the depiction of the convocation of Vallabha Sampraday, images of the royal devotees Maharao Umed Singh I and his son Maharao Kishor Singh with the chief priest, Dauji II. Another wall-painting program from the Kamvarpad apartments supplies the same religious and royal actors for a painting of Shri Nathji, who was once present as an icon painting. Here, a combination of picture practices allows paintings both to supply the religious context and to be the divine image itself.[39]

At the temple of Shri Brijnathji within the royal palace, a number of wall paintings, as well as paintings on paper framed behind glass, augment the viewing of Krishna in his sculptural form. Above the lion-throne (upon which Shri Brijnathji is often displayed) within an inner sanctum, a painting mounted behind glass shows Maharaos Bhim Singh I and Durjan Sal both worshiping Shri Nathji. The painting visually supplies the ontological equivalence of Shri Brijnathji with Shri Nathji, while also including the political rhetoric of the Kotah maharaos' long patronage and participation in Vallabha Sampraday practices. The program of paintings covering the upper walls and ceilings of Shri Brijnathji's inner

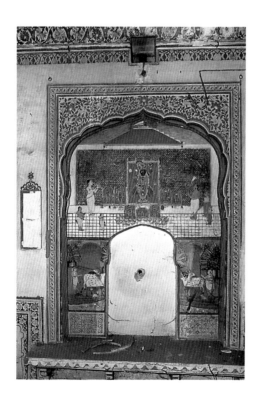

Figure 4
Wall paintings of a personal shrine in the Kamvarpad apartments at Kotah palace supplying the appropriate visual surround for a stone image, possibly of Garhu Mathureshji, which has since been removed from that space, c. 1820. Opaque watercolor on plaster.

sanctum offers additional scenes of worship at the pilgrimage center of Nathadvara. These include the celebrations of the spring festival Holi, when bright red powder is thrown on the images of Shri Nathji and Shri Navanitapriyaji, visually cuing priests and devotees at Kotah to the appropriate ways to celebrate this festival with Shri Brijnathji.[40]

Other painting programs were an essential visual part of the court ceremonial that took place within the architectural spaces they defined. Within the Raj Mahal, the main space where court ceremonial was performed, multiple wall-painting programs depict both the lineage of Kotah rulers and the story of Krishna. The painted portraits of Kotah rulers are located behind the area where the royal throne (*gaddi*) is arranged, where the current descendant of the painted genealogy of past rulers would be viewed when presiding over his court. The wall paintings of Krishna's narrative with a large central display of a mountain of rice surrounded by different varieties of his favorite foods visually codes this same space for its use during the annual Annakut Festival, when the titular deity Shri Brijnathji is brought to rule Kotah from the Raj Mahal. The painted mountain of rice is a visual cue to the display constructed in these spaces during Annakut, when a mountain of rice is piled high in the facing courtyard and an elaborate array of favorite foods is arranged around Shri Brijnathji.[41]

Picture Commentary: Framing Meanings
in Manuscripts and on Palace Walls

Paintings at Kotah also generated meanings for viewers by functioning as visual commentaries. In this picture practice, paintings may comment on other adjacent paintings or, within illustrated manuscripts, supply a visual interpretation of a text's meaning. By offering a visual commentary, these paintings intend to frame, and at times even constrain, possible meanings for the viewers of paintings or the readers of illustrated religious texts.

Within the extremely dense painted interiors of the Bada Mahal at the Kotah palace there are numerous juxtapositions — of wall paintings next to wall paintings, wall paintings next to framed paintings behind glass, and framed paintings next to each other — that create meaningful visual relationships. Viewed together, or in sequences, these relationships between paintings are visual semantic units essential to building the meanings generated by a whole painting program. In one explanatory relationship, a wall painting showing milkmaids throwing colors at Krishna during the Holi Festival supplies an interpretation of an adjacent wall painting in which the head priest Dauji II throws color at Shri Nathji, while Maharao Umed Singh I, along with his son Kishor Singh and grandson Ram Singh, look on (fig. 5). Here, the picture commentary visually informs viewers that throwing colors at Shri Nathji is

equivalent to playing Holi with Krishna. The painting-as-commentary supplies an interpretation consistent with Vallabha Sampraday belief.

Individual paintings can also supply visual commentaries on architectural spaces. The prominent placement of a painting showing Maharao Kishor Singh worshiping his personal deity, Shri Brijrajji, framed behind glass and above the Krishna Bhandar state treasury, acts as a visual commentary on the history and ownership of that treasury. The painting affirms that the state's assets belong to the titular deity Brijnathji, who is visually and ontologically equivalent to Kishor Singh's personal god, Shri Brijrajji. Through the figure of Maharao Kishor Singh, the painting also offered knowledgeable Kotah viewers a commentary on the history of the Krishna Bhandar itself. In his political maneuvers during 1821

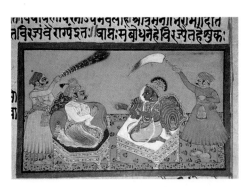

Figure 6
Painting commentary in an illustrated Bhagavata Purana *giving a Vallabha Sampraday explication of the text specific to Kotah, where Krishna is illustrated as the titular deity Brijnathji, here worshiped by the likeness of a maharao, possibly Durjan Sal, completed 1759, Kotah. Opaque watercolor, gold, and ink on paper, 16.5 x 40.6 cm. The Government Museum, Kota.*

against the combined forces of the regent Zalim Singh Jhala and British colonial forces, Maharao Kishor Singh not only insured the absolute power of the maharao but also negotiated the deposit of all Kotah state revenues into this very treasury.[42]

Paintings from an illustrated *Bhagavata Purana* manuscript produced at Kotah and kept in the Kotah royal library offer examples of picture commentary in which paintings give readers visual interpretations of the text they read (fig. 6).[43] Through a process of explicating the text, paintings take on the explanatory role normally accorded textual commentaries in classical Sanskrit tradition.[44] Here, painting commentary in an illustrated *Bhagavata Purana* gives a Vallabha Sampraday explication of the text specific to Kotah, where the Krishna narrative in the text is illustrated with the titular deity of Kotah, Brijnathji, worshiped by the likeness of a maharao, possibly Durjan Sal.[45] In this interpretive act, the painting localizes the story of Krishna for Kotah readers who would also have understood its Vallabha Sampraday interpretation, visually equating the living Krishna of the *Bhagavata Purana* text with a personal deity as pictured in the painting.

Manuscript Production and Painting Collections:
The Sarasvati Bhandar

Picture practices at Kotah were facilitated by the production and subsequent care and circulation of individual paintings and illustrated manuscripts at the royal palace. Although little is currently known about the location of workshops or production practices of artists employed at the Kotah court, by investigating various parts

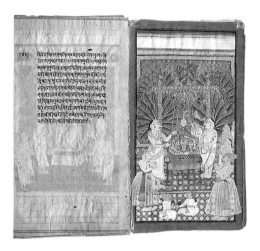

Figure 7
Shri Brajrajji ka Ghar ki Utsav Malika *manuscript indicating in text and image the arrangements for Shri Brijrajji's rainy-season public viewing during celebrations of a festival, from the Sarasvati Bhandar Royal Library, 1804, Kotah. Ink on paper, 21 x 24.7 cm. The Government Museum, Kota.*

of what once was a loosely constituted royal collection, it is possible to reconstruct a partial corpus of paintings and manuscripts used and viewed by members of the court.[46]

The main group of illustrated manuscripts known to have be-enproduced for the court were kept in the Sarasvati Bhandar, which served as a royal library. These illustrated manuscripts are exclusively religious, and most can be directly associated with Vallabha Sampraday practices. The only complete cycles of narrative paintings known to have been in the Sarasvati Bhandar illustrate the tenth chapter of the *Bhagavata Purana*, which, because of its recounting of Krishna's biography, is the most important religious text for the Vallabha Sampraday. The early set of forty paintings illustrating main episodes from the *Bhagavata Purana*, although without text, indicates a strong royal interest and monetary investment in

paintings that had a resonance for Vallabha Sampraday viewers (cat. 3–5).[47]

The other two major illustrated manuscripts from the Sarasvati Bhandar both include paintings that were probably used in conjunction with Vallabha Sampraday liturgical practices. Most of the thirty-eight paintings from the *Shri Brajrajji ka Ghar ki Utsav Malika* manuscript, composed to guide the performance of liturgical rituals for the image of Shri Brijrajji belonging to then Maharajkumvar Kishor Singh, visually specify displays to be constructed for public viewing sessions on all major Vallabha Sampraday festival days (fig. 7).[48] Similarly, the seven paintings included within the compilation of liturgical texts known as the *Panch Mel Gutkah* also directly relate to the liturgical activities performed by Maharao Kishor Singh for his personal deity, Brijrajji (fig. 8).

The bulk of the Sarasvati Bhandar consisted of unillustrated manuscripts, which are important sources for discovering which religious texts, liturgical manuals, and devotional poetry were known by members of the Kotah court.[49] Multiple copies of Vallabhacharya's Sanskrit commentaries indicate that court members were familiar with the tenets of purified nondualism ontology that facilitated the "picture turn" behind many picture practices at Kotah. Manuscripts that include poetry written by or composed for a number of devout maharaos and their queens reflect the active participation of court members in devotional practices of the Vallabha Sampraday.[50]

A "mock-up" manuscript preserved in the Sarasvati Bhandar also supplies rare evidence for the production processes by which an illustrated manuscript was produced at the Kotah court (fig. 9). The manuscript, which was probably used by artists working on the project and perhaps also by the patron, Crown Prince Kishor Singh, specifies the placement of paintings within a particular textual layout for Kishor Singh's liturgical manual, the *Shri Brajrajji*

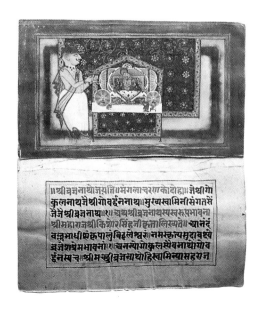

Figure 8
Painting of Maharao Kishor Singh worshiping Shri Brijrajji above the Sanskrit verses he composed praising Shri Brijnathji, from the Panch Mel Gutkah *manuscript, c. 1820, Kotah. Opaque watercolor, gold, and ink on paper, 21.5 x 14 cm. The Government Museum, Kota.*

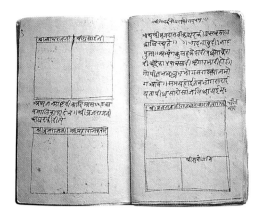

Figure 9
Artist's mock-up manuscript for the Shri Brajrajji ka Ghar ki Utsav Malika
*indicating the placement of specific paintings within a particular textual layout,
from the Sarasvati Bhandar Royal Library, before 1804, Kotah. Ink on paper,
26.4 x 16.3 cm. Rajasthan Prachyavidya Pratishthan.*

ka Ghar ki Utsav Malika (fig. 7).[51] In addition to specifying the order
of opening paintings for the final text, from portraits of Vallabhacharya, his son Vittalnath, and Kishor Singh to paintings of Shri
Brijnathji on specific occasions, the mock-up also includes specific
written instructions for artists. These written instructions at times
specify the placement of objects within paintings or indicate the
reactions of a patron or supervisor with orders such as "make the
painting larger" (*chitra baro*).[52]

Being literate in Sanskrit while also an accomplished poet in the
vernacular Braj Bhasha — a dialect precursor of Hindi used as a
poetic liturgical language by the Vallabha Sampraday — Kishor
Singh used his literary skills to construct an elaborate liturgical
cycle for Brijrajji, his personal deity, composing Sanskrit verses in
praise of him and even writing vernacular poetry to be sung during
daily and festival worship sessions.[53] In poetry composed to be sung
while viewing the scene pictured in catalogue number 56, Kishor
Singh describes how, while listening to sweet sounds of musical
accompaniment, he made Brijrajji's face red by throwing powdered
color on him.[54] Kishor Singh also supervised compilation of the
Shri Brajrajji ka Ghar ki Utsav Malika, a manuscript that, in text and
paintings, details the liturgical specifications for Brijrajji during

the yearly cycle of the religious festivals celebrated by the Vallabha
Sampraday community, to which the royal family had belonged for
six generations. The liturgical specifications for Holi include the
carefully color-coordinated pink rose garlands we see Kishor Singh
has draped around Brijrajji and his two accompanying milkmaids
in this painting.[55] The architectural details behind the seated deities
locate this liturgical celebration as taking place in the precise interior
palace courtyard where the temple of Brijrajji exists to this day.

The history, organization, and use of individual folio paintings
at the Kotah court is harder to reconstruct. Presumably, individual
paintings, like manuscripts, had their own storage unit (*pothikhana*)
within the royal palace. In addition to the significant number of
folio paintings framed behind glass and applied to many walls in
the Kotah palace, particularly in the Bada Mahal, there are three
distinct groups of paintings that can be connected positively with
court ownership and use at Kotah. The major intact royal collection,
from which this exhibition is largely constituted, came from a huge
stash of paintings discovered in a room at the Kotah palace, which
firmly places the paintings within the physical site of their use.[56]
The second group of folio paintings known to have been used by
the court is the collection of paintings given by Maharao Bhim
Singh II to the Government Museum, Kota.[57] The private collection of H.H. Maharao Brijraj Singh constitutes the third major
group of paintings whose provenance can positively be placed with
the Kotah rulers who commissioned and used them.

Conclusion

The variety of picture practices at Kotah necessitates the inclusion
of many different viewing contexts and physical painting formats
in any consideration of what meanings paintings generated for
Kotah viewers. This suggests that a critical study of Indian painting
must not only embrace a stylistics of artistic production but also
explicate paintings' post-production lives, when meanings were
generated by means of a dialogical negotiation between different
spectators and specific pictures. Going beyond any single meaning
for a particular painting, this art-historical move also unmasks the
social life of visual forms, when paintings were allowed a presence
and life of their own.[58]

This essay incorporates research funded by a Fulbright-Hayes Dissertation Fellowship (1993), during which Dr. Kapila Vatsyayan was my enthusiastic scholarly adviser. The question of possible religious uses for paintings at Kotah was first posed to me by Irene Winter; Norbert Peabody subsequently shared some specific examples he had noted from his earlier research in Kotah. I am particularly indebted to H.H. Maharao Brijraj Singh and Maharani Uttara Devi, who graciously facilitated my research and stay at Kotah.

1   Mitchell 1994, 10–14.

2   I initially developed this idea of an object's "post-production life" when considering the uses of an illustrated Mughal *Ramayana* manuscript by its patron and owner, Abdur Rahim (Taylor 1991).

3   In focusing on a viewer's negotiation of meaning from paintings, I am taking a cue from the critical literary theory on readers' interactions with texts found in Iser 1989 and the brilliant elaboration by M.M. Bakhtin of the dialogical negotiations that take place in speech acts (Bakhtin 1981).

4   For processes that sustain the long cultural duration of a mentality within a community's memory, see Halbwachs 1992. In using an anthropology of continuing practices to recover past uses of paintings, I follow Williams 1990.

5   For a history of the initiation of Maharao Bhim Singh I (r. 1707–20) into the Vallabha Sampraday Hindu community and the subsequent establishment of his personal deity, Brijnathji, as Kotah's titular ruler, see Peabody 1991b.

6   Vallabhacharya's new ontological system was initially called Brahmavad, positing that the world is constituted out of a divine Brahma; this was contrasted to the position of Shankara's followers, known as Mayavadins, who insisted that the world consisted of illusionary maya. Although one might question how many Kotah viewers were aware of these differences in ontological claims, a poem composed by Maharao Arjun Singh (r. 1720–23) specifically mentions Vallabhacharya's theory of Brahmavad attacking the Mayavadin, indicating a general knowledge of purified nondualism tenets among Kotah royalty. Arjun Singh's poem is included in a compilation of religious poetry formerly in the Sarasvati Bhandar Royal Library, now MS 3455 in the Rajasthan Prachyavidhya Pratishthan, Kota.

7   This variety of Shri Brijnathji paintings is illustrated in Bautze 1989a, where the relationship between representational realms is presented as an enigma.

8   The anomaly of a blue deity heading a hunting party was first identified in Kotah painting by S.C. Welch and Milo Beach, although at the time his identity as Kotah's Shri Brijnathji was not known (Welch and Beach 1965, 53).

9   During Arjun Singh's reign, the metal image of Brijnathji lost by Bhim Singh I in battle was physically located not in Kotah but in Hyderabad. This absence could be one reason for picturing Arjun Singh as visually equivalent to Brijnathji.

10   This convocation of Vallabha Sampraday images — when Shri Nathji and Navanitapriyaji, who already resided at Nathadvara, were joined by the other seven major images revered in the community — reunited the "nine treasures" that are the main images of the community. The convocation of 1740, which was funded by Kotah Maharao Durjan Sal, is commemorated in the poem *sri ji ke pas sato svarup padhare*, composed on the occasion when "seven divine images joined Shri Ji [Shri Nathji]." This poem is included in many compilations of religious texts that were kept in the Kotah royal library, indicating a poetic memory at Kotah that can be linked to the proliferation of paintings of this event. At Kotah, paintings of the "seven divine images join[ing] shri ji [Shri Nathji]" are often included in groupings of sculpture and paintings used in daily devotion (see fig. 1 in this essay). The main wall painting at the fort palace showing this convocation being viewed by a genealogy of maharaos, located above the main axis of the Bada Mahal's inner room, also visually broadcasts the long and close association between Kotah rulers and Vallabha Sampraday religious leaders. Two compilations of religious texts and devotional poetry from the royal library that include this poem are MSS 1226 and 3206, now housed in the Rajasthan Prachyavidhya Pratishthan, Kota.

11   A related wall painting showing Shri Brijnathji as charioteer in the *Bhagavad Gita* is located in the Bada Mahal's inner room, where it additionally comments on the activity in an adjacent wall painting picturing the Kotah maharao in battle against some of his royal relatives.

12   This affective experience of encountering Krishna is discussed in various parts of Vallabhacharya's *Subodhini*. For a translation of parts of the *Subodhini*, see Redington 1983. The vocabulary and operations of the classical *rasa* theory of aesthetics are explained in B. N. Goswamy 1986, 17–30.

13   This possibility of paintings or images having desires that elicit responses from viewers in a Western context has recently been proposed by W.T.J. Mitchell in a project entitled "What Does a Picture Want?" (Mitchell 1996).

14   Although a number of art historians, from A. K. Coomaraswamy to B. N. Goswamy, have used the classical aesthetic theory to explain aspects of South Asian visual arts, Vallabhacharya's use of it allows us to situate classical aesthetic theory historically for the first time with its known deployment in visual practices of a specific community that used both sculpture and paintings.

15   Here the honorific suffix *ji* has been added to the word *chitra* (painting). The ability of holy presences to reside in paintings has a long history in the religious practices of early and medieval Christianity. For a history of icon use in the West, see Belting 1994.

16   This account of Rasakhan is reproduced in Snell 1991, 79–83, taken from B. Sharma and Parikh 1951–53. Rasakhan is a fascinating example of a Muslim who was allowed to participate in a Hindu com-

munity's religious practices. Poems of praise to Krishna composed by him were even incorporated into the Vallabha Sampraday liturgy.

17   The phrase the account uses for this practice of religiously viewing a painting, *chitra ke darshan kare*, is probably the first direct reference to the Vallabha Sampraday practice of using paintings of divinity as the focus of public viewing sessions. For the context of this line, see Snell 1991, 81.

18   The earliest reference to the worship of a specific painting that is still the object of religious devotion comes from the court of Kishangarh, where rulers were also initiated into the Vallabha Sampraday from an early date. At Kishangarh, a portrait of Vallabhacharya, reputed to have been painted by an artist of Akbar's court and presented by the Mughal emperor Shah Jahan to Kishangarh Maharaja Rup Singh (r. 1643–58), continues to be cared for and worshiped at the royal temple within the Kishangarh palace. I am grateful to Maharaja Braj Singh of Kishangarh and Goswamy Shyam Manohar for corroborating this tradition of picture worship for the painting of Vallabhacharya, which was first mentioned in Dickinson and Khandalavala 1959, 2. As the earliest known representation of Vallabhacharya, this painting continues to be reproduced in painted and printed copies, which are worshiped by Vallabha Sampraday members.

19   A number of Kotah queens were well known for their devotional activity in the Vallabha Sampraday, some even sponsoring temple projects. Brajkumvar Bai, daughter of Mewar Maharana Jagat Singh and wife of Maharao Durjan Sal, built the Jag Mandir and Brijvilas Gardens. Maharani Phul Kanvar, Maharao Ram Singh's queen from Udaipur, established and then endowed the Phul Bihari Mandir in the Kotah bazaar, which remains a temple mainly patronized by women. See Lakshmandan n.d., 32 and 108.

20   Vallabha Sampraday tableaux include a number of different types of backdrop hangings, some of which are simply different colors of cloth, others of which are embroidered with decorative designs. The focus here is on the genre of representational backdrops, which most often are painted. For a discussion of different backdrop types, see Ambalal 1987, 76–77; for the variety of representational painted cloth backdrops, see Krishna and Talwar 1979; for the range of painted cloth backdrops produced at the pilgrimage center of Nathadvara, see Skelton 1973.

21   These passages come from Vallabhacharya's commentary on verse 3–4 of chapter 5 of the tenth book of the *Bhagavata Purana* (Redington 1983, 5–6 and 443–44.)

22   This background painting packed with lively narrative scenes is about the same size as the monumental cloth painting of Maharao Ram Singh's visit to Emperor Bahadur Shah in 1842 (cat. 65). Given their striking similarity in scale and details, both paintings were likely executed by the same workshop of artists, led by Lacchi Ram and Kishan Das, who probably belonged to traditional painters'

families from the pilgrimage center of Nathadvara. This would explain their familiarity with painting large programs on cloth, their intimate knowledge of Vallabha Sampraday liturgical traditions, and their use of a painting style associated with Nathadvara.

23 This painting comes from the same set as catalogue numbers 56–62, all showing Maharao Kishor Singh worshiping his personal deity, Brijrajji, during the main religious festivals of the Vallabha Sampraday liturgical calendar.

24 H.H. Maharao Brijraj Singh very graciously allowed me to witness these royal ritual traditions, still being enacted at Kota during my dissertation research there in 1993.

25 M. B. Singh 1985, 14.

26 For this practice of distributing royal portraits to Kotah nobility, see Peabody 1991b, 49.

27 For an example of one of these Hanuman and Sita cloth paintings still in the royal collection, see M. B. Singh 1985, fig. 27. There is some question whether the sculptural images of Shri Brijnathji and his consort were actually the gods taken to the final battle scene, and were more recently replaced by the image pair of Lakshmi and Narayan, who reside in the temple within the zenana of the royal palace.

28 This painting from the royal collection was probably intended to be used for this culminating action during Dashahra.

29 I remain grateful to Bada Devtaji, who allowed me to view his personal painted deities, as well as introducing me to a number of merchants in Kota who granted me a viewing of their shrines. This pairing, which to my knowledge is specific to Kotah, explains the number of Kotah paintings depicting the convocation of Vallabha Sampraday images; these paintings probably were initially integral parts of personal shrines. For an example of one of these "nine treasures" (*nava-nidhi*) or "seven images" (*sat-svarup*) paintings, see M. B. Singh 1985, fig. 26.

30 *Jagat Sinhji ke Kumvarpade ke mahal banaye ta ko kavita* describes this special room as having depictions of a lamp for the lamp-waving ceremony being raised by Shri Vittalkuvar (probably a head priest) and Shri Nathji "in the form of a painting" (*chitrarup*). This describes the very picture practice of wall-painting programs that include both Shri Nathji and those worshiping him and that are found in many rooms throughout the Kamvarpad section of the Kotah royal palace. The poem is within a collection of poems composed to commemorate historic royal occasions at Kotah. The manuscript of poems was initially kept in the Sarasvati Bhandar Royal Library and is now MS 3206/3422 in the Rajasthan Prachyavidya Pratishthan, Kota.

31 An interesting wall-painting program that similarly depicts the initiation of many Mewar maharanas into the Vallabha Sampraday by members of the family of Vallabhacharya, including Dauji II, is located at Nathadvara within a complex known as the Mahuavala Akhara. That both programs use the same conventions for depicting this important religious event seems to indicate an artistic sensibility

and stylistic vocabulary shared by artists in Nathadvara and Kotah. In addition, both programs refer to the polity of the descendants of Vallabhacharya by including a long horizontal depiction of Dauji II mounted on an elephant while in procession with troops. These programmatic similarities, along with shared stylistic features associated with paintings produced at Nathadvara, again suggest the employment of artists from Nathadvara families by the Kotah court, possibly after 1821, when Maharao Kishor Singh spent many months there. I am grateful to Amit Ambalal for initially mentioning these paintings, which for him had a Kotah "look," and to Tryna Lyons and Joanna Williams for sharing photographs of them with me.

32 Maharao Kishor Singh insisted on the implementation of the tenth article in the 1817 treaty between the British agent and his father, Umed Singh, which states that "the Maharao, his heirs and successors, shall remain absolute rulers of their country." When in asylum at Nathadvara, Kishor Singh additionally negotiated that the allowance for Kotah maharaos' household expenses be substantially increased to equal that allotted the maharanas of Udaipur (Tod 1983 ed., 456 and 470; Lakshmandan n.d., 80).

33 Both Maharao Kishor Singh and Prithvi Singh are identified in this painting by a prominent and easily read gold inscription.

34 An inscription written on the walls of a building in the upper corner of the painting begins by identifying Dauji using his given name, Damodar, "Gusaiji Shri Damodarji." Amit Ambalal was the first to recognize Dauji in this painting; Milo Beach had earlier correctly identified him as the "chief priest of Nathadvara" (Ambalal 1987, 67; Beach 1974, 43–44, fig. 119).

35 This central painting of Shri Nathji visually positions the religious affiliation of Kotah maharaos and Mewar maharanas, while also implying the political alliances between the two royal families, which were cemented through many marriages. It also refers to the politics of the two historic convocations of Vallabha Sampraday images, in 1740 and 1822, the first funded and the second facilitated by Kotah maharaos. These convocations were also used as important occasions for Kotah maharaos and Mewar maharanas to consult on their relationships to other political forces in Rajasthan.

36 The history of these political events is detailed in Tod 1983 ed., 452–70, and Lakshmandan n.d., 72–80.

37 An inscription on the painting supplies the date for this event as v.s. 1885, equivalent to 1828 c.e. In many ways, the Bada Mahal's wall-painting program is Ram Singh's posthumous tribute to his uncle's religious affiliations and astute political maneuvering. The program could well have been painted during renovations of the Bada Mahal known to have been made during Ram Singh's reign, as mentioned by Lakshmandan n.d., 105–6.

38 The current location of Garhu Mathureshji is within a temple on the ground floor of the Kamvarpad.

39 That this program was painted in a highly refined

style with a distinctly Nathadvara "look" signals its probable execution by artists brought to Kotah from the pilgrimage center of Nathadvara. Earlier wall paintings of the same religious scenes with the same royal devotees (see fig. 4 in this essay) and community priest have a very different look. The presence of these new artists can be explained by Maharao Kishor Singh's extended stay in Nathadvara during 1820 and his extremely close relationship with Dauji II, who, as head of the Vallabha Sampraday, was the main patron of artists at Nathadvara. After the new treaty with the British was put into effect, Maharao Kishor Singh's treasury had more monies than ever before to fund new commissions, some of which, such as this and wall paintings at the Shri Brijnathji temple, included the extensive use of gold paint. This new group of artists undertaking royal commissions also explains the distinct shift in painting styles that took place at Kotah after 1820; these styles had previously been associated exclusively with the rule of Maharao Ram Singh.

40 This wall painting, which is identical to a painting on paper in the Kotah royal collection (cat. 55), was probably painted around 1830, when a whole group of paintings (including cat. 54–62) minutely detailed liturgical specifications for the worship of Vallabha Sampraday images at both Nathadvara and Kotah. The artists' familiarity with these details and the permission given them to paint walls within the inner sanctum indicate that they belonged to traditional painters' families from Nathadvara who, as members of Brahman subcastes, are allowed periodically to repaint temple interiors in Nathadvara (Ambalal 1987, 85).

41 In October 1993 at the Annakut celebrations at the Kotah royal palace, I witnessed this visual display of Shri Brijnathji with Annakut foods, and I was told that in previous years the mountain of rice had been much greater in size than the small pile I saw.

42 In his negotiations, Maharao Kishor Singh forced the British to concede to the contested Point 10 of Umed Singh's 1817 treaty with them, and to agree to Point 7 of his additional demands of September 16, 1821. These conditions were agreed to by the British and Zalim Singh Jhala on the last day of 1821 (Tod 1983 ed., 463 and 617).

43 The manuscript, which is dated v.s. 1816, equivalent to 1759 c.e., was originally part of the Sarasvati Bhandar Royal Library and is now MS 1950.1138 in the Government Museum, Kota.

44 In effect, these paintings take the role of a Sanskrit text's primary (*tika*) and secondary (*tippani*) commentaries, which explicate the core text through a particular author's interpretation.

45 Although the manuscript was completed after Durjan Sal's death, the project could have been initiated by him. With 1,190 folios and 4,760 small paintings, it would have taken a long time to complete. We do know of Durjan Sal's other lavish expenditures on Vallabha Sampraday projects, particularly his funding of the 1740 convocation of community images at Nathadvara and his orchestration of both the return of Shri Brijnathji to Kotah from Hyderabad and the movement of Shri

Mathureshji from Bundi to Kotah. The artistic conceit of depicting both the maharao and Shri Brijnathji with the same beaklike nose is found in other paintings commissioned by Durjan Sal, most notably in a posthumous portrait of his eldest brother, Arjun Singh, worshiping Shri Brijnathji (cat. 19).

46 Recent research on painting at Udaipur and Jaipur has yielded this sort of information. See Topsfield 1995 and Das 1995.

47 This set of folio paintings, with incomplete borders and no verso text, appears to be an unfinished project. Associated with the period of Jagat Singh (r. 1658–83), the set signals a royal involvement in the worship of Krishna predating the first initiation of a Kotah ruler into the Vallabha Sampraday community — that of Maharao Bhim Singh I, which took place in 1719. An inscription on the verso of the set's first painting, "Of the court / Aum / Picture of the Sarasvati Bhandar" (*sarkari / aum / chitra sarasvati bhandar*), establishes that the set belonged to the royal court's Sarasvati Bhandar. That it elicited an appropriate religious invocatory *aum* at its beginning is a sign that even as a set of paintings it was treated reverently, as a religious text. For a complete listing of the subject matter of these paintings, see M. Shastri 1961, 13–17.

48 The illustrated *Shri Brajrajji ka Ghar ki Utsav Malika* manuscript was completed in v.s. 1861, equivalent to 1804 C.E., when Kishor Singh, then the crown prince, was twenty-eight years old. The manuscript was catalogued as the *Vallabhotsava Chandrika* by librarians of the Sarasvati Mahal (M. Shastri, 46–47; see also K. Singh n.d.a).

49 These unillustrated manuscripts from the Sarasvati Bhandar, which number almost five thousand, are currently housed in the Kota branch of the Rajasthan Prachyavidya Pratishthan. I am extremely indebted to Director O. P. Sharma for granting me access to this important collection, and to Khyali Ram Mina, Head Kota Branch, and his assistant Kamal Kishore Sankla for guiding me through this rarely used resource.

50 This forgotten corpus of poetry written or commissioned by Kotah royalty, once recited and sung at the court, includes poems composed for Maharao Durjan Sal, a devotional poem by Maharao Arjun Singh, a poem by a Kotah queen, and a religious treatise and numerous devotional poems by Maharao Kishor Singh.

51 To my knowledge, this "mock-up" for an illustrated manuscript is a unique extant example of an artistic practice used for the production of illustrated manuscripts at workshops within Rajput and even Mughal courts. Now MS 3447, preserved in the Rajasthan Prachyavidya Pratishthan, the text also refers to itself as the *Shri Brajrajji ki Nitiprati Sevaprakar* (Manual for the Daily Worship of Lord Brijrajji; see K. Singh n.d.a).

52 I am grateful to Khyali Ram Mina for first pointing out and then deciphering this notation.

53 Two compilations of Kishor Singh's devotional poetry separate poems to be sung for specific religious festivals, *Utsavan ki Bhavana ke Kirtan*, from those that can be sung any day, *Nitya ke Kirtan*. A manuscript from the Sarasvati Bhandar Royal Library including both these collections has been generically catalogued as *Chaupai Janmashtami ka Utsav ka Radhashtami ka Kirtan ki* (Rajasthan Prachyavidya Pratishthan, MS 3474). In all these poems, Maharao Kishor Singh includes his pen name, Kishor Das, in the last line, as is the convention in medieval north Indian poetry. The identity of Kishor Singh and verification of his authorship of these poems is supplied by the text ending the *Utsavan ki Bhavana ke Kirtan* section on page 16 of this manuscript: *iti srimaharaj brajraj prabhu ki maharav kishor sinhji krita utsavan ke kirtan sampurna* (Here are completed the poetic songs for festivals composed by Lord Maharaj Brajraj's [devotee] Maharao Kishor Singhji) (K. Singh n.d.c). Additional evidence that Kishor Das is indeed the pen name of Maharao Kishor Singh comes at the end of the *Shri Brajnathasya Svarupa Bhavana*, which was composed by Kishor Singh when he was the crown prince (K. Singh n.d.e). A couplet (*doha*) in vernacular Braj Bhasa that paraphrases a Sanskrit couplet (*shloka*) praising Shri Brajrajji as Kotah's ruling "god of love" includes his abbreviated pen name, Kishor.

54 Maharao Kishor Singh's *Utsavan ki Bhavana ke Kirtan* includes two poems under the heading of the Holi Festival, both to be sung in the musical mode of Kafi (K. Singh n.d.c, 11).

55 These specifications are listed after the heading *phagun sudi 14, tadin holi mangalani ko utsav* (the bright fortnight of the month Phagun, the day for the festival celebrating Holi), in K. Singh n.d.b, 35.

56 This is the paintings collection of the Rao Madhu Singh Trust Museum, Fort Kotah, established by H.H. Maharao Brijraj Singh.

57 These paintings, which number at least fifty-eight and which include paintings from other Rajput courts, were given to the Government Museum, Kota, in 1954 or before. For a description of them, see M. Shastri 1961, 17–24.

58 In this I take my cue from Arjun Appadurai (Appadurai 1986).

NORBERT PEABODY

The King Is Dead, Long Live the King!
Karmic Kin(g)ship in Kotah

On the fifteenth day of the bright fortnight of the month of Jeth, in v.s. 1777 — or June 20, 1720 c.e.[1] — Maharao Bhim Singh I of Kotah, while fighting in the service of the Mughal emperor Muhammad Shah, was slain in battle on the banks of the Narmada River, north of Burhanpur in Madhya Pradesh, by Nizam-ul-Mulk (Chin Qilich Khan), a rebellious Mughal governor of Hyderabad.[2] This unfortunate turn of events — from Kotah's perspective, at least — is vouchsafed by numerous historical sources, some Mughal, some Rajasthani, some from Kotah, and some from other Rajput polities, making it one of the earliest episodes in Kotah's history with a date amply substantiated by diverse contemporary documentation.[3] This date, moreover, witnessed a double loss for Kotah: along with the war booty carried away by Nizam-ul-Mulk to Hyderabad was the golden image of Shri Brijnathji, Kotah's tutelary deity, that always accompanied Bhim Singh in battle.

Up until this event, Bhim Singh I had been Kotah's most illustrious ruler. During his thirteen-year reign (1707–20), he had transformed Kotah from a petty principality into one of the first important "successor states" that emerged during the protracted decline of the Mughal Empire. He not only brought under his control all of Hadauti (the traditional region of southeastern Rajasthan), but also conquered the neighboring kingdoms of Rajgarh, Narsinghgarh, Raghugarh, Sheopur, Umri, Bhadora, Diglodi, and Kilchipur, to name just a few. In addition, for his services to the Mughal emperor — which included the battle in which he lost his life — Bhim Singh garnered great favor at the Mughal court in Delhi. In September 1713, Emperor Farrukh Siyar (cat. 18) bestowed upon Bhim Singh the title of Maharao, making him Kotah's first ruler to enjoy the honor. In the following years, he received from the Mughal emperor highly revered regalia, including large ceremonial kettledrums and the fish-and-dignities standard (cat. 68), which was reserved for only a handful of the most eminent Mughal courtiers.

Shortly after the ill-starred battle on the Narmada, the greatest of Kotah's artists, the Kotah Master, commemorated the event with a monumental (approximately 2.09 by 3.31 meters) but curious painting on cloth. Apart from its unusually large size — north India being famous for its *miniature* paintings, after all — the composition is remarkable insofar as, in the climactic confrontation between Bhim Singh and Nizam-ul-Mulk (fig. 1), the artist did not depict Bhim Singh being killed by Nizam-ul-Mulk, but just the opposite! Inscriptions above the two antagonists clearly indicate that Bhim Singh is decapitating his rival, who we know from numerous other historical sources actually lived for a further twenty-eight years after this battle.[4] How are we to interpret this apparently shameless misrepresentation of historical facts? Does it make a case for the accusations made by British colonial officials in the nineteenth century that India had an easily excitable imagination and an undisciplined historical consciousness? Could it be that Bhim Singh's defeat and death were so emotionally bruising for the people of Kotah that this large painting expresses a psychological state of denial and repression? Or is it evidence of a peculiar Rajasthani historical sensibility — and, if so, what could that possibly be?

These questions will be addressed below through an examination of the specific ways in which royal legitimacy was established, substantiated, and traced in the kingdom of Kotah. In doing so, it will be necessary to reevaluate the dominant historiography of eighteenth-century Rajasthan, which typically has been portrayed as suffering from political chaos, economic decline, and cultural stagnation. This was the era when much of Rajasthan was dominated by "foreigners," whether Marathas from the Deccan or, in the case of Kotah, Zalim Singh Jhala, a Rajput from Gujarat, whose exploitative influences have been blamed for the region's sorry state of affairs. Not all was in decline in Rajasthan during this era, however, and the forms of rule established by "outsiders" often enjoyed a considerable degree of "indigenous" support and legitimacy precisely because the boundaries between insider and outsider, or native and foreigner, were traditionally much less fixed than has been assumed by Western-trained scholars. With a better understanding of the mutable boundary between different communities in the precolonial polity, we shall be able to understand more fully the unusual painting by the Kotah Master. Crucial to this understanding is some background on how kinship between individuals was established both in terms of shared blood and through the common performance of archetypal actions informed by the Hindu-Buddhist belief in metempsychosis (the transmigration of souls) and karmic retribution and reward.

In India, a number of Hindu scriptural sources appear to restrict sovereignty rigidly to one group only, the Kshatriyas — the hereditary caste of warriors and rulers. Maharao Bhim Singh 1 of Kotah was a Rajput, a group that claimed Kshatriya descent; the term *Rajput* is often said to derive from the Sanskrit *rajaputra*, meaning "son of a king," reflecting the belief that all Rajputs have a royal ancestry even if they are not kings themselves. Unsurprisingly, Rajputs, who claimed unique Kshatriya status in Rajasthan, made extensive use of genealogical reckoning based on biological descent in order to regulate inclusion in this privileged category. However, this was by no means the sole criterion through which the right to rule was established. Notions of biological descent were always supplemented and crosscut, and occasionally overruled, by genealogies of incarnations and avatars. These lineages, founded on the belief in reincarnation through the transmigration of the soul, were pedigrees that revealed "genetic" connections through the performance of similar exemplary and virtuous deeds and actions.[5]

The cultural constitution of these nonbiological lineages was based on three interrelated Hindu concepts: karma, dharma, and samsara. The

> theory of karma postulates that every action has its inevitable "fruit" or consequence, so that a person's condition is determined by good or bad deeds in this and previous lives. In Hinduism, karma is inseparable from dharma, understood as the moral code by which good and bad are evaluated, and samsara, the eternal cycle within which a person is reborn.[6]

Because the soul is, in most cases, considered to be undying, when the mortal body expires the soul is reborn in another being, who need not be kin or even human, and the quality of the rebirth is determined by the excellence of the individual's past karma.

The most famous application of these beliefs to the succession to high office occurs among the Dalai Lamas of Tibet, where there is ideally no genealogical connection between successive lamas. Rather, "soul-ful" continuity is revealed through the common appearance of agreed-upon signs among unrelated personages. Similarly, in India those claiming to be righteous kings (*dharmarajas*) had to do so, in part, on the basis of their personal achievements in culturally specific arenas of action. Thus, positions of authority were not simply inherited, but had to be proven by individual karma and meritorious conduct.

This emphasis on karmic attainment in establishing the legitimacy of Kotah's kings informed portions of the *Maharao Shatru Salji ki Vamsha Prashasti*, a panegyric composed during the last half of the nineteenth century by Kaviraja Lakshmandan to honor the lineage of Kotah's then ruler, Maharao Shatru Sal 11 (r. 1866–89).[7] Although written after nearly fifty years of colonial domination,[8] this panegyric still shares several features with similar praise poems from the precolonial era insofar as, at least with regard to most of the historical portions prior to the nineteenth century, it continues to link royal legitimacy to the exemplary actions of Kotah's rulers. The emphasis on the monarchs' personal deeds in establishing their authority differs from the rather more "institutionalized" footings of such status based on biogenetic descent or tenure of office.

This point is well illustrated in that portion of Lakshmandan's account dealing with Bhim Singh 1's reign, particularly starting with the period in 1719, less than a year before his death, when he paid homage in Delhi to the Mughal emperor Muhammad Shah. Although Muhammad Shah had recently succeeded to the majesty of the Peacock Throne, he was little more than a puppet of his prime minister, Vazir Sayyid Husain Ali, whose cabals Bhim Singh conspicuously supported. The audience with Muhammad Shah was ostensibly convened by Husain Ali to reward Bhim Singh for this assistance. Of the event, Lakshmandan wrote:

> Emperor Muhammad Shah ascended the throne in the Samvat year 1775,[9] and Vazir Sayyid Husain Ali beseeched him that "Your Majesty should take recognition of the fact that your good fortune is due to Maharao Bhim Singh." Thus Muhammad Shah summoned Maharao Bhim Singh and said, "Ask for whatever land you want and consider it granted." To which the Maharao replied, "I ask only that whatever land I subdue through the strength of the sword be mine." Sayyid Husain Ali objected, "This liberty is unacceptable and will lead to great destruction." But Maharao Bhim Singh insisted, "If you are freely granting something, then don't grant that which I do not want." So at this time Muhammad Shah gave Maharao Bhim Singh nine gold coins [symbols of royal authority] and said, "I grant you in perpetuity whatever land you seize by the strength of your sword and bravery." This proclamation was written and taken by Maharao Bhim Singh who, having offered his respects to the emperor, departed for his capital at Kotah.[10]

This passage is interesting because it not only portrays the maharao as wanting to display his worth through conquest and the merit of his own deeds but also shows him specifically discounting other means of establishing his authority, especially through his "institutional" association with the Mughal emperor. Bhim Singh rejects the emperor's outright gift of land,[11] and, although he accepts the emperor's sanction of his actions, he insists on establishing sovereignty himself.

Although positions of authority could not be inherited in this system of beliefs, they at least could be retrospectively validated through claims of being incarnations, or avatars, through the transmigration of souls of archetypal warrior heroes. In Rajasthan, the most frequently invoked heroes are the kings Prithvi Raj Chauhan and Rana Pratap, both of whom gained fame for resisting the

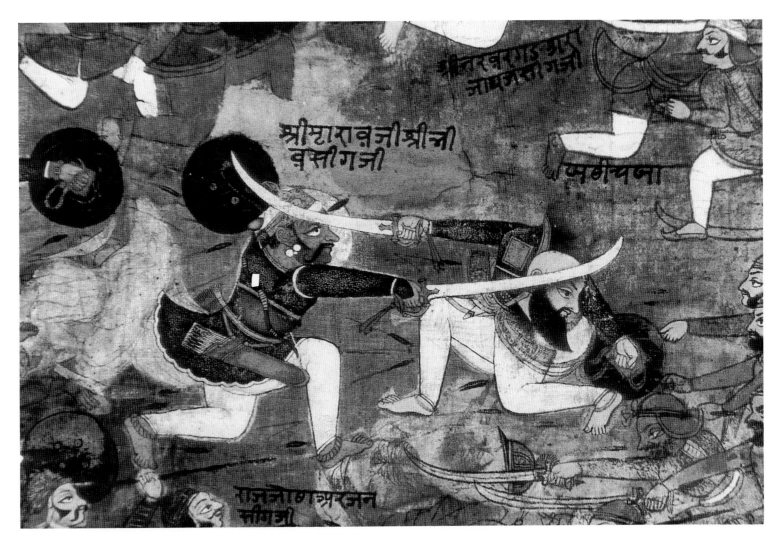

श्रीतारावजी श्रीजी वसी गजी

भीतरखगढ़ भुत जोमजरसी गजी

जगींचला

राजनोगणप्रजन सीगजी

Figure 1
Maharao Bhim Singh 1 of Kotah Beheads Nizam-ul-Mulk, *attributed to*
the Kotah Master, 1720, Kotah. Watercolor and opaque watercolor on cloth, 209 x 331 cm.
Rao Madho Singh Trust Museum, Fort Kotah.

penetration into India of various Central Asian groups; in Kotah, Maharao Bhim Singh 1 is often included along with these other exemplars. From the late seventeenth century on, one of the most important means of retrospectively establishing one's claim to karmic descent from such heroes in Kotah was through possession of sacred statues that had been worshiped by the earlier champions. Through the history of their worship by previous kings, these images became repositories for their merit; possession of them conferred some of that merit upon new owners.[12]

Much of this highly esteemed religious statuary was associated with the bhakti, or devotional practice, of the Vallabha Sampraday, of which the preeminent image, a shiny black stone statue of the manifestation of Krishna known as Shri Nathji (cat. 54), is now located in the busy pilgrimage town of Nathadvara (Mewar, Ra-

jasthan).[13] Since the late seventeenth century, the history of several important Vallabha images (all manifestations of the god Krishna) has become entwined with Kotah's history. For example, the image of Shri Nathji briefly sojourned in Kotah during the monsoon months of 1672 under the protection and patronage of Jagat Singh of Kotah (r. 1658–83); Shri Mathureshji, perhaps the sect's second most revered image, has remained there over much longer periods. However, one deity in particular has come to be especially associated with Kotah's ruling dynasty: the image of Shri Brijnathji (fig. 2), which was given to Maharao Bhim Singh 1 during his initiation into the practice in 1719 shortly after his audience with Muhammad Shah in Delhi. Since that date, Shri Brijnathji has been the kingdom's tutelary deity, and possession of this deity has played an important role during civil wars and succession disputes in establishing the legitimacy of rival claims to the throne. For example, during the civil war (1723–28) between Maharao Durjan Sal of Kotah (r. 1723–56) and his elder brother, Shyam, Durjan Sal's recovery of the image of Shri Brijnathji from Hyderabad was crucial in legitimating his "usurpation" of the throne.

While "genealogical" connections could be established between different individuals through a belief in the reincarnation of the soul within cycles of life, death, and rebirth, which was then validated by the performance of exemplary actions and possession of revered statuary,[14] similar connections, subject to the same processes of validation, could be forged through what has been called "the transfer of karma"[15] among more or less contemporary individuals for whom there can be no question of sharing the same reborn soul.

In large measure because of the distinctiveness of the belief in reincarnation, it has become commonplace to think that the moment of reckoning at which karmic reward and retribution are decided occurs at the time of death/rebirth — that is, a particular soul is reborn with an innate karmic imprint, or "headwriting,"[16] based on actions in previous lives. This belief is true enough. However, it has also been argued that the transfer of sin and merit associated with karma also occurs while individuals are alive.[17] There are detailed ethnographic examples of how karma is reckoned to be transferred between living individuals through various mediums, such as blood, cooked food, and coresidence or physical proximity.[18] And, intriguingly for our present purposes, there are similar textual examples in which a victorious king incorporates the qualities and virtues of his vanquished rival in the course of battle through the medium of sacrifice.[19] Furthermore, because it is karma that defines and differentiates one soul from another — at least when caught in the web of samsara — transfers of karma between contemporary individuals have the effect of causing different souls to be qualified similarly, thus becoming more alike.[20]

The fluid notions of self that attend the belief in the transfer of karma readily accord with mutable conceptions of community identity, "insider" and "outsider," or "native" and "foreigner," in Kotah during the eighteenth century. The indigenous bases on which political legitimacy was established in Rajasthan and, by extension, much of the conventional Western historiography of the region, require reconsideration in this light.

The Maratha Insurgency and the Jhala Regency: "Native" Princes and "Others" in Kotah during the Eighteenth Century

Since the first appearance in the early nineteenth century of what remains the most famous study of Rajasthan, Lieutenant Colonel James Tod's two-volume *Annals and Antiquities of Rajast'han*, the eigh-

teenth century has been treated as a "dark age" characterized by political disarray, shrinking commerce, declining agriculture, and cultural decadence. Tod himself succinctly dismissed the eighteenth century as an era of "civil strife and external spoliation,"[21] and his opinions broadly fall in line with other British colonial commentaries on the condition of Indian politics, which tend to see strong governance, economic prosperity, and cultural vitality in unmitigated decline everywhere on the subcontinent during the 1700s.[22] C. A. Bayly's revisionary history of burgeoning commerce and cultural florescence in many of the subimperial market (*qasba*) towns of the Gangetic plain during the age of British expansion[23] provides a valuable corrective to these ideas, which appear to have been informed principally by observations of what was happening in the old imperial centers such as Delhi and Agra — or in Tod's much beloved Mewar. More recently, Ronald Inden has shown how these colonially inspired denigrations of Indian social conditions were part of a self-serving campaign that aimed to delegitimate indigenous society and politics on the eve of British mastery over India, in order to justify a colonial intervention.[24]

Since Tod's time, much of the blame for the apparently chaotic situation in Rajasthan during the eighteenth century has been directed toward the intervention of "outsiders" in the region. In Tod's estimation, the principal alien culprits were the Marathas, a "warrior" (but non-Rajput) caste whose "homeland" was the Deccan, but who had expanded their empire northward into Malwa, Rajasthan, and the interfluvial Doab between the Jamuna and Ganges rivers. In the late eighteenth and early nineteenth centuries, the Marathas were also the principal indigenous rivals of the British in north India. No fewer than three Anglo-Maratha wars were waged between 1774 and 1818, when the British were finally able to achieve a decisive victory.

Up until 1818, Maratha military success rested on the use of lightly armed and highly mobile cavalry. In British eyes, the Marathas' superb horsemanship was symptomatic of their unsettled, "nomadic" way of life, which Tod considered to be "lawless" and "predatory." Thus, it was claimed that the defining characteristic of Maratha rule was that the rights and prerogatives of the government vis-à-vis the people were in no way defined or codified. The Maratha penal regime was portrayed as irregular and arbitrary, and its revenue "system" as random and wanton pillage.[25] Tod pulled no punches when he wrote that the Marathas were "distinguished for mean parsimony, low cunning, and dastardly depredation"[26] or likened them to "vampires, who drained the very life-blood wherever the scent of spoil attracted them."[27]

The fly in the ointment of Tod's thesis was Kotah.[28] Despite the fact that Kotah had been in the Maratha sphere of influence longest of all the Rajasthani kingdoms (Kotah first began paying an annual indemnity to the Marathas in 1738), it was an extremely

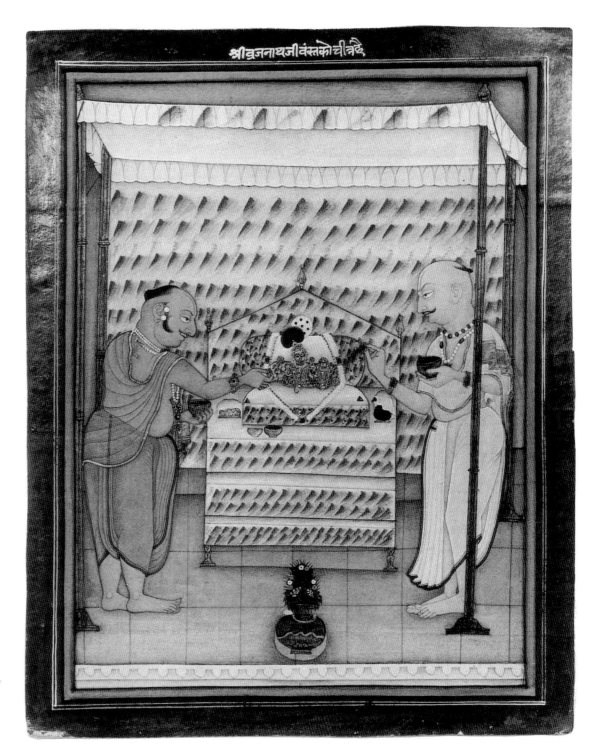

श्रीव्रजनाथजीवंस्तकोचीवदे

Figure 2
Maharao Kishor Singh of Kotah
Assisting Tilkayat Damodarji of
Nathadvara in the Worship of
Shri Brijnathji, *c. 1831, Kotah.*
Opaque watercolor, gold, and metallic gray
watercolor on paper, approx. 25 x 20 cm.
Rao Madho Singh Trust Museum,
Fort Kotah.

prosperous place when Tod visited it in 1820. On his arrival, he wrote:

> The appearance of Kotah is very imposing, and impresses the mind with a more lively notion of wealth and activity than most cities in India. A strong wall with bastions runs parallel to, and at no great distance from, the [Chambal] river ... The scene is crowded with objects animate and inanimate. Between the river and the city are masses of people plying various trades.[29]

Moreover, in the surrounding countryside, agriculture flourished to such an extent that Tod made the following startling admission: "[Kotah possesses] one of the richest and most productive soils in India, and *better cultivated than any spot even of British India*" (emphasis added).[30]

As this confession indicates, Tod himself recognized that Kotah's economic prosperity was not merely the byproduct of its incorporation in 1817 into the British sphere of influence, but had earlier, eighteenth-century roots. It was during the eighteenth century, for example, that many of Kotah's largest merchant houses first established themselves in Kotah's capital city. Thus, the famous merchant and moneylender (*seth*) Bahadur Mal, after whom Kotah's Bahadur bazaar is reputedly named, moved his headquarters of operations from Jaisalmer to Kotah around 1757 C.E.[31] Moreover, the size of the walled city expanded more than threefold during the century prior to the British presence, and much of the expansion was undertaken to accommodate new emporiums, such as the Bahadur bazaar, the Rampura bazaar, and the Ladpura bazaar, all of which stretch along the banks of the Chambal River north of the inner city from the Patan Pol gate.[32] The Comte de Modave, who visited Kotah for a month in July/August 1776, estimated that the city's population at the time was a bustling twenty-five to thirty thousand "souls," or just slightly less than the population of Ujjain and more than twice the population of Indore at the same time.[33]

Agriculture also throve in the Kotah region during the late eighteenth century; Modave specifically contrasted the intensive and prosperous agriculture of eastern Rajasthan (including Kotah) with the declining farming conditions that he had observed around Delhi and Agra.[34] It was also during this period that the royally patronized Kotah school of painting achieved its greatest volume of output and many of its most stunning artistic successes — as is amply confirmed by this catalogue. Similarly, the elaborate performance of Kotah's royally sponsored public pageant-plays, such as the *Ramlila*, also apparently date to the eighteenth century.

According to Tod, Kotah was "saved" from the Marathas thanks to the diplomatic and military skills of its long-serving prime minister, Zalim Singh Jhala, who dominated Kotah's affairs for over fifty years, from the later half of the eighteenth into the early nineteenth century. Zalim Singh was a Rajput from the Jhala clan whose great-grandfather, Madho Singh, had first come to Kotah from Gujarat in 1696 and had successfully worked his way into various positions of importance in Kotah's army and court, the most important of which was military commander (*faujdar*) of Kotah City. This position was held hereditarily by Madho Singh's descendants until Zalim Singh assumed it in 1758. In 1761, Zalim Singh directed Kotah's stunning victory over Jaipur at the battle of Bhatwara (cat. 44), which finally laid to rest Jaipur's claims to suzerainty over Hadauti, and following which Kotah's eight largest feudatories, known as the Kotriat Thikanas and occupying the frontier "netherland" between Kotah and Jaipur, first paid allegiance to Kotah.[35] After the battle of Bhatwara, Zalim Singh rose quickly to prominence in court circles. In 1764, Maharao Guman Singh of Kotah (r. 1764–71) elevated Zalim Singh to the position of prime minister (*musahab-i-ala*). In 1771, after a brief falling-out with Guman Singh, during which time he left Kotah to join the service of the maharana of Mewar (Udaipur), Zalim Singh was appointed by the dying maharao to be regent for his ten-year-old son and heir, Umed Singh I (r. 1771–1819). After Umed Singh

reached his majority, however, Zalim Singh retained power, and the Kotah maharao remained more or less a puppet of his prime minister. Paintings of the period bear witness to the extraordinary influence of Zalim Singh over Umed Singh, as time and time again the maharao is depicted in the watchful company of his prime minister (cat. 45, 46, and 49).

During his tenure as prime minister, Zalim Singh is credited with having kept the Maratha menace at bay and thus preserving Kotah from Maratha "spoliation." Still, despite nobly resisting the Marathas (and thus indirectly serving colonial interests at the same time), Zalim Singh never earned unconditional British approval — no doubt because he commanded the best-trained army in Rajasthan, which, though nominally allied to the British, nevertheless remained a potential threat. Tod branded Zalim Singh a "usurper," a "tyrant," and a "despot." Among his offenses were the summary seizure of lands from their "hereditary" holders, a reliance on extensive networks of "spies" and "newsrunners" to inform him on his enemies, and his employment of an army of "foreign mercenaries" to maintain his political position. In short, Zalim Singh did not respect the rights of private property and failed to sustain basic civil liberties; most important, his apparatus of government was not indigenous and therefore not truly "national."

With reference to Kotah's economic good health, therefore, Tod posed, and then answered, an important question:

> But is this propriety? Is this the greatness which the Raja Goman [Maharao Guman Singh of Kotah] intended should be entailed upon his successors, his chiefs, and his subjects? Was it to entertain twenty thousand mercenary soldiers from the sequestered fields of the illustrious Hara, the indigenous proprietor? Is this government, is it good government according to the ideas of more civilized nations, to extend taxation to the limits in order to maintain this cumbrous machinery? We may admit, for a time, such a system may have been requisite … to preserve the state from [the Marathas] … and now could we see the noble restored to his forfeited estates, and the riot [landholding farmer] to his hereditary rood of land, we should say that Zalim Singh had been instrumental in the hand of Providence for the preservation of the rights of the Hara. But as it is, whilst the corn which waves upon the fertile surface of Kotah presents not the symbol of prosperity, neither is his well-paid and well-disciplined army a sure means of defense; moral propriety has been violated; rights are in abeyance, and until they be restored, even the apparent consistency of the social fabric is obtained by means which endanger its security.[36]

As this condemnation clearly indicates, much of Tod's censure rested on the fact that Zalim Singh, while holding the reins of power in Kotah, was not of the royal Hara clan, which Tod (and other British officials) saw as indigenous to the Hadauti region of southeastern Rajasthan.[37] The Rajput caste in northern India is divided into numerous clans (nominally thirty-six), each of which is defined by a common descent through the male line from a unique mythical ancestor. Unlike Kotah's maharaos, who were from the Hara subclan of the Chauhan clan, Zalim Singh was a Jhala. Moreover, Tod pointed out, Zalim Singh's forefathers did not even hail from Rajasthan; rather, they immigrated from Gujarat, further to the west. Tod used Zalim Singh's putative foreignness to Kotah, as he had that of the Marathas, in order to delegitimate his rule, and this is how Zalim Singh continues to be remembered in most histories of the region.[38] But were Zalim Singh Jhala and the Marathas castigated as foreign and not native by the inhabitants of Kotah themselves at the time? Were the social boundaries between Maratha and Rajput, or between Hara and Jhala, really as sharply defined, nonnegotiable, and mutually exclusionary as Tod thought them to be?

In fact, the relationship between the Marathas and Rajputs (and among the various Rajput clans) were not always as sharply delineated and antagonistic as has commonly been thought. Indeed, it appears that much of the good fortune enjoyed by Kotah under the stewardship of Zalim Singh Jhala was achieved not *in spite* of the Marathas (as Tod would have it) but *because* of them. Furthermore, many of the alleged differences between Rajput and Maratha were often blurred as the two groups found important arenas in which they shared common interests and ambitions. Although Maratha demands for tribute from Kotah at times placed a heavy burden on Kotah's treasury, the Maratha presence facilitated Kotah's political and economic development in other respects. Under Maratha supremacy, Kotah became a strategic "central place" from which Maratha policy in the rest of Rajasthan was directed and administered. Kotah's centrality was due in part to its geographic position on the northern side of the Ghatoli and Dara gaps, which breach the Mukandara range separating Rajasthan from Malwa and the Deccan. Thus, Kotah became an important staging town on the caravan routes that linked Ujjain in the south with the rest of Rajasthan, as well as with Agra further north.[39] Much of the Maratha "plunder" that passed through Kotah was redirected to support patterns of "conspicuous consumption" in Kotah itself. For example, Balaji Yashwant Gulgule, the Saraswat Brahman who in 1738 was appointed by Ranoji Shinde to be the Maratha civilian revenue collector (*kamavisdar*) and agent (*vakil*) in Kotah, also had under his charge at various times revenue collectors stationed at the courts of Bundi, Mewar, Rajgarh, Sheopur, and Indragarh. Some of the huge inflows of tribute that passed through the hands of Balaji Yashwant Gulgule and his adopted son, Lalaji Ballal, who succeeded as agent in 1759/60, were steered to Kotah's benefit through the Gulgule family's moneylending operations. Ultimately, the Gulgule fortune became so bound up with Kotah that after the establishment of the Pax Britannica in 1818, when most Maratha agents were encouraged by the British to leave Rajasthan, the Gulgule family chose to remain behind, fearing

that if they left, the Kotah darbar, or court, would never make good on the extensive debt owed them.[40]

Finally, it was with Maratha collusion, if not outright support, that Kotah was able to (re)assert dominion over many neighboring tracts of land. When Kotah wrested direct authority over the eight Kotriat Thikanas on its northern frontier from Jaipur in 1761, it did so with Maratha backing. In 1779, the Maratha general Mahadji Sindhia (cat. 53) transferred the district of Shahbad, on Kotah's extreme east, from one of his clients to Zalim Singh Jhala, and during the same year another Maratha general, Tukoji Holkar, made over to Kotah the administrative districts (*parganas*) of Suket and Bakani on a revenue farming (*ijara*) basis. Around the turn of the nineteenth century, the Chau Mahala and Sat Mahala regions (straddling the Mukandara range) were also given to Kotah by the Marathas on the same terms.[41] Although each of these additions to Kotah's territory deepened its financial obligations to the Marathas, they also enabled Kotah to exercise authority over significant tracts of land that had not recognized Kotah's rule since the reign of Maharao Bhim Singh I.

Given these arrangements, it is not surprising that many Rajputs self-consciously sought to identify with the Marathas in more symbolic ways. For example, during the height of Maratha power in Rajasthan in the eighteenth century, many Rajputs eagerly established "fictive" kin relations with the wives of important Maratha leaders through a rite of protection (*rakhi bhandan*) that is paradigmatically performed among brothers and sisters.[42] Moreover, the claims to Rajput descent by the great seventeenth-century Maratha king Shivaji were turned around by eighteenth-century Rajputs to claim that they themselves were Marathas and thus entitled to various privileges, such as tax concessions, that were typically enjoyed by Marathas within the Maratha Empire.[43] For their part, the Marathas joined the Rajputs in becoming enthusiastic patrons of Rajasthani religious institutions, particularly of the temples of the Vallabha Sampraday; important members of the leading Maratha families undertook highly public pilgrimages to leading Vallabha Sampraday temples, such as the Shri Mathureshji temple in Kotah.[44]

Similarly, within Kotah among Rajputs the boundary between Hara and Jhala was capable of being blurred. During the period of Zalim Singh Jhala's ascendancy, he undertook to secure his dominant position in Kotah by establishing his legitimacy in socially relevant terms as defined by the Hara dynasty. This does not mean that Zalim Singh did not attempt to reduce the material influence of the Hara nobility by sequestering their estates or to dilute Hara power by flooding Kotah's court with substantial numbers of non-Hara nobles. Nonetheless, Zalim Singh was less interested in forcibly and completely replacing the Hara royal line with his own than he was in merging the identity of the two lineages. He never attempted to delegitimate the Hara dynasty or to efface its memory. Rather, he attempted to demonstrate that he was a sympathetic and rightful receptacle of the Hara legacy.

This aim was accomplished by several mechanisms. First and foremost was the utmost respect that Zalim Singh outwardly showed to the maharao. Even as he was pulling the strings of power, he was always careful to maintain the dignity of the maharao on public occasions. At the same time, he carefully forged important marriage links between his family and Kotah's ruling line, as well as with that of its parent state of Bundi, also ruled by Haras. Indeed, the terms of address in both the direct correspondence between Zalim Singh and Maharao Umed Singh I and third-person administrative documents stressed their kinship links.[45] To the same end, Zalim Singh publicly engaged in the construction and renovation of the Hara royal cenotaphs, monuments erected on the cremation sites of Kotah's Hara rulers, which had become — and remain to this day — popular objects of local veneration.

However, perhaps the most important single aspect of Zalim Singh's legitimizing program was his patronage of the Vallabha Sampraday, the spiritual practice with which Kotah's Hara dynasty had become so closely affiliated. His crowning achievement was to harbor the deity of Shri Vitthalnathji, the sect's third most important deity, in Kotah from 1802 until 1820. Similarly, he maintained a small force of troops, known as the army of worship or service (seva ki sena), in Nathadvara for the protection of the temple of Shri Nathji, following in the tradition of Jagat Singh of Kotah in offering protection to this preeminent deity. Zalim Singh also became an ardent devotee of Shri Nathji, and the apartments of his villa (haveli; now unfortunately in a state of ruin), situated just behind the maharao's palace, were filled with wall paintings showing the worship (seva) of this god.

In sum, Zalim Singh's "usurpation" of the throne would be better seen as the slow conquest of a political order by colonizing it from within. In taking this long-term strategy, Zalim Singh was perhaps attempting to effect a type of transfer of karma between the Hara dynasty and himself that would eventually render him a legitimate successor to the Hara line. Significantly, this strategy earned him influential local support, including backing from powerful members of the Hara clan. For example, Sheodan Singh of Gainta, a Hara Rajput, was Zalim Singh's agent to the British when the first treaty of alliance (which included a secret clause recognizing Zalim Singh Jhala's position as de facto ruler of Kotah) was negotiated.

Intriguingly, although Tod did not take into full account indigenous processes of legitimation based on the transfer of karma, he was not totally blind to what eventually may have been the outcome of Zalim Singh's course of action had the British not brought the kingdom under its "protection" in 1818. Although his characterization of the details of this process owed too much to the European historiography of eighth-century France, Tod nevertheless astutely surmised that

> It would have been considered as a matter of course, where "Amurnath to Amurnath succeeds," that the Maharao Kishore should continue the same puppet in the hands of Madhu Singh [Zalim Singh's son] that his father had been in Zalim's. This would have excited no surprise, nor would the proceeding have afforded speculation for one hour. Nay, the usurper might have advanced to the ulterior step; and like the Frank maire du palais, have demanded of the Pontiff of Nat'hdwara [i.e., the head priest of the Shri Nathji temple], as did Pepin of Pope Zacharius, "whether he who had the power, should not also have the title, of king"; and the same plenary indulgence would have awaited the first Jhala Raja of Kotah as was granted to the first of the Carolingian kings![46]

In the end, however, because Tod's own conception of legitimacy was based on a patriarchal model in which royal succession was based on an "affinity in blood," he saw lawful rule as ultimately resting with the maharao, who, by official accounts, was of the same Hara bloodline as the kingdom's founder, Madho Singh. With the arrival of the British in Rajasthan during the early nineteenth century and the imposition of colonial "indirect rule," the Jhala slow conquest was thus first halted and then reversed. Although the British treaties initially (albeit secretly) recognized Zalim Singh Jhala's prime ministership as a right to be hereditarily passed on to his heirs, and although it was invested with all state power, Zalim Singh's position became increasingly untenable. Under colonial influence, the rhetoric of political legitimacy, as expressed by officials such as James Tod, was tied exclusively to paternal descent, while older forms of divine rule associated with the transfer of karma lost social currency. In this environment, Zalim Singh Jhala's claims to "righteous rule" progressively lost their cultural meaning, and eventually Maharao Ram Singh (r. 1827–66) was able to mount an effective campaign against Madan Singh Jhala, grandson of Zalim Singh. The result of this agitation was that a small portion of Kotah was separated in 1838 for the creation of a new state, known as Jhalawar, to be ruled by Zalim Singh's descendants, while the remaining portion of Kotah was returned to the authority of the Hara line.

This transformation in how legitimacy was reckoned is witnessed in the paintings of the nineteenth century. As late as the reign of Maharao Kishor Singh (r. 1819–27), the maharao still portrayed himself in righteous terms as a pious devotee of the Vallabha Sampraday performing the worship of various Vallabha deities, especially his personal deity, Shri Brijrajji (cat. 56–62), and the state deity, Shri Brijnathji. Moreover, wall paintings in the inner apartments of the Bada Mahal in the Kotah palace glorify his association with the most important of the Vallabha Sampraday priests, Tilkayat Damodarji II (also known as Dauji II), the head priest of the Shri Nathji temple in Nathadvara. The most impressive of these compositions depicts the head priest's visit to Kotah in 1826, at which time Maharao Kishor Singh apparently assisted him in the worship of Shri Brijnathji (see also fig. 2).[47] Clearly, by emphasizing his close association with the Vallabha Sampraday, Kishor Singh was attempting to counter similar claims made by Zalim Singh Jhala at the time. By the middle of the nineteenth century, however, such demonstrations of religious merit had largely disappeared from the repertoire of Kotah's royal atelier. Under the mature patronage of Maharao Ram Singh, kingship is represented in largely secular terms: darbars, royal portraits, marriage feasts, hunts, and other entertainments, as well as genre scenes. In this secular age of Indian kingship, notions of karmic attainment had little or no role to play, as British power recognized only the role of biological descent in establishing the ruler's charisma.

Conclusion

Given this understanding of how legitimacy was reckoned in Kotah, particularly as it was informed by Hindu beliefs about the transfer of karma, we are finally in a position to understand the curious battle scene of Maharao Bhim Singh I and Nizam-ul-Mulk by the Kotah Master. The powerful effect of this painting, apart from the sheer wizardry of the Kotah Master's draftsmanship, derives from a contrapuntal polyphony in which the visual cues available in the painting by itself are self-consciously and purposefully held in opposition to other well-known historical narratives concerning the event. This serves to blur the identities of hero and rival precisely at the moment when Nizam-ul-Mulk demonstrates himself to be the worthy receptacle of Bhim Singh's karma by virtue of both his military success and the capture of Shri Brijnathji. Even though we know that the bodily Bhim Singh was defeated and killed in the battle on the banks of the Narmada in 1720, the fruit of his meritorious life, or karma, continued to be manifest in this world — and in none other than the person of Nizam-ul-Mulk. By virtue of his defeat of Maharao Bhim Singh I, Nizam-ul-Mulk *had become* Bhim Singh — and Bhim Singh, Nizam-ul-Mulk. The king is dead, long live the king!

NOTES

1 While there is very near unanimity about the Samvat date of Bhim Singh I's death, there remains considerable confusion about its equivalence in the Gregorian calendar. The concordance cited here is taken from Shyamaldas 1886, 2:1415. For other reckonings, see, for example, Mathur 1986, 202, and M. L. Sharma 1939, 296.

2 From his base in Hyderabad, Chin Qilich Khan later succeeded in establishing one of the largest and longest-lived Mughal "successor states," and became better known under his assumed titles of Nizam-ul-Mulk and Asaf Jah I.

3 For a partial recitation of this documentation, see Bautze 1992b, 313, and Mathur 1986, 202–3.

4 Joachim K. Bautze, who first noticed this, supports the inscriptional evidence with a wealth of other comparative evidence based on well-identified portraits of the two rivals (see Bautze 1992b, 310–14).

5 D. H. A. Kolff has suggested that in the pre-Mughal era, genealogical descent was not as singularly important in defining Rajput status as it became later with the growth of Mughal, and then British, power. During this earlier period (prior to the late sixteenth century), "Rajput" was more of a generic name applied to any "'horse soldier,' 'trooper,' or 'headman of a village,'" regardless of biogenetic origin, who achieved his status through his personal ability to establish a wide network of alliances

by means of military service and marriage. But "during the sixteenth and seventeenth centuries, the top layer of Rajputs, encouraged by openings presented by the Mughal state and helped by the expertise of their bards, tended to close ranks and articulate new forms of Rajput behavior ... [and] the political power and social status of the more successful lineages tended to be legitimized exclusively in the language of descent and kinship" (Kolff 1990, 711–16). As we shall see, however, the capacity of, and indeed the incumbency on, Rajput rulers to demonstrate their personal merit and ability remained vitally important even after the seventeenth century.

6 Fuller 1992, 245.

7 Peabody 1991a.

8 Kotah first came under colonial "indirect rule" in 1817, when Maharao Umed Singh signed a treaty of "subsidiary alliance" with the British.

9 According to R. S. Mathur, Muhammad Shah's installation took place on September 14, 1719 (Mathur 1986, 199).

10 Lakshmandan n.d., 24–25.

11 See Dirks 1987, 128–38.

12 Peabody 1991a.

13 The Shri Nathji temple is reputed to be one of the wealthiest in all of India.

14 Peabody 1991a. At first blush, it would appear that

this analysis would have only limited applicability to the Rajput dynasties of western India, where unbroken succession through bloodlines can often apparently be traced for hundreds of years (indeed, to the sun and the moon in some instances). However, the ease with which genealogies can be fabricated is well known. Although there is no firm evidence to prove that the type of continuous royal succession as reconstructed in this catalogue (see chart) for Kotah rests to some extent on concocted pedigrees, there is plenty of circumstantial evidence to indicate that this practice was not unknown elsewhere in Rajasthan. Any reader of the royal family histories collected by James Tod will be familiar with the extraordinary legends of posthumous birth in exile of male heirs to apparently extinguished royal lineages, and tales of Rajput kings who were left for dead on the battlefield only to be dragged to some forest or mountain retreat from whence their heirs later reconquered their patrimonies; these are just two common Rajasthani narratives through which warriors of obscure origin established their biogenetic legitimacy (Tod 1829 and 1832).

15 O'Flaherty 1980, 28–37; see also S. B. Daniel 1983, 35–40.

16 S. B. Daniel 1983, 30–35.

17 O'Flaherty 1980, 27–37, and S. B. Daniel 1983.

18 S. B. Daniel 1983, 28–29.

19 Hiltebeitel 1976, 153, 323, and 352.

20 See also Marriott 1976 and E. V. Daniel 1984.

21 Tod 1832, 438.

22 This line has also greatly influenced twentieth-century Indian historians such as K. S. Gupta, Beni Gupta, A. C. Banerjee, Jadunath Sarkar, and Dilbagh Singh.

23 Bayly 1983.

24 Inden 1990.

25 For a very different appraisal of the long-term effects of the Maratha conquest of Malwa, see Gordon 1977.

26 Tod 1829, 406.

27 Ibid., 438.

28 Even in Mewar, Tod could have painted a very different picture had he concentrated less on what was happening at the court of the maharana in Udaipur and more on what was happening in important "feudal" estates (*thikanas*) such as Badnor. Badnor grew rapidly during this period, becoming an important center of commerce and seat of culture.

29 Tod 1832, 662.

30 Tod 1829, 14. Bishop Reginald Heber, who passed through Rajasthan five years later, described Kotah as "a sort of Eden amid the surrounding misery" (Heber 1828, 2:39).

31 This information is based on a family-history interview with Seth Budh Singh Baphna on October 14, 1987. See also p. 79 of this catalogue for the history of the Gulgule family, who established themselves in Kotah in 1738.

32 According to N. L. Mishra, in 1695 C.E. the walls of Kotah City enclosed only about 160 acres. This initial, "inner" fortification had three gates (all still standing): Patan Pol to the north, Kethuni Pol to the east, and Bhilwari Pol to the south (now also known as Kishorpura Pol). The western side of the city was (and is) flanked by the Chambal River. By 1723, new fortifications had been constructed east and north of the "inner" city to bring an additional 244 acres under protection. Two new gates were established then: Suraj Pol to the east and Rampura Pol to the north. At the close of the eighteenth century, the walls were again extended northward to include a further 160 acres. This addition had yet another northern gate, Ladpura Pol (N. L. Mishra 1987, 113–15).

33 Modave 1971, 478, 497, and 501. The establishment of the Pax Britannica in Rajasthan in 1818, which was supposed to stimulate urban commerce, in fact did little to swell the city's population. Ida Pfeiffer estimated that, when she visited Kotah in February 1848, the city's population remained at about thirty thousand (Pfeiffer c. 1852, 200).

34 Modave 1971, 467–86. For similar observations by Charles Metcalfe in 1802, see Kaye 1858, 2:56.

35 In 1753, the Mughal emperor Ahmad Shah awarded the military command (*qiladari*) of Ranthambhor to Raja Madho Singh of Jaipur. Not only did the Kotriat Thikanas fall within the Ranthambhor command at that time; historically so did Kotah itself.

36 Tod 1832, 546–47.

37 The strong and natural connection that Tod saw between the Haras and the region around Kotah is witnessed in his popular but somewhat suspect etymology of the term *Hadauti*: "land of the Hadas."

38 For a fuller account of Tod's attitude toward Zalim Singh Jhala and the factors informing it, see Peabody 1996. For more recent accounts of Zalim Singh which reproduce these attitudes, see M. L. Sharma 1939 and R. P. Shastri 1971.

39 When the Comte de Modave traveled from Agra to Hyderabad in 1776, he passed via Kotah, Mukandara, and Ujjain. Along the route (as far as Ujjain at least), he found caravanserais and thriving bazaars where he could outfit his company, hire guides, and buy camels and horses (Modave 1971, 459–96). In fact, he identified Kotah, along with Delhi and Jaipur, as one of the principal horse markets in "l'Indoustan" (Modave 1971 ed., 327). At the end of the eighteenth century, Kotah remained the principal transit point between Agra and Ujjain. William Hunter traveled this route via Kotah in March 1793 (see Hunter 1801), as did Charles Metcalfe in March/April 1802 (see Kaye 1858, 1:55–56).

40 In 1738, Maharao Durjan Sal granted Balaji Yashwant Gulgule a small estate in the village of Birakhedi (see B. Gupta 1979, 26). Thirty-three years later, Lalaji Ballal Gulgule was hypothecated the lucrative Sarola estate in southeastern Kotah as a surety against a debt owed him by the Kotah darbar.

41 B. Gupta 1979, 63–66.

42 Ibid., 121–23.

43 I am indebted to Sumit Guha for bringing this information to my attention.

44 B. Gupta 1979, 119.

45 For example, see R. P. Shastri 1971, 77 and 79.

46 Tod 1832, 454.

47 Woodman Taylor, in his essay in this volume, above, first recognized that it was Maharao Kishor Singh who was performing the worship in this series of pictures. Heretofore, the individual depicted in this series has been commonly misidentified by many scholars, including myself (Peabody 1991a, pl. 4), as a priest.

CRAIGEN W. BOWEN WITH AMY SNODGRASS

Line and Color: Painting
Materials and Techniques in Kotah

The paintings and drawings produced in Kotah from the sixteenth through the nineteenth centuries can be broadly characterized as opaque watercolor on paper or, occasionally, cloth. Rajput painting has been studied by art historians,[1] but no single school has been looked at in depth by conservators and scientists. Many months spent in Kota conserving the works and preparing them for exhibition extended a unique opportunity to delve into the brilliant world of line and color conceived by Kotah artists. Observations of the physical nature of pictures that were produced for the ruling family of Kotah, and that have remained there since, provide the basis for this study.

There are few historical sources about the painting techniques of the region, and those that do exist focus on Persian and Mughal traditions; additional problems in the literature arise from the translation, either historical or contemporary, of common names of materials and their manufacture. While it is clear that painting techniques and materials traveled constantly throughout the Middle East to the Indian subcontinent, it is helpful to investigate the regional differences that must have existed. Availability of materials, as well as variations in method, play a role in defining an indigenous style such as the one that developed in Kotah. Therefore, extensive visual examination was augmented by scientific analysis to identify the pigments and binders.

Kotah's graphic production falls into two classes. The first is drawings (khakas), including sketchy ones done in charcoal or black ink on single sheets of paper, highly detailed finished ink drawings, and wash drawings with line and color. The second is paintings — heavily painted layers of transparent and opaque watercolor over transparent ink underdrawings on opaque watercolor grounds laid down on thick multilayered paper supports. The range of pigments and implements used to produce the pictures is relatively narrow: the extensive range of effects derives from the artists' mastery of the handling of their materials, using brushes, pens, and burnishers.

The artists' working techniques evolved from Persian antecedents, which remained remarkably unchanged through the transformation into Mughal, Deccani, Rajput, and other Indian styles. Perhaps this was the case in part because the tools, pigments, and binders were generally available throughout the Islamic and Indian worlds, apparently with some variations depending on local pref-

erence and availability. Paper, pigments, water-soluble gums and glues, brushes, and pens made from reeds or feathers were found throughout this vast region — and, indeed, the world — and remained the primary materials for the production of pictures for some half a millennium.

In Europe during this time, tremendous changes were made in the materials and techniques used for making pictures, with fresco giving way to tempera paintings on panel and then to oil paintings on canvas. Watercolor and opaque watercolor, which had existed from antiquity, continued to be used primarily for illustration and, later, in imitation of oil painting. It was not until the eighteenth and nineteenth centuries that watercolor technique developed in its own right.[2]

Rapid changes in painting materials in Europe resulted in continuous changes in technique and development of style, as artists attempted to translate their images into different media. During this same period, the invention of movable type and the subsequent evolution of printmaking techniques provided further outlets for artistic expression. In India, these technologies arrived later and were much less often embraced by artists and patrons. Although practiced today by many Indian artists, European painting and printmaking techniques were not significantly influential at Rajput courts until the end of the nineteenth century.

The ongoing political alliances and military campaigns carried out by the Mughal emperors and local princes assured interaction between artists. Artists generally were employed by the heads of state in studios that included many craftsmen. They often traveled with the court during military campaigns and could be considered part of the spoils of war, so that they may have begun their careers under one ruler and later moved to an entirely different part of India. As has been described in the first essay in this volume, the artist known as the Kotah Master most likely underwent such dislocation, probably beginning his work in Golconda and maturing fully in the kingdom of Kotah.

The interaction of artists from various places brought about the lively development of styles of painting, but the limited range of artists' materials and the practice of training artists as apprentices from a very young age under the strict eye of a master ensured the continuance of traditional methods. Artists are shown in some

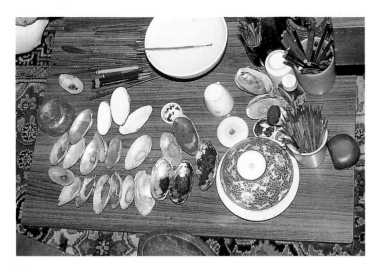

Figure 1
The materials of Jaipur painter Ved Pal Sharma (known as Bannu), 1996.

paintings sitting in their workrooms, surrounded by their implements. They traditionally sat on the floor and worked on boards or low tables, a practice followed even today, as can be seen among a family of artists in their workrooms above a store in a narrow street in the Kota bazaar. At hand are selections of brushes, including ones with only a few hairs for the finest lines; shells containing pigments; pots of binding media, usually gum (fig. 1); and stacks of paper, along with drawings and paintings that were used as models from which to build compositions. There are also tools for grinding pigments from minerals and organic secretions (fig. 2), together with burnishers and burnishing stones (fig. 3). Since the painter's craft was handed down in families from generation to generation, a continuing succession of artists was ensured, and stocks of artists' materials might have accrued in a given studio over time. Even today, it is possible to see historic materials in the workroom of a traditionally trained painter.

The artist would begin a painting by laying out the composition with charcoal or thin black ink applied with either a brush or a pen. The sheet might or might not have been burnished beforehand, depending on its texture. After the initial underdrawing was done, a thin ground was brushed in broad strokes across the sheet, covering the paper but still translucent enough that the underdrawing could be seen. This ground — a layer of opaque watercolor — differed from the ground of a Western oil or tempera painting in that it was composed of the same materials that were used subsequently to create the upper layers. This ground was sometimes white, but was often tinted yellow or blue or whatever color would be complementary to the upper layers of paint in a given area.

Broad areas of different-colored grounds could be employed loosely to define major areas of composition such as the sky, jungle, or water. On the ground, another underdrawing was done with a brush in thin watercolor (fig. 4; detail of cat. 50). The underdrawings generally were red or black or both. Often, red appears to have been used as the material with which the composition was worked out. The red is a transparent color, which is rarely visible in the final picture; one of its merits seems to have been that the subsequent black lines would render it almost invisible.

At this point, the painting was usually burnished. In this process, it was placed face down on a smooth slab of stone and its back rubbed with a smooth stone, traditionally inset into a symmetrical wooden holder vaguely ellipsoid in shape (see fig. 3). Burnishing compacted the paper fibers and paint layers, making them both smooth and dense. It was repeated frequently during the process of making a painting until, near the end, it might take place on the painted side, using a smaller burnisher to produce local areas of gloss.

On the ground with its ink or watercolor underdrawing, further layers of paint were added, working from larger to smaller areas of color and from more diffuse to more detailed definition of the composition. Often, the final areas to be completed were the human figures or more important compositional elements, such as the lions or tigers in the spectacular hunting scenes. This was not always the case, however, as is apparent in catalogue numbers 21 and 22, in which the architecture appears to be somewhat unfinished while the figures are complete.

Final outlining of the design elements occurred at some point near the completion of the painting. Usually, the outlines were done in black, but often there was an additional color, frequently red or brown, included for reasons of naturalistic shading. The order in which the final elements were added seems not to have been overly rigid. The principle that usually prevailed was that the most important bits were added last, but, as we have seen in catalogue numbers 21 and 22, that was not always the case. All of the pigments could be used in any part of the process, as can be seen in figure 5, a detail of catalogue number 50 in which gold was used for the final outlining, or figure 6, a detail of catalogue number 51 in which gold paint apparently was used for an underlayer.

Because of the continual burnishing, the paint layer was generally smooth. In addition, discrete areas of the composition were burnished further to create highly reflective surfaces. However, to enliven the surface and provide emphasis, areas of impasto were frequently created in the jewelry or decoration of the major figures and left unburnished. Metallic pigments were also used for visual appeal and to emphasize important figures.

One final step was the painting of the red borders so often seen in Rajput and Kotah compositions. The red was built up in layers to form a brilliant border, sometimes highly reflective and sometimes matte.

The process described above led to the completion of a highly finished painting — one that had little, if any, paper showing. To produce a drawing, wash drawing, or less elaborately finished work, virtually any of the steps could be eliminated. Works in all stages of progress remained in the studio for copying by apprentices and for use as models in other compositions by the master.

The papers used for drawings and paintings tend to fall into two groups: those produced from finely prepared off-white paper pulp, resulting in thin, smooth, whitish papers; and those produced from fibrous, brownish, nonuniform paper pulp, resulting in rougher buff papers. There is latitude in these types of papers, so that some buff-colored sheets are smooth and regular while some of the whiter sheets are porous and rough. The practice of burnishing the papers during the production of the images helped modify the rougher papers, giving them smoother surfaces. Drawings and paintings of all kinds were produced on both kinds of paper, and paper type does not appear to indicate relative importance of any type of image over any other type. Rather, it seems that availability of paper of a certain size, regardless of color and texture, might have been a limiting factor. Kotah drawings and paintings could be tiny, intimate objects, in dimensions of just a few inches, or elaborately finished works three feet or more across, comprised of a number of pieces of paper joined together. The various papers seem to have been continuously manufactured throughout the time period spanned by the pictures in this exhibition.

Cloth seems to have been reserved for use when a painting's large size mitigated against the joining of multiple sheets, or when

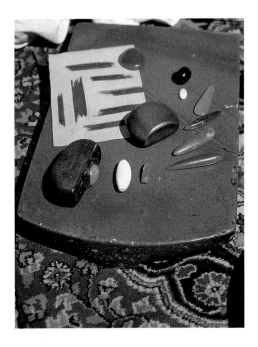

Figure 3
Burnishing stone and implements in Ved Pal Sharma's studio, 1996.

Figure 2
Ved Pal Sharma grinding red pigment, 1996.

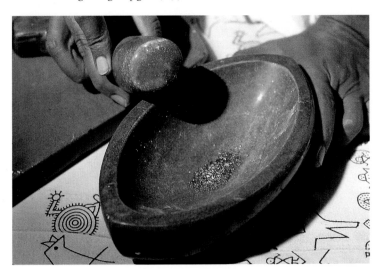

the size was so large that the strength of cloth was required. Such paintings on cloth (cat. 44 and 65) could be up to fifteen feet or more in length or height. Although there has been no systematic visual study or instrumental analysis to confirm this, drawing and painting techniques appear to have been the same as those employed on paper when cloth was utilized as a support.

Visual inspection of the paintings raised a number of questions about the artists' materials. General curiosity to know what pigments were used to produce the dazzlingly colored paintings inspired pigment analysis to identify the Kotah palette, but specific problems also emerged during examination and conservation treatment. Foremost among these was the composition of the red paint used on the borders and the identity of the silvery pigment present in many paintings. Also, the use of a wide range of greens throughout the paintings, especially in the hunting scenes, was of interest. There is extensive use of gold in many pictures, but its appearance and lack of tarnishing, as well as its documentation historically, conjoin to suggest that it is actually gold, ground and applied as a water-based paint. That expectation was confirmed during analysis, as will be seen.[3]

At the initial stage of this research, the inaccessibility of the paintings in Kotah led to the analysis of a number of paintings and drawings from the Department of Islamic and Later Indian Art, Sackler Museum, Harvard University Art Museums. These works were examined with a binocular microscope, an infrared vidicon, and in ultraviolet light — techniques not available during work in India. Eventually, some samples were taken from pictures in the royal collection. Hence, the analysis was performed on some pictures that are included in the exhibition and on others that are not.

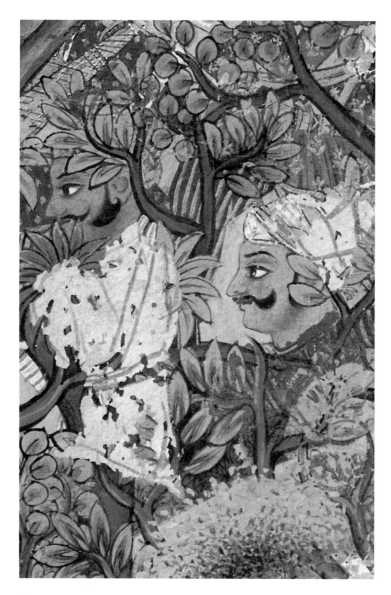

Figure 4
In the flaked areas of cat. 50, the red lines of watercolor comprising part of the under-drawing are clearly visible.

However, the images and artists' techniques displayed by all the pictures are typical of Kotah painting from the seventeenth to the nineteenth centuries.

The physical characteristics of the materials were established by polarized light microscopy and fluorescence microscopy. Their elemental composition was determined using energy dispersive spectroscopy in a scanning electron microscope (SEM-EDS). Fourier transform infrared spectroscopy (FT-IR) identified the pigments, dyes, and binding medium by comparing the samples to known reference materials. Finally, any crystalline materials not sufficiently characterized by the previous techniques were analyzed by X-ray diffraction (XRD).

The pigments identified on the paintings and drawings will be described here grouped by color. Unless a pigment's identification

was confirmed by several analytical methods, it was not included in the results; therefore, this list does not include every pigment ever used by Kotah artists, but rather, most of the pigments used routinely.

White, used either pure or mixed with other pigments, was found in virtually every painting, and, as expected, lead white was found in the majority. This basic lead carbonate has been produced since ancient times by exposing lead metal to acetic acid vapors in the presence of fermenting manure. More interesting is the identification in five paintings of tin white, the oxide of tin corresponding to the mineral cassiterite. Tin white is an unusual pigment, used in Europe by watercolorists in manuscript illumination and by enamelers until the early seventeenth century, according to the literature. It is reported to have declined in use as manuscript illumination ceased; the pigment's reputation for turning gray may

Figure 5
Detail of cat. 50, in which gold was used as the final outlining color.

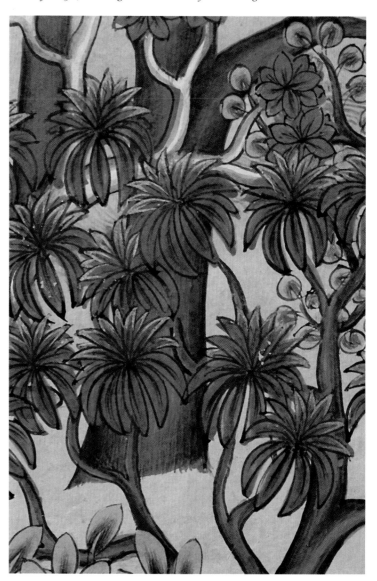

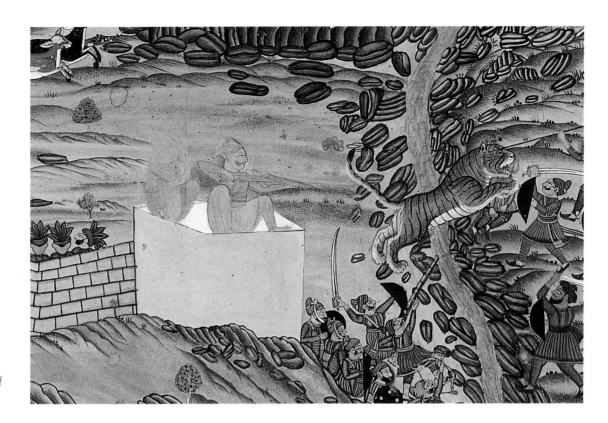

Figure 6
Detail of cat. 51, showing the unfinished central figures painted largely in gold.

also have contributed to its disuse.[4] Its positive identification by analysis on Western manuscripts is rare, and its use has never been reported on Indian paintings. As a corrosion product, it is easy to manufacture: tin oxide forms on tin metal exposed to weathering. Most likely, though, the process was accelerated by exposing the tin to acid vapors: European medieval manuscripts describe producing tin white by the same method as lead white.[5] The reason this pigment has not hitherto been identified in Indian paintings may be because it is not as prevalent as lead white. In fact, in one painting, it was found mixed with the greens and seems to have been used more as an extender than as a colorant. Why this unusual pigment might have been used in Kotah is not clear; perhaps tin oxide was a byproduct of a local industry.

Other whites were found as minor constituents. Calcite was used as a carrier for indigo, and clay was found mixed with Indian yellow. In one painting, a barium pigment was used as an extender for one of the reds. Zinc white was found on one painting, but it is uncertain whether it was used by the artist or during a later restoration. Zinc white was commercially available in Europe in 1834 and is supposed to have been used by Indian artists, although this has not been confirmed analytically except in the isolated instance reported here.

Lampblack, a fine-grained amorphous carbon pigment, was the only black identified in the paintings. Charcoal, characterized by its woody structure, was not seen; it was used by Indian artists for underdrawing, and this study did not look at the underdrawing materials analytically.

Indian yellow is ubiquitous in Kotah paintings. It was found mixed with clay, tin white, and lead white, and as a constituent of almost all the greens. This brilliant yellow, a calcium or magnesium salt of euxanthic acid, is an organic extract from the urine of cows that have been fed mango leaves. Yellow ochre, an earth pigment of hydrous iron oxide and quartz, was mixed with indigo in one sample. Orpiment, a sulphide of arsenic, was possibly found on one painting, but was not confirmed. In their study of Indian pigments, Purinton and Newman found orpiment to be as common as Indian yellow, but they found it in Mughal paintings; the paintings they studied from Rajasthan — from Kotah, Jaipur, and Bikaner — all exhibited Indian yellow. Whether the Rajasthanis simply preferred the brilliant Indian yellow or whether orpiment was not easily available is not clear. Orpiment reacts with some lead and copper pigments, and artists may have observed the resulting discoloration, leading them to avoid its use.

The vegetable dyestuff indigo was the most common blue. It was used by itself or mixed with yellow to make green. Smalt, a pigment made from crushed glass colored blue by cobalt, was confirmed in one painting (and possibly observed, but unconfirmed, in two others). Natural ultramarine, the mineral lazarite extracted from the semiprecious stone lapis lazuli, was also found in three paintings. Indigo and ultramarine were expected, but smalt has not generally been reported. Areas in which smalt was used are significantly different from areas of other blue pigments: visually, they are sparkly and the texture is coarse, while the surface is very hard. The glassy characteristic of smalt was exploited to good effect by Kotah artists. In one case, it seems to have been used for Krishna's face, emphasizing his divine nature by using a substance quite different from the other pigments employed.

Vermilion and red lead were the most commonly used reds. Vermilion — mercuric sulphide — has been produced artificially since the eighth century. Red lead is manufactured by heating lead white to obtain the tetroxide of lead and has been known since ancient times. Red ochre, an earth colored by iron oxide, was found as well. Finally, red dye from an insect source was found, when the difficulty during conservation treatment of reproducing the shiny red borders found on many Kotah paintings led to the search for an explanation of how they were made. Analytically, the red of the borders was easily and clearly identified as vermilion, but no amount of burnishing vermilion could produce the almost iridescent shininess often seen on the paintings. Because vermilion does not have a spectrum in the mid-infrared, it was assumed that an organic material would show up easily if one were present, but none was observed initially by FT-IR. However, a conversation between Stuart Cary Welch and the Jaipur artist Ved Pal Sharma (known as Bannu) yielded the information that "lac" (derived from the insect *Laccifer lacca*) was added to the vermilion for the borders. Mr. Sharma graciously demonstrated the technique and donated a sample for analysis. The FT-IR analysis was repeated with a larger sample, and this time the dye was found. The addition of information gleaned from a conversation was extremely fortunate given that the initial analysis did not reveal the presence of the organic material. This

points out the need for persistence in such analyses, since the presence of an expected mineral pigment, in this case vermilion, only partially elucidated the artist's method.

Kotah paintings display a rich array of greens, with verdigris being the most common. Verdigris is copper acetate, but according to Gettens and Stout the term can be used to describe the general category of green corrosion products of copper. The verdigris found on these paintings is basic copper chloride in the form of the mineral atacamite, rather than copper acetate. The reaction of copper metal with salt water or other chloride solutions produces this pigment.[6] The literature describes a method of producing basic copper chloride by combining ammonium chloride solution with copper scraps.[7] Verdigris was found in the paintings by itself or mixed with various amounts of indigo and Indian yellow. Mixtures of indigo and Indian yellow were also used without verdigris to produce green, as has been described above.

Several other greens were found, though much less frequently than those discussed above. Emerald green, an artificial copper aceto-arsenate first produced in Germany in 1814, was found in one nineteenth-century painting. Its presence in an Indian painting seems to indicate that imported pigments were in use in India at that time. The claylike hydrous magnesium-iron-aluminum silicate known as green earth was found in one drawing. Although its use is mentioned in texts, it had not previously been identified on a painting or drawing.

The final class of pigments examined was metallic pigments. Gold was found on many of the paintings in a painted powder form rather than gold leaf. One method of preparing gold paint is by grinding gold leaf with honey, glue, syrup, or egg and applying it with a size as the binder (figs. 5 and 6).[8]

A silvery gray pigment appears on many paintings, sometimes in a glossy form and at other times almost matte. Despite its silver color, the complete absence of any sign of tarnishing indicated that it was not silver. Identified as powdered tin metal, it was found both by itself and mixed with lead white and/or lampblack. It has been noted that the painters of Jaipur used tin in preference to silver in order to avoid the oxidation of silver, which significantly alters its color.[9] This makes eminent sense, because Kotah painters often used the tin to portray water, and the black oxidation products of silver would not be visually effective in that context. The tin paint has a characteristic appearance, which, once observed, can be seen in paintings from many other Indian schools. However, further analysis is necessary to confirm the supposition that tin was indeed used on these paintings.

The binders for the pigments have been supposed to be traditional gums. The results of the FT-IR spectroscopy confirmed the presence of gum arabic in some samples and a close relative of gum arabic and gum tragacanth in others. Gums seem to have been used

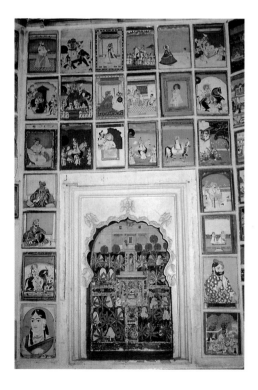

Figure 7
Bada Mahal, Kotah
palace, 1987.

exclusively, based on visual analysis and the lack of identification of other media in several FT-IR analyses. In fact, one of the authors of this essay was told by a contemporary Kotah artist to just "go to the market to buy gum."[10] The binders for the gold and tin paints, however, were not analyzed, and they may differ significantly from those for nonmetallic pigments.

It is valuable to note here the physical preservation of the paintings, which is related to their use and storage. In general, the paintings share problems of mechanical damage to both the paper supports and the paint layers, probably caused by the traditional storage system, which consisted of wrapping groups of pictures in cotton cloths and placing them in trunks in palace godowns. Extensive edge tears and losses are evident, and the paint layers often exhibit flaking due to past flexing of the supports. Although the technique of building up the images in paint layers and burnishing between steps seems to compact the paint, it also contributes to the tendency of the paint to cleave and flake between layers. However, usually the pigments retain their vibrant color, since they were not routinely exposed to light. Paintings that have been mounted under glass on the palace walls in important apartments are not mechanically damaged, but the pigments have often faded and discolored dramatically. It is thought that the pictures were mounted on the walls in individual "plaster" surrounds and pieces of glass in imitation of the British way of framing pictures; this may be the case, but the visual result is very different, with the wall-to-wall presence of separate paintings embedded in the plaster of the walls (fig. 7).

In the end, it is not to scientific analysis that we turn for a vision of Kotah painting, but to the pictures themselves. Linear and coloristic virtuosity define the school, along with its predilection for elephants, hunting scenes, and religious stories. Although some of the individual pigments might differ from those used in the Turko-Indo-Iranian antecedents of this painting style, the actual techniques remained the same. What changed was a sensitivity to line and color that reached its peak in the auspicious collaboration of the artists with the rulers of Kotah.

NOTES

First and foremost, Stuart Cary Welch must be acknowledged for his conception of this project and the enthusiasm he has sustained for the last decade or so during its progress. His vision gave shape to the exhibition and all its parts, and his liveliness and insight made the hard work a joy. H.H. Maharao Brijraj Singh welcomed and housed the influx of Americans, sometimes for lengthy stays, as work continued. Working with him was a wonderful collaboration, and he and his family became dear friends.

Marjorie B. Cohn, then head of the Paper Conservation Lab at the Fogg Art Museum, was gracious in allowing my absence for months at a time and in being continually supportive of the project. I will forever be grateful for the opportunity. Edith I. Welch gave tremendously, in general support of the project and in long hours of photography and rehousing of the paintings. To James Cuno, director of the Harvard University Art Museums, and Vishakha N. Desai, director of the galleries of the Asia Society, go a multitude of thanks for their commitment to the exhibition.

Nancy Purinton, then at the Los Angeles County Museum of Art, generously assisted in treating the paintings in Kota in February 1987.

A number of Harvard students contributed to this project through their research in Fine Arts 202 or as research assistants in the Straus Center for Conservation. They are: Julia Bailey, Lisa Barro, Aren Cohen, Alison Hill, Kristina Kalan, Nuha Khoury, and Beatrice St. Laurent-Lockwood. Without their hard work, and that of Amy Snodgrass and Eugene Farrell, we would know far less about Indian painting materials.

My thanks also go to Anne Driesse for shouldering the burden of the operation of the Paper Lab while I was in India, to Victoria Bunting for enduring my three-week absence, and to Ellen Young and Norene Leddy for picking up the slack.

Finally, and most of all, I thank Mark, Andrew, and Anna Bowen: for supporting my work, for putting up with my absence, and for their love, I am deeply grateful.

1   See Beach 1974 and Lee and Montgomery 1960.
2   Cohn 1977.
3   Most of the analysis was carried out by Amy Snodgrass, but Harvard undergraduates Lisa Barro, Aren Cohen, Kristina Kalan, and Alison Hill carried out analysis of pigments from Kotah drawings and paintings housed at Harvard's Sackler Museum. Eugene Farrell graciously supervised students during Fine Arts 202.
4   Harley 1970, 172.
5   Ibid.
6   Dana 1944–62.
7   Ibid., 110; M. Chandra 1949; and Dickson and Welch 1981.
8   M. Chandra 1949, 30.
9   Ibid., 32.
10 Lukeman Mohamed, in conversation with Craigen W. Bowen in his painting studio in Kota, March 1987.

Catalogue

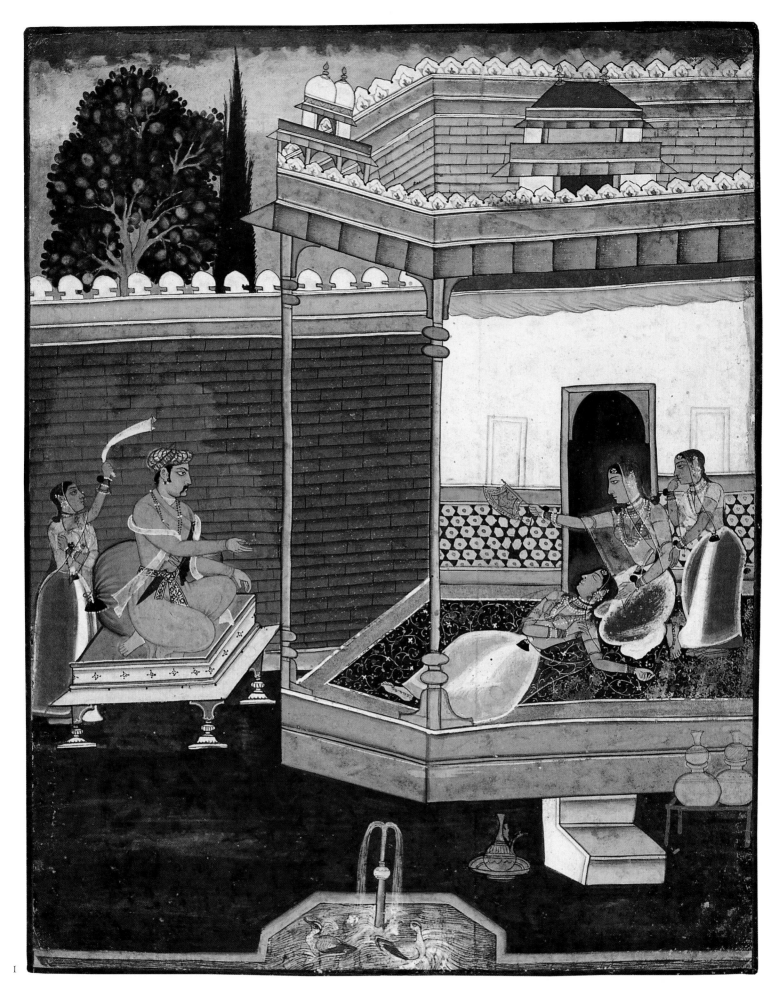

1

A Lady Swoons
Folio from a
Madhavanala Kamakandala-chaupai

Perhaps by the Master of Elephants
c. 1620–30
Opaque watercolor, gold
25 x 20 cm
Rao Madho Singh Trust Museum, Fort Kotah

2

Conversation Scene
Folio from a
Madhavanala Kamakandala-chaupai

Perhaps by the Master of Elephants
c. 1620–30
Opaque watercolor, gold
24.4 x 20 cm
Rao Madho Singh Trust Museum, Fort Kotah

Following the death of Emperor Akbar in 1605, Jahangir (r. 1605–27), his connoisseur-son, cleared the imperial workshops. Primarily concerned with artistic subtleties, the new emperor demanded ever greater creativity and artistic imagination from a small number of favored artists. Less admired painters were forced to find new jobs. Usually, they joined the commercial workshops of the Agra bazaars, to cater to a clientele composed mostly of Mughal courtiers, wealthy merchants, and visitors, whom they supplied with a stock-in-trade ranging from portraits — usually based on imperial likenesses — to manuscripts of the Persian classics, sets of Hindu epics, *Ragamalas*, and other standard subjects. However talented, the artists of these commercial establishments lacked the enthusiastic and discerning direction found at courtly centers and rarely scaled artistic heights.

Some of the more fortunate painters eventually found work with Rajput courtiers who had admired Mughal art at Agra. It is highly likely that one of these was the artist who created this series, who probably joined the budding workshops of Kotah's first independent ruler, Madho Singh (r. 1631–48), during the first half of the seventeenth century. At the outset, the painting studio at Kotah probably included artists from Bundi, the birthplace of Madho Singh and the senior center of the Hara clan. That studio's work, however, has been lost, and our understanding of early Kotah painting, largely based upon the collections at Kotah, demonstrates that the Master of Elephants, the artist to whom this series may be assigned on stylistic grounds, played a major role in the formation of the Kotah style. In the second of these earliest known Kotah pictures — the Kotah "primitives" — a distinguished gentleman with drooping mustaches appears to be Madho Singh himself. Architecture, characterizations, trees, and compacted power of design all reflect the energy of Kotah's innovative and dynamic founding lord.

SCW

The *Madhavanala Kamakandala-chaupai* is a love story by Vachaka Kushalabha, written in Jaisalmer, Rajasthan, in the year 1559 C.E. (V.S. 1616).[1] Another manuscript of this story was illustrated in 1603 C.E. (V.S. 1660, on Saturday, the third of the bright fortnight of the month Shravana, to be precise). Stylistically, it shares a number of features with the two present folios. The bulk of the 1603 manuscript is in the Museum für Indische Kunst, Berlin; one folio is in the Goenka Collection, Bombay, and another is in the Earnest C. and Jane Werner Watson Collection.

JKB

---

1 For a summary of the story and a bibliographical reference to the original text, see Khajanchi Cat. 1960, 28.

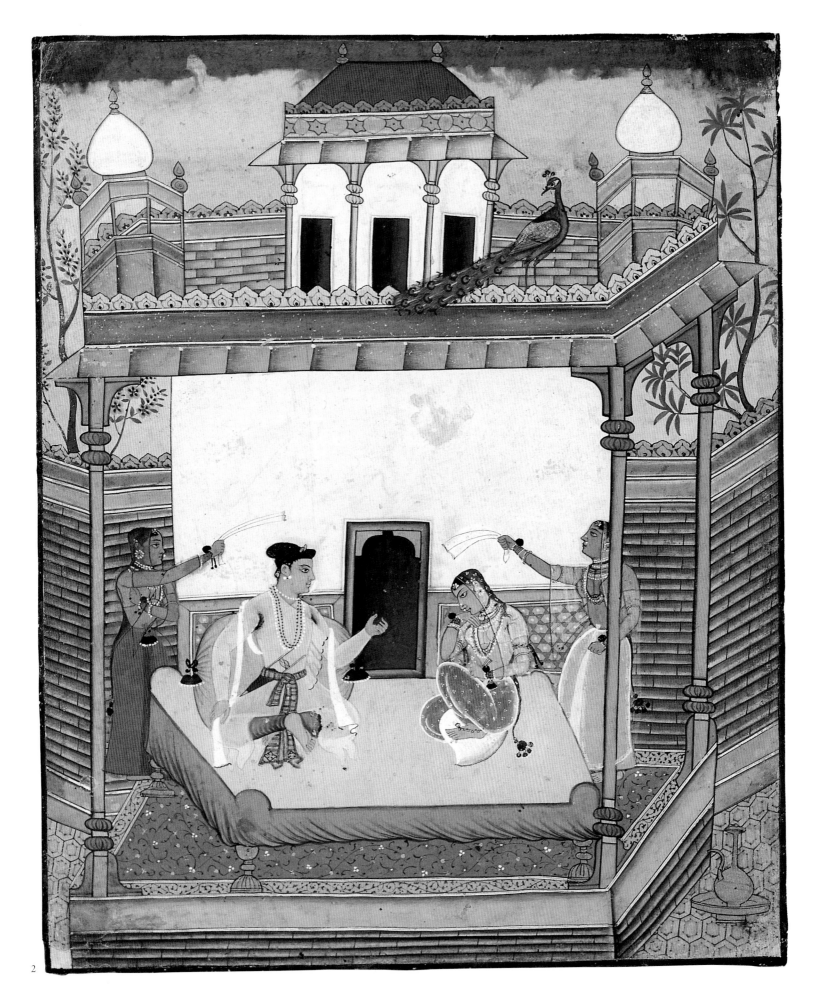

3

The Naming of Krishna by Gargacharya
Folio from a
Bhagavata Purana

Attributed to the Master of Elephants
c. 1630–40
Opaque watercolor
34 x 21.6 cm
The Government Museum of Kota
(Not in exhibition)

4

Krishna Quells the Snake, Kaliya
Folio from a
Bhagavata Purana

Attributed to the Master of Elephants
c. 1630–40
Opaque watercolor
32.8 x 20 cm
The Government Museum of Kota
(Not in exhibition)

5

Krishna Slays the Elephant Kuvalayapida
of Kamsa's Court at Mathura
Folio from a
Bhagavata Purana

Attributed to the Master of Elephants
c. 1630–40
Opaque watercolor
34.1 x 21.8 cm
The Government Museum of Kota
(Not in exhibition)

When this remarkable set of illustrations to a *Bhagavata Purana* — the story of Krishna — was painted at Kotah, presumably for Madho Singh, the early Kotah style had been formed. Credit for this achievement should be shared by the ruler and by the powerful artist whose brilliant depictions of elephants entitle him to be known as the Master of Elephants. A greatly talented specialist, he was less adept at painting men, women, architecture, landscape, trees, flowers, gods, birds, and other animals. Like a musician who comes alive when performing, say, Bach preludes, but whose Chopin, Mozart, and Beethoven are undistinguished, this Kotah artist scintillated only for elephants; he seems to have devoted much of his time to studying their anatomies, habits, and psychology. Because Kotah is ideally situated for elephant breeding and training, and because elephant combats were held there, he could study these animals in depth, and in every mood. His patrons, evidently sharing his delight in the great animals, wisely encouraged this inclination.

Although the Master of Elephants might also have illustrated the *Madhavanala Kamakandala-chaupai* set (cat. 1 and 2) at Kotah earlier in his career, the *Bhagavata Purana* series may more surely be ascribed to him on stylistic grounds. One of the paintings shown here, *Krishna Slays the Elephant Kuvalayapida . . .* (cat. 5), includes an idealized crowned ruler resembling Madho Singh. It also contains a remarkably observed study of the elephant-demon's corpse, drawn and colored in the unmistakable style of the Master of Elephants.
SCW

These three paintings illustrate Book X, chapter 8, verses 11–19; Book X, chapter 16, verses 31–53; and Book X, chapter 43, verses 13–14, respectively, of the *Bhagavata Purana*.[1]
JKB

1 For an English translation, see Tagare 1978, 1300–1, 1363–69, and 1515–16.

Published (cat. 3): (without illustration): M. Shastri 1961, cat. 157, under "Nama Karana"; (cat. 4): M. Shastri 1961, cat. 171 (= Shastri 1961, 8th unnumbered pl. = Barrett/Gray 1963, 141); (cat. 5): M. Shastri 1961, cat. 190.

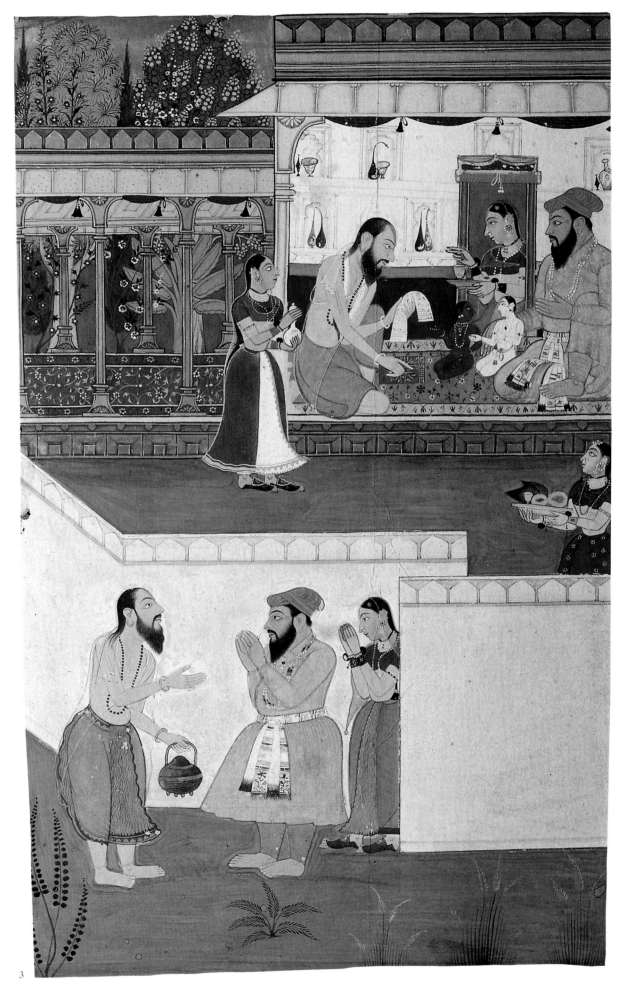

3

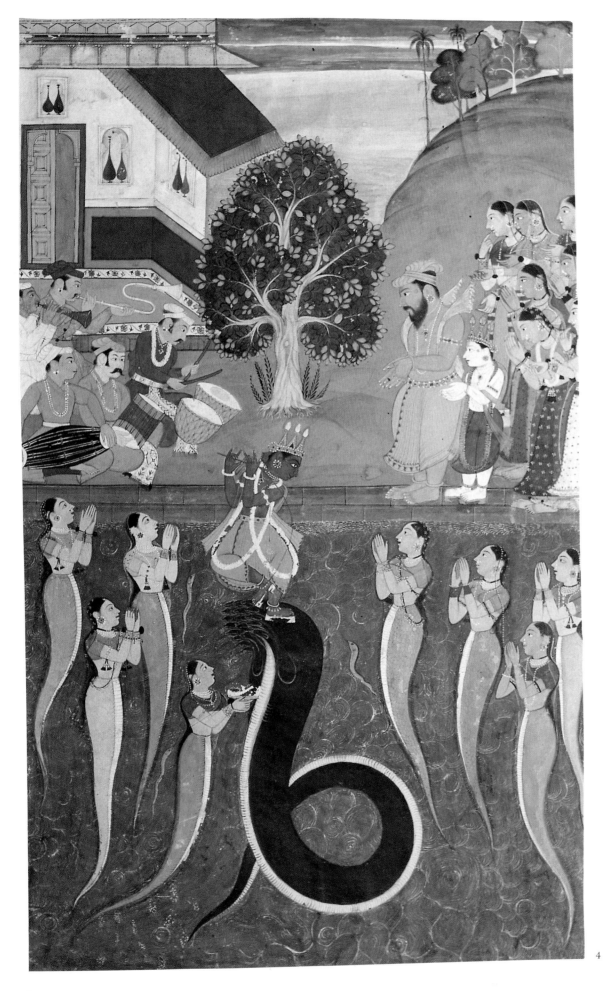

4

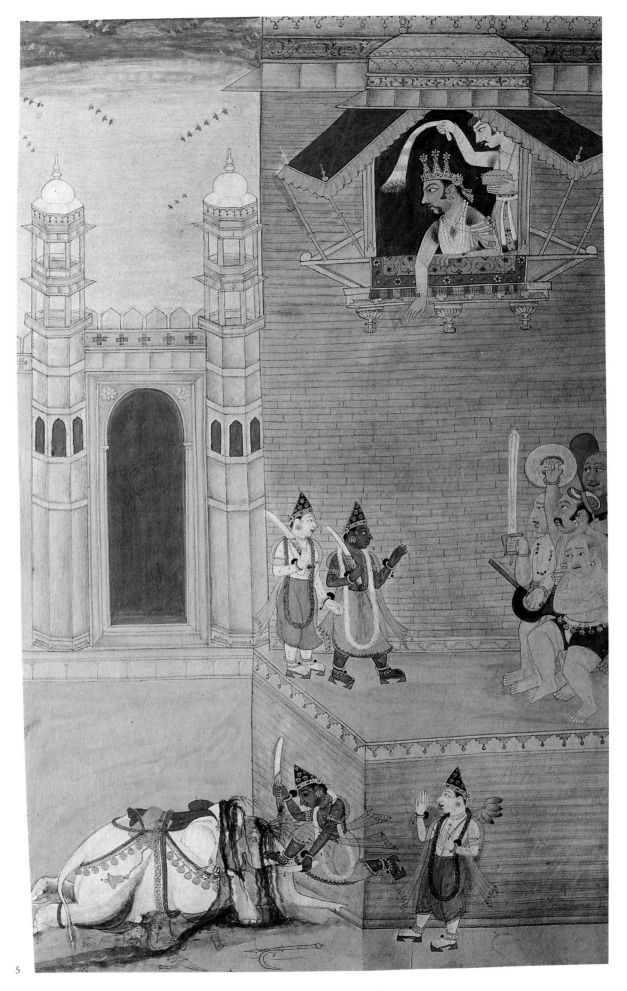

5

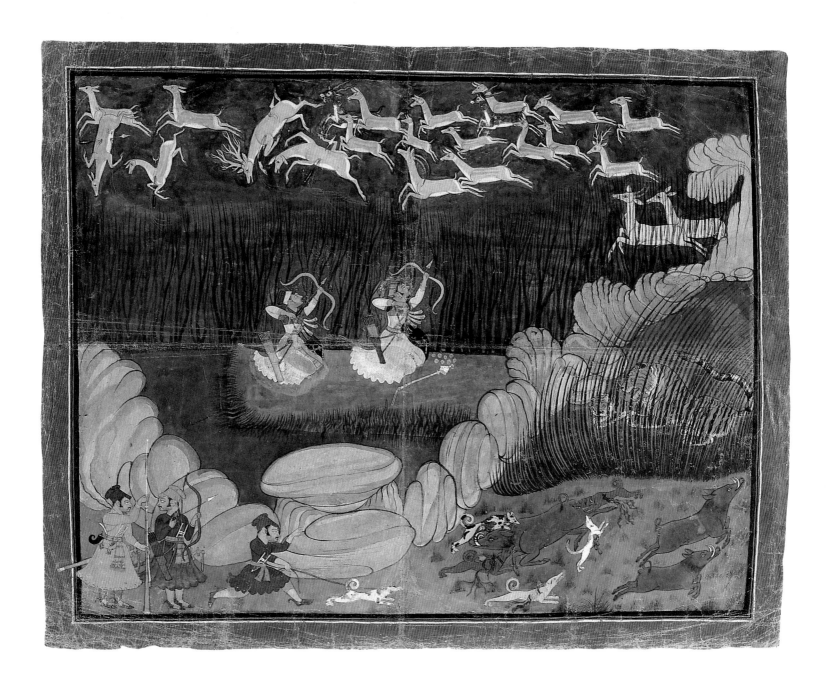

6

Two Princes Shooting Deer; Dogs Hunting Down Boar

c. 1660
Opaque watercolor, gold
50.2 x 62.8 cm
H.H. Maharao Brijraj Singh of Kotah

The work of a Bundi artist, this picture repeats a passage from the jewel-like painted chamber known as the Baddal Mahal in the fort at Bundi.[1] Few hunting pictures in Rajput art are as lyrical as this portrayal of a pair of huntsmen, gracefully congruent as a dance team, firing seemingly painless arrows at inappropriately happy animals. Here, killing — as in English metaphysical poetry — could be a metaphor for love. The brotherly, godlike hunters bring to mind Ram and Lakshman, heroes of the *Ramayana*.

Stylistically, this lilting painting does not resemble other works from the Kotah collection. Probably it was painted at Kotah by a Bundi artist who adjusted his style to Kotah ways, especially in his treatment of the rocky landscape, with its richly patterned trees and rhythmically arranged grasses.

SCW

1 See Bautze 1989b.

Published: M. B. Singh 1985, fig. 17.

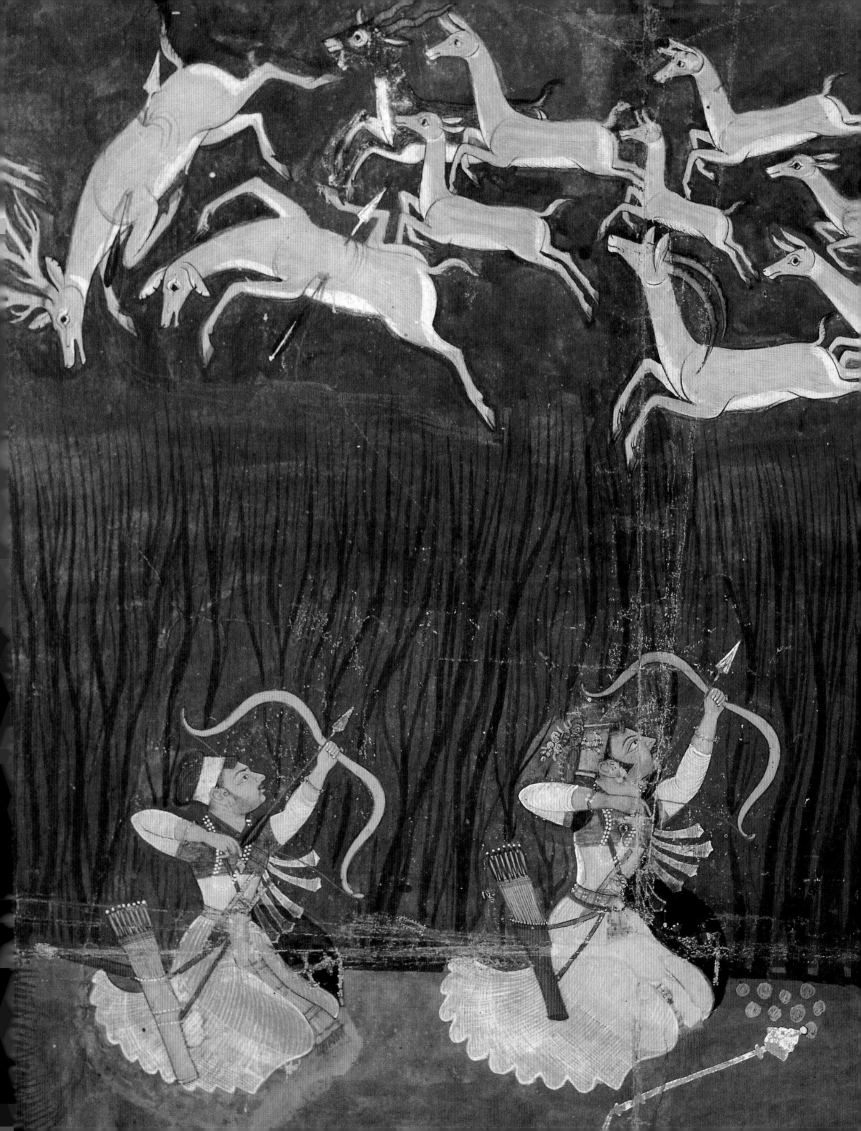

7

A Tortoise Supports a Multihooded Snake,
Which Lifts the Earth
Folio from a
Rukminimangala Series

c. 1660–70
Opaque watercolor
34.4 x 26.5 cm
Rao Madho Singh Trust Museum, Fort Kotah

8

Opening Page from a
Rukminimangala Series

c. 1660–70
Opaque watercolor, gold
32.4 x 26.5 cm
Rao Madho Singh Trust Museum, Fort Kotah

9

Marriage of Vasudeva and Devaki
Folio from a
Rukminimangala Series

c. 1660–70
Opaque watercolor, gold
36.3 x 26.7 cm
Rao Madho Singh Trust Museum, Fort Kotah

The Kotah collection includes many pictures that cannot be assigned to known artists. The opening page of the richer *Rukminimangala* set, illustrated in the Kotah style of the third quarter of the seventeenth century, includes a portrait of a tall, lean prince standing before a holy man. The prince can be identified as Jagat Singh (r. 1658–83), who spent many years in the Deccan serving the Mughals in their continuing campaigns against the Deccani sultans. The artist of this elegant likeness was unstinting in his detailed treatment of Rajput court life. Architecture, costumes, horses and elephants and their trappings, ornaments, still life, and weapons are noted with encyclopedic detail, and the crowds of heroes, heroines, holy men, retainers, and servants are animatedly, interactingly expressive. This strongly "Rajput" group of pictures was most likely carried out by an artist — or artists — trained and working at Aurangabad, the imperial camp-city where Rajputs such as Jagat Singh spent many years in the imperial service. Further support for this provenance is provided by the markedly Deccani palette, which is lavish with purples, violets, and sparkling passages of gold.
SCW

Rukmini, the heroine of this love story, does not want to marry the man selected for her by Rukma, her brother; she loves Krishna and decides to marry only him. She contacts Krishna in due course and is carried off by him on the day of her wedding with Shishupal, the selected bridegroom. Shishupal pursues Krishna and gives battle, but is defeated.

The version of the story that frequently served painters as a basis for their illustrations was written by Vishnudas, whose text was published by N. P. Joshi and Mukandilal in 1973. The text of these Kotah folios, however, does not follow Vishnudas's text.
JKB

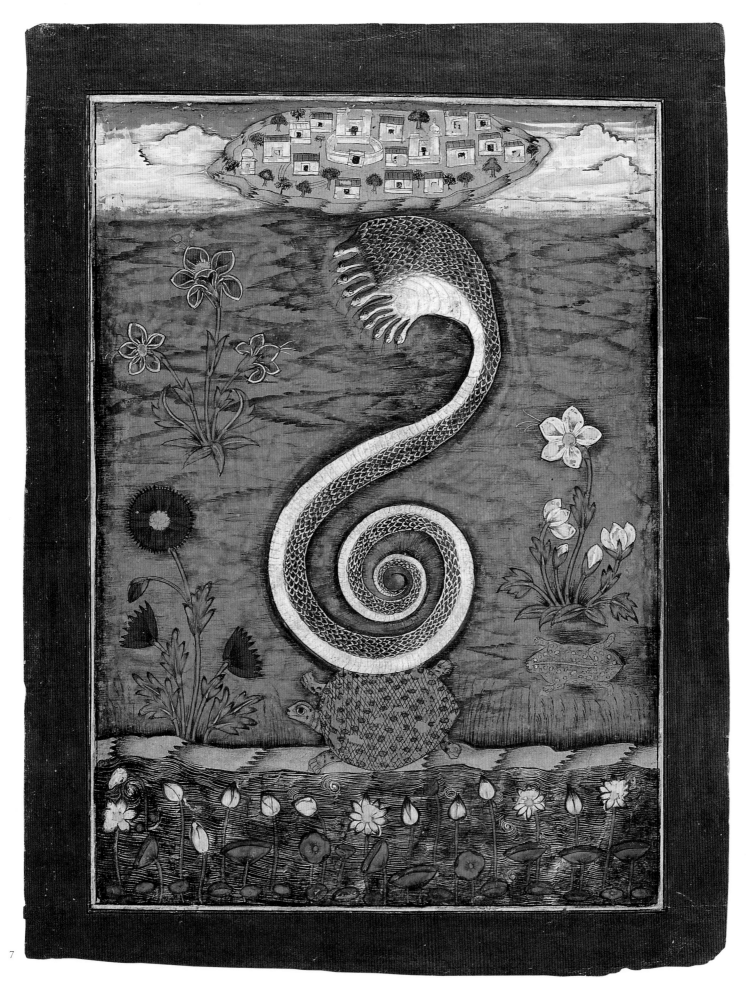

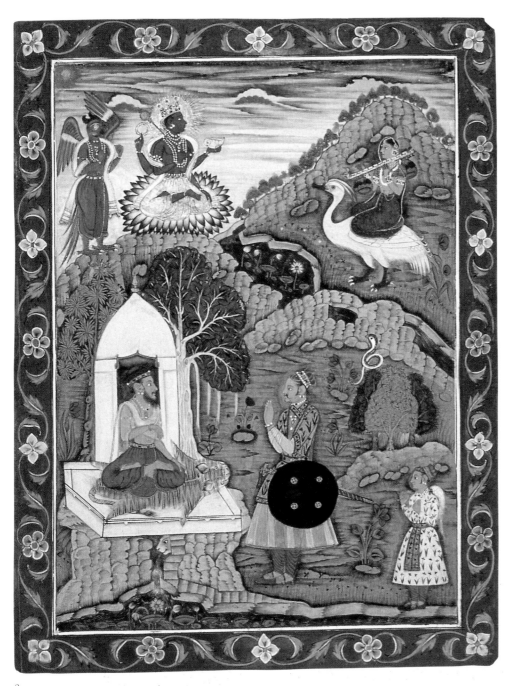

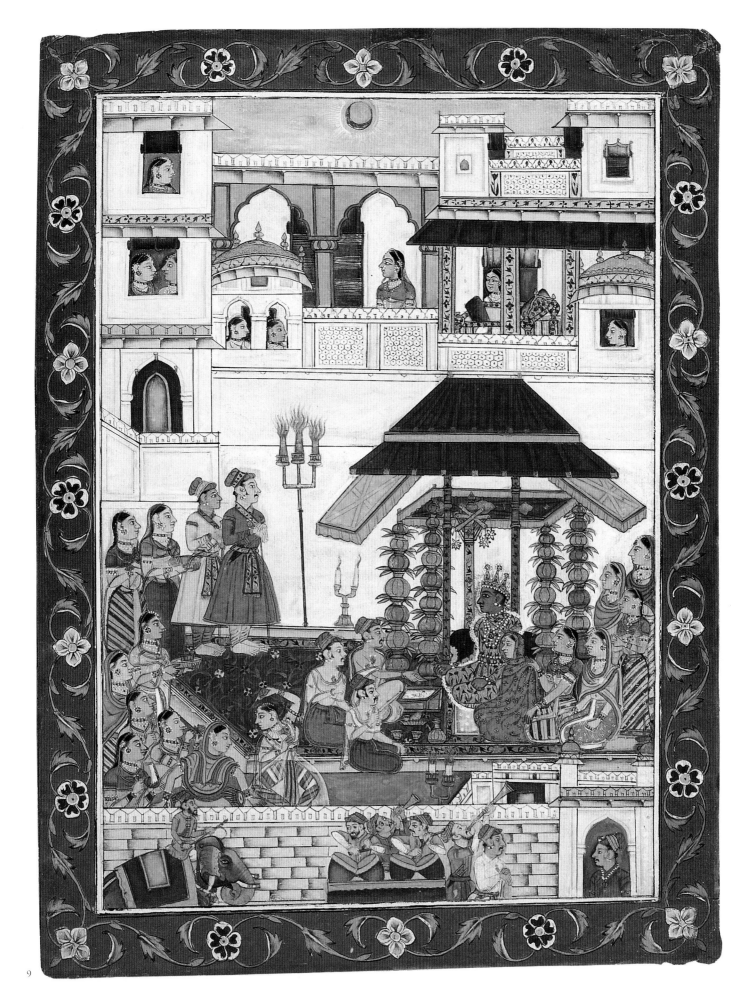

10

*The Musical Mode for Spring
(Vasanta Ragini)*

c. 1675–1700
Opaque watercolor
31.1 x 24.5 cm
Rao Madho Singh Trust Museum, Fort Kotah

Elegantly lilting, this cheerful picture ranks high among Rajput depictions of its familiar theme. A strongly typical image, it evolved from the mind's — or spirit's — eye, not from observation. At many Rajput courts, including Kotah, pictures can be divided into two categories: religious ones, such as this, which retain their traditional Hindu idioms, and secular ones, in which Mughal or Deccani elements are combined with sketches from life. Most court artists worked in both modes — and, not unexpectedly, often blended the two. Here, for instance, old-fashioned ways are evident in the bright, flat color, symmetry of composition, the scale of figures to setting, and the musically dancelike rhythms that animate every figure, tree, flower, and bird. The women's figures and costumes are reminiscent of those painted by the artist I call the Kotah Master, in his portrait of Jagat Singh (Welch essay, fig. 4).
SCW

By visually rendering a musical mode, this painting uses an iconography of appropriate seasonal activities, actors, and musical instruments to cue viewers to the resonance of nuanced notes and poetic text. Poems set to Vasanta musical modes (*ragini*), sung to celebrate the advent of spring, often detail the amorous spring sporting of Krishna with the milkmaids. Musical instruments that accompany the singing of spring songs most notably include the large round tambourine (*duff*) played by one of the milkmaids, while others keep time to Krishna's dancing with cymbals (*jhanj*) and the double-headed drum (*mridangam*). Sexually explicit poetic metaphors specific to spring are also visually supplied, where Krishna's right hand makes the hand gesture (*mudra*) used in dance for a bee, while a milkmaid's opened hand refers to a receptive lotus, for which the blooming lotuses below are additional visual clues.

Although the Kotah court was not known as a center of any great musical tradition, Kotah rulers were certainly conversant with the intricacies and nuances of Indian classical music. The most comprehensive *Ragamala* project ever undertaken, with individual paintings illustrating 240 musical modes, was completed in 1768 for Kotah Maharao Guman Singh (r. 1764–71).[1] Temple musicians (*kirtaniya*s), who sang and accompanied the seasonally appropriate poetry for the elaborate liturgy at Vallabha Sampraday temples within the royal palace, were retained by the Kotah court and are pictured in many religious paintings. This rich religious musical tradition, called Vallabha Sampraday music (*sangit*) or temple music (*haveli sangit*), maintained all the musical specifications of north Indian classical music.[2] Recent discoveries of religious poetry composed to be sung in specified modes written by the maharaos Arjun and Kishor Singh are indicative not only of the sophisticated knowledge of this religious musical tradition by some Kotah rulers but also of their participation in musical performances.[3] For them, viewing this painting could have generated musical responses — the singing of a tune or composing of new springtime lyrics praising Krishna.
WLT

This painting illustrates the following text from the *sangitadarpana* (mirror of music):

> He, in whose crest plenty of peacock feathers are fastened up, whose earrings are embellished with beautiful mango-sprouts, who has a body as dark as the blue lotus-blossoms, who [dances] full of mirth, charmingly gleaming like a bee, is Vasantaka.[4]

JKB

1 This set, with paintings by Dalu and accompanying text written by the court poet Ram Kasan, ended up in the Sarasvati Bhandar of the Udaipur court. For a description and illustrations, see Ebling 1973, 217–20.
2 For a description of this important musical tradition, see Goswamy and Goswamy 1975.
3 For the most comprehensive study of songs composed and sung at Rajput courts, see T. J. Singh 1990. This previously unknown repertoire from the Kotah court merits an additional volume of this invaluable resource for the study of Rajput musical culture.
4 Quoted after Waldschmidt 1975, 36; for further examples, see Bautze 1987a, fig. 85, and index under "Vasanta."

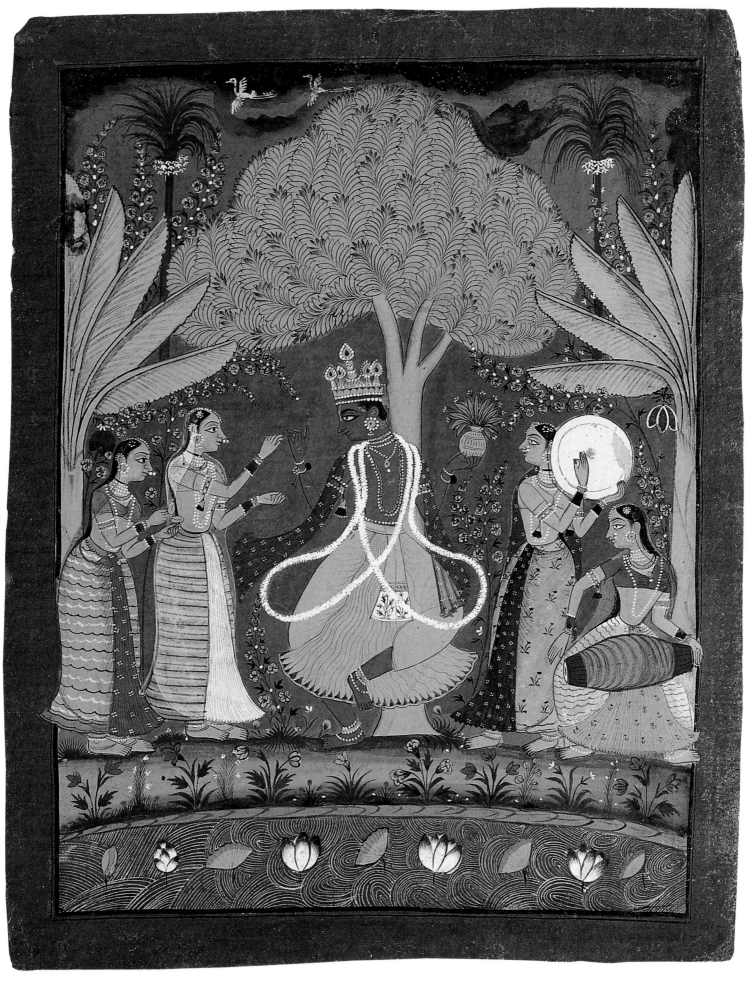

11

The Round Dance (Rasamandala) of Krishna and the Milkmaids

c. 1680
Opaque watercolor, gold, metallic gray watercolor
35.4 x 27.1 cm
Rao Madho Singh Trust Museum, Fort Kotah

The divine lovers, peacock-crowned Krishna and Radha, embrace while seated on a throne (*takht*). Dancing around them, the milkmaids enhance the ecstatically amorous mood. Although stars and moon imply night, the palette is bright and clear as noon, radiating the inner light of bliss. Like all purely Rajput pictures, this one was envisioned with religious faith, not traced from the world of appearances. The "heart" of the composition, the circle of dancers, is traditional; remembering and delighting in it, the artist seems to have used it like a favorite old song, as the basis for his improvisation. Although this charming picture was apparently derived from a damaged, earlier version of the subject still in the royal collection, architecture, foliage, and figures are in fully evolved Kotah style.
SCW

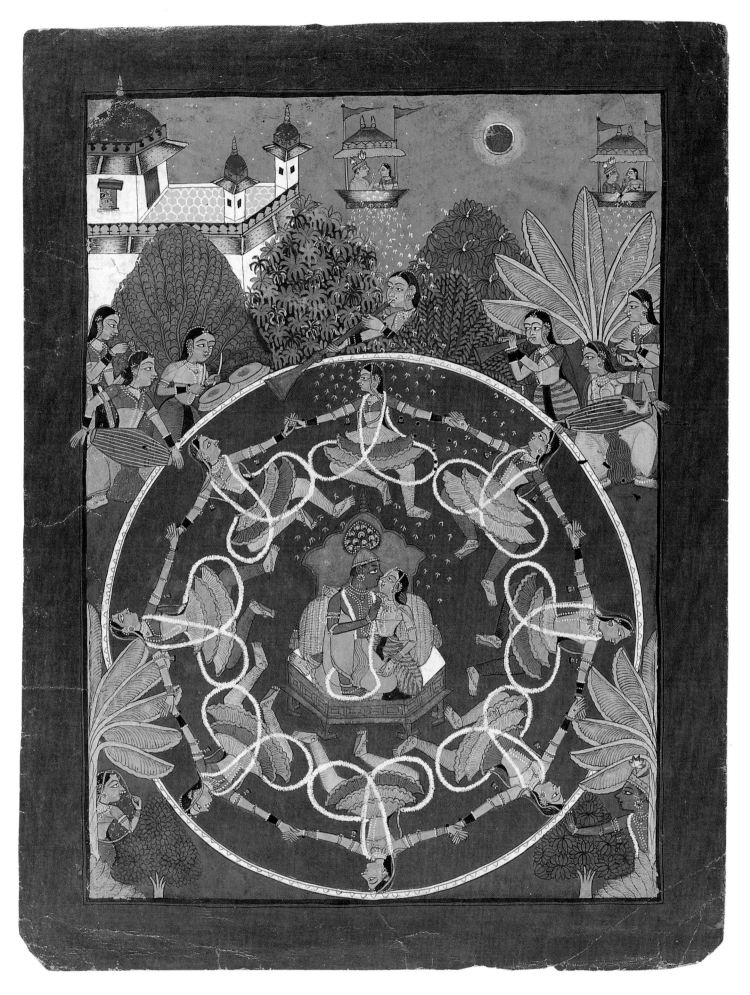

107

12

An Angry Elephant Breaks Its Chains

Attributed to the Master of Elephants
c. 1680
Drawing (*khaka*): black ink, opaque watercolor
Approx. 46 x 61 cm
Rao Madho Singh Trust Museum, Fort Kotah

Elephant combats, a Kotah specialty, were staged in the great courtyard near the fort gate. Victorious elephants, like Sumo champions, became cult figures, whose adulation extended to their owners and mahouts, specialists in elephant health, grooming, and psychology. The stakes were high: mahouts were often injured or killed in combats, and occasionally their huge charges turned against them with deadly results. Like artists, mahouts usually followed the family specialty. Fathers, grandfathers, uncles, and cousins knew the ancient lore of elephants and passed on "trade secrets" from one generation to the next.

This powerful drawing — the most vital and dynamic elephant included here — is by the early Master of Elephants (see cat. 3–5). In a composition that gained expressive compactness from accidental cropping at every edge, little remains of the noble animal's keepers, who are attempting to control (or worsen) his frustrations by using fireworks on the ends of poles (*charki*s). The artist can be considered a Rembrandt of elephant portraiture; his animal's head in profile deeply explores the hulking creature's pent-up, intense emotions. Close observation of this drawing from life reveals the artist's faint but sensitive outlines, which were strengthened and refined as the work progressed. Although he concentrated on the head and trunk, the edges of every limb and of the massive body ripple with life, and the chains bring to mind Laocoön's dread snakes.
SCW

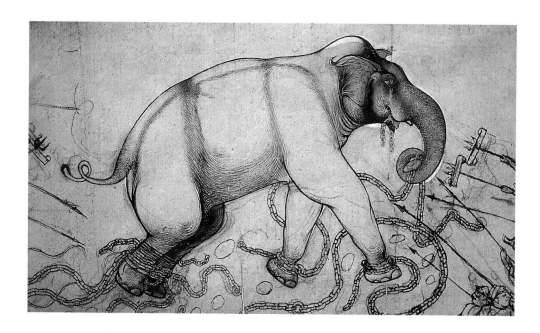

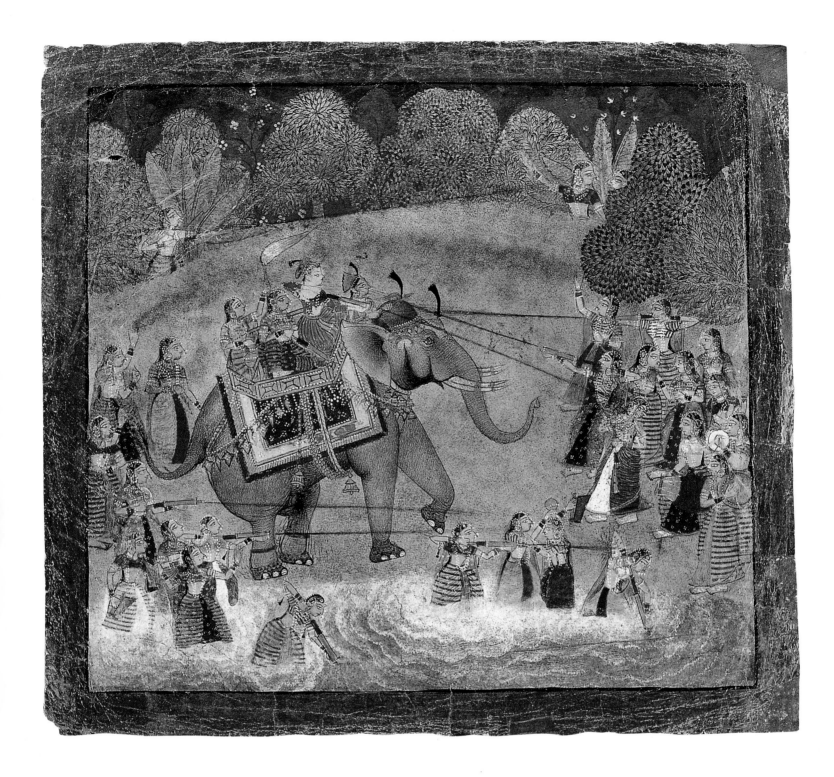

13

Elephant with Four Tusks at Holi

Attributed to the Master of the Zenana
1675–1700
Watercolor, opaque watercolor, gold
26.3 x 29.2 cm
Rao Madho Singh Trust Museum, Fort Kotah

Religious and secular modes meet in this diverting scene of court ladies disporting in celebration of spring. It is the earliest of several Kotah pictures in which the spring festival of Holi is celebrated with elephants, in this case not the archetypal Kotah animal, but one with four tusks. Not a curious natural phenomenon, these are iconographically explained as attributes of the god Indra's wondrous vehicle, Airavat. Somewhat frayed, paled, and muted by the devotions of admirers, this picture by a nameless artistic personality who might be called

the Master of the Zenana exemplifies zenana taste. Ladies, trees, water, and ground are meltingly feminine, in contrast to the boldly masculine elephant, suited to the men's quarters (*mardana*). His vigorous silhouette stems from the artist's use of a tracing (*charba*), which might very well have been taken from an elephant study by the Master of Elephants. The use of such aids was not only acceptable but encouraged in the workshops of Kotah and throughout the Turko-Indo-Iranian world.
scw

14

Maharao Bhim Singh I Received by Emperor Farrukh Siyar
("Emperor Aurangzeb [sic] in Darbar")

Attributed to Sheikh Taju
c. 1707–20
Drawing (*khaka*): charcoal, black and red ink, white opaque watercolor
25.4 x 32.7 cm
Rao Madho Singh Trust Museum, Fort Kotah
Inscribed on recto: "Picture of the king of kings (*padishah*), Aurangzeb."

15

A Darbar at a Mughal Palace

Attributed to Sheikh Taju
c. 1707–20
Drawing (*khaka*): charcoal, black and red ink, traces of white opaque watercolor
51.1 x 62.2 cm
Rao Madho Singh Trust Museum, Fort Kotah

16

Darbar of Shah Jahan

Attributed to Sheikh Taju
c. 1707–20
Drawing (*khaka*): black ink, red and white opaque watercolor
31 x 24.5 cm
Rao Madho Singh Trust Museum, Fort Kotah

All of these drawings can be attributed to Sheikh Taju and provide evidence of his intimate connection with the imperial ateliers prior to his arrival at Kotah. The first drawing, in red and black ink whited over for corrections, was mistakenly inscribed at a later date with the name of Emperor Aurangzeb. The most freely worked, it is the least Mughal in style and probably the latest of the group. Of great historical and art-historical significance, it depicts Maharao Bhim Singh I of Kotah (r. 1707–20) being received by Emperor Farrukh Siyar (r. 1709–19) in a small, domed pavilion within a tent enclosure. As Joachim K. Bautze has pointed out, although Maharao Bhim Singh was an apparently devoted and well-rewarded supporter of Emperor Farrukh Siyar, he was eventually one of those responsible for the emperor's death in 1719. Inasmuch as Sheikh Taju's pictures attest to im-

perial affiliations during the early eighteenth century, when relations between Kotah and the Mughal court were strongest, it is not unlikely that the artist met Maharao Bhim Singh at Farrukh Siyar's court and was there invited to enter Kotah service.

The second drawing, *A Darbar at a Mughal Palace*, is in the less formal mode known from Sheikh Taju's work after coming to Kotah and influenced by the calligraphic, lively draftsmanship of the Kotah Master. In this strictly formal scene, in which every personage from the emperor to his least prestigious attendant is ramrod stiff, only the jaunty tiger cub is undaunted by the dead weight of imperial protocol. Since Kotah courtiers, attendants, and musicians dominate the foreground, it seems likely that they brought the animal as a gift.

The third, and perhaps the earliest of these paintings, and the most imperial in style, drawn in lean black line and evidently before the sheikh moved to Kotah, was clearly directly inspired by the painted darbars known from Shah Jahan's magnificent illustrated history of his own reign, the *Padshahnameh*, most of which is now preserved in the Royal Library at Windsor Castle. Although this accomplished drawing is not directly related to any of the surviving illustrations of this watershed manuscript, it conforms to Shah Jahan's compositional formula. The emperor is seen enthroned in the grand courtyard of the fort at Agra. He is haloed and facing three of his four sons, the princes Dara Shikoh, Shah Shujah, and Murad Baksh. Behind him stands his omnipresent personal attendant (*khidmatgar*), Khan Hayat, wielding a yak-tail whisk. Courtiers are placed according to rank, the more elevated nearer the throne, the lesser ones and visitors beyond an openwork fence. As usual, every figure is a portrait based on sketches from life available in the workshop's archive, to which even a junior painter would have had access.
scw

In the first of these drawings, the artist has blended two paintings of the *Shah Jahan Nama*. The top part was inspired by a painting now in the Bodleian Library, Oxford.[1] The lower part is an adaption from a painting in the collection of Her Majesty The Queen in Windsor Castle.[2]
jkb

1 Published in Binyon 1921, pl. XXXVI, and frequently thereafter.
2 Published in 'Inayat Khan 1990 ed., pl. 23.

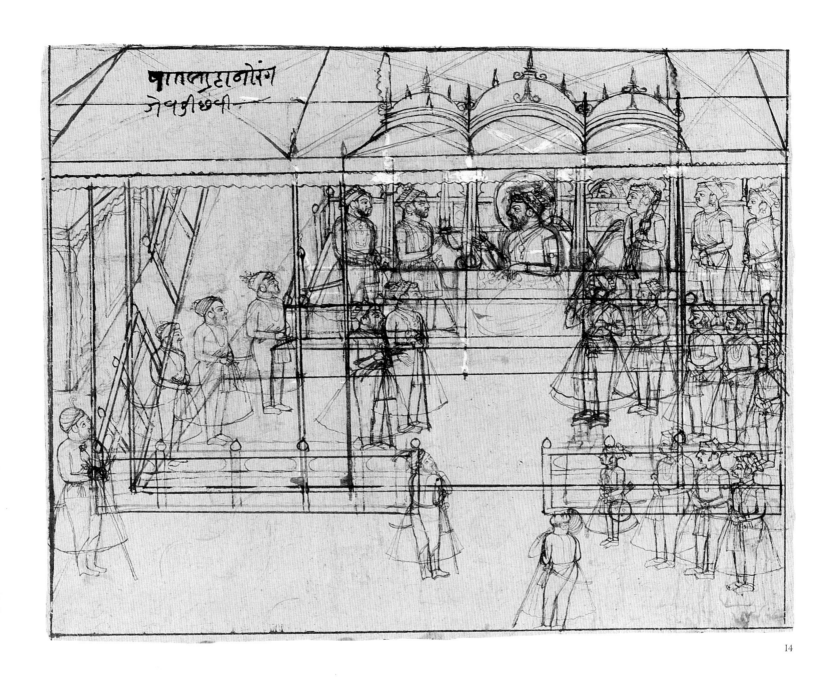

14

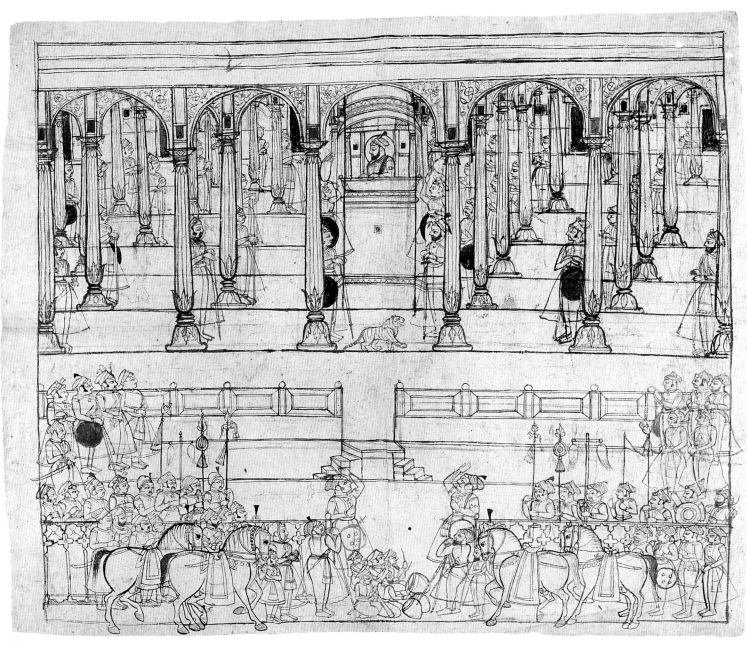

15

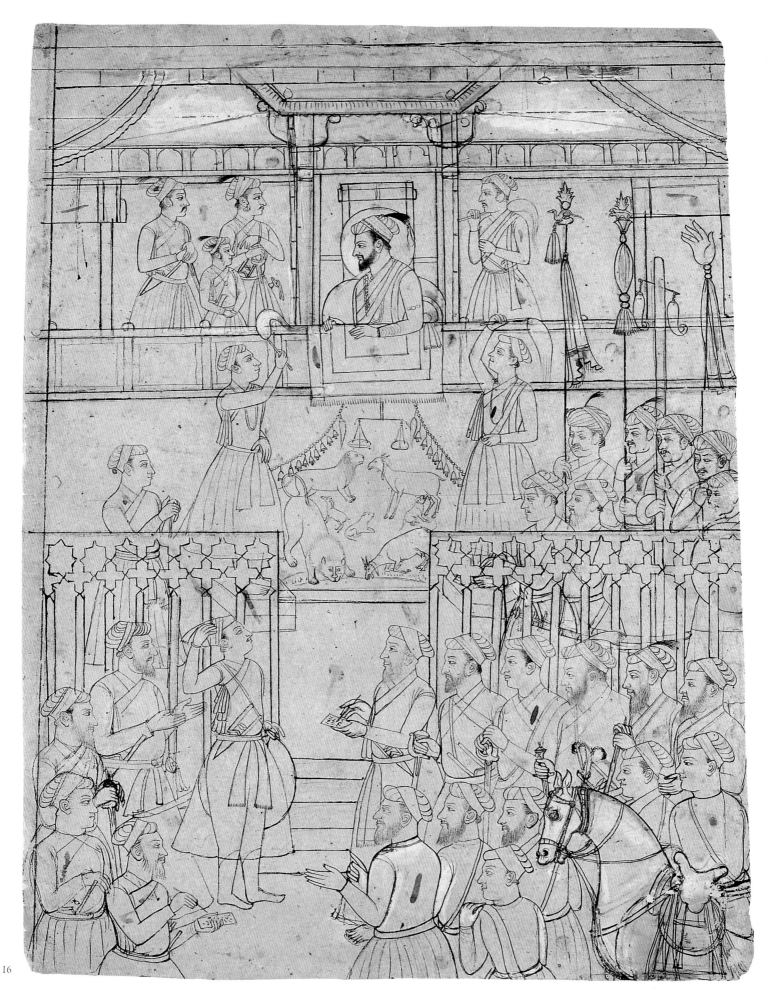

16

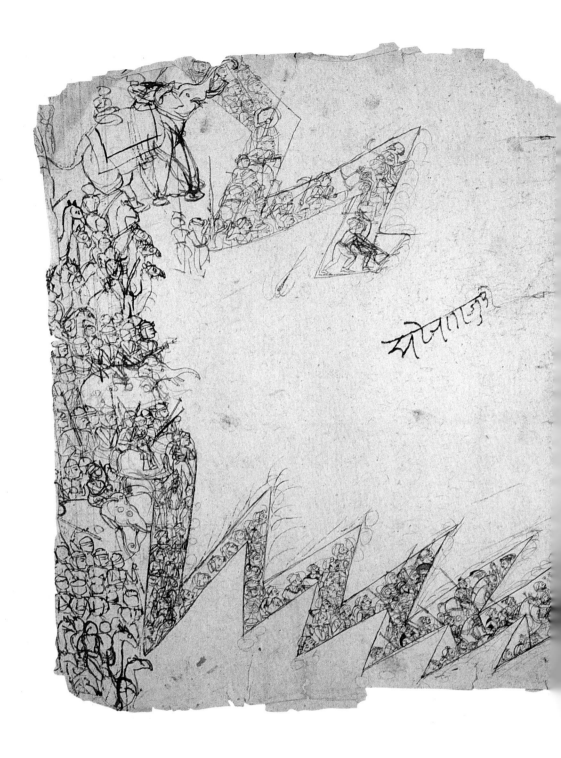

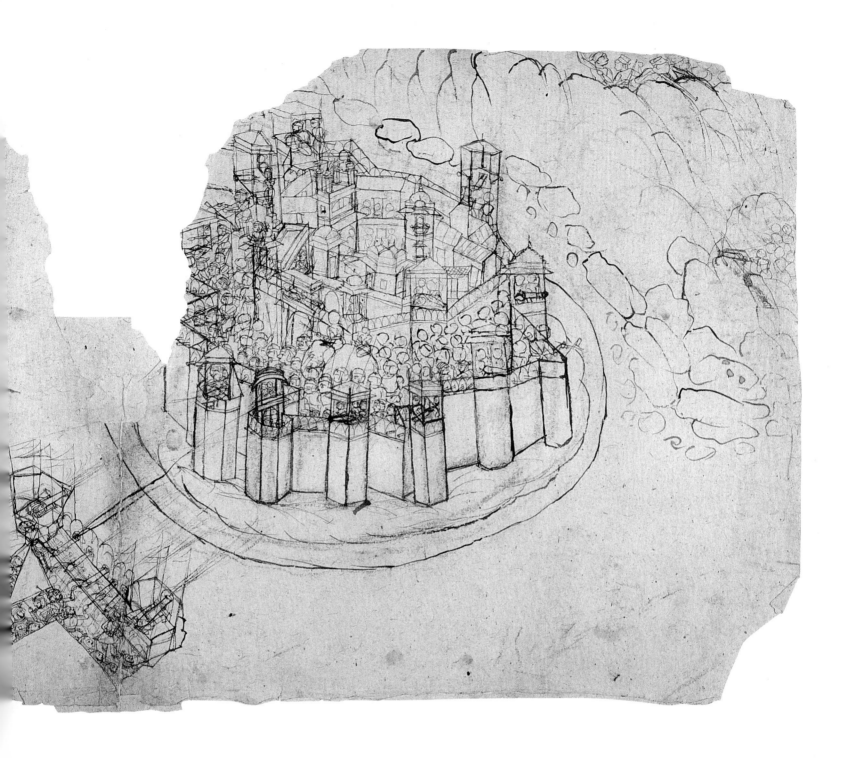

17

Siege of a Strong Fort

Sheikh Taju
c. 1720
Drawing (*khaka*): charcoal, black and red ink, traces of
white opaque watercolor
27.5 x 58.5 cm
Rao Madho Singh Trust Museum, Fort Kotah
Inscribed on left half: "By Sekh Taju."

Sheikh Taju's many depictions of military subjects suggest that he — like other Mughal artists — experienced military service. His forts,
soldiers, elephants, and horses are itemized in
knowing detail, even when, as here, he deliber-
ately seems to have soared beyond technicalities
of strategy and logistics. Although the viewer
might accept matter-of-factly each zigzagged
trench, mobbed battlement, camel, elephant,
and horse, in combination they evoke not a
battlefield but a vision.
SCW

18

The Mughal Emperor Farrukh Siyar Carried in a Palanquin

Attributed to Sheikh Taju
c. 1720
Watercolor, opaque watercolor, gold
27.4 x 26.8 cm
Rao Madho Singh Trust Museum, Fort Kotah
Inscribed on verso: "Emperor (Padishah) Farrukh Siyar." This seems to be the Hindusthani rendering of another inscription, apparently in Nastaliq, below.

Is this august, goggle-eyed, almost solarly radiant, rotundly sleek presence a hero or a slug? When Sheikh Taju portrayed his erstwhile but probably seldom-observed patron, Emperor Farrukh Siyar (r. 1709–19), in his new Kotah style, he seems to have sensed and expressed his new patron's ambiguous feelings toward the Mughal emperor. Although the emperor had rewarded Maharao Bhim Singh's loyalty, he had also aroused the Rajput's scorn and enmity. Conjuring up an imperial image poised between might, pride, heroism, and loathsomeness, Sheikh Taju's Farrukh Siyar is a plum of Kotah mannerism.

Rajput connoisseurs must have examined such pictures with amused satisfaction. Invariably, their imperial overlords were suspect, and when this portrait emerged from the studio and was presented in the men's quarters, it might well have raised eyebrows and prompted more than sly giggles. Pity the poor palanquin-bearers, laboring beneath the weight of a massive litter and even more massive ruler! And pity anyone else at the beck and call of such an eminence! After its moment before royal Rajput eyes, this mildly impudent characterization would have been returned to its stack of imperial likenesses, tied into its bandanna, and stacked in the room set aside for picture storage (pothikhana).
SCW

Published: Bautze 1993b, 83, fig. 5.

19

Brijnathji and Maharao Arjun Singh aboard a Hunting Barge on the Chambal River

Attributed to the Kotah Master
c. 1720–23
Opaque watercolor, gold
35 x 51.4 cm
H.H. Maharao Brijraj Singh of Kotah
Inscribed on verso in a later hand: "Maharao Shri Arjun Singhji." Inscribed below on verso, in the typical hand of a Kotah scribe: "Picture (chavi) of Shri Brijnathi [and] Maharao Arjun Singhji hunting in the Kara ... [Karai, Karay?]."

The Kotah Master's later style is exhilaratingly represented in this ensemble of religiosity, hunting, and the pleasures of river-boating on a sunny day. Everyone — from the god to the maharao, the seated devotee, assorted musicians, attendants, the huntsmen, and the promenading bears — is infectiously delightful. If the haughty, nose-in-the-air finial on the vessel's prow harks back to Turkman dragons, the rest of the picture celebrates the Kotah Master's profound adjustment to — and understanding of — Kotah. After decades of happy employment at the Kotah court, he appears to have been totally, enthusiastically at ease in a world that initially must have seemed outlandishly foreign. From his paintings and drawings, it is evident that his relationship to a succession of Kotah patrons was mutually satisfying. Never does one sense flagging spirits. Indeed, as time passed, rapport seems to have increased and deepened. Joyous heights were reached during the reign of Maharao Arjun Singh (r. 1720–23), whose intertwining strands of the worldly and otherworldly, of pious devotion and mundane fun, and of loving devotion to both mortals and immortals seem to have been shared with the great artist. For Arjun Singh, it seems, the Kotah Master broadened and deepened his style. Although his vitally expressive, all-defining line still rules, color plays a larger role, and brushwork gains breadth and painterly strength.
SCW

Maharao Arjun Singh is shown worshiping the tutelary deity of Kotah, Shri Brijnathji. Significantly, all three principal figures in the painting (each with white nimbus) — the bare-chested and bare-headed devotee sitting before the deity, the courtly, turbaned attendant standing to one side, and the blue-faced god — bear the distinctive sharp-nosed profile of Arjun Singh. In showing the "three faces" (tin murti) of Arjun Singh, the artist has tried to capture the different manifestations of the ruler's constituent identity (householder, warrior-ruler, and deity) and express his mastery over the three worlds of family, polity, and cosmos. The fact that the image of Shri Brijnathji is depicted not as a statue (the actual image is gold and only a few centimeters tall) but as an animate being reflects the belief within the Vallabha Sampraday that their religious images are not mere representations of that deity, but contain his immanent presence. The sentient capabilities of Vallabha images account for the elaborate care with which worship (seva) is performed. The various ritual actions are not merely symbolic, but aim to bring real pleasure to both devotee and deity. The form of worship depicted here, with musical accompaniment, on a finely carved and decorated barge gently floating in the middle of a river, surely must have brought great pleasure to Shri Brijnathji.
NP

Published: M. B. Singh 1985, pl. IV.

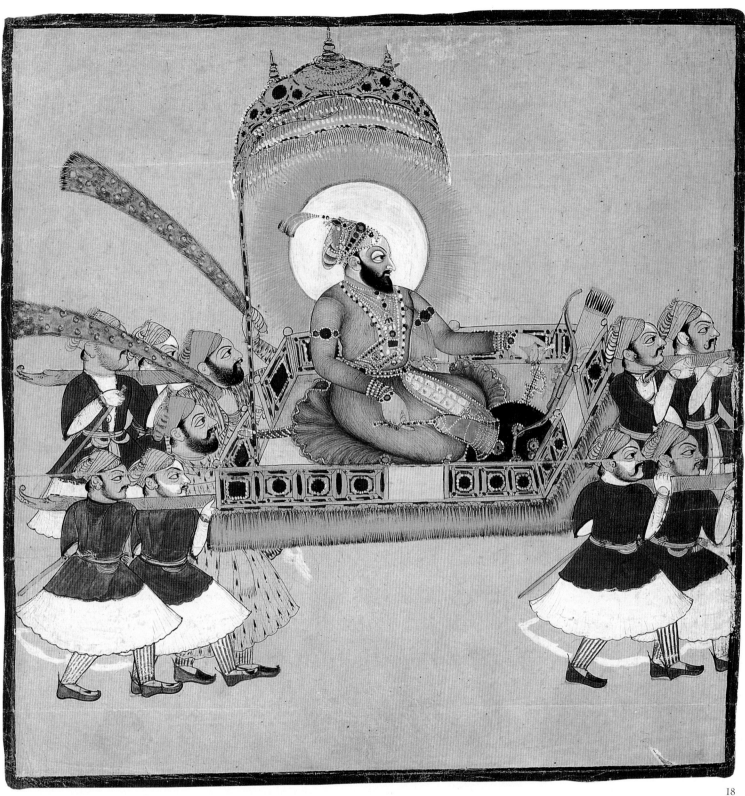

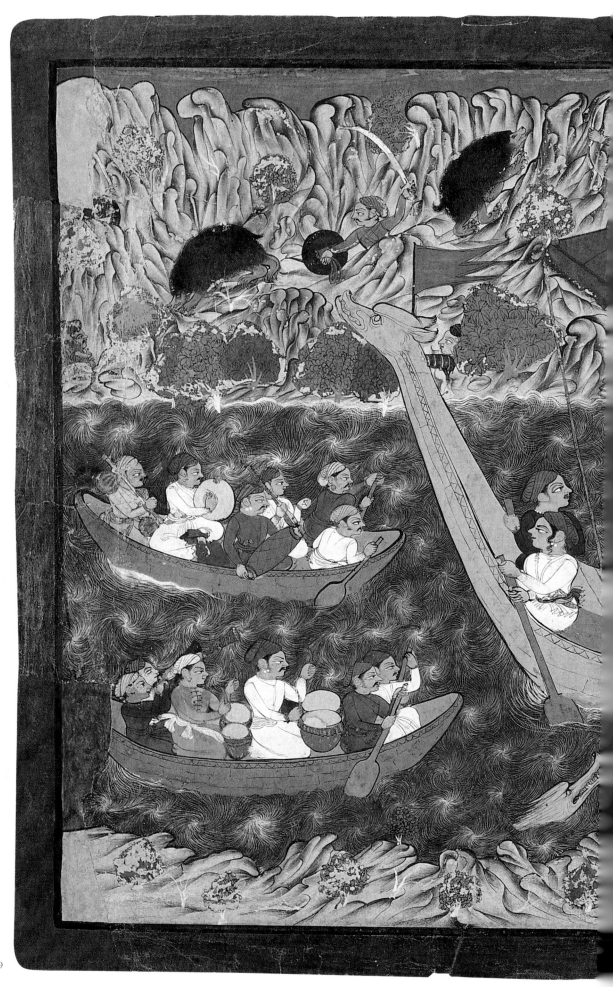

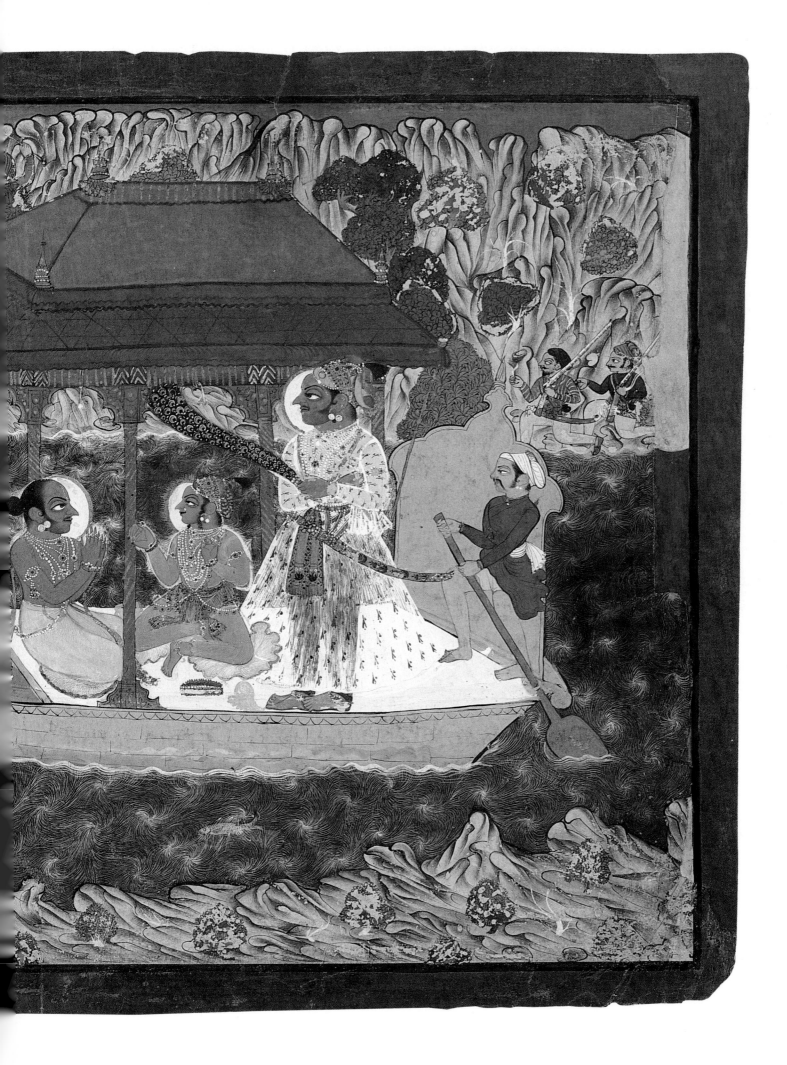

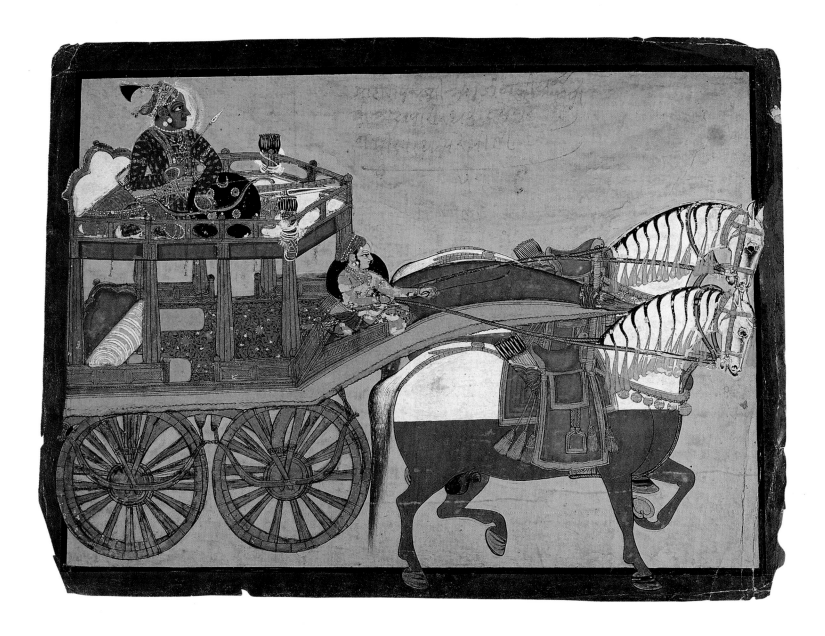

20

*Maharao Arjun Singh as Brijnathji
on a War Chariot*

Attributed to the Kotah Master
c. 1720–23
Opaque watercolor, gold
29.2 x 40.4 cm
Rao Madho Singh Trust Museum, Fort Kotah
Inscribed on verso: "Picture of Maharao Arjun Singhji."

This painting continues the practice of representing Maharao Arjun Singh in divine form. In portraying the god-king on a war chariot, the painter may have been alluding to the custom observed by Kotah's rulers of carrying the image of Shri Brijnathji with them on the battlefield. This custom had especially poignant consequences for Arjun Singh as, according to legend, the image of Shri Brijnathji was first brought to Kotah by his father, Maharao Bhim Singh, but was lost in 1720 when Bhim Singh was killed in battle by Nizam-ul-Mulk (Chin Qilich Khan). Nizam-ul-Mulk is supposed to have taken the image back to his capital at Hyderabad, where it was given to a wealthy merchant (*seth*) in the bazaar, who spent a fortune

on the image's worship. Brijnathji remained absent from Kotah throughout Arjun Singh's reign (1720–23) and was only returned during the reign of his younger brother and successor, Durjan Sal (r. 1723–56). The numerous visual references to Shri Brijnathji during the brief reign of Arjun Singh may reflect the maharao's heartfelt sense of loss in the absence of the deity that had become closely associated with his late father.

NP

Published: Bautze 1992b, detail, fig. 37.4, and Bautze 1993b, full page, fig. 9.

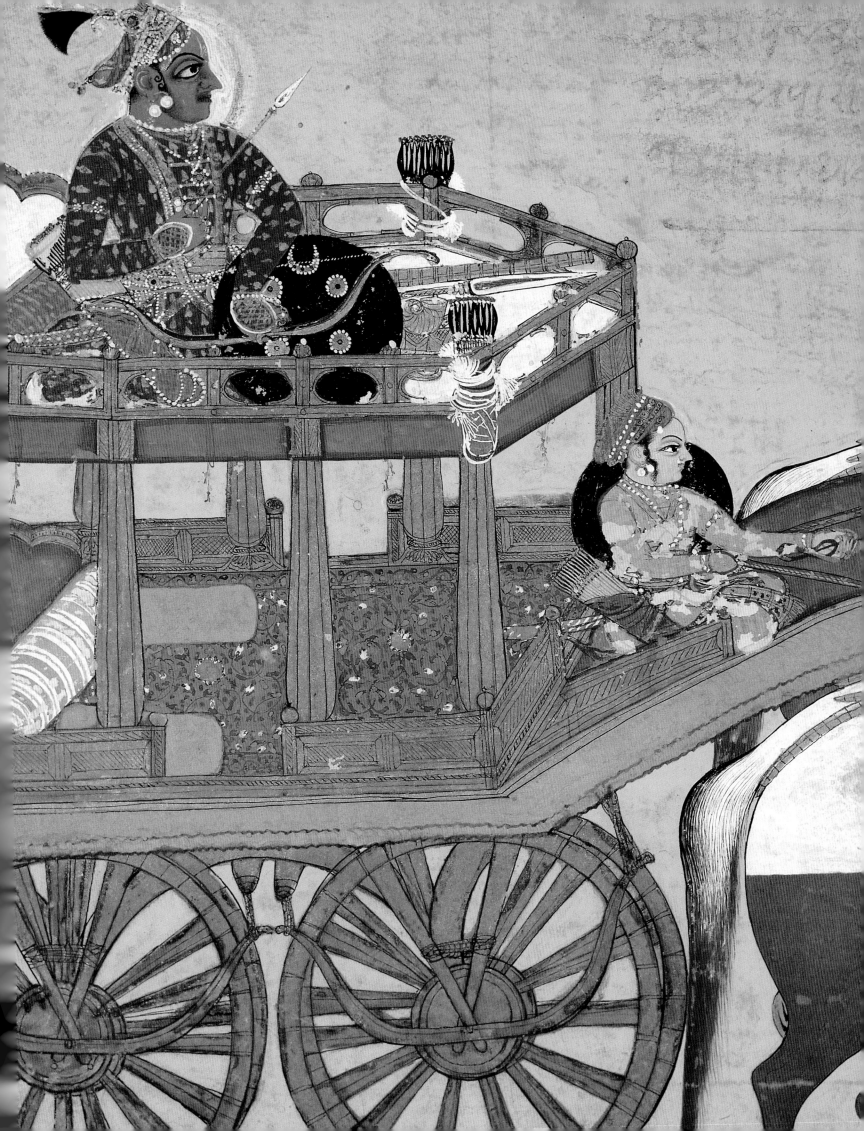

21

Maharao Arjun Singh Celebrating Krishna's Birthday (Janmashtami) in the Audience Hall (Darikhana) of the Raj Mahal at Kotah

Attributed to the Kotah Master
c. 1720–25
Opaque watercolor, gold
50.2 x 40.1 cm
H.H. Maharao Brijraj Singh of Kotah
Inscribed on recto: "The honorable Maharao Shri Arjun Singh at Krishna's birthday (Janmashtami) in the Audience Hall (Darikhana) of the Raj Mahal [royal palace, here meaning the older part within the fort (*garh*) of Kotah]."
Inscribed on verso, in a later hand: "The honorable Maharao Arjun Singh." A shorter inscription below the first line on the recto is partly obliterated by the black rule and hence unreadable.

22

Maharao Arjun Singh Celebrating Krishna's Birthday (Janmashtami) in the Audience Hall (Darikhana) of the Raj Mahal at Kotah

Attributed to the Kotah Master
c. 1720–25
Opaque watercolor, gold
51.3 x 39.9 cm
Rao Madho Singh Trust Museum, Fort Kotah
Inscribed on verso: "The minister (*divan*), the honorable Maharao Arjun Singh at Krishna's birthday (Janmash-tami) [celebrations] in the Audience Hall (Darikhana)."

Godly and mundane delight meet again here — twice. Although catalogue number 21, with its signs of trial and error in working out details of the design, appears to have been painted first, it was clearly deemed worthy of repetition, with slight variation. Both versions are painted in the Kotah Master's sprightly later idiom, when his brush, loaded with rich color, danced with all the majestic spring associated with Rajput music. Sharing his patron's and the devotees' spiritual exhilaration, the artist, who may have come under the influence of Sufi mysticism from an early age, gave form to their ecstatic mood. The chromatic notes of the oboe (*shahnai*) and flutes soar, wind, and undulate above the sharp, linear rhythms of plucked strings and romp to the earthy thuds and sharp taps of tablas. Few Rajput pictures are more joyous.
SCW

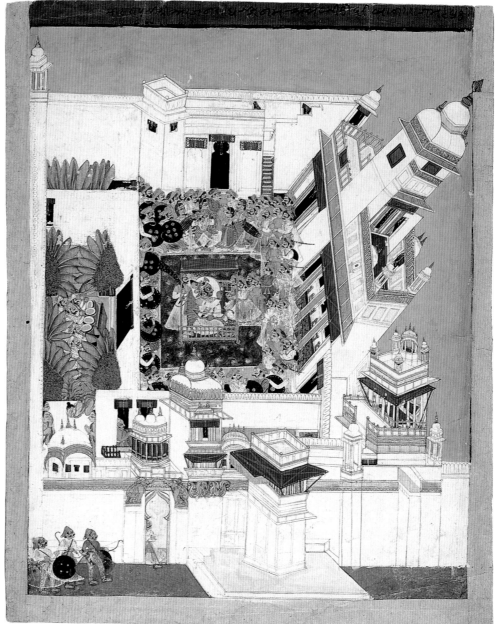

21

Published (cat. 21): Bautze 1992a, fig. 43.

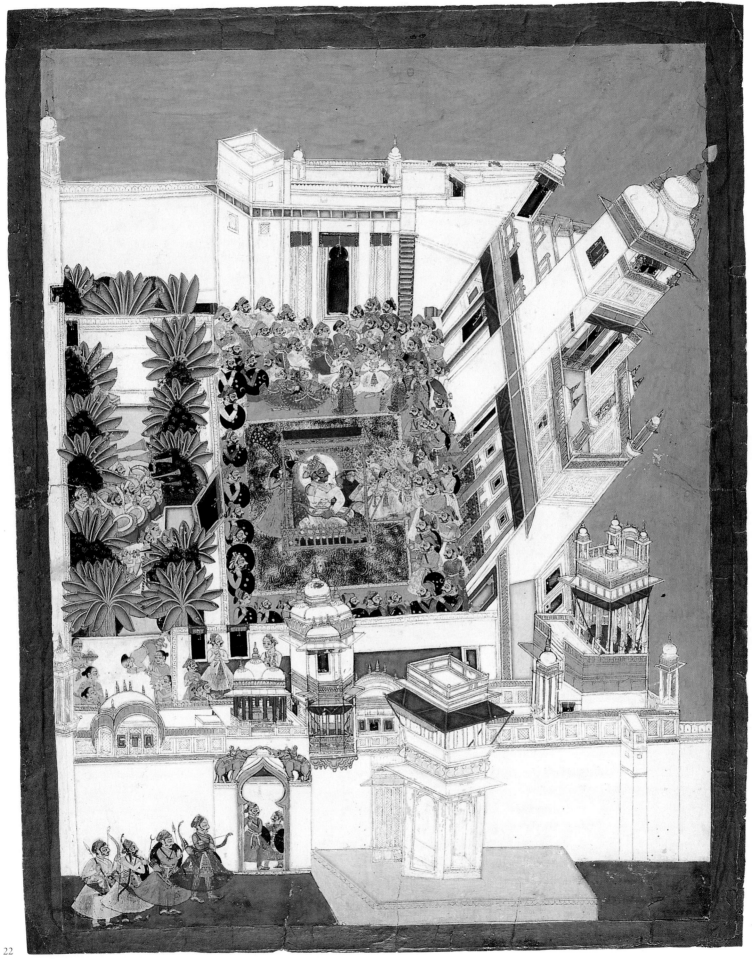

22

23

Great Siege: A Fantasy

Attributed to Sheikh Taju
c. 1725–50
Drawing (*khaka*): charcoal, black ink, watercolor
43 x 30.9 cm
Rao Madho Singh Trust Museum, Fort Kotah

The real and the imagined are sometimes hard
to sort out in Rajput art. Here, however, the
very large fort atop a very narrow pinnacle belongs to a universal fairyland, not to any known
site in admittedly astonishing Rajasthan. In
painting this military fantasy, Sheikh Taju's
soldierliness combined with his ever-increasing
awareness of Hindu epics, such as the *Ramayana*
(which he may have helped the Kotah Master to
illustrate; see Welch essay, fig. 19, for a scene
from the *Ramayana* that is entirely the work of
the Kotah Master). It is fascinating to speculate
upon the development of Sheikh Taju's art had
he remained at the imperial court, where no
picture of this sort would have been entertained.
If his observed imperial accomplishments
enriched the art of Kotah, Kotah's otherworldliness seems equally to have enriched and
liberated him.
SCW

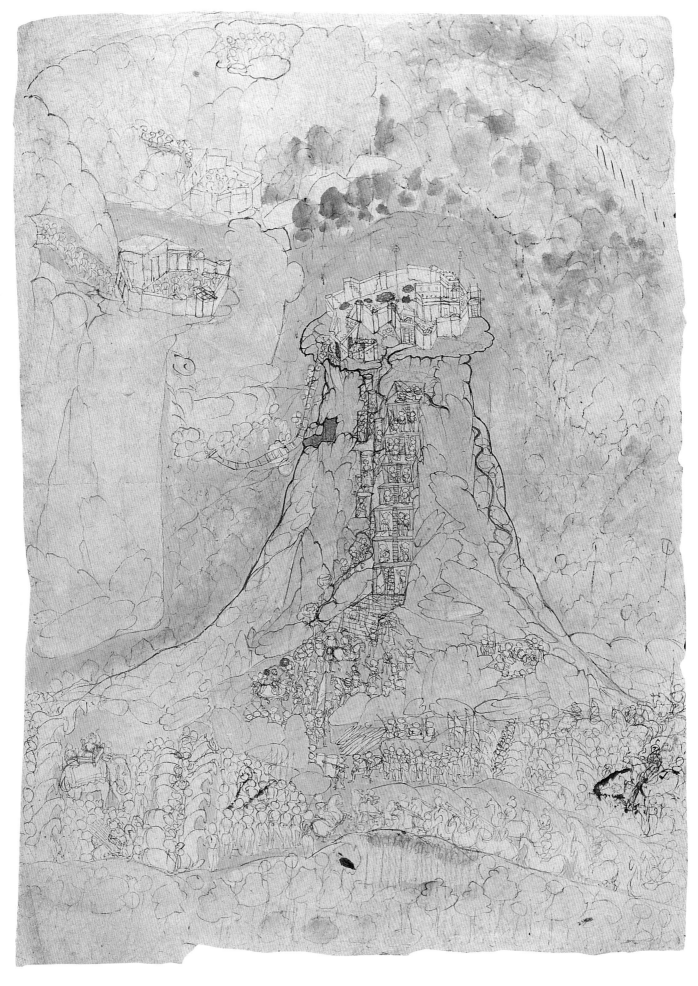

24

An Elephant near a Palace Gate

Attributed to Sheikh Taju
c. 1730
Drawing (*khaka*): black ink, white opaque watercolor
34.3 x 58.9 cm
Rao Madho Singh Trust Museum, Fort Kotah

This spirited portrayal of a prince somewhat apprehensively examining a splendid elephant eager for combat exemplifies the brilliant draftsmanship of the Kotah school. It can be assigned to Sheikh Taju, who, like the Kotah Master, seems to have based many of his silhouettes not only on sketches from life, but on drawings and paintings by the Master of Elephants. This logically observed composition, with its credible scale, specific buildings, trees, portraitlike figures, and animals (even the elephant appears to be a portrait), conforms to Mughal practice. The accomplished, wire-thin line points to Sheikh Taju's early training in the imperial workshops, from which he most likely was recruited for the Kotah ateliers during the first quarter of the eighteenth century.

SCW

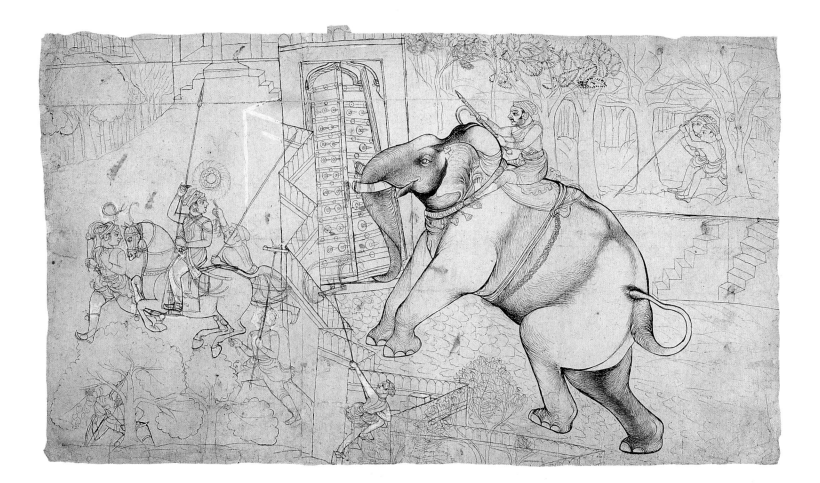

126

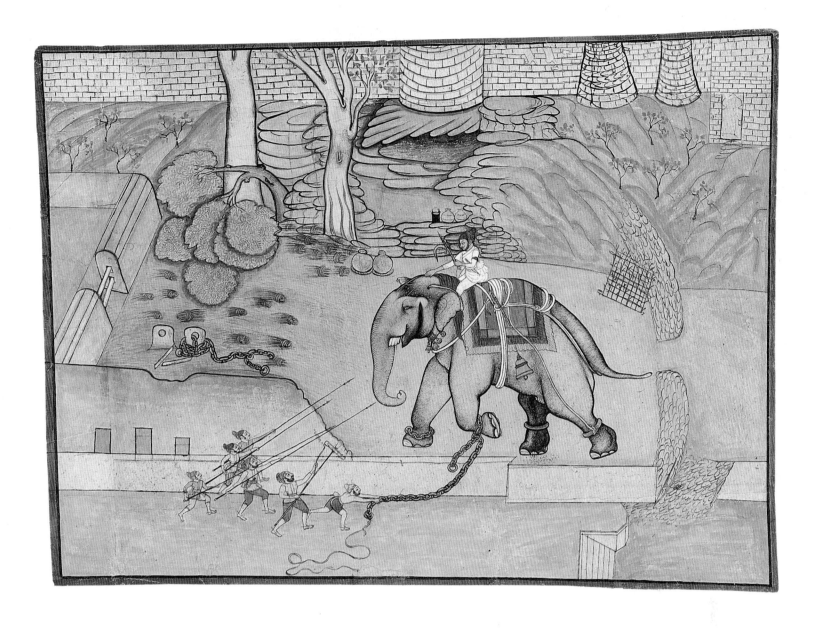

25

Controlling an Elephant

c. 1730
Opaque watercolor, watercolor, metallic gray watercolor
36.9 x 50.9 cm
Rao Madho Singh Trust Museum, Fort Kotah

Elements apparently borrowed by tracing from pictures by Sheikh Taju such as catalogue number 31 elevate this picture beyond its artist's innate limitations. The composition, dominated by the elephant, walls, and a pair of tree trunks, is forceful, but the central animal brings to mind a paper cutout, awkwardly related to the surroundings. Like the elephant, the figures seem secondhand, lacking in observation and understanding of movement. The nameless, modest artist seems to have been happiest when rendering still life, as in the evocative passage of two pierced stones and chains at the left. He would probably have achieved more in the studio of the eighteenth-century French painter Jean-Baptiste-Siméon Chardin.
SCW

26

A Craftsman Making a Toy Matchlock of Wood

Attributed to the Kotah Master
c. 1730
Opaque watercolor
25.4 x 14.3 cm
Rao Madho Singh Trust Museum, Fort Kotah

The Kotah Master's artistic universality is evident from all of his work. Animals of every
sort, architecture, landscape, still life, complex
battle and hunting scenes, were all within his
compass, along with portraiture. At Kotah, he
recorded a Balzacian cast, ranging from rulers
and courtiers to soldiers and craftsmen. One of
his most captivating painted likenesses is this
intent matchlock-maker shaping a stock —
probably the finished version of a sketch from
life. The craftsman's prominently furrowed
brow, sharply focused eye, and mouth and chin,
better suited to a quiet artisan than to a soldier,
bring him brightly before the viewer.
SCW

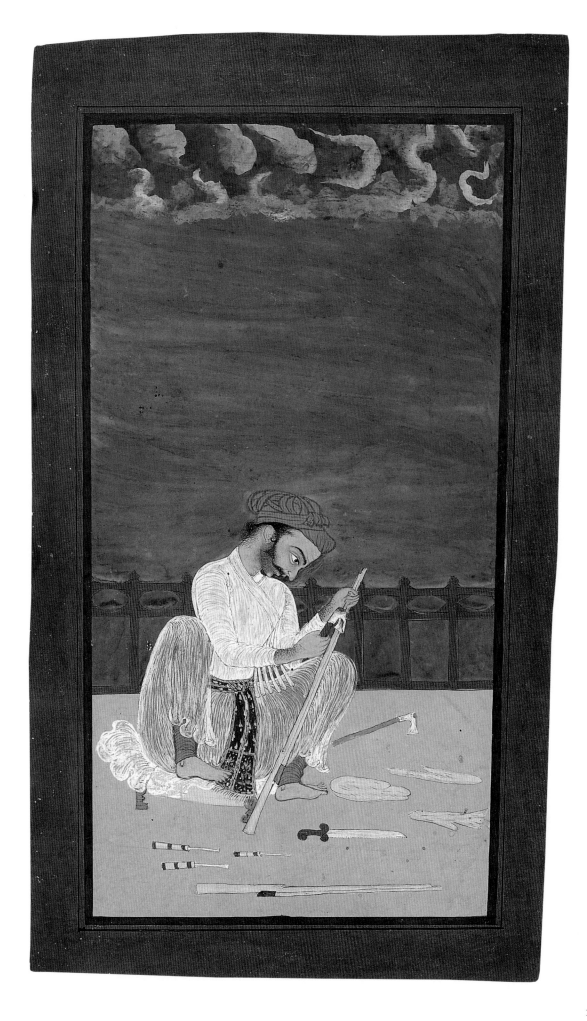

27

Maharao Durjan Sal's Elephant, Kisanprasad

Attributed to Sheikh Taju
c. 1730
Black ink, opaque watercolor, gold, metallic gray watercolor
45.8 x 51.7 cm
Rao Madho Singh Trust Museum, Fort Kotah
Inscribed on recto: "The elephant of the honorable Maharao Durjan Sal, Kisanprasad."

Kotah art is not always for the squeamish. Proud as the patron must have been of his elephant's deadly squeeze, not everyone is sufficiently unsentimental to savor such details as the blood spurting from the panther's eyes. Although the episode isolated so compellingly here — and recorded for the maharao's file of hunting subjects — must have happened, it is reminiscent of Sheikh Taju's two great predecessors' brilliant animal studies, from which he borrowed in characterizing Kisanprasad and the struggling panther.

Sheikh Taju's ability to record such incidents so convincingly and dramatically must have astounded the maharao's friends from other Rajput courts, where elephants, cheetahs, and all other animals were depicted far less movingly. In comparison with Kotah's animal pictures, those of Mewar, Bikaner, Jaipur, and every other Rajput school appear to be drearily bland and devoid of empathy.
scw

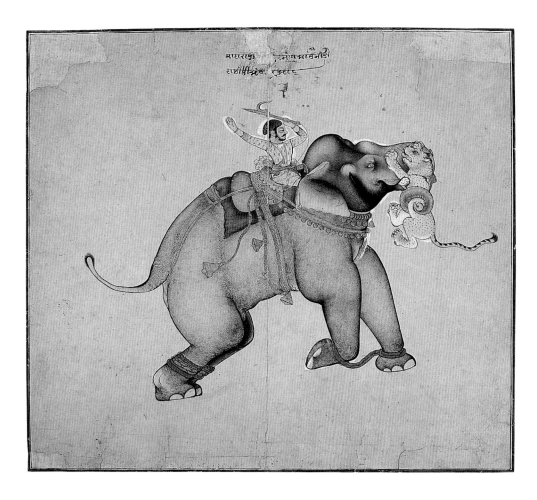

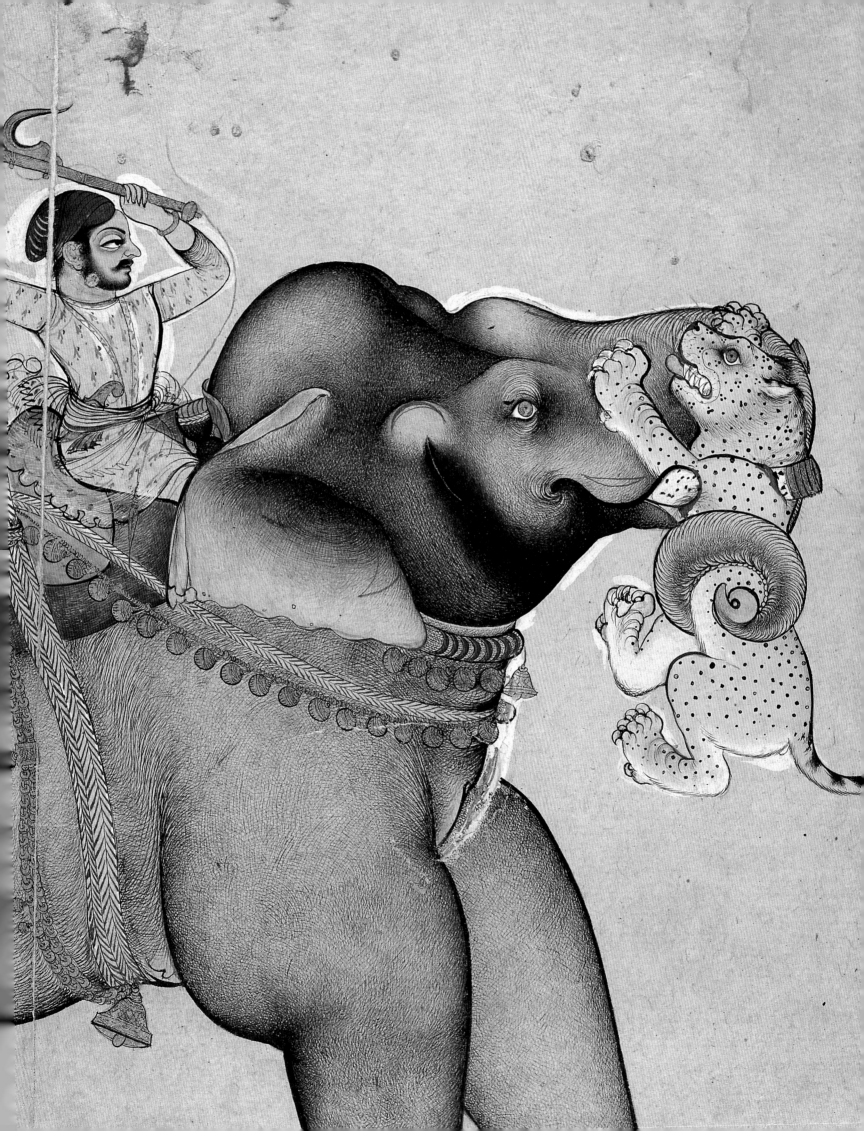

28

Krishna Hiding the Milkmaids' Clothing
(Gopivashtraharana)

Attributed to the Kotah Master and Sheikh Taju
c. 1730
Opaque watercolor, gold
35.6 x 24.6 cm
Rao Madho Singh Trust Museum, Fort Kotah

At times, it seems that nothing was sacred to the Rajputs, not even the gods. This painted romp, in which Lord Krishna teases bathing milkmaids by hanging their clothing, like banners, in a treetop, would have enjoyed wide appeal at court, in both the zenana and the men's quarters. To the pious, it would have been appealingly *spirituelle;* to the worldly, it may have seemed rewardingly naughty. The artists, probably the Kotah Master and Sheikh Taju, may themselves have enjoyed the "field work" that enabled them so perceptively to characterize the blushingly embarrassed gestures of charming young ladies subjected to a love-god's playfulness. Two middle-aged monkeys, peeping through the foliage, wittily bring to mind portrayals in European art of Susannah being ogled by the elders.
SCW

This painting basically illustrates an incident from the *Bhagavata Purana:* book x, chapter 22, verses 9 ff.[1]
JKB

1 For an English translation, see Tagare 1978, 1396 ff.

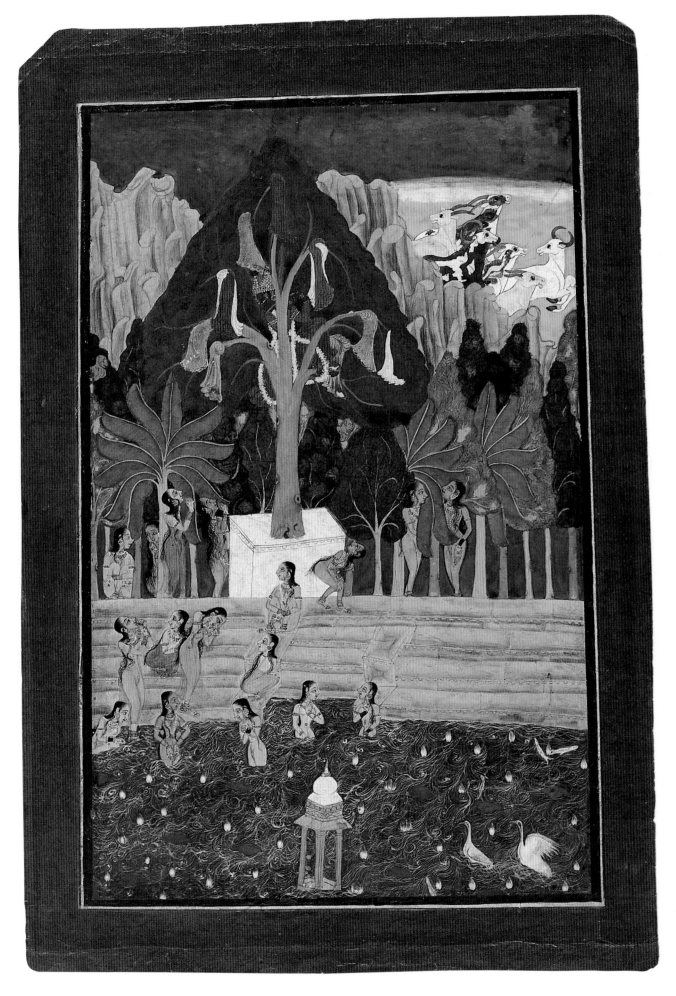

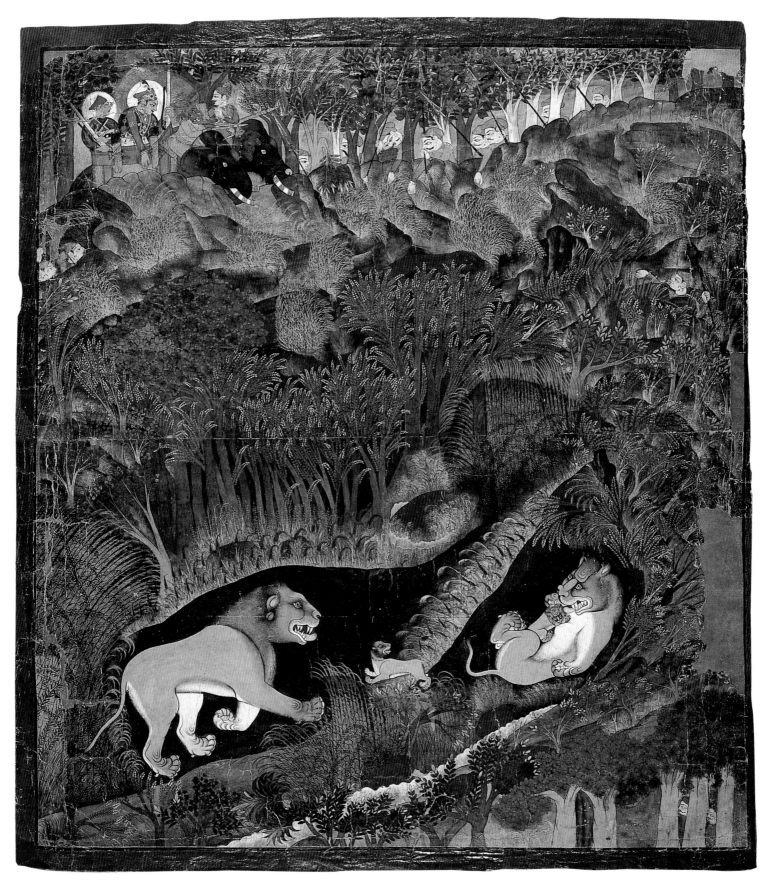

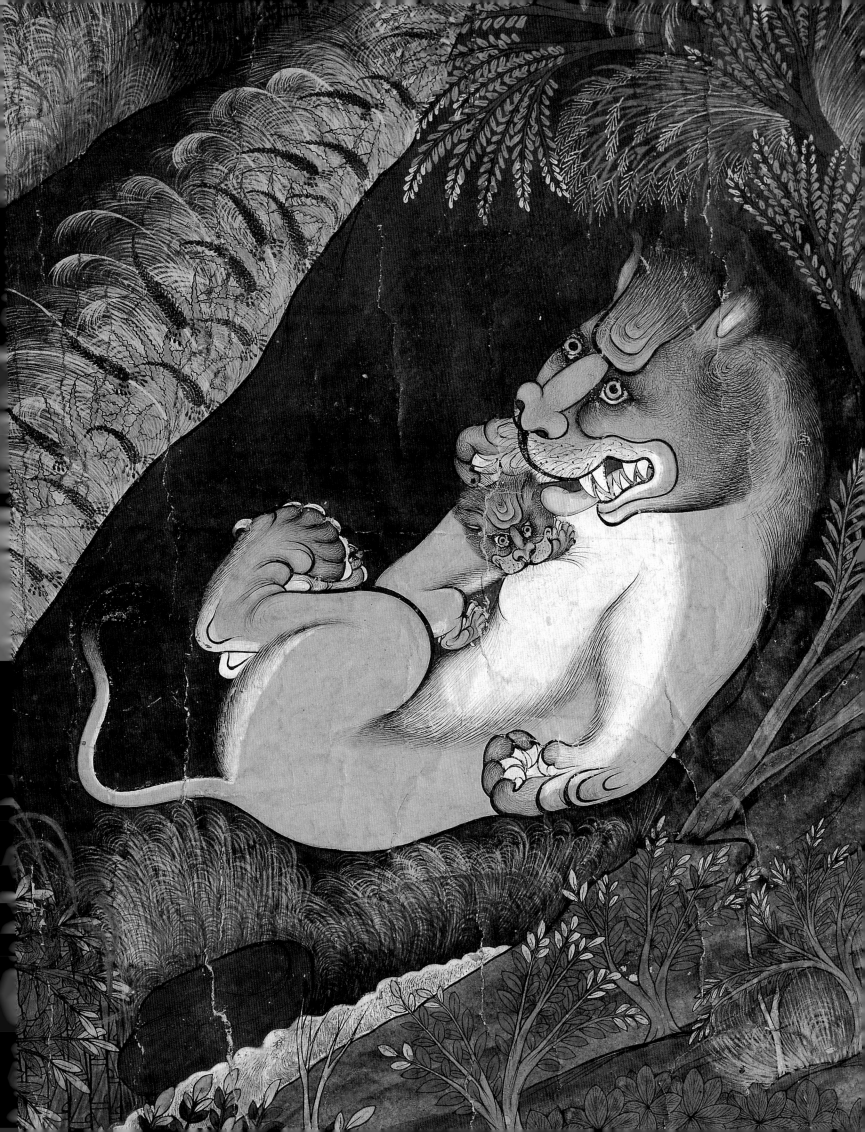

29

Brijnathji and Durjan Sal Sight
a Pride of Lions

Attributed to the Kotah Master assisted by Sheikh Taju
c. 1730–35
Opaque watercolor, gold
66.9 x 59 cm
Rao Madho Singh Trust Museum, Fort Kotah
Inscribed on verso: "Picture of Shri Brijnathji and the
honorable Maharao Durjan Sal and the honorable Jaswant[?] Singh hunting with the elephant [name not
given] and the elephant Shondargangaji[?] [meeting] a
strong lioness with cubs."

During a long, fulfilling life that most likely led
from Golconda to Aurangabad and, finally, to
Kotah, the Kotah Master synthesized many cultures, forming a powerful new harmony. Lions
as well as elephants replaced Turkman dragons
in his repertoire, and with time his blend of
humor and fierce power mellowed into sagacious sweetness. Exhilarating proof of the
Kotah Master's artistic triumph is this dark
junglescape in which the patron and his godly
companion, whose face and hands are rendered
in glistening gold, come upon a beguiling family of lions in a feline paradise. Hauntingly, it
proves that elements from Turkman and Safavid
Tabriz — the rhythmically composed trees,
lions, and calligraphic line — have not only
survived the move through time and space to
Kotah, but have united with Rajput elements,
creating a thrillingly fresh idiom. Although the
composition and much of the execution can be
credited to the Kotah Master himself, parts of
the figure painting are attributable to Sheikh
Taju. As the Kotah Master's most gifted follower, who came to Kotah from Delhi fully trained
in Mughal style and technique, he now absorbed
the traditions of Turkman and Safavid Iran,
which he in turn combined into a compelling
personal synthesis.
scw

A highly finished, closely related drawing is in
a Washington, D.C., private collection.[1] The
main figure in that drawing is identified as Rao
Bhoj of Bundi; this is hardly surprising, since
the lioness with cubs already figured in the
great hunting scene within the Baddal Mahal
of the Bundi palace, datable to about 1630.
JKB

1 See Topsfield and Beach 1991, 94, n. 3.

Published: M. B. Singh 1985, pl. III (= Gorakshkar/
Nigam 1988, cat. 23).

136

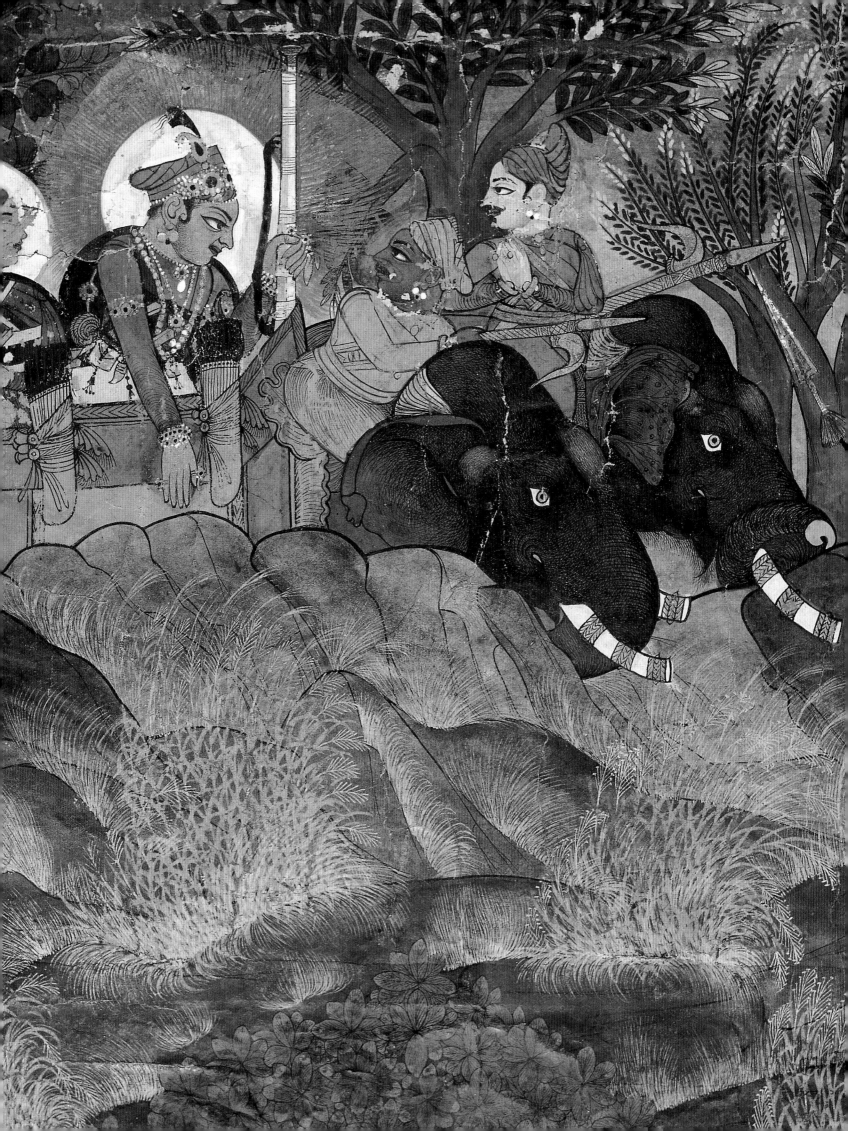

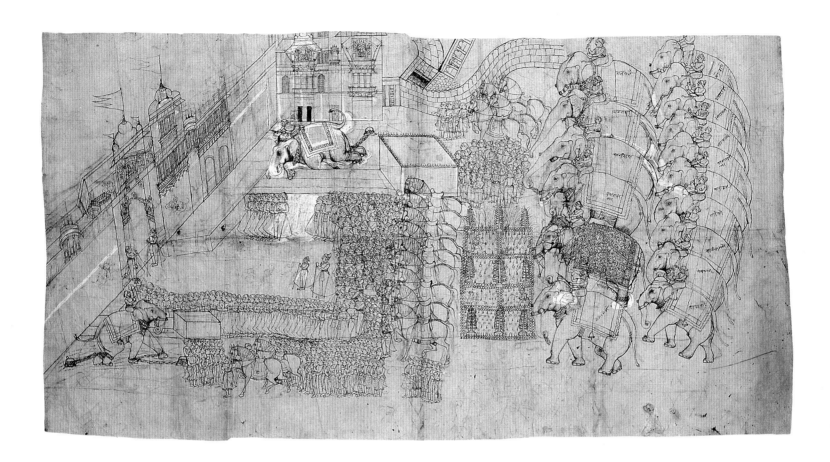

30

*Elephants and Horses Assembled before the
Image of Brijnathji, Who Is Seen Looking
Down from a Balcony in the Palace*

Attributed to Sheikh Taju in collaboration with the
Kotah Master
c. 1730–40
Drawing (*khaka*): black ink, opaque watercolor
109 x 208.4 cm
Rao Madho Singh Trust Museum, Fort Kotah

This exceptionally large, thoughtfully improvised, but finely worked drawing was probably
the preparatory sketch for a major painting, perhaps for a wall. Every skill learned by Sheikh
Taju in the imperial ateliers, enriched by the
spirited calligraphic line expounded by the
Kotah Master, was employed to describe a major
Kotah festival in honor of Brijnathji. The god
appears in an upper window facing the assembled Kotah nobility, army, cavalry, and corps
of elephants. Lampstands (*jha*) and a formal
"garden" of oil lamps illuminate the nocturnal
celebration. Behind the vigorously prostrating
elephant — apparently rendered from life in
Sheikh Taju's most vital manner — is a large
and mysterious square container, identified by
Maharao Brijraj Singh as a cage, long since removed, in which tigers were kept before being
released in the courtyard for animal combats.
Space is handled in the imperial mode, reminiscent of the artist's drawings of Mughal darbars
(cat. 14–16). The massed elephants at the right,
although akin to equivalent passages in Mughal
art, possess the élan and individuality associated
with Kotah's trio of great elephant artists.
Characteristically, the sheikh sketched a small,
humble, open-mouthed personage, seated in
front of the picture plane in the right foreground; this empathetic figure in effect invites
the viewer to share his curiosity about the pro-
ceedings at this remarkable Kotah festival.
scw

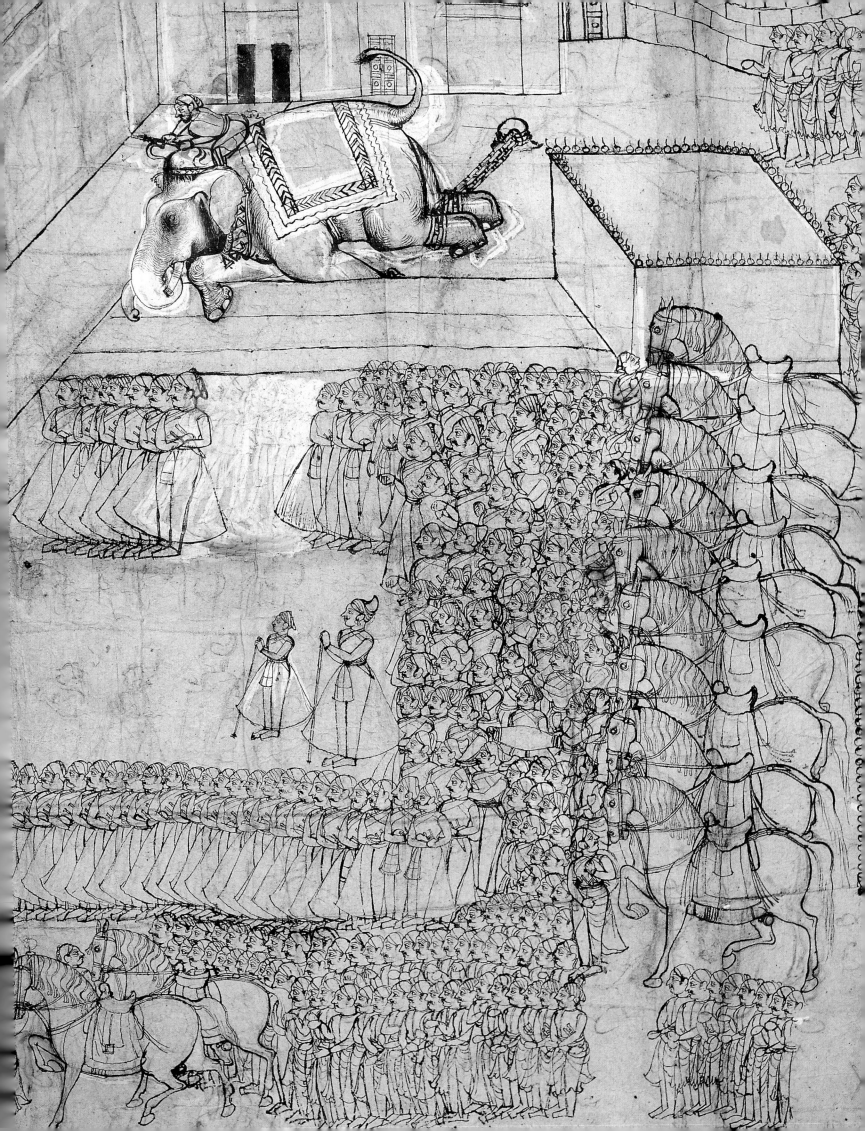

31

A Chained Elephant

Attributed to Sheikh Taju
c. 1730–40
Opaque watercolor, watercolor, gold, metallic gray
watercolor
35.6 x 50.1 cm
Rao Madho Singh Trust Museum, Fort Kotah

This is one of Sheikh Taju's exemplary pictures. Starkly simple — a single animal and two small figures in an enclosure — it is compellingly dramatic. The elephant is firmly chained, with his trunk between his teeth, apparently pondering his fate as a beast of combat. The viewer can hardly help sympathizing with this gladiator confined in the very field — gouged by recent triumphs and defeats — where he will risk his life. The champion's mood has been expressed in the manner of the Master of Elephants and the Kotah Master, which is high praise for the third of the school's major artists. Comparison with the preceding picture confirms the striking talent of the creator of this one.
scw

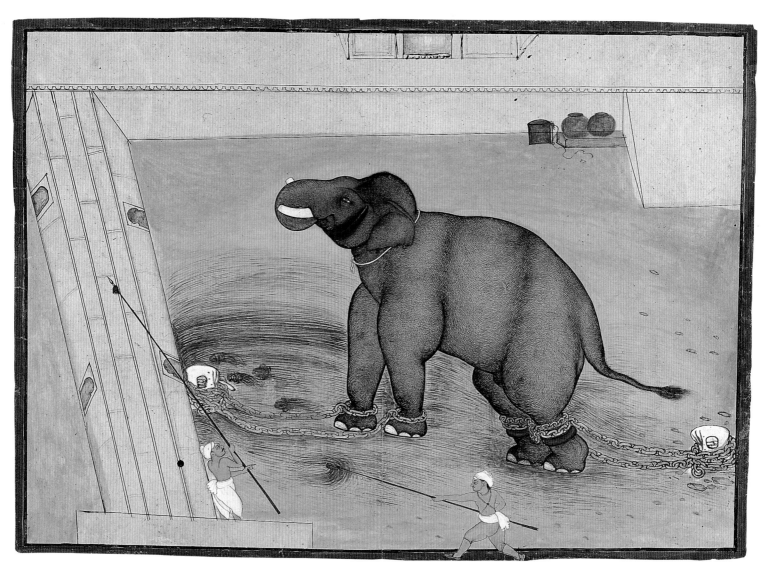

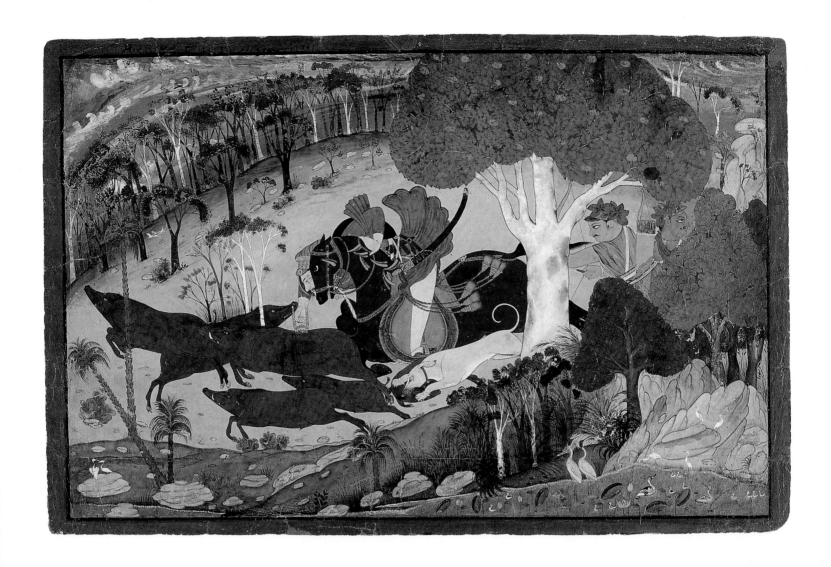

32

*Madho Singh of Kotah Hunting Boar
from Horseback*

Attributed to Sheikh Taju
c. 1730–40
Opaque watercolor, gold, metallic gray watercolor
30.1 x 46.9 cm
H.H. Maharao Brijraj Singh of Kotah
Inscribed on recto, at top border: "The honorable
Madho Singh killing boar . . ."
Inscribed on verso: "The king of kings, the honorable
Maharao Madho Singh . . . with dagger . . . horse." Some
passages are illegible, but it is clear that this inscription
captions the painting.

This small painting is a reduced and later version of a picture attributable to the Kotah
Master, now in the collection of Sir Howard
Hodgkin. Perhaps it was created as an educa-
tional assignment at the behest of the earlier
artist. Tightly and meticulously rendered, it follows every twist, turn, and flair of the original
— which, however, is more spontaneous —
and qualifies as a tinted drawing rather than as
a painting in full color. The Hodgkin picture
was painted as the pendant to *Bhoj Singh of Bundi
Slays a Lion* (Welch essay, fig. 10), which contains
particularly vital lions in markedly Turkman/
Safavid style. Compositional elements of this

Rajput boar hunt may have been remembered
from one of the standard illustrations to the
Iranian *Shahnameh*, in which Byzhan slashes a
scurrying pack of wild pigs. It is not unlikely
that the Kotah Master could have been called
upon to paint this popular subject at Golconda.

scw

Published, together with its Bundi prototype, and
discussed: Bautze 1986e, fig. 14.

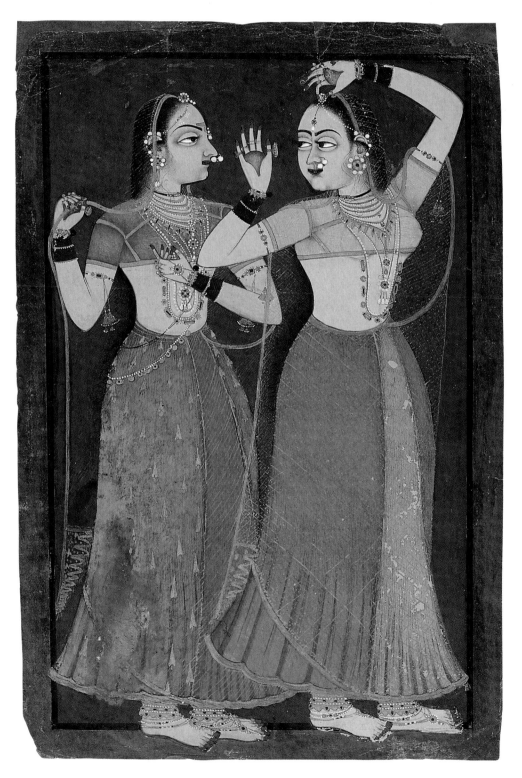

33

Dancers

Attributed to the Kotah Master
c. 1730–40
Opaque watercolor, gold
40.3 x 27 cm
Rao Madho Singh Trust Museum, Fort Kotah

When news reached Kotah of the death of
Maharao Bhim Singh I (r. 1707–20), two of his
queens and five concubines immolated themselves (became *sati*). These two dancers, seen
under happier circumstances, were probably
concubines. As in traditional Japan, Kotah
women were unapproachably formal in public,
assuming masklike expressions that cosmetics
made even more impenetrable. Increasing their
mysterious impersonality, they were schooled to
move in prescribed ways. This pair, painted in
all their ritualized coyness, lack the engaging
individuality found in the Kotah Master's
craftsman (cat. 26), who is plausible, palpable,
approachable, even smellable. The ladies are
not. Even while dancing, or posing for their
portraits, culturally imposed protective barriers,
filtering out every trace of individuality,
psychologically confine them to the zenana.

In painting this double portrait, the Kotah
Master respected the ladies' courtly exclusive-
ness. In private, however, constraints would
most likely have vanished, and the artist would
not only have been welcomed in the dancers'
practice rooms, but allowed to sketch there at
leisure.

SCW

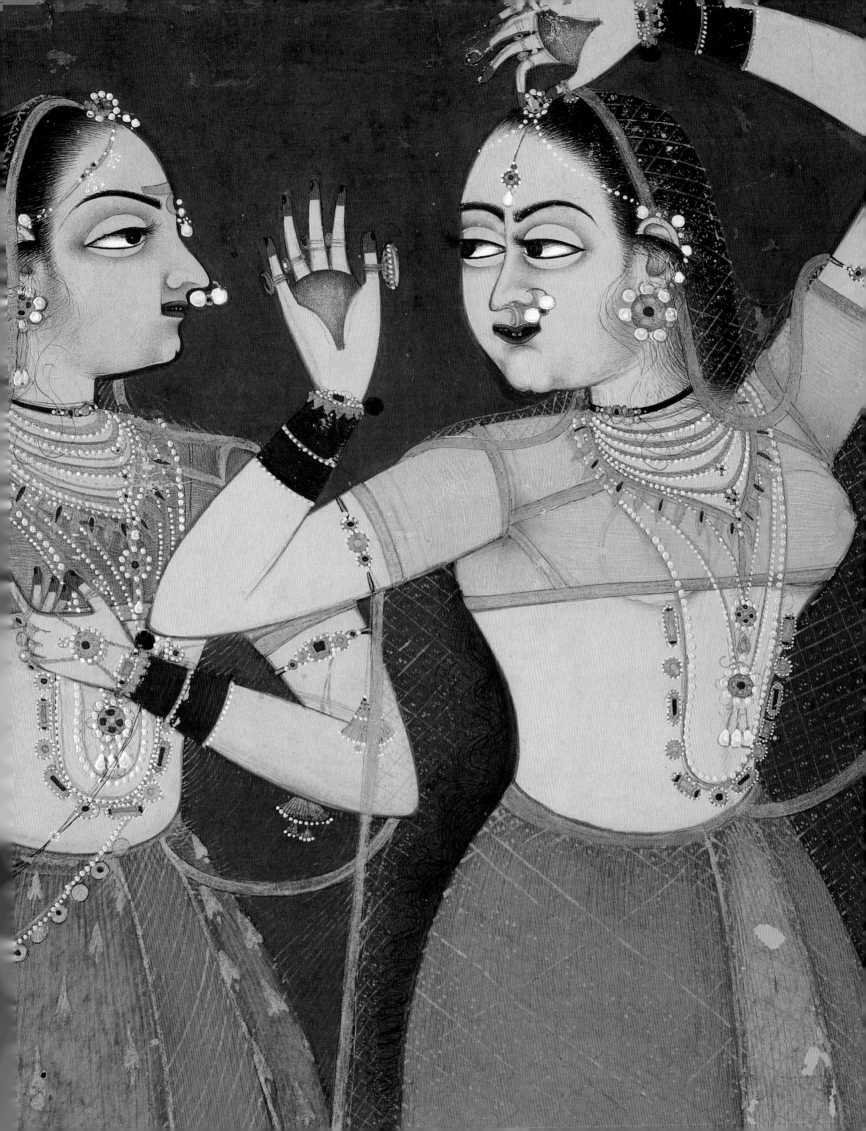

34

Ganesh Attended by Riddhi and Siddhi

Attributed to Sheikh Taju
c. 1735
Drawing (*khaka*): charcoal, black ink, traces of watercolor
27.6 x 19.1 cm
Rao Madho Singh Trust Museum, Fort Kotah

The divine elephant, cushioned by lotus petals,
is attended by Prosperity (Riddhi) and Wisdom
(Siddhi) bearing yak-tail whisks, and is being
fanned veneratingly by graceful palm trees. He
is saluted by his vehicle, a perky rat, with ears
as winglike as the god's. Although traditionally
Rajput in subject, this humorous yet devout
drawing of a Hindu god can be assigned to
Sheikh Taju, the Mughal-trained Muslim
master better known for his elephant combats,
hunts, and other secular subjects. Adjusting
from the visible to the envisioned, he reanimated
a traditional composition. In sketching Ganesh's
benevolent countenance, however, he repeated
one of his own idiosyncratic formulas: the left
side of the mask, including the plump god's
sweets-eating trunk, is an independent profile
— looking ahead, perhaps, to Picasso's animated multiplicity of viewpoints.
SCW

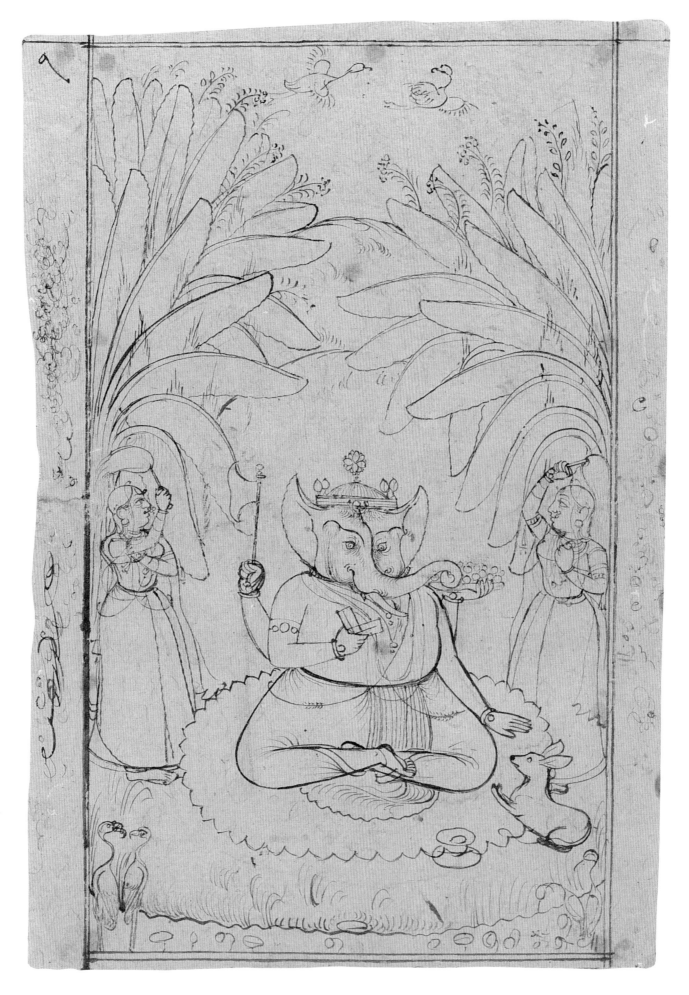

35

Brijnathji and Durjan Sal Hunting Deer

Attributed to the Kotah Master
ca. 1735–40
Opaque watercolor, gold
20.7 x 25.8 cm
Rao Madho Singh Trust Museum, Fort Kotah
Inscribed on verso: "Picture of Shri Brijnathji [and] the honorable Maharao Durjan Sal out hunting deer."

Intense and glowing, this picture might be the last by the Kotah Master. Handled in a less masterly fashion than earlier works, it has soft outlines, and the artist's once crisply jewel-like crosshatches and massed arcs are muddled. But his artistic conviction seems never to have been stronger. Feelings and expressive powers, like those of the great Titian in old age, seem to have gained intensity, transcending the uncertainties of eye and hand. This small painting's weaknesses are its strengths.

SCW

During the reign of Maharao Durjan Sal (r. 1723–56), much of Kotah's court ceremonial was reorganized around the worship of Shri Brijnathji. Although the deity spent most of his time relatively secluded within his temple sanctum sanctorum, located in a shady courtyard in the heart of the palace, on state occasions he was brought out into more public areas of the palace such as the maharao's Raj Mahal (Throne Room), where the enthroned god was worshiped by the entire nobility (see also cat. 30). At the same time, Durjan Sal continued the practice of having himself portrayed with an appearance almost identical to that of the deity, whose figure overlaps his. In this way, Durjan Sal sought to merge his identity with that of Shri Brijnathji; thus, the nobility's worship of Shri Brijnathji became combined with devotion to Durjan Sal.

This painting shows Durjan Sal and Shri Brijnathji engaged in one of the quintessential royal pursuits: the hunt (*shikar*). The hunt was important to Indian rulers not only because it served as an excellent form of training for more martial pursuits but also because it demonstrated that the king's mastery extended beyond the social into the natural realm. Indeed, Indian rulers were held responsible for many natural phenomena, from the coming of the life-replenishing monsoon (a type of royal boon) to invasions of locusts (a type of royal punishment).

NP

Published: M. B. Singh 1985, pl. v.

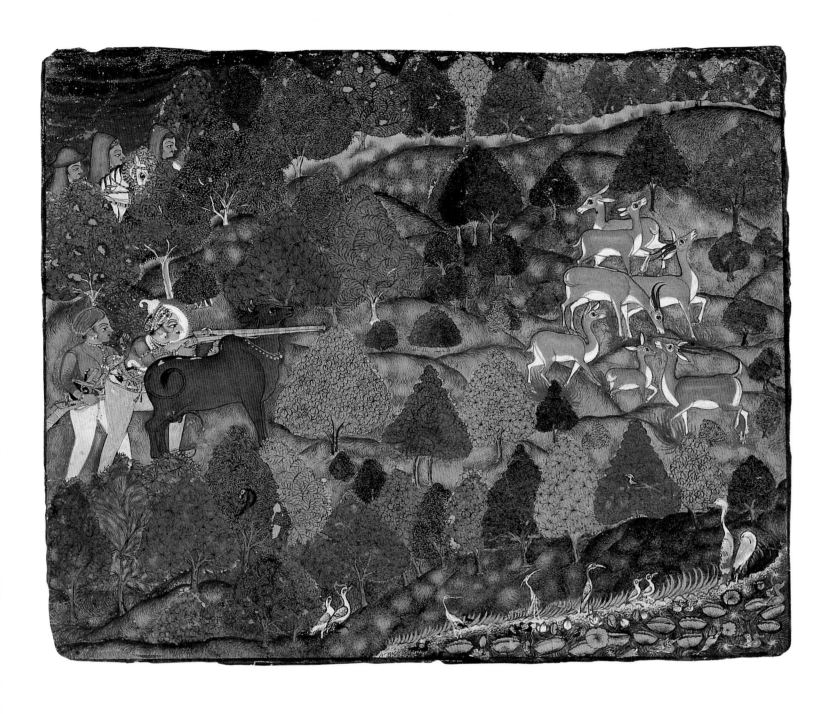

36

Maharao Durjan Sal and Maharana Jagat Singh in a Palanquin, Surrounded by Royal Courtiers

Attributed to Sheikh Taju
c. 1735–40
Opaque watercolor, gold
49.7 x 73.1 cm
Rao Madho Singh Trust Museum, Fort Kotah
Inscribed on verso: "Ram! The king of kings, the honorable great king Maharana Jagat Singh [and] the honorable Maharao Durjan Sal [seated] in a [traveling] throne [surrounded by] riding kings and chieftains [including] the honorable Maharaja Takhat Singh, the honorable Maharaja Nath, the honorable Maharaja Bakhat Singh, Prince Prithviraj, the honorable Chhitra Singh Rajavat [and] the foster brother Udairam. This folio is obtained from the artist Sekh Tajun, the painter, obtained by His Highness [Hazur] as a present [*nazar*]."

A one-line Nastaliq inscription runs parallel to the second line of the Devanagari inscription.

Processions were often painted at Kotah, especially by Sheikh Taju, whose magisterial bejeweled portraits, painted in Mughal technique with finely layered and burnished pigments, were well suited to royal display. In this picture, a haloless Maharao Durjan Sal faces the senior-most Rajput, Maharana Jagat Singh of Mewar, whose portliness well supports not only a chestscape of opulent necklaces, but the largest and brightest of halos. The artist meticulously doled out his skills here: the important personages in this painting are lavished with gems and gold, whereas those lower in the pecking order are accorded less refulgent costumes and fewer sparkles. In such courtly pictures, following imperial precedent, individualization and psychological nuances also increased according to rank. The artist, who may have preferred the freedom of sketching quirkier, less noble personalities, was here compelled to honor court protocol.

SCW

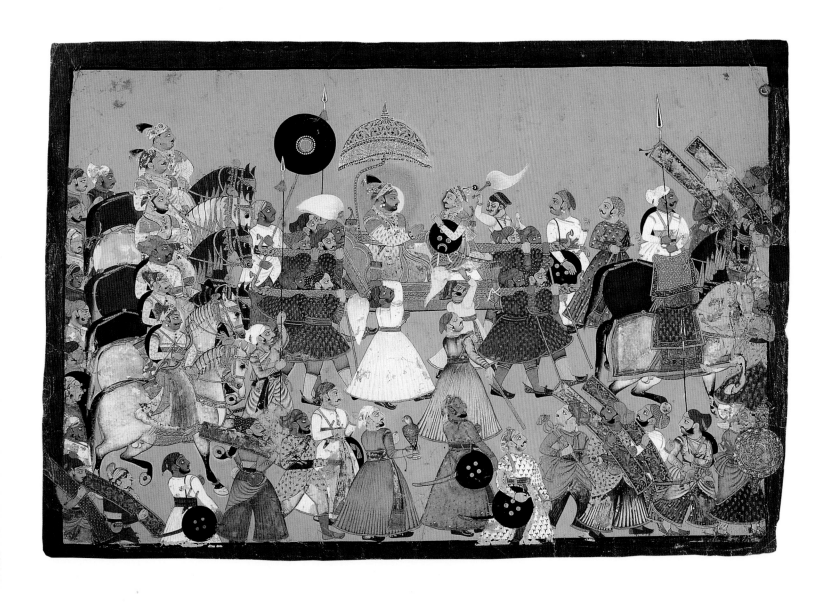

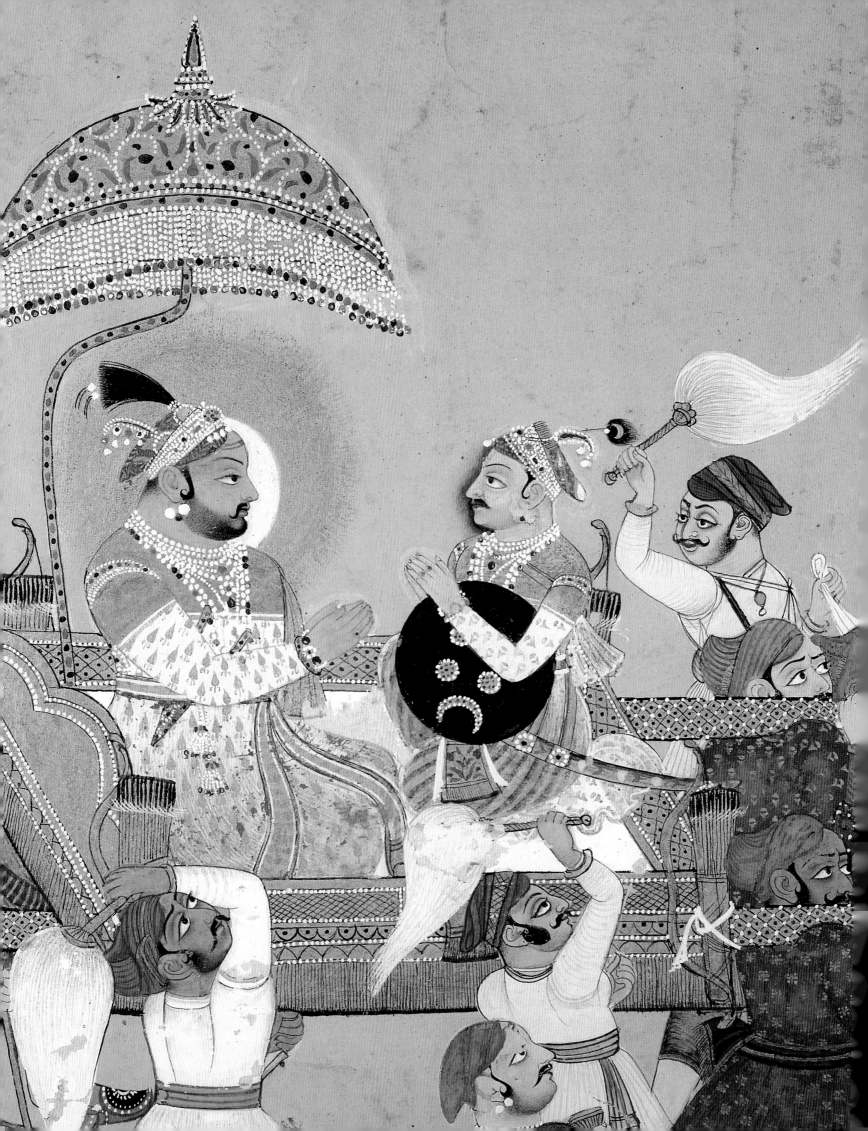

Here, Maharana Jagat Singh II kneels under an umbrella in a palanquin (*palki*) carried in a procession. His fleshy, nimbate head faces right while he greets his son-in-law Maharao Durjan Sal, seated next to him. Jagat Singh II was the eldest son of Maharana Sangram Singh II of Mewar and his third wife, Ummed Kunwar, daughter of Mukund Singh of Banbori.[1] He was born on September 29, 1708,[2] and first ascended the throne (*gaddi*) of Mewar on February 2, 1734;[3] he died on June 16, 1751.[4]

The last three horsemen from the top riding behind the palanquin belong to the retinue of the maharana. Nath Singh, second from the top, was a younger brother of Jagat Singh, who was given the estate (*jagir*) of Bagor and who created some trouble during the short reign of Jagat Singh's eldest son, Maharana Pratap Singh II.[5] Maharajas Takhat Singh and Bakhat Singh frequently occur in Mewar paintings showing Maharana Sangram Singh II and/or his son, Jagat Singh II.[6] The shape of the pointed turbans indicates that the other three horsemen belong to Maharao Durjan Sal's retinue. It is difficult to tell who Prince Prithvi Singh is, but Chhitra Singh Rajawat and the foster brother Udairam accompany Maharao Durjan Sal in a well-known Kotah hunting scene.[7]

No other Mewar ruler was more often portrayed than Jagat Singh II; probably five hundred pictures of this "hedonistic and ineffectual ruler" exist.[8] His paintings also attest to the fact that he traveled in a palanquin, as shown here.[9] The use of this mode of transport as a "double planquin" carried by eight porters is, however, unusual; the more common use is demonstrated by catalogue number 18. A flywhisk (*chauri*) bearer accompanies each ruler, while the (higher) status of the maharana of Mewar is indicated by an additional bearer with the regal insignia (*chamhagi*) of Mewar, "the golden sun in the sable disk," "a disc of black felt or ostrich feathers, with a plate of gold to represent the sun in its center, borne upon a pole."[10]

The beardless face of Maharana Nathji indicates that the original painting was done around 1734–35 and probably owes its existence to the Hurda conference in 1734, at which the more important rulers of Rajasthan officially formed a league against the Marathas. Further portraits of Durjan Sal done by Mewar artists

are known;[11] they all show him without a nimbus. It should be remembered that the Haras served the Sisodia clan of Mewar before accepting Mughal suzerainty — a fact the Sisodias probably never forgot: in those days, they did not accept the Haras as their equals despite their strong matrimonial relations.

The inscription on the back of the painting is in a Kotah hand, and so is the invocation to it; its contents were probably copied from the original Mewar painting, since it so strongly emphasizes the maharana's titles. That the original painting was done by a Mewar artist is shown by the absence of a nimbus around Durjan Sal's head. It has been suggested that the painter, Sheikh Taju, originated in Mewar, but this assumption is based on a series of wrong observations, which resulted in confounding two different artists working for Hara and/or Naruka patrons: Sheikh Taju and Taju. The works of the latter are inferior to the works of the former.[12]

JKB

1 Shyamaldas 1886, 2:981.
2 Ibid., 2:1245 (Saturday, 10th day of the dark fortnight of [the month] Ashvin, v.s. 1766). Somani 1976, 335, writes that he was born on September 9, 1709.
3 Shyamaldas 1886, 2:1217 (13th of the dark fortnight of [the month] Magh, v.s. 1790, and the 13th of the bright fortnight of [the month] Jyeshtha, v.s. 1790, respectively). The diverging dates given by Somani 1976, 335, are January 11, 1734, and June 3, 1734.
4 Shyamaldas 1886, 2:1245 (7th day of the dark fortnight of [the month] Ashadha, v.s. 1808). According to Somani 1976, 352, he died on June 5, 1751.
5 Shyamaldas 1886, 2:981; Somani 1976, 334; and Somani 1985, index under "Nathji." For his portrait, see Topsfield 1980, nos. 111 and 132, and Sotheby's, Inc., 1996, no. 40.
6 Topsfield 1990, nos. 5–7; Bautze 1995b, fig. 129, 288; Sotheby's, Inc., 1994, nos. 25, 31, and 37; Sotheby's, Inc., 1996, no. 37, just to mention a few.
7 London, Victoria and Albert Museum, IS 563–1952.
8 Topsfield 1995, 193f.
9 Topsfield 1980, nos. 119–20.
10 Tod 1920 ed., 1513 and 659f.
11 Bautze 1995b, 136, pl.; Topsfield 1990, 47, no. 12; and Sotheby's, Inc., 1994, no. 39. Note the absence of the nimbus in all these (Mewar) portraits of Durjan Sal.
12 M. B. Singh 1985, 23.

37

Heroine Going to Meet Her Lover
(Krishna Abhisarika Nayika)

Attributed to Sheikh Taju
c. 1750
Opaque watercolor, watercolor, silver
41.8 x 28.6 cm
Rao Madho Singh Trust Museum, Fort Kotah

The extent of Sheikh Taju's emotional reach is
demonstrated by this extremely romantic painting, in which the heroine (*nayika*), dressed in
flaming red, churns through dark jungle toward
her lover. Identifiable as Krishna the blue god,
the lover waits tranquilly, his passions colorfully
expressed in the reds of the surroundings. The
paired reds reach out, balanced by a pair of
stark, static palm trees silhouetted against the
darkly moody sky, soon to be activated by wind
and rain — like the lovers they symbolize.
Monsoon rains are about to fertilize the land.
One wonders if this remarkable picture was left
unfinished because the artist and patron feared
that further brushstrokes might weaken its
spell.
SCW

The Abhisarika is a heroine (*nayika*) who,
"being affected by love, pride, or passion," goes
to meet her beloved.[1] According to the *Rasikapriya* of Keshavdas Mishra (1555–1617), who
composed this text for Raja Indrajit Deo of
Orccha in 1591, there are three different types of
Abhisarikas. None of the eight major types of
heroines described by Keshavdas in the seventh
chapter of his work seem to apply to this painting more than the Abhisarika, although an
exact correspondence with Keshavdas's text[2]
cannot be detected.
JKB

1 Bahadur 1972, 110.
2 See ibid., 119–22, or Coomaraswamy 1914, 106–8.

Published: M. B. Singh 1985, pl. VI.

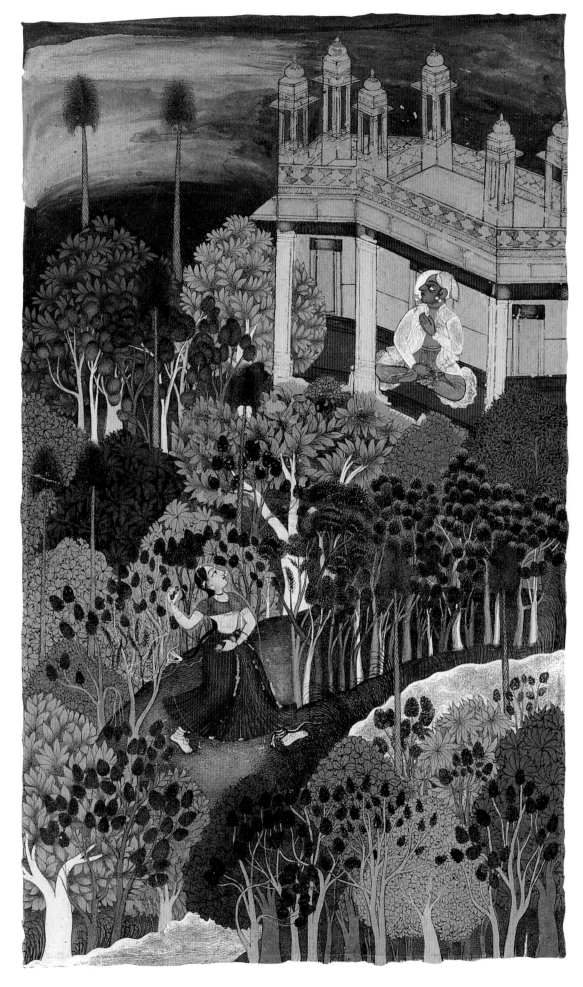

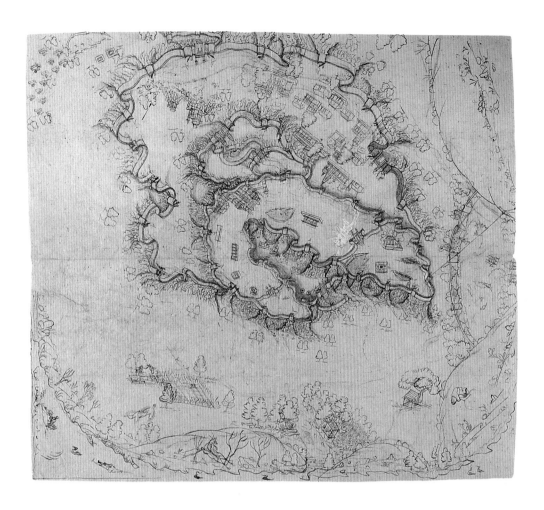

38

Bird's-Eye View of a Fort

Attributed to Sheikh Taju
Mid eighteenth century
Drawing (*khaka*): charcoal, red and black ink, white
opaque watercolor
61.9 x 55 cm
Rao Madho Singh Trust Museum, Fort Kotah

Like European Renaissance artists, Rajput
painters were called upon to carry out tasks not
always deemed "artistic," but often, as in this
drawing of a fort, aesthetically rewarding and
innovative. Because the sprawling complex set
on high ground appears to be real, it is probably safe to assume that it was commissioned
either as a record for the Kotah archive or as a
map for military purposes. Like other pictures
of forts by Sheikh Taju, this one must be
turned around and upside down to be compre-
hended fully. Doing so reveals an unexpected
touch of whimsy — two tightrope-walking
daredevils, accompanied by a drummer, crossing from hilltop to fort. Datable to the artist's
maturity, this attractive sketch recalls his variants on Mughal historical pictures (cat. 14–16).
SCW

39

Fort Walls and Garden

Attributed to Sheikh Taju
Mid eighteenth century
Drawing (*khaka*): watercolor, opaque watercolor
24.1 x 19.5 cm
Rao Madho Singh Trust Museum, Fort Kotah

Nostalgia and loneliness, rare in Rajput art, are notable in this little picture — an Indian early de Chirico — of a small, entirely uninhabited fort. Once again, Sheikh Taju — who could be dubbed the "Master of Levitation" — invites the viewer to soar with him and to share his poetic impression of fort walls, a formal garden, and a gracefully shaped moat or pond. Like many of his particularly rewarding pictures, this one was drawn and painted in a starkly economical, highly personal palette: modulated yellows, white, and black, accented by the sensuous greens, reds, and blues of flowers and leaves.

scw

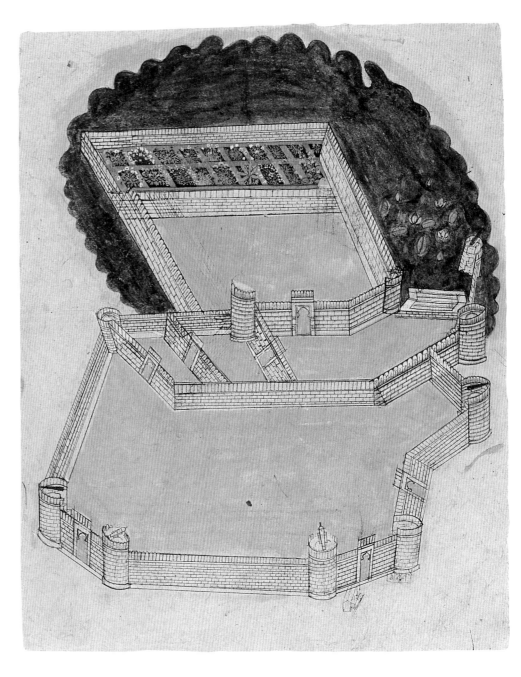

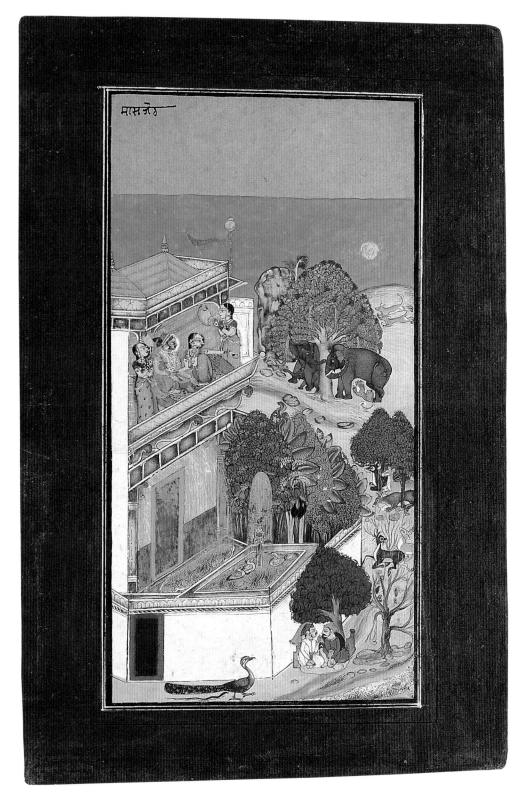

40

May/June (Jeth Masa)
Folio from a
Twelve Months (Barahmasa) Series

Attributed to the Kotah Master working with
Sheikh Taju
c. 1750—60
Opaque watercolor, gold
40.2 x 26.4 cm
Rao Madho Singh Trust Museum, Fort Kotah
Inscribed: "The month May/June (Jeth)."

41

August/September (Bhadon Masa)
Folio from a
Twelve Months (Barahmasa) Series

Attributed to the Kotah Master working with
Sheikh Taju
ca. 1750—60
Opaque watercolor, gold
40.1 x 26.1 cm
Rao Madho Singh Trust Museum, Fort Kotah
Inscribed: "The month August/September (Bhadon)."

Genre figures apparently sketched from villagers
enliven the foreground of *May/June (Jeth Masa)*,
which also contains delightful studies of deer
and elephants enjoying shade on a hot day. The
monsoon is about to bring refreshment to god,
mankind, animals, and parched vegetation in
August/September (Bhadon Masa), which also contains closely observed vignettes from life. Both
pictures were finely but freely carried out, apparently by two different hands, most likely
those of the Kotah Master and his younger
co-worker, Sheikh Taju. In such pictures, the
artists improvised vivid combinations of boldly
brushed reds, oranges, and yellows in palettes
reminiscent of Bonnard and Vuillard.

scw

The first of these paintings illustrates Keshav-das's *Kavipriya*, chapter 10, verse 26:

> The sun is so bright and scorching that the five elements — air, water, sky, earth, and fire — have become one, that is, hot as fire. The roads are deserted and the tanks are parched dry, seeing which the elephants do not go out. Even the cobra and lions sleep inside in this weather (and dare not go out because of the heat). Thus even the powerful creatures have become weak in this season and the whole world is at unrest. Poet Keshavdas says that the elders are of the opinion that one should not go out in this season (that is, should stay home with his beloved).[1]

The second painting illustrates chapter 10, verse 29, of the same work:

> The dark clouds have gathered all around and are thundering loudly. The rain is pouring in torrents. The cicadas are chirping continuously and a strong wind is blowing fiercely.
> Tigers and lions are roaring and herds of elephants are breaking trees. There is no longer any difference between day and night (because of the constantly clouded sky). One's own home is like nectar and outside is like poison. The poet is of the opinion that one should not leave his home during this month.[2]

JKB

1 After Dwivedi 1980, 131; see also Randhawa 1962, 136f.
2 Dwivedi 1980, 134; see also Randhawa 1962, 142.

Published (cat. 40): M. B. Singh 1985, pl. x.

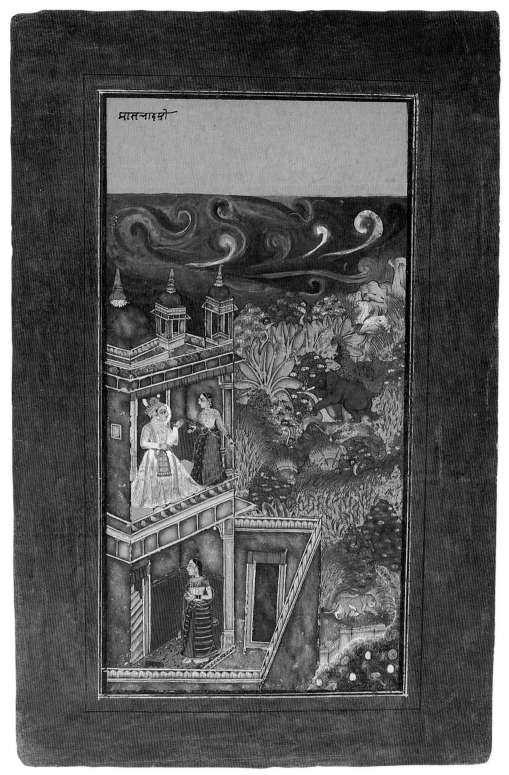

41

42

Brijnathji Mounting His Garuda

c. 1750–75
Opaque watercolor, gold, metallic gray watercolor
22 x 14.4 cm
Rao Madho Singh Trust Museum, Fort Kotah

While heavenly musicians serenade overhead, Brijnathji steps firmly but carefully on the polite and obliging birdlike sky-vehicle's extended left calf and climbs aboard. Not an "important" picture, this is one of many ingratiating stock subjects turned out in the Kotah studios. Because the Garuda is virtually totemic to Kotah and appears on Kotah banners, the design was invented, refined, and perfected by a succession of artists long before this version was painted. Every line, squiggle, zigzag, and dot had been learned so well by the artist that they could be performed in much the same way that eighteenth-century Cantonese children scrambled blue and white fairylands onto pottery. The results, even if carried out blindfolded, are satisfyingly spirited, because the artist clearly deeply respected their symbolic implications.
SCW

The image of Vishnu and Lakshmi aboard their mount Garuda, the sunbird, was first introduced by painters around 1630 in Bundi, where the couple can be seen in the murals of the Baddal Mahal.[1] A similarily mounted Garuda appears in the murals of Indargarh.[2] Maharao Bhim Singh introduced the Garuda, with neither Vishnu nor Lakshmi, as the state emblem of Kotah in 1719. The present picture, however, might well be identified with Lakshmi and Narayan, in accordance with present-day Dashahra celebrations in Kotah. According to these, Ravan is ceremoniously killed by Lakshmi and Narayan, who are carried in a howdah atop an elephant from their temple in the fort (*garh*) to the Ram Lila grounds outside the walls of the city.

The two Garuda standards of Kotah are specially worshiped during the Shastra Puja as part of the Dashahra celebrations. On the tenth and last day, they are involved in the consecration of the bow, arrows, and shield with which Ravan is to be killed the same evening. A modern painting of the Garuda is placed side by side with a modern painting of Shri Nathji on the occasion of the Puja at the Lakshmi-Narayan temple, before the idols are transferred to the howdah. Narayan holds the arrow with the sickle-shaped head that will decapitate Ravan, while a therio-anthropomorphic Garuda wields the bow and the shield. It is therefore not improbable that the riders of Garuda in this case are Lakshmi and Narayan.
JKB

1 Bautze 1986d , fig. 3.
2 Ibid., fig. 4.

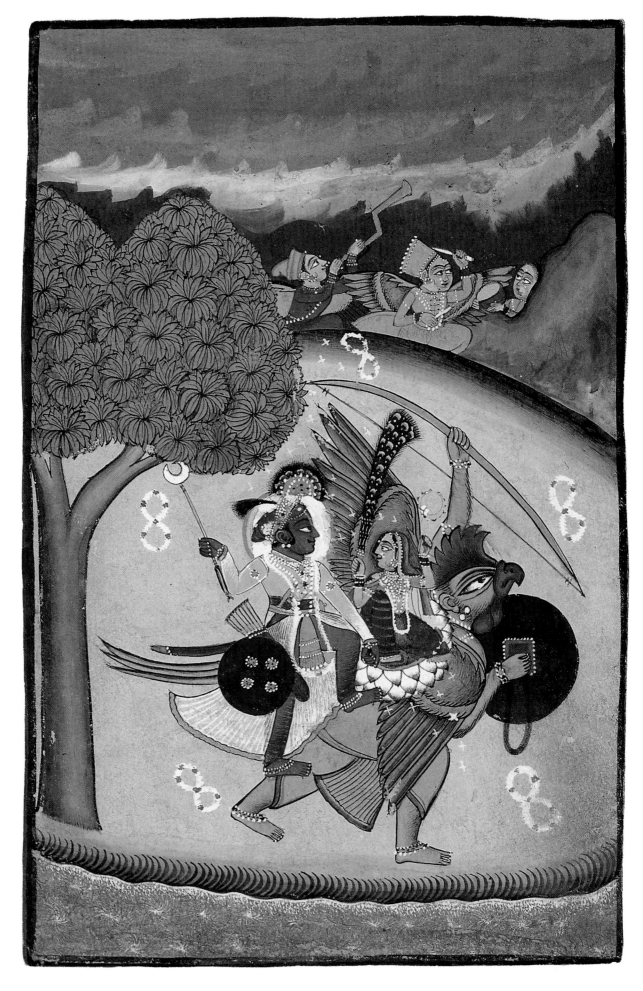

43

*Young Prince on Horseback near
a Shiva Shrine*

Workshop of Sheikh Taju
Mid to late eighteenth century
Opaque watercolor, gold, metallic gray watercolor
36.1 x 24.5 cm
H.H. Maharao Brijraj Singh of Kotah

The divine and the secular never quite meet in
this partly serious picture of a haloed young
prince before a shrine to Lord Shiva. Eight
ladies in court dress carry out their devotions
to the god beneath a large tree with snakelike
branches shaped like the sinuously jointless
arms of Shiva's ash-clad devotees in the distance. While the elegant prince stands patient-
ly, one of his musicians turns distractedly —
and comically — to fasten his gaze on a lady
worshiper who reveals somewhat more than
an ankle while reverently removing her sandals.
This courtly picture, as unexpected as a sacred
subject by François Boucher or Fragonard, can
be assigned to the workshop of Sheikh Taju.
SCW

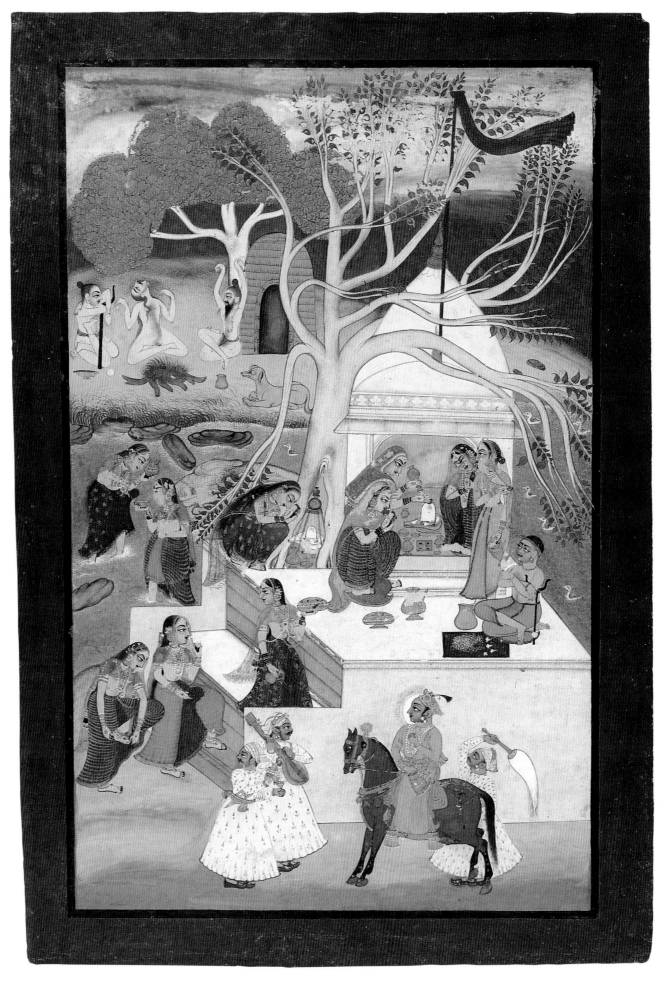

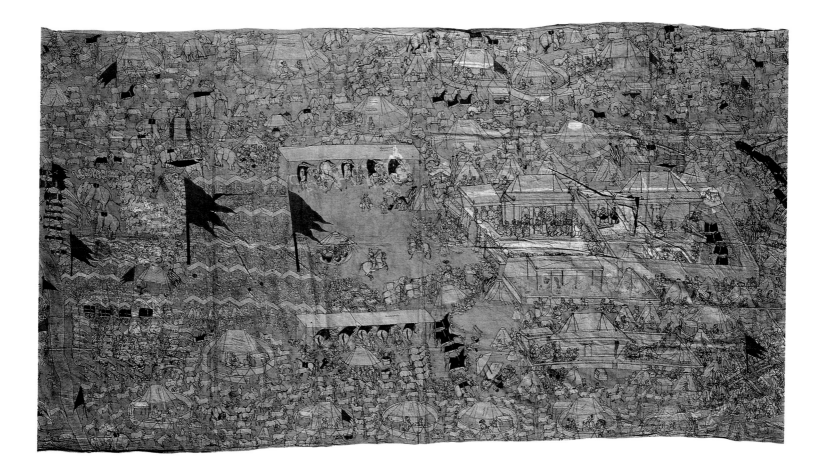

44

Camp of Maharao Shatru Sal I

Attributed to Sheikh Taju
1764
Black ink, watercolor
261 x 504 cm
H.H. Maharao Brijraj Singh of Kotah
Inscribed on recto (see below)

No other picture so vividly describes Rajput outdoor festivities. Glimpses of Maharao Shatru Sal I (r. 1758–64) and the prestigious statesman Zalim Singh Jhala are tiny jewels in this panorama of lesser beings and animals. The artist seems to have roamed, sketchpad in hand, for many hours, recording from life the elephants, camels, horses, mahouts, grooms, cooks, stewards, clean-up squads, and more. Anecdotal portraits so abound that this huge tinted drawing, probably created as an ephemera to adorn a tent wall, must have fascinated everyone represented in it.

Although a compilation of improvisations, this work was carefully planned. Its myriad activities are viewed as though from a hilltop or cliff, in a grand — if unscientific — per-spective, akin to those Sheikh Taju might have studied while apprenticed in the Mughal ateliers, where perspectives inspired by European prints of battlegrounds and the like, by such masters as Stefano della Bella and Jacques Callot, might have been available for study. Orange banners and ochre patches of ground provide major accents, as does the placing of tents, the net-work of vital black lines, and the multitudes of figures and animals, such as the elephant in the lower left-hand corner. All indicate Sheikh Taju's disciplined, artful planning. His free spirit emerges in an appealing afterthought, the Charlie Chaplinesque seated figure in the lower right margin, open-mouthed with awe at the nocturnal festivities.

Major and minor evidence supports an attribution to the third great talent in the devel-opment of Kotah painting. Although with the help of the Kotah Master, Sheikh Taju pro-gressed from the somewhat hesitant rigidity that lingered from his Mughal apprenticeship and continued to gain mastery through constant sketching, he always retained several "habits of hand" that enable us to recognize his work. Varied as were his artistic modes, all emanated from the same mind and touch, and certain formulas were constant. Found many times in this major work is the almost automatically rendered arrangement of outlines, dots, and dashes that read as the angles, brows, noses, and chins of beardless young faces.

scw

This painting yields a large number of inscrip-tions, often not neatly written. Following are translations of the more important ones.[1]

The large rectangular enclosure made of plain tent walls (*qanats*) in the center of the right half of the painting surrounds the two major tents, called "camp" (*deri* or *dero*) in each case. The left tent is called "camp of the 'carpet house'" (*darikhana*) — generally used as a royal part of the palace in which important functions take place — where the rao is surrounded by seated nobles as in a darbar. The larger tent to the right of this royal tent is the "tent for the royal attendants." The next important camp is just in front of the royal tents, in the lower part of the right half of the unfinished painting. It is the tent of Zalim Singh, inscribed as the "camp of the honorable uncle [Zalim Singh], the 'boss' (*sahib*)." The five royal horses, all but one of which have red covers on their backs, are fed below a large awning on which the inscription reads, "The royal [or 'first-class'] horses of His Highness." Similarly inscribed is the awning of the other group of five horses, all seen from the back, and also called "first-class horses." The awning of the drummers and trumpeters in the square, formed by the stables of the first-class horses and the enclosure of the royal tent, is inscribed as "the camp of the drumhouse."[2]

To the left of the camp of Zalim Singh are the military commander's six horses, which do not enjoy the luxury of an awning. A water-carrier (*bhishti*) pours water out of the container made of animal hide in order to water the horses in the center of this group. The inscription behind the water-carrier reads, "The first-class horses of the honorable uncle [Zalim Singh]."

The remaining inscriptions mostly give the names of the persons present, with some clues as to their origin or function. In general, they appear on the tents. Several of these inscriptions were either erased or painted over in white, and a few are written upside down. At the lower left, to the right of the river, is the camp of "the honorable Navab Namdar Khan," who is being offered drinks by an attendant. The next to the right is the camp of "the honorable Jagat Singh from Rajgarh," who is followed by "the honorable Fateh Singh from Jalwara," who keeps a small post with a red flag within his tent enclosure and two kettledrums in front of it. Two tents to the right of this is the camp of "the honorable Sawant Singh, son of Man Singh," followed by the camp of "the sister's son, the honorable Jagat Singh," who looks like a Rathor Rajput from Bikaner. The tent of "the honorable Bhuvani Singh" terminates the lower row of the important larger camps.

The nobles who pitched their tents in the top part of the painting include, from left to right: "the honorable Ghatya," with two pairs of kettledrums in front of his tent enclosure; "the honorable warrior, the respected Burjanand," who is shown seated with his son below a square awning in front of his tent; and "the honorable brother Zorawar Singh from Khatoli," whose small camp is just behind Burjanand's. To the right of Burjanand's large tent is the camp of "brother Sobhag Singh," a man from Ratlam, who has two striped streamers in front of his tent enclosure; next is the camp of "the honorable brother Megh Singh," with similar streamers in front of its enclosure.

Behind these two camps, "the honorable brother Samar Singh from Palaitha" has pitched his tent, to the right of which stands the camp of "the honorable Hardava Bhai Nath from Pipaldau," with a red flag within its enclosure. Further to the right stands the camp of "the honorable Chand Singh from Ramkot"; it has a square awning shielding two pairs of large kettledrums below. In front of Chand Singh's camp is the enclosed tent of "brother Girvar Singh," and to the right of Chand Singh's camp is the tent-enclosure of "the honorable landholder Thanur Khan," who is being offered a drink by his servant. At the extreme right of the painting is the camp of "the honorable Rajawat Surajmal from Bathali[?]."

The numerous simple tents without enclosure are mainly inhabited by servants, merchants, wrestlers, and the like. Often the tent is shown without its inhabitant, as in the case of "the honorable Son Singh from Ramkot," standing just in front of the camp of Girvar Singh. The tent of the paymaster (*bakshi*), Sukhram Dev, is right behind the camp of Pandit Lalaji.

The tent of the "provision store" (*tosha khana*) is right in front of the entrance to Zalim Singh's camp enclosure. The tent of the Hall of Private Audiences (Divan-i-Khass) stands near the entrance to the enclosure of the royal tent. The Tent of the Elephant Stables (Phil Khana)

is marked by two Garuda standards flanking it in the left half of the painting, behind the market area. The different markets, with their peculiar zigzag awnings between two large flagpoles with red standards, are all called "bazaars." The second from the top, for example, is labeled "grocery market." To the right of the elephant stables and behind the markets, people flock to "the camp of the grain-dealer Kaniram."

The carts (*garis*) are parked to the right of the royal servants' camp and are labeled "Vehicle House" (Gari Khana) accordingly. The inscriptions on the horses for the most part give the names of their owners and not, as might be thought, the names of the animals.
JKB

1 It must be remarked here that only the clans and localities coincide with the names of the participants at this gathering given by R. P. Shastri (R. P. Shastri 1971, 41). The names as such do not, and hence the possibility that the painting might portray a later historical event cannot be excluded. The enclosed tent of Pandit Lalaji, who was the agent (*vakil*) to Sindhia in 1776, stands in front of the enclosure of the tent of the royal servants.
2 The drumhouse or drumhouse-gate (*naqqar khane darvaza*) belongs to the earliest buildings of the Kotah palace and is still in use. The band, now reduced to one drummer and one oboe (*shahnai*) player, performs almost every day around noon.

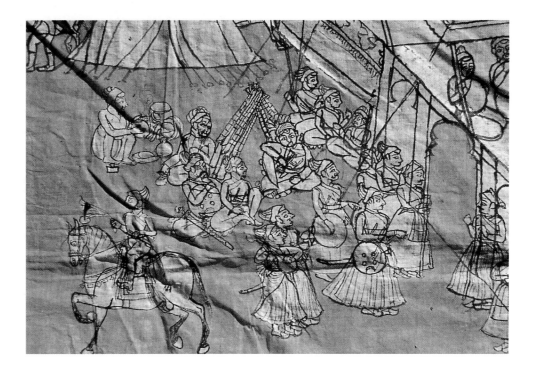

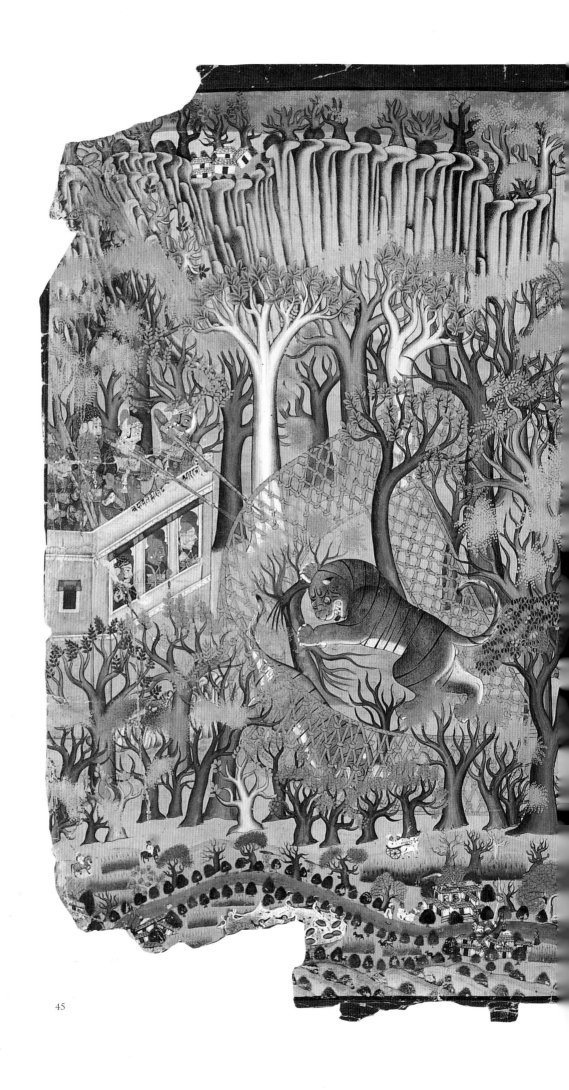

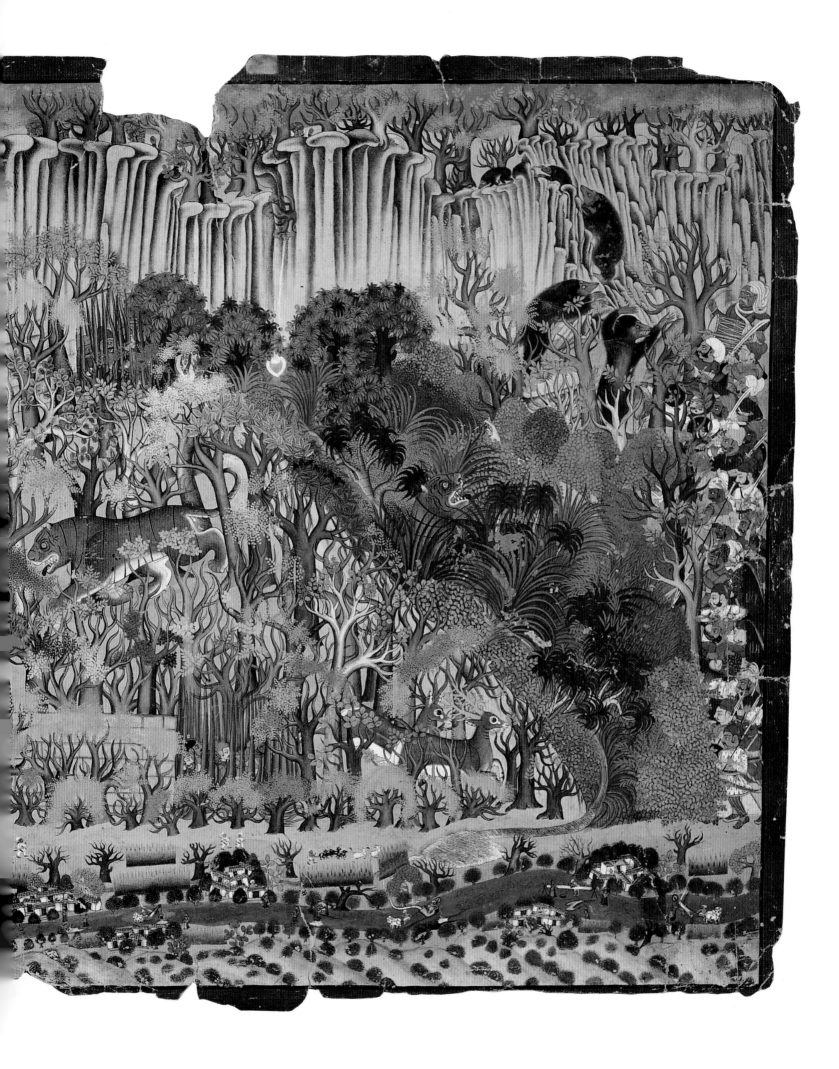

Maharao Umed Singh 1 and His Chief Minister, Zalim Singh Jhala, Tiger Shooting

Attributed to Sheikh Taju
c. 1770
Opaque watercolor, gold
57.8 x 84.6 cm
Rao Madho Singh Trust Museum, Fort Kotah
Inscribed on verso: "Honorable Ram! On Monday, the
11th day of the dark fortnight of [the month] April/
May (Vaishakha) in the year 1770 C.E. (V.S. 1827), at the
well of Dolya, Maharao Umed Singh [hunted] one
tiger ... [part of the text is missing here and recom-
mences:] ... at the Vakedar spring, in the Sundaram
grasslands of the forest terrain (ajada), at the camp,
estate (jagir) Dolo, near Raipur, hunting [at] Raipur
through the authority [or: through the arrangement]
of the honorable uncle of His Highness [Zalim
Singh Jhala], together with the honorable Khan Anvar
Khan, the honorable Yadu Singh, the honorable prince
Bhuvani, the honorable Barat Singh, Arjun Pota, the
honorable Joshi Devkaran, the honorable Pyardhan
Thakur Puran Singh, the paymaster (bakshi) of the ruler
(hakim), Akhairam. This is obtained from the hand of
the painter Seikh Taju, given by him."

An inscription on the verso of this painting
includes the names of further nobles and ends
with "from the hand of the painter S[h]eikh
Taju, given by him." He may perhaps have been
assisted by his followers in painting it.

This major Kotah hunting scene continues
an ancient tradition. Rajput rulers accepted as
one of their responsibilities the protection of
their people from beasts, and from this grew
the view of the royal hunter as the embodiment
of good, in opposition to his quarry as the embodiment of evil. Thus, when Maharao Umed
Singh 1 (r. 1771–1819) slew lions or tigers, he not
only was enjoying a sport but also was on the
side of the gods. Such scenes bring to mind
ancient prototypes: Assyrian and Achaemenid
hunting reliefs, scenes painted for the Turkmans, Safavids, and Mughals, and Hindu portrayals of gods vanquishing demons.

In the painting Bhoj Singh of Bundi Slays a Lion
(Welch essay, fig. 10), which I attribute to the
Kotah Master, Iranian and Deccani artistic
traditions converge to describe the heroism of
a Bundi ancestor of the Kotah rulers. The remarkable Brijnathji and Durjan Sal Sight a Pride of
Lions (cat. 29) appears to have been painted by
the same artist, with the assistance of Sheikh
Taju. These compositions document the evolution of hunting pictures at Kotah and prepared
the way for the later hunting pictures, of which
this is a prime example. Although its style is
deeply rooted in the earlier works, there are
several differences. Because Maharao Umed
Singh was an especially ardent hunter, eager to
document the precise location and circumstances of each drive and bag, he commissioned
his court artists to paint highly detailed descriptions such as this one. His chief minister
(divan) and fellow huntsman, Zalim Singh Jhala,
moreover, seems to have brought to Kotah
several young artists from the Mewar court.
These talented painters appear to have been
trained to paint far less lively animals than
those of the Kotah school; Sheikh Taju seems
to have been called upon to set up a finishing
school in zoological art. This picture, which
might have served as a demonstration, incorporates the richly patterned, almost tapestrylike
vegetation so admired in Mewar painting. The
all-important animals, which might have
strained the capacities of the Mewar protégés,
are rendered more sleekly but less naturalistically. Conveniently and credibly, their sizes are
diminished in relation to pictorial space, and
they are concealed in tangles of jungle grass and
hence harder to see. Many ornamentally appealing hunting pictures like this one were created
for Umed Singh.

SCW

"Uncle" (mamaji) was the usual designation of
Zalim Singh Jhala, whose sister was married to
Maharao Guman Singh. Zalim Singh was
hence a maternal uncle (mama or mamaji) to
Maharao Umed Singh 1.[1] "Kanwar Bhavani,"
possibly identical with the prince (kanwar)
Bhuvani of the inscription, is mentioned by
R. P. Shastri;[2] he was an officer. Devkaran Joshi,
probably identical with the "Joshi Devkaran"
of the inscription, also mentioned by Shastri,
assisted the agent (vakil)[3] and is said to have
been an important landlord (jagirdar).[4] Akhairam's position as paymaster (bakshi) is also confirmed by Shastri.[5]

JKB

1 R. P. Shastri 1971, 75.
2 Ibid., 108.
3 Ibid., 111.
4 See ibid., 119.
5 Ibid., 106 and 185.

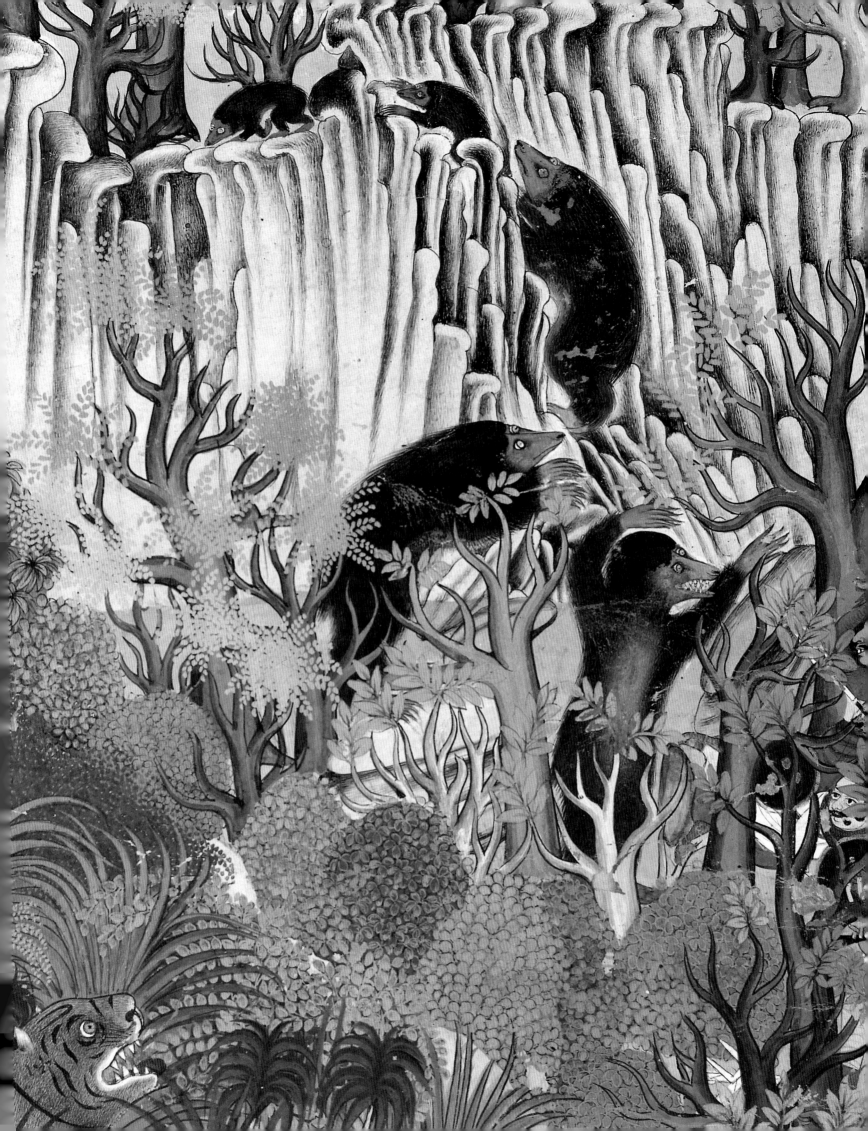

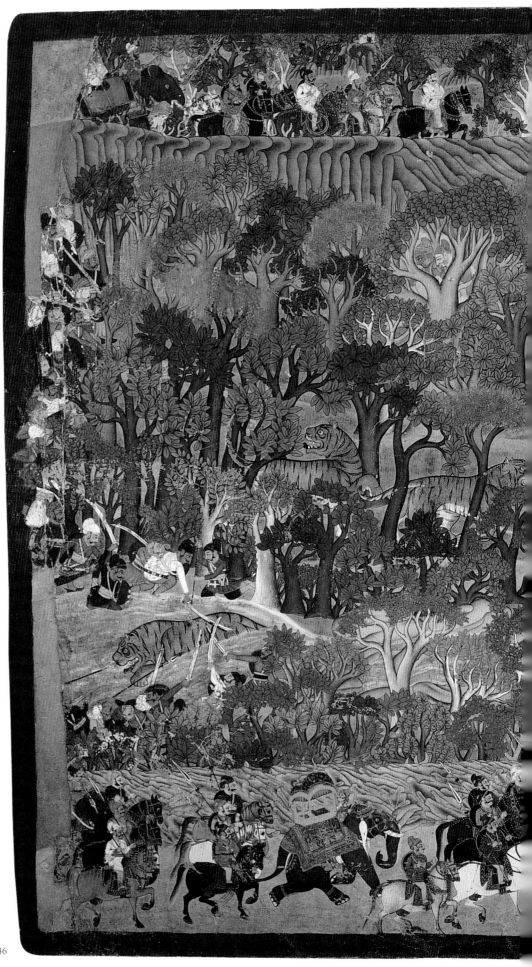

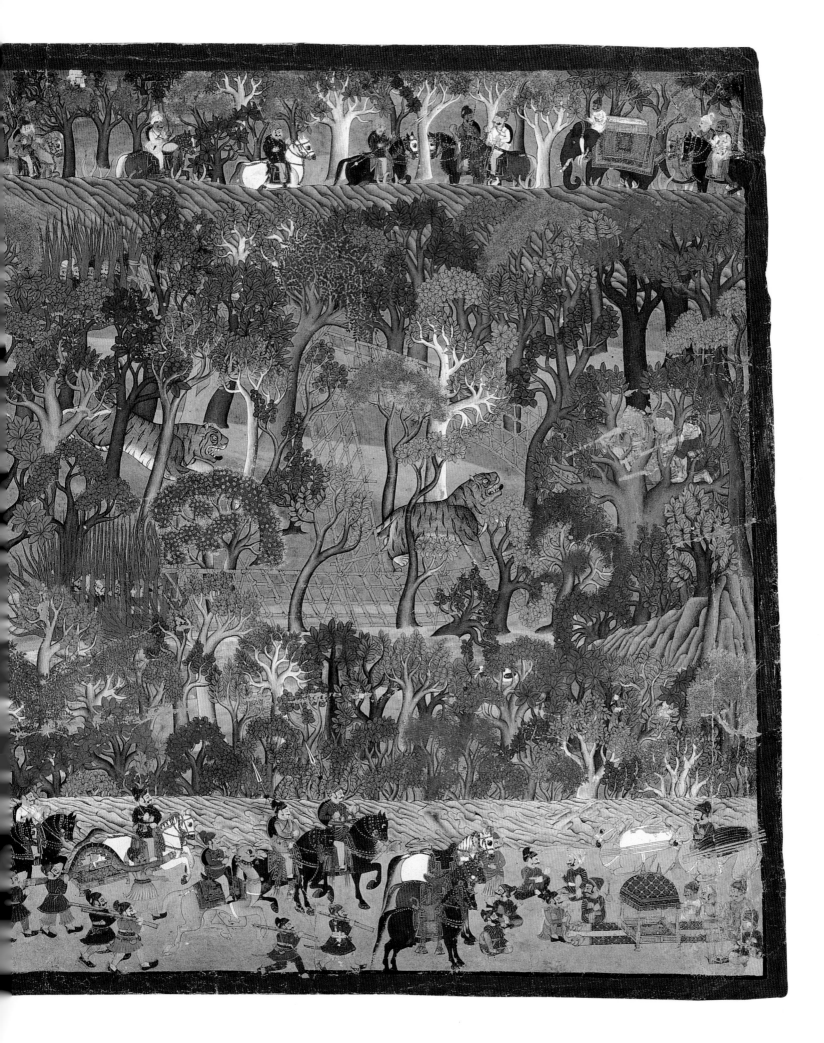

46

*Maharao Umed Singh I and His Chief
Minister (Divan), Zalim Singh Jhala,
Tiger Hunting*

Joshi Hansraj
1774
Opaque watercolor, gold
56.8 x 81.7 cm
Rao Madho Singh Trust Museum, Fort Kotah
Inscribed on verso: "Honorable Ram! On Sunday, the
11th of the dark fortnight of [the month] May/June
(Jyeshtha) in 1774 C.E. (V.S. 1831), at the forest terrain of
the Alnia, a pair [consisting] of one tiger and one
tigress was killed, 2."
Inscribed below, in a different hand and partly obliter-
ated: "On the third of the bright fortnight ... of 1779
C.E. (V.S. 1836), the honorable Maharao Umed Singh
and the honorable Raja Zalim Singh at the Alainya
River killed a tiger and a tigress ... tiger, tigress through
the ruler (*hakim*). Tigress: 1, tiger: 1."
Inscribed below, in a third hand: "Given by Joshi
Hansraj."

Most likely painted under the eye of Sheikh
Taju, this crowded hunting scene shows how
well the Mewar artist Joshi Hansraj had adapted
his style to Kotah by 1774. Eagerness for hard
work is also evident, in the parade of figures
and animals in the foreground, the quantity of
beaters in the game preserve, and the curious
spectators on the cliffs beyond the action. Close
inspection of the tigers, however, reveals that
Joshi Hansraj could not have been reared at
Kotah, where he would have been compelled
to sketch animals until he had mastered their
anatomies and psyches.
SCW

It must be noted that two different dates are
mentioned in the inscriptions here. The inscriptions appear to record the date of the hunt
or hunts, but not necessarily the date of the
painting.
    Alnia, mentioned in this and following in-
scriptions, is a hunting preserve well known to
H.H. Maharao Brijraj Singh.[1]
JKB

1 See M. B. Singh 1985, 24.

47

Floral Design for an Embroidery

c. 1775–1800
Charcoal, black ink, opaque watercolor
62.5 x 58.6 cm
Rao Madho Singh Trust Museum, Fort Kotah

An enthralling, too often neglected factor in
Indian painting is ornament. Whether this
splendidly rhythmic, sunny all-over pattern of
flowers was intended to guide embroiderers or
wall decorators matters little. The highly accomplished artist, whose religious or hunting
scenes might also be among those considered
here, showed thorough enjoyment in designing
and painting this liberated growth of vegetation. Most of the forms seem to have emerged
melodiously from mind and hand; but when
errors crept in, the artist followed the usual
practice of scumbling over them in white and
unself-consciously redrawing. Almost hidden
among the blossoms, leaves, and vines are delightful butterflies. This artist would have been
admired by the comparably gifted Ottomans,
whose brilliant patterns are best known from
Iznik ceramic painting, and by the wizardly
screen painters of Momoyama and Edo Japan.
SCW

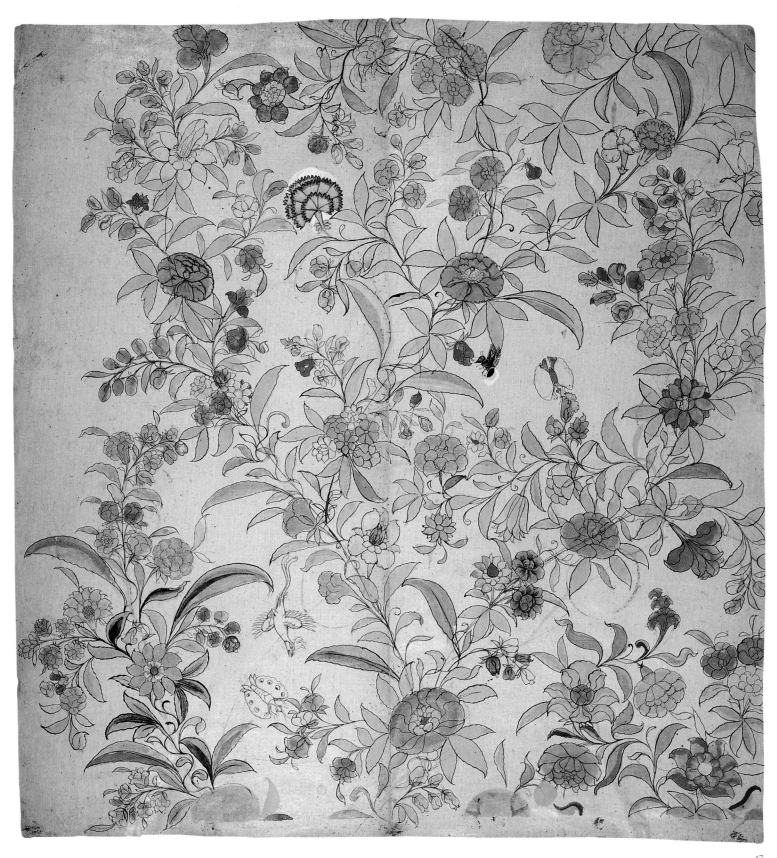

48

Maharao Umed Singh I and Nobles
Shooting Lions in Alnia

Joshi Hatuva
1784
Opaque watercolor, gold
55.4 x 67.7 cm
Rao Madho Singh Trust Museum, Fort Kotah
Inscribed on verso: "Honorable Ram! On the 13th of
the bright fortnight of [the month] March/April
(Chaitra), the year 1784 C.E. (V.S. 1841), in the forest
terrain of Alnia, three lions were killed."
Inscribed below, in a later hand: "From, and given by,
Joshi Hatuva."
Inserted between the first and second line, in a later
hand: "Honorable Maharao Umed Singh."

By 1784, Sheikh Taju's disciples had learned a
great deal about drawing and painting animals.
After several years of being painted at reduced
scale and camouflaged by vegetation, they increased in stature and visibility. The viewer
may sympathize with these powerful, graceful
lions — desperate at being trapped, shot at, and
slaughtered — and, at the same time, admire
the hunter's skill and the artist's success in
turning a scene of heroism and violence into a
dazzling, almost kaleidoscopic arabesque of
trees, men, and animals.
SCW

Published: M. B. Singh 1985, pl. 1.

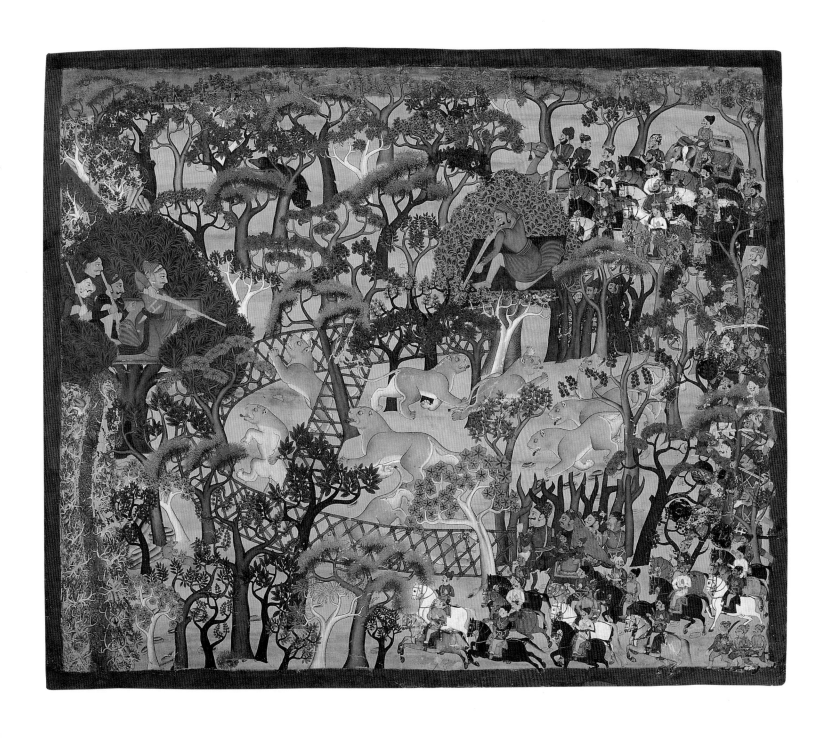

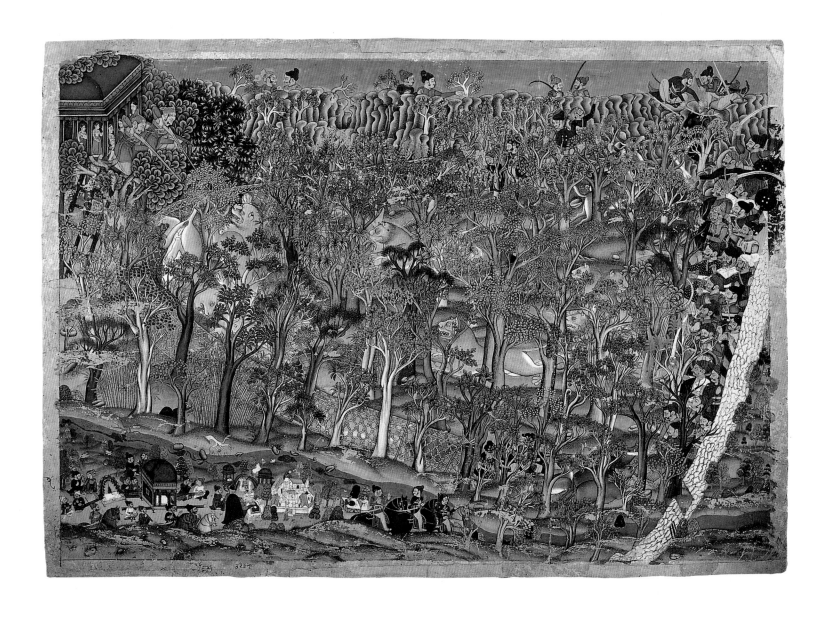

49

*Maharao Umed Singh 1 and Zalim Singh Jhala
with the Zenana Shooting Lions*

Chateri Gumani
1784
Opaque watercolor, gold
58.4 x 82.1 cm
Rao Madho Singh Trust Museum, Fort Kotah
Inscribed on verso: "Honorable Ram! On Wednesday,

the 1st of the dark fortnight of [the month] February/
March (Phalgun), the year 1784 C.E. (V.S. 1841), in the
forest terrain of Hamalajhamar, male and female strong
lions were killed, three (altogether), of which were
male: one; and female: two."
Inscribed below, in a different hand: "By the hand of
the painter Gumani and given by him."
Inscribed, again in a different hand, below the central
top part of the verso of the painting: "Shri! The honorable Maharao Umed Singh having come for hunting
with the honorable Zalim Singh Jhala in the hunting
(with) his harem."

Gumani's topsy-turvy lions attest to devoted
study from life, augmented by full use of the
paintings, drawings, and tracings stored for
reference in the ateliers. More than most Kotah
hunting pictures, this one carries the viewer
into the fray. With particular explicitness, it
documents the way beaters noisily drive the
animals into an enclosure and keep them there.
SCW

174

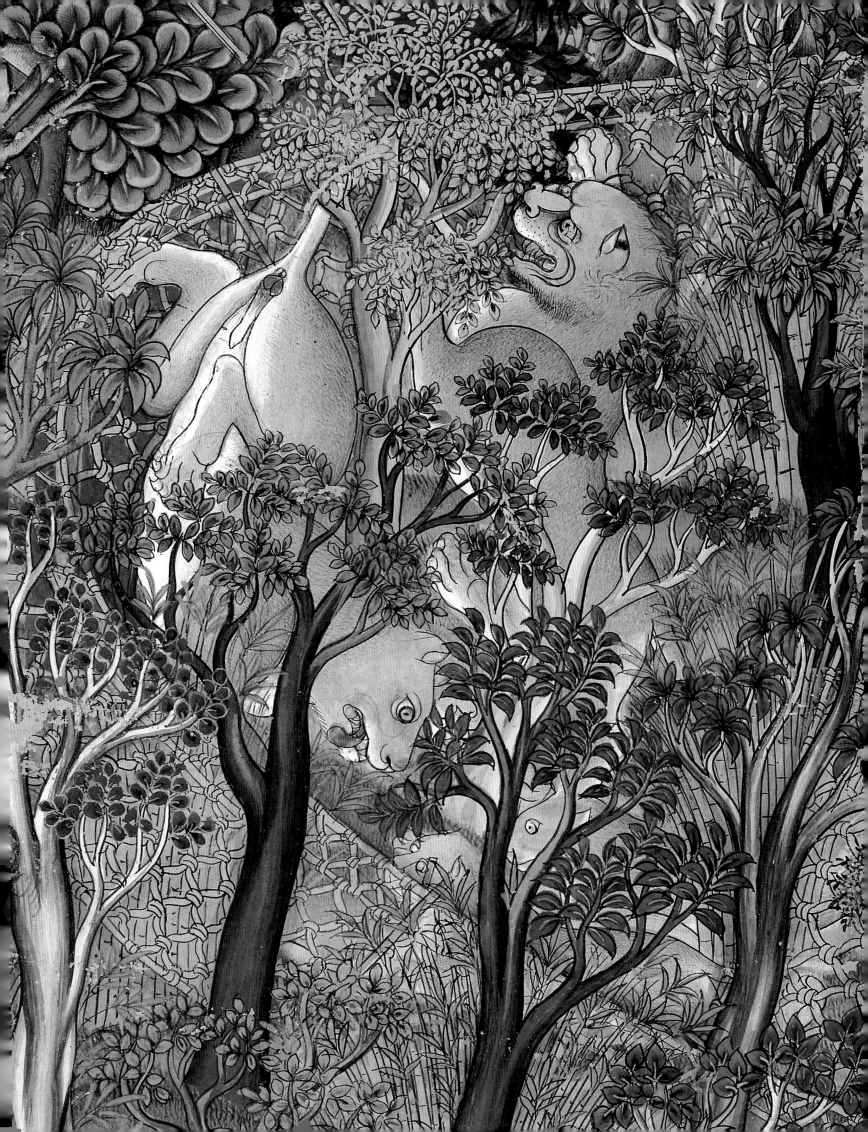

50

A Tiger Shoot in the Jungle at Raipur

Sita Ram, son of Pandu Garsi
1787
Opaque watercolor, gold
56.4 x 88.2 cm
Rao Madho Singh Trust Museum, Fort Kotah
Inscribed on verso: "Honorable Ram! On Thursday,
the 1st of the bright fortnight of [the month] Decem-
ber/January (Posh), the year 1786 C.E. (V.S. 1843), in
Raipur, in the forest terrain of the Kiradi Patel Rupa, a
strong tiger was killed."
Inscribed below, in a different hand: "By the hand of
Sitaram, son of Pandu Garsi, [and] given by him."
Inscribed beside the first inscription, in the same hand:
"Honorable Ram! On Tuesday, the 1st of the dark fort-
night of [the month] November/December (Agahan),
in Raipur, in the forest marsh of the Kiradi Patel Rupa,
a strong tiger was killed."

Kotah hunting scenes of the 1770s and 1780s
pleasingly bring to mind the rhythmic com-
plexities and spirited sounds of Indian music.
Coming upon this density of trees, tigers, and
hunters, relieved in the right foreground by a
schematically rendered hunting palace, is equivalent to entering a recital by Ali Akbar Khan or
Kishori Amonkar. Like many true works of art,
these pictures transcend their subjects. Man's
struggle against animals — order versus chaos?
— might seem to be the theme. But is it?
Maharao Umed Singh I (r. 1771–1819), who
deserves much of the credit for their creation,
must have been attuned to the purity of their
unique artistic vision, which transcended the
gory reality of killing animals.
SCW

It is noteworthy that, while the place name
remains identical, two different dates are given
side by side, and by the same scribe, on the back
of this painting.
JKB

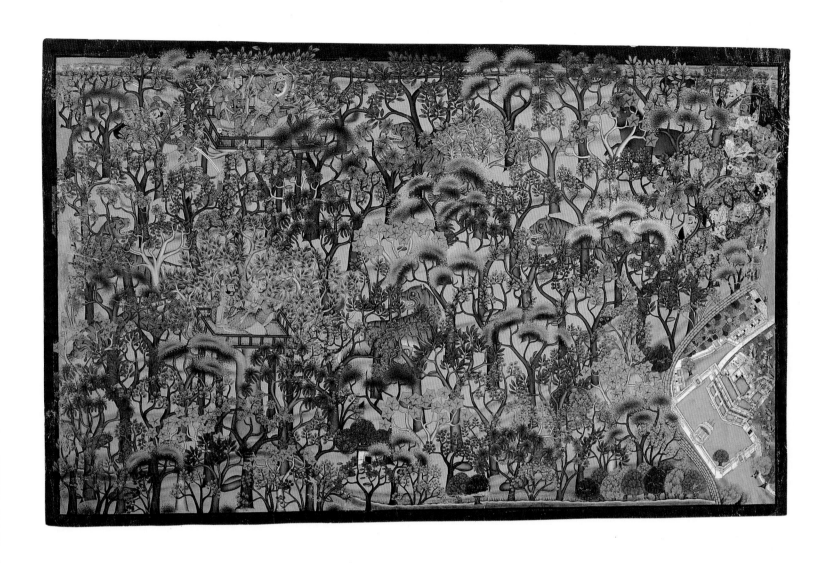

51

A Tigress Shoot in Open Landscape

1788
Opaque watercolor, gold, metallic gray watercolor
58.2 x 69.2 cm
Rao Madho Singh Trust Museum, Fort Kotah
Inscribed on verso: "On Friday, the 3rd of the bright
fortnight of [the month] February/March (Phalgun),
the year 1788 c.e. (v.s. 1845), in the forest terrain of the
Watchman[?] of His Highness, Sadaram Ravat, one
strong tigress was killed."

Tigers, deer, hunters, and beaters are all subservient to landscape in this very odd "hunting
picture," which may have been left unfinished
for this reason. If so, one is moved to differ
with the decision; for if the artist was a slouch
as an animalier, he ranked high as a composer
of exciting patterns based on Kotah's rocks and
rills, scrub, and the narrow stream across which
a tiger bounds directly at the water-buffalo-
hide shield of a foolishly brave huntsman.
Wiser heads, including a graybearded fogy at
the lower right, remain cautiously out of danger.
The patron's negative reaction to all this survives in ghostly form: his almost invisibly faint
likeness is a mere sketch not far from the leap-
ing tiger, at whose rump he fires point-blank.
It is probably safe to conjecture that landscape
artists were frustrated in a kingdom that doted
on pictures of people, animals, and gods.
scw

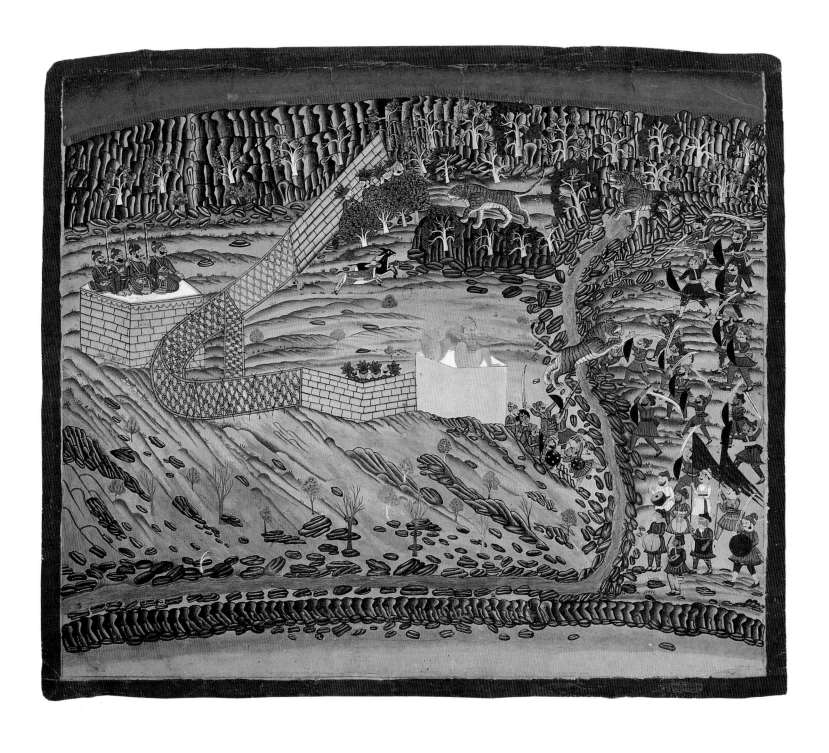

52

Tiger Approaching a Waterhole

c. 1790
Watercolor, opaque watercolor
27.1 x 49.8 cm
Rao Madho Singh Trust Museum, Fort Kotah

More thirsty than hungry, the tiger approaches
a waterhole, oblivious to three perturbed hares
sheltered behind rocks. Sharp of tooth and
bright of eye, the handsome feline brings to
mind earlier Kotah tigers and lions, some of
which had probably influenced its painter. This
picture is unusual in being presentably large in
scale, hence suitable for the maharao, and at
the same time thinly worked. It seems to have
been drawn by one of the artists brought from
Mewar, and apparently from comfortably
accessible works of art rather than from far
more challenging reality.
scw

Published: M. B. Singh 1985, pl. XII, and Bautze
1991–92, detail, fig. 20.

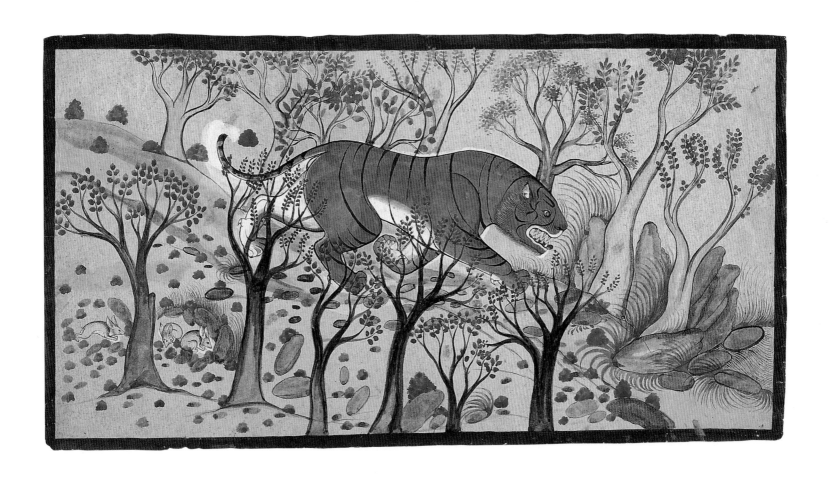

53

Shrimant Patelji Mahadji Sindhia
on Horseback out Hawking

c. 1800
Opaque watercolor, gold
36.1 x 51.4 cm
Rao Madho Singh Trust Museum, Fort Kotah
Inscribed on verso: "Shrimant Patal Mahaji Sidhya."

Every part of this picture, from the central portrait to the horse, birds, subsidiary figures, and landscape, was improvised on the basis of elements from existing repertoires. Such was the pattern of most art and music in traditional India, where artists, like musicians, were appreciated for their masterly techniques and talent for animating reinvention. It would be unfair to expect the artist of this equestrian portrait to breathe psychological profundity into the Maratha ruler's profile; the painter's enticing colors, the graceful gallop of the horse, and such pleasing details as the leaf-shaped pattern on its hoofs are sufficient to provide enjoyment. This appealing picture was once one among many thousands of portraits kept in the royal Kotah archive.

scw

Mahadji Sindhia became one of the most powerful Maratha leaders — as powerful as the Mughal emperor, who had come under his protection by 1784.[1] His numerous military campaigns were successfully led by the Savoyard Benoit de Boigne from Chambery, besides numerous other European soldiers of fortune.[2] For quite some time he operated from Gwalior, which is still the seat of the Sindhia family.

Mahadji Sindhia is not remembered with pleasure in Rajasthan,[3] where his tactics during the regency of Zalim Singh Jhala of Kotah are described by a Kotah historian:

> The usual strategy of the Maratha chiefs was to threaten destruction and devastation in case a certain amount was not immediately paid. This amount used to be fixed so high as to be not within the means of Zalim Singh to pay. When immediate payment was not made, the threat used to be put into practice and great havoc used to be wrought.[4]

Despite all the raids, threats, and fines levied by the Maratha chief, Zalim Singh's shrewd diplomacy somehow managed to appease the "Patelji," and Kotah was to some extent spared Maratha depredations.

The glove on the raised right hand of Mahadji Sindhia indicates that it was he who released the hawk that attacks its prey in the upper right corner of the painting. For this sport, which was favored by the Mughal emperors,[5] hawks of both long- and short-winged species were used. Mahadji Sindhia follows the hawk on the back of a trotting horse, since "it is necessary . . . that those following this sport should ride very hard, and the eye and mind being intent on the birds in the skies, renders the work of a hazardous nature."[6] A second hawk is kept in reserve by a falconer in the left foreground, whose dress is of a darker green than that of the other three assistants on foot — one of whom has already collected a bird previously slain.

jkb

1 Sarkar 1938, 287–91.
2 Young 1959, 74ff; Compton 1893, 26–80; and Keene 1907, 23–56.
3 For Mahadji Sindhia's devastations in Rajasthan and Malwa, see R. P. Andhare 1984, 101–24; K. S. Gupta 1971, index, under "Mahadji"; Parihar 1968, index, under "Mahadaji Sindhia"; R. P. Shastri 1971, 106 and 116.
4 R. P. Shastri 1971, 105f.
5 For a detailed description, see Abul Fazl 1977 ed., 1:304–7; and Jahangir 1978 ed., 1:164 and 2: index under "hawking."
6 M. Archer 1833, 1:78. For more detailed descriptions of early nineteenth-century hawking in India, see M. Archer 1833, 1:12f, 28, 76ff, and 80ff; and G. C. Mundy 1858, 10f, 33, 172, 195, 201, 204, and 241.

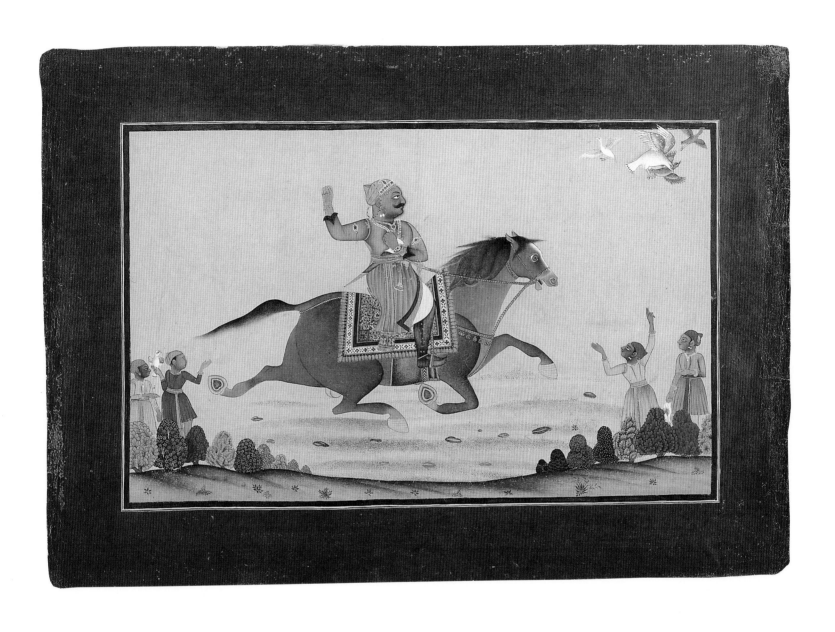

54

Worship of Shri Nathji

c. 1810
Opaque watercolor
36.1 x 26.1 cm
Rao Madho Singh Trust Museum, Fort Kotah

Crisp, peculiarly colorful, and suggestive of subtly modeled relief, this Vaishnava picture is akin only to a pair of others in the Kotah collection. Presumably, it is a royal Kotah version of its subject, commissioned by Maharao Umed Singh I (r. 1771–1819) or, more likely, his son, Kishor Singh (r. 1819–27). On stylistic grounds, it is clear that the artist was trained at Nathadvara, in Mewar, the center of the cult of Shri Nathji, whose image was brought to Mewar from Mathura to escape the religious intolerence of the Mughal Emperor Aurangzeb (r. 1658–1707). As Woodman Taylor points out in his essay in this catalogue, Kishor Singh was a devout Vaishnava, and probably it was he who brought not only the painting but also its artist from Nathadvara to Kotah, where, in collaboration, the two created royal Kotah variants of the Nathadvara idiom. This picture is admirable for its remarkably fine craftsmanship, strikingly innovative color, and unprecedented — almost Mondrianesque — elaboration of geometrical shapes. These, along with the draperies and figures, glow with an inner light.
SCW

The shiny black stone statue of Shri Nathji that today resides in the busy pilgrimage town of Nathadvara in Rajasthan is the preeminent image of the Vaishnava practice of the Vallabha Sampraday. Like all statues in the sect, the image is an anthropomorphic manifestation of Krishna, the sect's paramount deity. More than simply representing Krishna, Vallabha statues are believed to contain the deity's immanent presence and to possess (and emanate) his mystical powers. In order to partake of these powers, the worship of images is a regular feature of Vallabha religious practice, and pilgrimage to important temples, such as the Shri Nathji temple, is a cherished goal of all members of the sect.

Followers of the Vallabha Sampraday, or Pushtimargis, as they are often called, make a strong distinction between the terms *svarup*, meaning "essential form," and *murti*, meaning "statue," to differentiate their religious statues from those of other Hindu groups. *Murti* is used (somewhat pejoratively within the sect) to mark non-Vallabha statues that pass through a consecration rite such as the life-breath ceremony (*pran-pratishtha*) before being suitable for worship. During such ceremonies, the immanent presence of the deity is activated in the statue by Brahman priests who transfer their vital energies to it through the recitation of Sanskrit mantras. After performance of the life-breath ceremony, however, the deity may choose not to reside permanently in the statue. The deity is free to come and go as he or she pleases, and should the statue ever be damaged accidentally, it would no longer be suitable for worship. By contrast, the immanent presence of Lord Krishna eternally inheres in the material substance of a Vallabha *svarup*, which always remains divine. Hence, there are no periodic rites in which the deity is inveighed to retake residence in the image, and a divine image must be worshiped continuously, as represented in this painting, lest the deity suffer any deprivation.

Among their own statuary, Pushtimargis further distinguish between a limited group of images that enjoy the attribution of divine genesis (*nidhi-svarup*s), such as Shri Nathji, represented here, and an unnumbered group of man-made images (*pushti-svarup*s), such as Shri Brijnathji. Numerous popular texts recount the mystical origins of the divinely originated images. Vallabhacharya, the sect's founder, and his early disciples typically discovered the divine images, which miraculously appeared from the earth in full iconic form unblemished by a human sculptor's imperfections. For example, *Shri Nathji ki Prakatya Varta* (An Account of the Manifestation of Shri Nathji) narrates how Shri Nathji emerged partially from the earth on Mount Govardhan near Mathura before the birth of Vallabhacharya (c. 1479), but was misidentified and improperly worshiped by the local inhabitants of the land. Later, when Vallabhacharya was a young man, Shri Nathji summoned him to Mount Govardhan, where the guru revealed the true identity of the deity and instructed people about the image's proper worship.
NP

This painting offers viewers a sight of that moment during the morning Shringara viewing session (*darshan*) when, after having been properly dressed for celebrating the Thakurani Tij Festival, Shri Nathji is allowed by the presiding priest to inspect himself in a mirror. Thakurani Tij, which honors Krishna's consort Radha as "the Lord's Queen," was a festival initially celebrated by women from royal Rajput households and later incorporated into Vallabha Sampraday liturgy.[1] Held on Tij, the third day of the bright lunar fortnight in the month Savan, this morning audience finds Shri Nathji dressed in red and surrounded by a red cloth hanging (*pichhavai*) — specifications included in liturgical manuals from Kotah. The inclusion of two devotees with hands folded in a gesture of devotion (*pranam*) and a pair of temple musicians (*kirtaniya*s), one singing from an open book of religious poetry while strumming the drone (*tanpura*), with the other accompanying him on a double-headed drum (*mridangam*), supply other performative activities constitutive of a public viewing session within temples of the Vallabha Sampraday.[2]
WLT

1 Ambalal 1987, 27.
2 The inclusion of these additional actors outside the ritually restricted area directly in front of Shri Nathji, as well as the checkerboard pavement design, are reminiscent of manuscript and wall paintings commissioned for Maharao Kishor Singh during the early nineteenth century, particularly the illustrations for his manual for worshiping Shri Brijrajji (see K. Singh n.d.a). Possibly two artists worked on the painting, one from Nathadvara taking responsibility for correctly depicting Shri Nathji with attending priests from the Tilkayat family, while a local artist added actors normative in earlier Kotah paintings picturing Vallabha Sampraday liturgies.

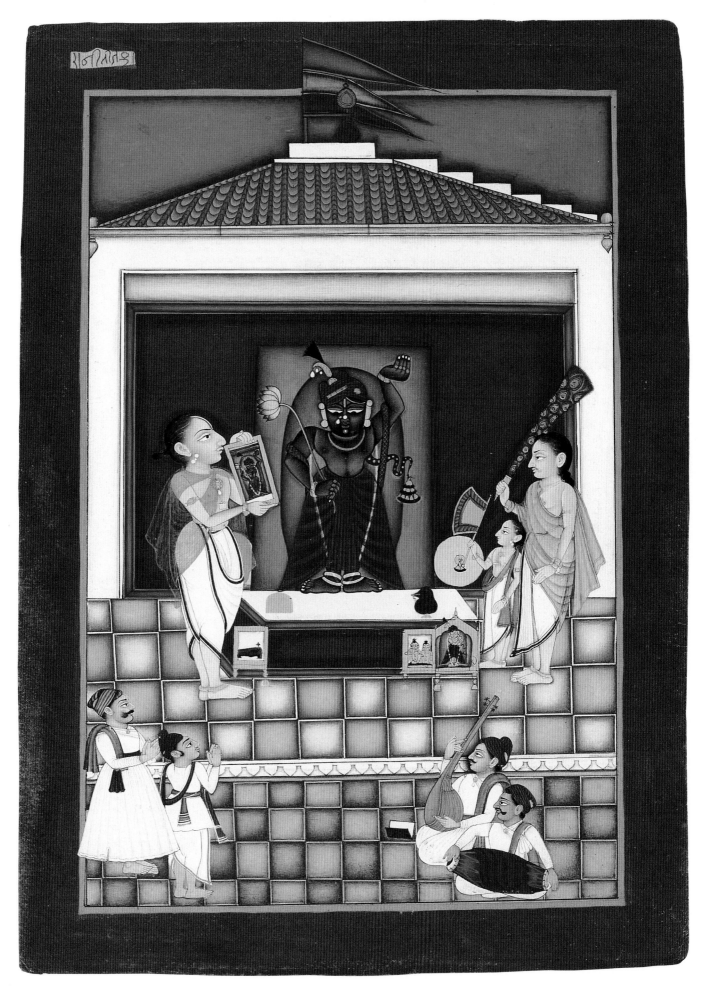

55

Shri Nathji and Navanitapriyaji during the Flower Swing Festival (Phuldol)

c. 1831
Opaque watercolor, gold
25.3 x 19.4 cm
Rao Madho Singh Trust Museum, Fort Kotah
Inscribed on top border: "[This] is Shri Nathji's swing festival." (WLT)

Spiritual aspiration, artistic sensibility, and profound royal devotion combined to create this serious small picture and the seven that follow. As Woodman Taylor has shown, many of them contain portraits of their patron, Maharao Kishor Singh (r. 1819–27), as worshiper. Probably the most inspired Vaishnava among nineteenth-century Kotah rulers, he must have brought at least one Nathadvara artist to Kotah and established him there. The gifted artist of the liturgical series represented here — perhaps helped by one or two assistants — was capable of delicate nuances and seems to have adjusted to the Kotah idiom. Although all of these pictures rank high in Kotah art, *Maharao Kishor Singh Bathing Govardhanji with Milk during the Festival of Awakening (Prabodhini)* (cat. 60) is especially moving in its overall luminosity, finesse of finish, and vibrantly jewel-like squares and rectangles. These recall the special qualities already apparent in catalogue number 55. On the basis of his excitingly original, masterly accomplishment, this artist may be ranked with Kotah's major artistic innovators. Seemingly, he was instrumental in bringing about another great flowering of art at Kotah, as can be seen in the mostly religious pictures commissioned by Maharao Kishor Singh and in the secular ones associated with Maharao Ram Singh (r. 1827–66). Although this artist's likenesses of Maharao Kishor Singh at worship reveals him to have been a remarkable portraitist, and his depictions of offerings are among Indian art's major still lifes, his purest achievement was his painterliness. Transcending subject matter, this capacity — evident in the colors, proportions, and surfaces of the spaces he painted — marks him as one of Rajasthan's most rewarding artists.
SCW

The flower swing festival is celebrated by Vallabha Sampraday members on the day after the spring festival of Holi. In this painting, we see elaborate arrangements and festive activities taking place at the pilgrimage center of Nathadvara, where the Tilkayat head priest Girdharji (1769–1807) throws red powder (*gulal*) on the image of Shri Nathji, while his son Dauji II (1797–1826), aided by assistants, applies it to Navanitapriyaji, who is seated in a "flower swing" placed within a specially constructed bower.[1] A group of temple musicians (*kirtaniyas*) energetically accompanies this spring frolic on drums, cymbals, and a large tambourine (*duff*) used specifically for spring songs.

An identical wall painting located in the inner room of Brijnathji's temple within the Kotah palace indicates that the painter or painters of this set of liturgical paintings, which mostly depicts Maharao Kishor Singh worshiping his personal deity, Brijrajji, also executed the wall-painting program within Brijnathji's temple. These artists' familiarity with liturgical practices at Nathadvara and their use of a style virtually indistinguishable from that of works painted there support the claim that artists from this religious center were brought to Kotah sometime after Kishor Singh's triumphant return from Nathadvara in 1821. Members of the Nathadvara artists' families were Brahmans, which made it permissible for them to enter and paint the ritually pure interior rooms of Brijnathji's temple.[2]
WLT

1 For a description of this very arrangement during the flower swing festival at Nathadvara, see Ambalal 1987, 34.
2 Amit Ambalal has pointed out that Nathadvara painters traditionally come from two Brahman subcastes (Ambalal 1987, 85).

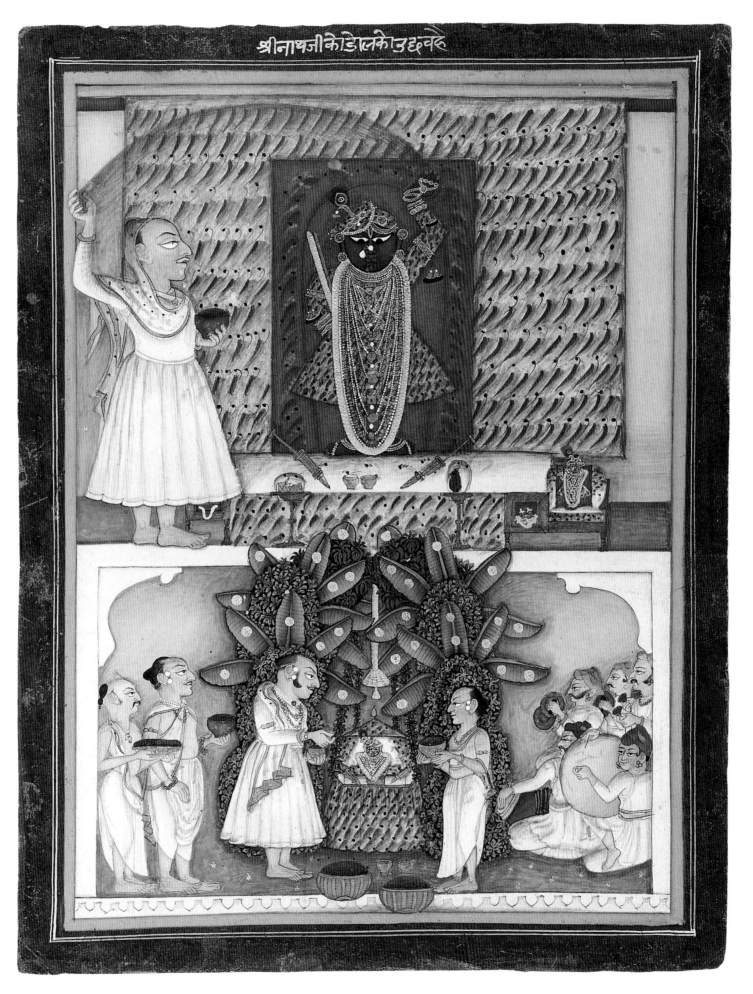

56

Maharao Kishor Singh Performing the Lamp-Waving (Arati) Ceremony of Brijrajji during the Holi Festival

c. 1831
Opaque watercolor, gold, metallic gray watercolor
25.2 x 20.2 cm
Rao Madho Singh Trust Museum, Fort Kotah
Inscribed on top margin: "Lamp-waving [ceremony] from Shri Brijrajji's Holi festival." (WLT)

Maharao Kishor Singh, one of the most devout and religiously knowledgeable of all Kotah rulers, performs the elaborate liturgy of Holi for his personal deity, Brijrajji.[1] Before the waving of the lamp (*arati*) — shown in the painting — Kishor Singh has played Holi with his deity by throwing bright red color at him, while also carefully creating a pattern of red stains on what started out as a white throne cover. Through his intensely personal, even playful participation in Brijrajji's life, Kishor Singh is aiming to experience the bliss (*ananda*) associated with intimately interacting with Lord Krishna. In poetry composed to be sung while viewing this scene, Kishor Singh describes how, while listening to sweet sounds of musical accompaniment, he made Brijrajji's face red by throwing powdered color on him.[2]

Brijrajji was the personal deity given to Kishor Singh when he was formally initiated into the Vallabha Sampraday religious community. His initiation, which is the subject of a wall painting in the Bada Mahal of Kotah palace, was from the community's head priest, Tilkayat Damodarji II (also known as Dauji II). This took place before 1804, the date of the illustrated manuscript detailing in text and image the precise seasonal liturgy for Brijrajji that was completed for the then crown prince, Kishor.[3] The small size, use of gold, and iconography of Brijrajji, with his left hand raised to play a flute and right hand extended, ready to hold edible offerings, exactly matches the image of Brijnathji, the titular deity of Kotah given to Maharao Bhim Singh I (1707–20) on his own initiation in 1719. This homology between Brijrajji and Brijnathji even extended to their respective names of Krishna, which both mean "ruler of Braj." Kishor Singh plays with this intentional ambiguity at the end of a text he

wrote ostensibly to describe the physical features of Brijnathji: after stating that Brijnathji and Brijrajji are visually indistinguishable, he praises Brijrajji rather than Brijnathji as ruler of Kotah![4] As Kishor Singh states in his text, the only way to distinguish between these two deities is by noticing how many milkmaids are seated beside them. Brijnathji is flanked by one female companion (*svamini*), whereas Brijrajji is always seated between two, as pictured in this painting.[5]

The precision with which liturgical arrangements have been meticulously recorded by the artists of this series, which includes more than thirty paintings, cues us to their intimate knowledge of Vallabha Sampraday liturgy. These artists would not only have witnessed the whole yearly cycle of festivals as Kishor Singh celebrated them for Brijrajji; they probably also belonged to hereditary artists' families that traditionally painted the elaborate liturgy enacted for their religious community's main deity, Shri Nathji, at Nathadvara.[6] A few paintings in the series, particularly those showing Shri Nathji in worship, are hard to distinguish stylistically from known Nathadvara paintings.[7] That Kotah artists from before and during the early period of Kishor Singh's reign did not depict these liturgical arrangements in such a hyperreal way also suggests that the artists were brought to Kotah from Nathadvara, possibly after 1821, when Kishor Singh spent three months of political asylum from British colonial forces as the guest of Dauji II, his spiritual mentor and head priest of the Vallabha Sampraday.

A painting from this series depicts Kishor Singh's nephew and successor, Maharao Ram Singh (r. 1827–66), waving a lamp in front of the Kotah tutelary deity of Brijnathji.[8] This is the last religious act captured in the set, signaling Ram Singh's desire to be seen as heir not only to his uncle's religious allegiances but also to the artistic traditions brought to Kotah by Kishor Singh.[9]

WLT

1 Previous scholarship on paintings from this set has consistently misidentified Maharao Kishor Singh as an unknown Brahman priest. For a genealogy of this mistaken identity, see Bautze 1987b.

2 Two compilations of Kishor Singh's devotional poetry separate poems to be sung for specific religious festivals (K. Singh n.d.c) from those that can be sung

any day (K. Singh n.d.d). The former includes two poems under the heading of the Holi Festival, both to be sung in the musical mode (*rag*) of Kafi (see K. Singh n.d.c, 11).

3 Here, I am referring to a manuscript written and illustrated for Kishor Singh when he was crown prince (*maharajkumvar*; see K. Singh n.d.a). Once part of the Sarasvati Bhandar Royal Libary, it is now incorporated into the collections of the Government Museum, Kota. For an artist's "mock-up" for this manuscript, see K. Singh n.d.b.

4 This visual similarity between the two images has confused many scholars, as has the variation "Brijrayji" on Brijrajji's name — which also translates as "ruler of Braj." Even though inscriptions above some paintings from this set use the designation "Brijrayji," reflecting an early usage of this variant name, in his writings Kishor Singh always refers to his deity as "Brijrajji." An additional interesting variation preserved in the inscription on this painting is the spelling of Brijrajji with an initial long "i," reflecting the way his name is pronounced in Kota rather than the orthographically correct spelling that normally would be transliterated as "Brajrajji." Many copies of Kishor Singh's *Shri Brajnathasya Svarupa Bhavana*, describing Brijnathji, were in the collections of the Sarasvati Bhandar Royal Library, indicating its use and circulation among members of the royal family. A deluxe clothbound copy even ended up in the Jhalawar State Library, reflecting the religious allegiance of the chief minister Zalim Singh Jhala's family to Kotah's titular deity. See K. Singh n.d.e.

5 Kishor Singh's text reads: *tahan koi prashan kare shri vrajnathji ki pas ek svaminiji biraji he aur shri vrajrajji ke pas to doi svaminiji viraje hen tate ek bhavan kaharahi* (Then if anyone asks [but] one companion is seated next to Shri Brijnathji while two are seated next to Shri Brijrajji tell them that the emotional affect is the same). See K. Singh n.d.e, 11–12.

6 Kalyan Krishna's interviews with contemporary Kotah painters revealed an earlier migration to Kotah by members of Nathadvara artists' families. This connection between Kotah and Nathadvara artists appears to have been initiated when Maharao Durjan Sal (r. 1723–56) recruited the painter Rajrup Hansraj from Nathadvara, as recalled by his twentieth-century descendant Omkarlal in Krishna and Talwar 1979, 74–75. The artistic traditions of these families is the focus of Lyons 1995.

7 Both Amit Ambalal and Milo Beach have pondered the extremely close artistic relationship between paintings from Kotah and Nathadvara of this period that depict Vallabha Sampraday liturgical performance. See Ambalal 1987, 154, and Beach 1992, 219–20.

8 This painting is in the collection of H.H. Maharao Brijraj Singh, Kota; see Bautze 1987, 256, pls. 5, 6.

9 1831 C.E. (V.S. 1888) should be considered an approximate completion date for the artistic project that produced this series. Whether any of these paintings of Kishor Singh or a number of related wall paintings in the Kotah palace were painted before Kishor Singh died is still an open question. Many of the greatest paintings depicting Kotah maharaos at worship were executed posthumously.

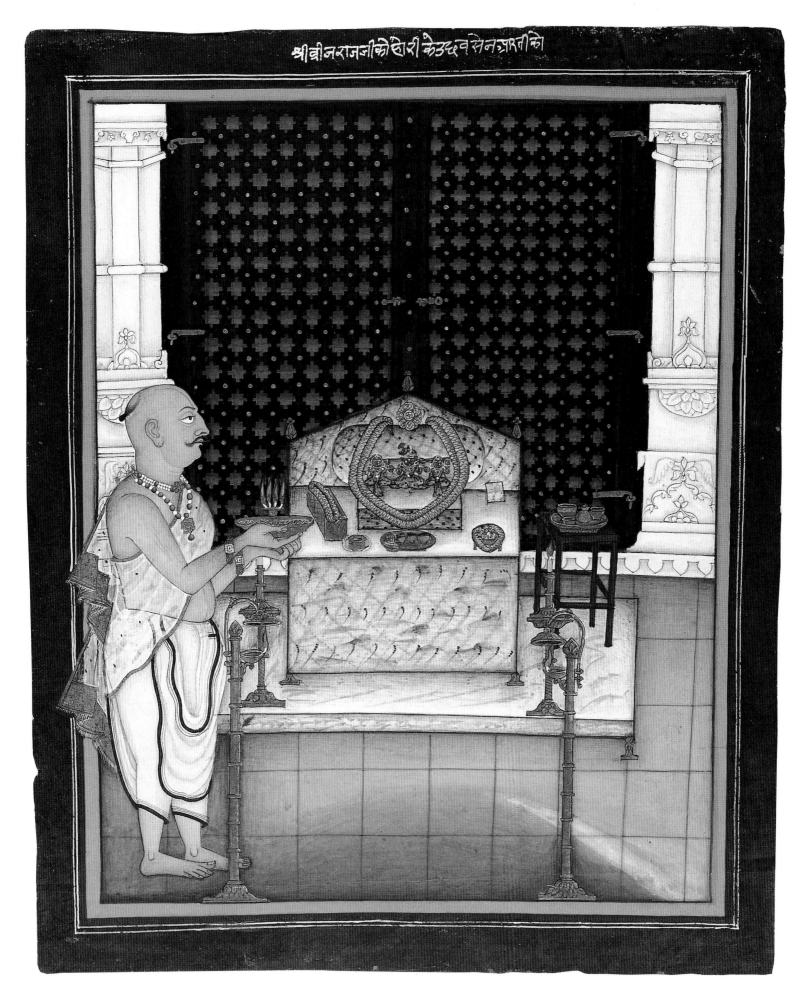

श्रीव्रजराजजीको ठारी कैउद्धवसेन आरती को

57

Maharao Kishor Singh Performing the Lamp-Waving (Arati) Ceremony of Brijrajji during the Festival for Religious Merit (Akshatritiya)

c. 1831
Opaque watercolor, gold, metallic gray watercolor
26.7 x 20.7 cm
Rao Madho Singh Trust Museum, Fort Kotah
Inscribed on top margin: "[This is] Brijrajji's Akhatij festival." (WLT)

Maharao Kishor Singh waves a lamp before a depiction of Brijrajji and his two flanking female consorts during liturgical celebrations of Akshatritiya (festival for religious merit), which secures the permanence of everything performed that day.[1] Kishor Singh's liturgical manual tells us that before this viewing session, he had already applied auspicious and sweet-smelling sandalwood paste to Brijrajji's body, as well as to himself as part of the forehead mark (*tilak*) visually signifying his membership in the Vallabha Sampraday religious community.[2] In poetry he composed to be sung during the viewing session pictured in the painting, Kishor Singh also refers to this special ritual use of sandalwood paste during Akshatritriya. In the musical mode of Rag, Sarang Kishor sings:

> He's been made handsome, that joy of Nanda,
> seductively dark Krishna with lotus petal eyes,
> smear him with sandalpaste!
>
> Make his whole body beautiful,
> in the middle place a bunch of saffron flowers.
>
> Kishor Das — Krishna, that destroyer of evil,
> brings happiness to the eyes.[3]

This festival occurs during the month that falls during April/May (Vaishaka), when the days become increasingly hot, particularly at Kotah, and the liberal use of sandalwood paste would have had the pleasing effect of cooling Shri Brijrajji. Kishor Singh's liturgical manual also specifies that hand-fans (*pankhi*) be placed, ready for use, among the objects assembled on Shri Brijrajji's lion-throne (*sinhasana*), which we see in the painting. The diaphanous white cloth of Kishor Singh's tunic (*angarkha*), which is also used for the cloth backdrop hanging and the lion-throne covering, is a textile specific to

Kotah, made in the village of Kaithun by traditional Muslim weavers whose families were brought from the Deccan by Maharao Bhim Singh. Cotton and silk threads are woven into a grid that allows air to ventilate freely, making saris from Kotah, ideal for summer wear, the envy of women throughout India. Kishor Singh here wears a turban tied in his favorite, easily distinguishable style.[4]

WLT

1 Apte 1986, 9. Robert Skelton reported that this therefore was also the day favored to settle spring harvest accounts; see Skelton 1973, 86.

2 These liturgical specifications are listed under the heading *vaishakh sudi 3, akshatritiotsav* in K. Singh n.d.b, 43–44.

3 K. Singh n.d.c, 12v. The heading for the poem reads: *atha vaishaka sudi 3, akshayatritiya chandan yatra,* which supplies the proper Sanskrit spelling for the festival day, as well as its more colloquial designation as the "sandalwood festival."

   As is the convention in all medieval north Indian vernacular poetry, the last line of Kishor Singh's poem begins with a pen name, known as the poet's "seal" (*chhap* or *bhanita*). Kishor Singh used the pen name Kishor Das, which preserved his own given name and is also a name for Krishna, while adding the ending name Das, designating him as a Vallabha Sampraday member dedicated to being a "servant of Krishna." This poetic signature also identified Kishor Singh as following the tradition of the great eight poets (*ashtachhap*), whose names all end with *das* and whose poetry was also composed to be sung during different viewing sessions at Vallabha Sampraday temples.

4 Numerous portraits of Maharao Kishor Singh within court contexts, some even with identifying inscriptions, depict him wearing his turban in this particular style. Previous studies of this series fixated on the "curve of the head," his tied tuft of hair, and such details as his arching eyebrows, yet failed to consider what Maharao Kishor Singh would look like without his turban. Certainly, Maharao Kishor Singh's distinctive nose is an element of his physiognomy that all Kotah artists knew and used in their depictions of him.

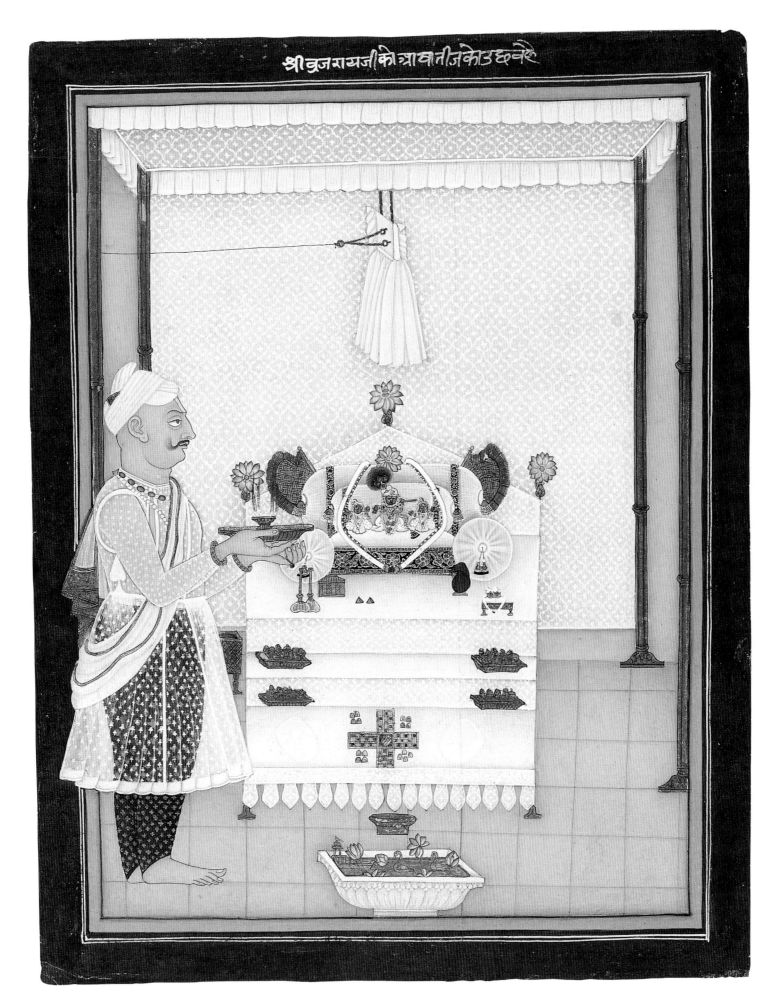

58

Maharao Kishor Singh Bathing Brijrajji during the Bathing Festival (Snan Yatra)

c. 1831
Opaque watercolor, gold, metallic gray watercolor
25.1 x 20.8 cm
Rao Madho Singh Trust Museum, Fort Kotah
Inscribed on top margin: "Picture of Shri Brijrajji's
Bathing Festival." (WLT)

The holy river Jamuna, which passes through
the area of north India known as Braj, where
Krishna lived, has a special place in the Vallabha
Sampraday, where it is revered as an anthropomorphic goddess. As a newborn infant, Krishna
was saved from the cruel king Kamsa by being
carried across the Jamuna from Mathura to
Brindavan, and it was in her waters and on her
banks that he later sported with his favorite
milkmaids.

In the Vallabha Sampraday liturgical calendar, Jamunaji has her own festival, which is
followed on the next day by Snan Yatra (the
bathing festival), during which personal and
public images of Krishna are bathed in water
from the Jamuna.[1] In this painting, we are given
a viewing of Kishor Singh bathing his personal
deity, Brijrajji, in a large gold basin. A young
priest assists him by holding a jug (lota) with
Jamuna water, ready to replenish waters in the
conch shell through which Kishor Singh
expertly directs a stream onto Brijrajji.

From Kishor Singh's liturgical manual, we
know that the Jamuna water had been specially
prepared in the morning by placing sandalwood, saffron, and basil leaves (tulsi) in it, after
which the water was ritually worshiped with its
own lamp-waving ceremony.[2] Brijrajji's bath
took place during the evening, when the necessary apparatus was arranged in the courtyard
outside his temple. The repeated refrain in
poetry Kishor Singh composed to be sung for
the occasion supplies the perfect accompaniment for viewing this scene:

> Bathe beloved cowherd Krishna,
> Mother! fill the conch with cool, pure
> Jamuna water ...
> Bathe beloved cowherd Krishna.[3]

WLT

1 These two consecutive festivals are held during the
   summer month May/June (Jyeshtha), on Sudi 10
   and 15, culminating with the bathing festival held on
   the full moon of this month.
2 K. Singh n.d.a, 49r.
3 To be sung in the mode of Vibhas (K. Singh n.d.c,
   14). The Braj Bhasa refrain is: karata snan gopal kanhaiya.
   In the second line, sitala jal jamuna ko nirmala bhari sankh
   nhavavat maiya, Kishor Singh takes the voice of
   Krishna calling out for his foster mother, Yashoda.

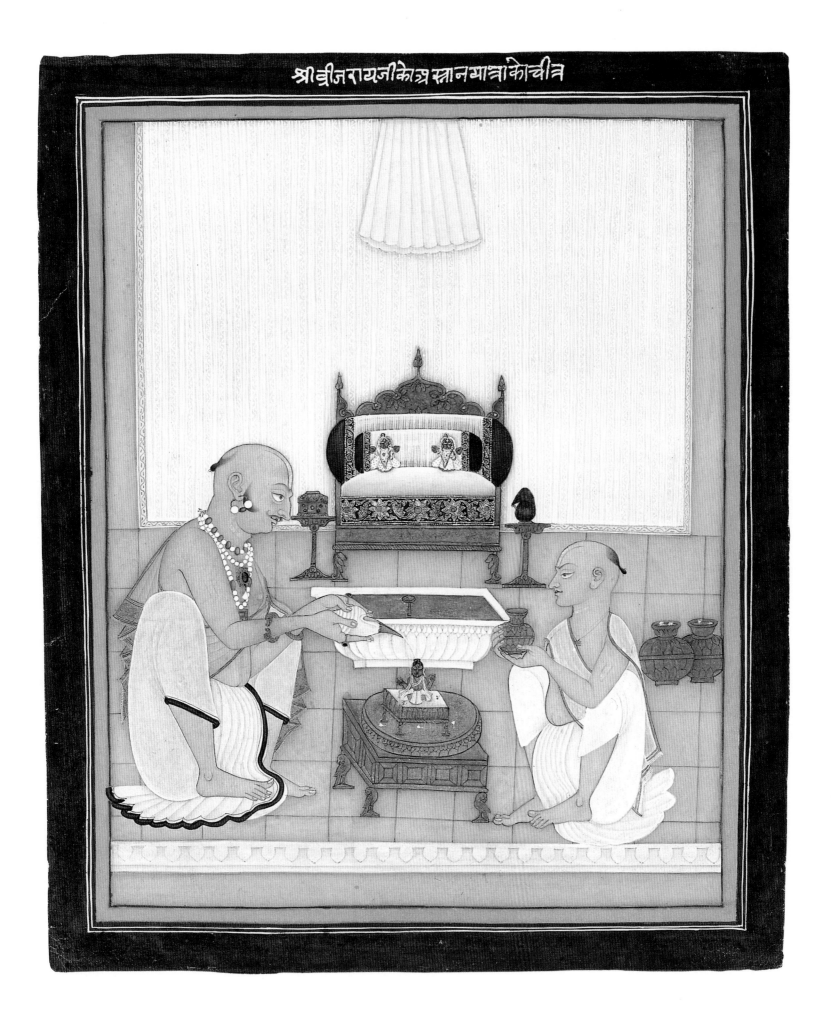

59

Maharao Kishor Singh Performing the Lamp-Waving (Arati) Ceremony of Brijrajji during the Festival of Water Sports (Jalakrida)

c. 1831
Opaque watercolor, gold, metallic gray watercolor
25.4 x 19.9 cm
Rao Madho Singh Trust Museum, Fort Kotah
Inscribed on top margin: "[This] is a painting of the water-sports (Jalakrida) [festival] on the 2nd of the bright fortnight of [the month] May/June (Jyeshtha)." (WLT)

During the intensely hot month of May/June (Jyeshtha), before the monsoon rains arrive, Vallabha Sampraday deities are often treated to cooling, playful water sports (*jalakrida*). Here, Maharao Kishor Singh has created an ideal water-sporting spot for Brijrajji, covering the floor with a shallow pool of water stocked with boats, lotuses, and toy ducks.[1] Brijrajji, who is scantily dressed, ready to jump right in, seems to be preparing for his sports by attracting milkmaids with sounds from the flute (*murali*) Kishor Singh has placed in his raised left hand.

The grandest water sports are normally played on the 10th of the bright half of this month, known as Yamuna Dashami or Yamun-aji ki Utsav (Jamuna's festival). According to the inscription above the painting, the water sports in this painting took place on the 2nd, little more than a week before the grander Jamuna festival.[2] Another painting showing a similar water-sports arrangement held on the 3rd for the major deity Mathureshji, who resides in the business district of Kotah, confirms that water sports are enjoyed by Vallabha Sampraday deities on many hot summer days.[3]

WLT

1 For a description of this festival as celebrated at Nathadvara, see Ambalal 1987, 43.
2 Jyeshtha Sudi 2 is not singled out for special treatment in either Kishor Singh's liturgical manual (K. Singh n.d.a) or his collection of festival verses (K. Singh n.d.c).
3 This painting from the Mittal Collection is published in Desai 1985, 120.

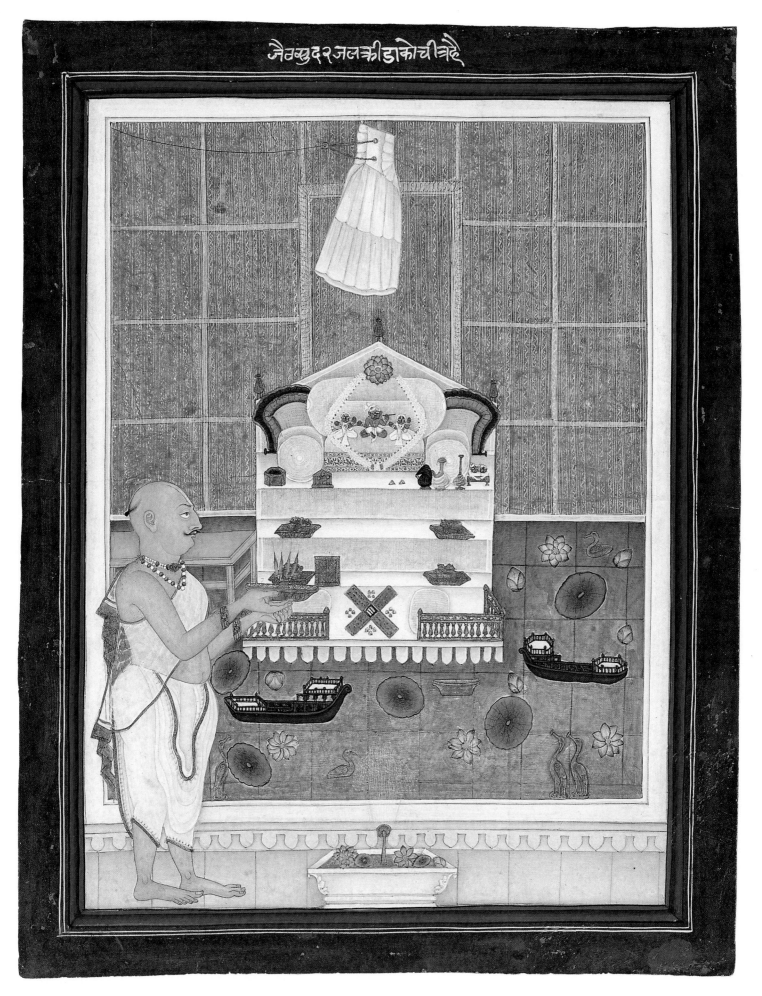

Maharao Kishor Singh Bathing Govardhanji with Milk during the Festival of Awakening (Prabodhini)

c. 1831
Opaque watercolor, gold, metallic gray watercolor
25.6 x 20.2 cm
Rao Madho Singh Trust Museum, Fort Kotah
Inscribed on top margin: "This is Shri [Brijrajji's] Awakening (Prabodhini) festival on the 11th of the bright fortnight of [the month] October/November [Karttik]." (WLT)

After four months of slumber, Vishnu is awakened in the Prabodhini Festival with the sounding of Sanskrit mantras followed by a bath in "five nectars" (*panch amrit*).[1] In the viewing scene depicted here, Kishor Singh begins the performed bathing sequence, pouring milk supplied by his assistant through a conch shell onto Vishnu in the form of a rock from Mount Govardhan, honorifically referred to as Shri Govardhanji.[2] Behind Kishor Singh's assistant, vessels containing the remaining sequence of bathing "nectars" — yogurt, clarified butter, honey, and sugar — are ready for use.

The grander arrangement created for the festival is the elaborate pavilion (*mandapa*) constructed for Brijrajji, from which he and his two consorts view Vishnu's bath. Within the courtyard adjoining Brijrajji's temple, an intricate design in white flour and colored powders was created on the floor. Above the central medallion of this floor decoration, a tentlike pavilion was then skillfully constructed, using four clumps of sugarcane stalks with their tops tied together. Sets of five oil lamps (*dipak*) mark the four corners of the floor decoration. As Kishor Singh mentions in his liturgical manual, with these arrangements complete, Brijrajji would have been brought out on his lion-throne and placed within this temporary festival pavilion.[3]

In poetry composed to be sung during a ritual viewing of this scene, Kishor Singh opens with the refrain "Today is Prabodhini, when god is awakened, which Vaishnavas observe." After lyrics describing arrangements for the pavilion in the courtyard and liturgical activities, from placing Brijrajji within the pavilion to reading an awakening mantra three times, he

ends with a reference to his own singing: "Sing auspicious songs to god Narayan [Vishnu], Kishor Das's lord."[4]

WLT

1   The Prabodhini Festival takes place during the month spanning October/November (Karttik), on the 11th day of its bright half. The word *prabodhini*, which means "awakening," is misspelled *pramodini* in the inscription above the painting. Another painting from this set, now in the San Diego Museum of Art, Binney Collection, depicting the same festival being liturgically celebrated at Nathadvara, is also inscribed *pramodini*. In contrast to the inscriber of these Kotah paintings, within his liturgical manuals and compilations of poetry Kishor Singh consistently spells the word correctly.

2   At times also called Shri Govardhanshila, or "rock from Govardhan."

3   K. Singh n.d.b, 25. A similar account of this visual display and the sequence of liturgical actions that constitute the Prabodhini Festival, including the specified three repetitions of a supplied Sanskrit mantra text, is found in another manuscript in the royal collections known as the *Utsavan ki Pranalika* (Tradition of Festivals) (Kota, Rajasthan Prachyavidya Pratishthan, MS 3206). This is additional evidence of the liturgical celebration of Prabodhini in Vallabha Sampraday temples located throughout the Kotah royal palace.

4   K. Singh n.d.c, 9

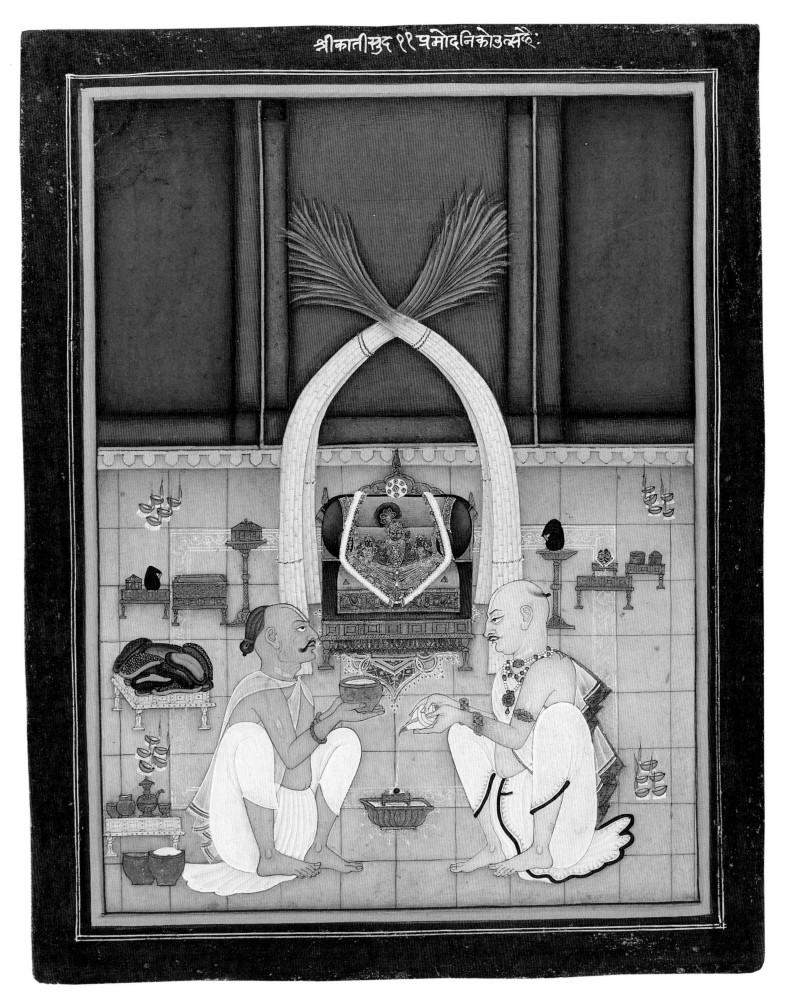

61

Maharao Kishor Singh Performing the Lamp-Waving (Arati) Ceremony during Brijrajji's Throne (Pat) Festival

c. 1831
Opaque watercolor, gold, metallic gray watercolor
25.1 x 20.5 cm
Rao Madho Singh Trust Museum, Fort Kotah
Inscribed on top margin: "Shri Brijrajji's Installation (Pat) Festival on the 5th of the bright fortnight of [the month] April/May (Vaishakha)." (WLT)

Although liturgical calendars for Vallabha Sampraday temples mark the same major festivals, one festival added to each cycle is specific to the local deity on view. Called the Pat (Throne) Festival, this celebration marks the day when the local divine image (svarup) first "took a seat" on his "throne."[1] For Brijrajji, the "5th day in the 'bright' half of April/May" marks the anniversary when Maharao Kishor Singh initially brought him to be "seated" with his two consorts on the lion-throne located in the temple especially built for him within the Kamvarpad apartments of the royal palace.

Kishor Singh's liturgical manual for Brijrajji, as well as poetry he composed to be sung on the occasion, both mention the saffron garments he dressed Brijrajji in.[2] A second painting from the set inscribed as also depicting Brijrajji's Pat Festival includes the specified auspicious color saffron for the throne cover, pillows, and cloth backdrop hanging. The second depiction of the festival is of the morning tableau-viewing session, when, after Kishor Singh has played with him by throwing red powder, Brijrajji is shown his reflection in a mirror held by Kishor Singh.[3] This painting probably depicts a later viewing session during the same festival day, after the red-stained throne cover and backdrop hanging have been replaced by clean white ones.[4] For this later viewing session, when we see Kishor Singh performing the auspicious waving of a lamp in front of Brijrajji, the visual display conforms to others designed for the hot season, in which two hand-fans are ready for use and a water basin with pink lotuses and toy ducks offers the possibility of cooling off by playing miniature water sports. In both paintings, Kishor Singh wears the same color-coordinated saffron upper cloth appropriate for this auspicious occasion.[5]

The two poems that Maharao Kishor Singh wrote to be sung in the musical mode of Vilaval during viewing sessions on this day include references to the performed sequences of the liturgy for Brijrajji's Pat Festival, from smearing him with oil and washing him in the morning to the festive distribution of money after the viewing session.[6] Specifications for creating Brijrajji's visual display included in Kishor Singh's poems even incorporate sets of words taken directly from his own liturgical manual, including, "fasten a lion-throne cover, throne pillows and a cloth backdrop, all of saffron."[7] This close intertextuality between Kishor Singh's poetry and his liturgical manual exemplifies the resonant poetics of Vallabha Sampraday visual display, in which the lyrics heard during viewing-session displays are closely cued to the activities and scenes devotees see and participate in. Kishor Singh ends both his poems for the occasion with references to the viewing session made possible by Brijrajji's presence in Kotah. In the last line of his first poem, he even includes the exclamation of praise, "jai," sounded by devotees as a response to viewing Brijrajji during viewing sessions, making this an appropriate sung response to viewing the session pictured in the painting: "Praise to [Jai!] Kishor Das's treasure of devotion, / whose viewing is experienced every day".[8]

WLT

1 Here, I translate the word viraje, which is always used in conjunction with describing the movement of sacred images, as "taking a seat." The word has an additional meaning of "ruling," which is particularly appropriate for both of the royal divine images, Brijnathji and Brijrajji, who were considered the living rulers of Kotah and were addressed with the title of Maharaja. I owe my understanding of the significance of throne festivals to Thakur Jaswant Singh.

2 For these liturgical specifications, see K. Singh n.d.a, 45. The two poems Maharao Kishor Singh wrote to be sung during viewing sessions on this day both include performed sequences of the liturgy, particularly the specifications for the visual display to be created, in which he even incorporated sets of words taken directly from his own liturgical manual (see K. Singh n.d.c, 13–14).

3 This second painting for Brijrajji's Pat Festival is in the private collection of H.H. Maharao Brijraj Singh of Kotah.

4 In his liturgical manual, Kishor Singh twice refers to "removing the saffron," which could refer to this change of cloth coverings during the progression of festival celebrations (K. Singh n.d.a, 45).

5 Kishor Singh's saffron cloth is the single visual clue the painter of this set has included to link these two paintings to the same festival day.

6 The entry for Shri brajrajji ko patotsav in Kishor Singh's liturgical manual and the first of his poems both begin with abhyang, specifying Brijrajji's early-morning anointment with oil. The last line of Kishor Singh's second poem ends with "Bring the nyochavar!" referring directly to the precise type of festive distribution of money first waved in circles around Brijrajji that is specified in his manual entry to take place directly after one of the performances of the waving of the lamp during the morning viewing session. See K. Singh n.d.a, 45, and K. Singh n.d.c, 13–14.

7 This appears as the initial line of the second couplet from Kishor Singh's first poem: singhasan vastra gadi takiya pichhavai kesariyan bandhavai (K. Singh n.d.c., 13), which incorporates all the words and specifications from the third line of his manual: pichhavai sinhasan vastra kesari gadi takiya kesari (K. Singh n.d.a, 45). The following line in the manual, sajya ko saj su[p]et upali chadari kesari (K. Singh n.d.a, 45), is also closely paraphrased in the second line of Kishor Singh's couplet as sijya saj taiso hi upali chadar taisi utavai (K. Singh n.d.c, 13).

8 Kishor Das kon bhakti nidhi jai jon nitaprati darasan pavai (K. Singh n.d.c, 13).

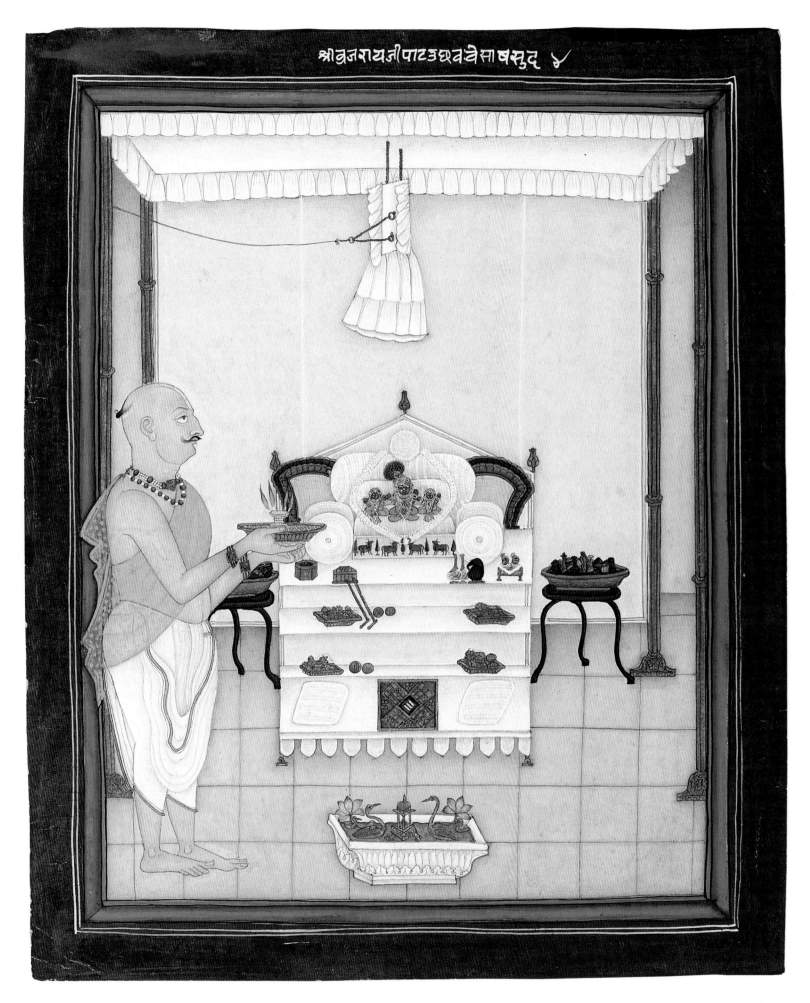

62

Maharao Kishor Singh Performing the Lamp-Waving (Arati) Ceremony of Brijrajji during the Festival Honoring Vyas

c. 1831
Opaque watercolor, gold, metallic gray watercolor
24.7 x 21.5 cm
Rao Madho Singh Trust Museum, Fort Kotah
Inscribed on top margin: "[This] is the Auspicious (Punyo) Festival on the 15th of the bright fortnight of [the month] June/July (Ashadha)." (WLT)

The day of the full moon in the month of June/July (Asadh) is an auspicious moment for honoring teachers, particularly the prototypical sage Vyas, who, by composing the epic *Mahabharata*, *Brahmasutra*s, and eighteen *Purana*s, as well as arranging all the ancient Vedas, embodies the rich scholarly and religious tradition of Sanskrit texts and textuality.[1] In the inscription above this painting and in Kishor Singh's poetic text to be sung on this occasion, the day is referred to as "auspicious" (*punyo*).[2] In the heading to his poem, Kishor Singh also refers to the day as "the day to worship Vyas" (*Vyas puja*).[3]

For members of the Vallabha Sampraday community, the attribution of the *Brahmasutra*s and the *Bhagavata Purana* to Vyas had specific resonance, as these were the two canonical Sanskrit texts that Vallabhacharya himself commented on, thereby generating his own texts, the *Anubhashya* and *Subodhini*. Through commentarial interjections in his *Anubhashya*, Vallabhacharya argued the premises of his radical ontology (*shuddhadvaita*). In the *Subodhini*, he explicated the narrative of Krishna's life in a way that guided members of his community such as Kishor Singh so that they could participate in it.[4]

In a brief entry for the festival day in his liturgical manual, Kishor Singh's only specification for the visual display is that both Brijrajji's turban and the cloth backdrop hanging behind him be "of roses."[5] In the painting, the presence of roses is evoked by having both a throne cover and a cloth backdrop hanging made with a field of embroidered or printed rose bushes against a saffron ground, each with a crowning cluster of flowering pink roses.

WLT

1 Apte 1986, 1520.
2 K. Singh n.d.c, 14v–15. The appearance of the word *punyo* in the first line of his poem and in the inscription above the painting (but not in his liturgical manual) is an important possible indication that the author of some of the inscriptions for this set was familiar with Kishor Singh's poetic text intended to be sung during the festivals depicted in the paintings.
3 According to V. S. Apte, this is a common designation for this day; see Apte 1986, 1520.
4 For a partial translation of Vallabhacharya's *Subodhini*, see Redington 1983.
5 *Pag pichhavai gulabya* (K. Singh n.d.a, 51b).

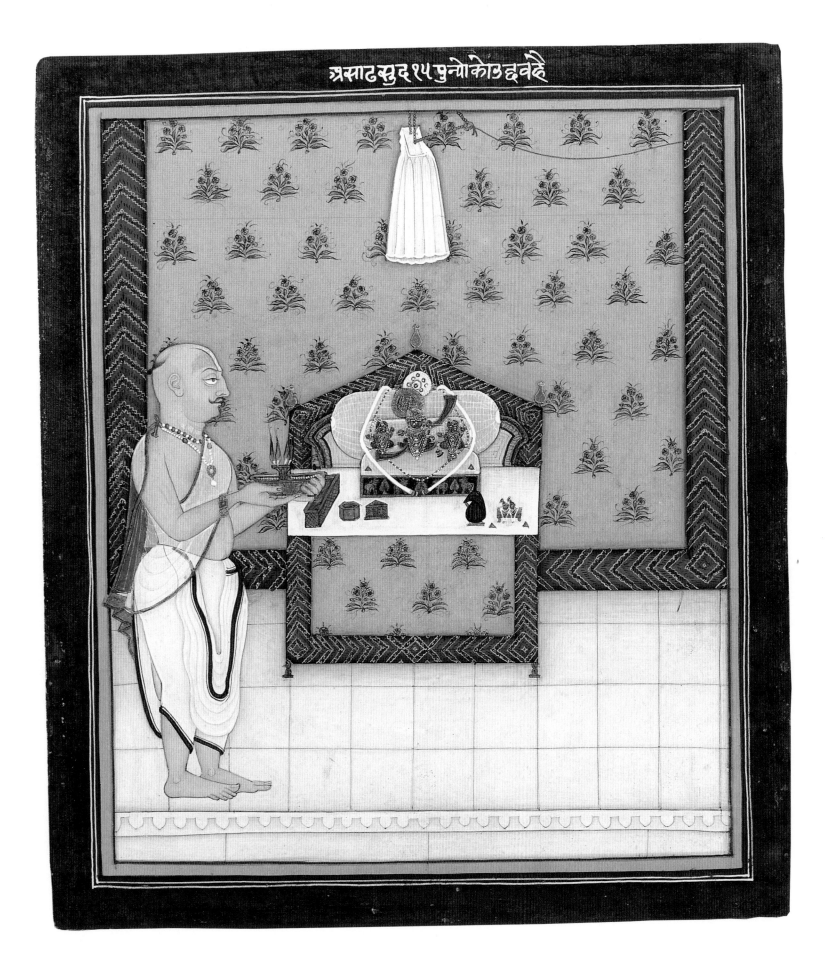

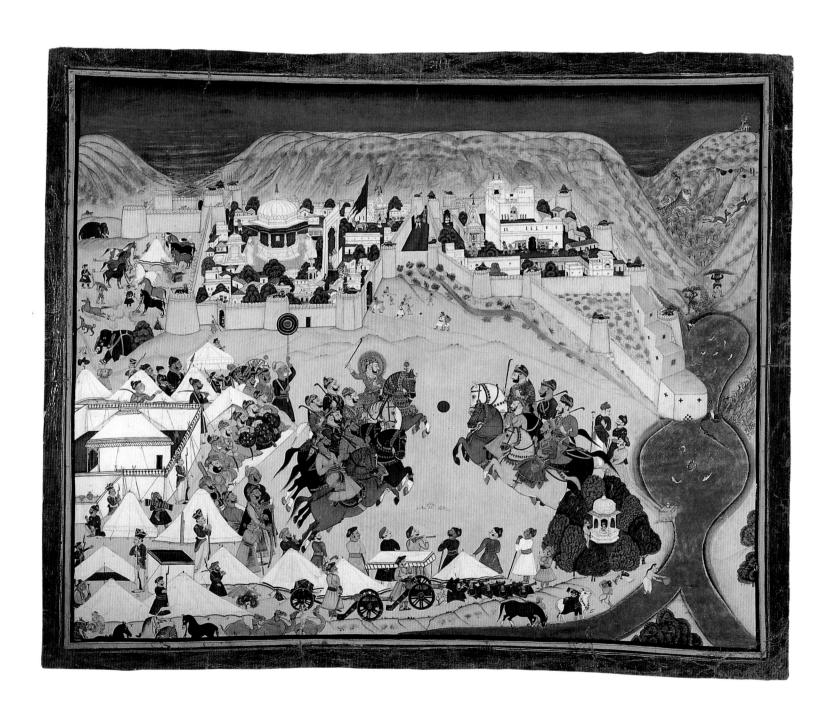

202

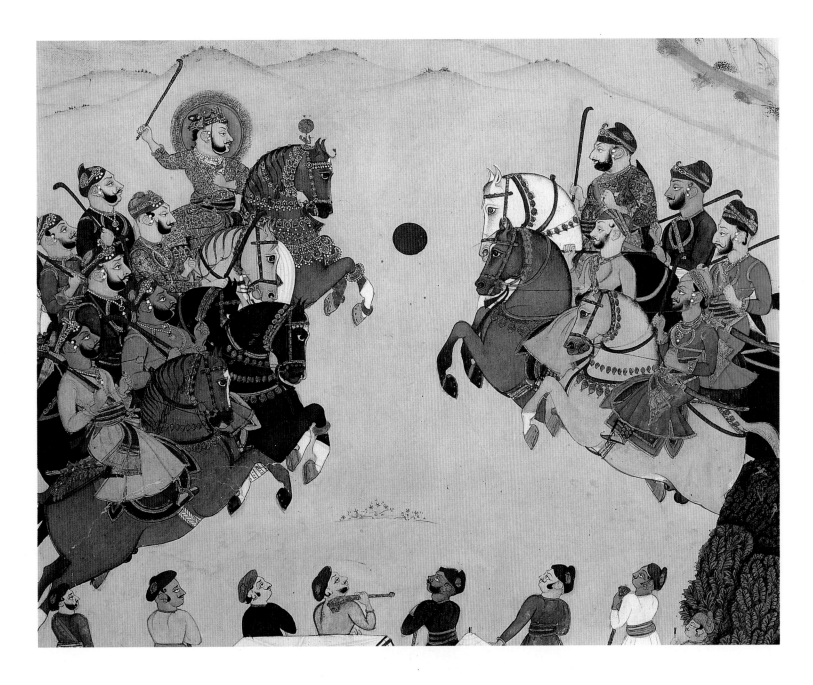

63

*Maharao Ram Singh Playing Polo
near Gagraon*

1838
Opaque watercolor, gold, metallic gray watercolor
61 x 74.6 cm
Rao Madho Singh Trust Museum, Fort Kotah
Inscribed on recto on the top margin: "Shri."
Inscribed on verso: "Honorable Ram! The king of
kings, the lord of the earth, the honorable Maharao
Ram Singh went to the district of Gagraon and played
near the camp … with the noblemen in the year 1838
C.E. (V.S. 1895)."

Maharao Ram Singh (r. 1827–66) was a sociable, charismatic, and lively ruler noted for his outrageous sense of humor. Hunter, polo player, and ardent lover, he commissioned artists to portray the royal rounds in uncompromising depth. A record of one of the merry monarch's pranks, showing an elephant defying death by walking on the narrow skirting of Kotah Fort, is mounted on the walls of the Bada Mahal. Another painting exhibits him atop an elephant, simultaneously making love with several lady guests and shooting a tiger. In the cheerful and sunny picture shown here, he leads his team, mallet in hand, and is about to whack a red polo ball almost as large as his halo. In the distance, boys play stick polo — echoing the royal game — and at the left, grooms look after their not entirely obliging horses. Gagraon, one of Kotah's major forts, is explicitly rendered, along with a schematic but accurate presentation of the terrain and surroundings. Although the artist accurately and carefully noted walls, tents, animals, people, colors, and textures, proportions and sizes conform to the later Rajasthani mode, as known from the art of Jodhpur, Udaipur, and most of the other schools. Human figures are shown larger or smaller according to rank. The mighty maharao is elephantine, soldiers — some of them in British-style uniforms — are lilliputian, and two standing courtiers, perhaps scorekeepers, seem to be giants.

SCW

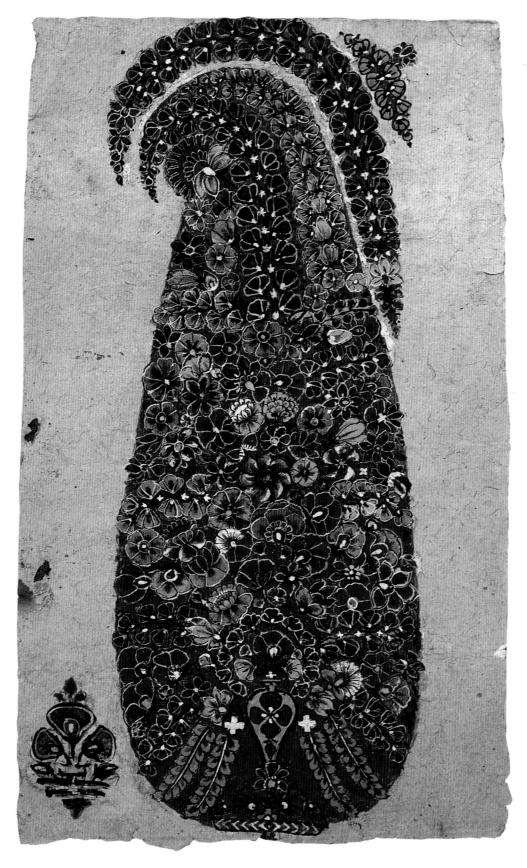

Floral Design (Buta) for a Tapestry

c. 1840
Opaque watercolor
32.3 x 20 cm
Rao Madho Singh Trust Museum, Fort Kotah

Little is known of embroidery or other textile work at Kotah. This appealing design was carefully painted as a guide for a weaver or embroiderer, presumably at Kotah. The pattern is a familiar one, of a traditional Indian type that appears more naturalistically in Mughal floral ornament and was geometricized and further ornamentalized by Kashmiri textile designers, who employed it as a repeat pattern in shawls. Widely traveled, it was employed by industrial weaving manufacturers in Scotland (such as those in Paisley, from which the pattern takes its Western name), who often marketed their wares in India. Still popular, it can be found on twentieth-century British and American neckties and other clothing and decorative items.
SCW

65

Maharao Ram Singh's Visit to Delhi

Attributed to Kishan Das and Lacchi Ram
1842
Opaque watercolor on cloth
445 x 259 cm
Rao Madho Singh Trust Museum, Fort Kotah

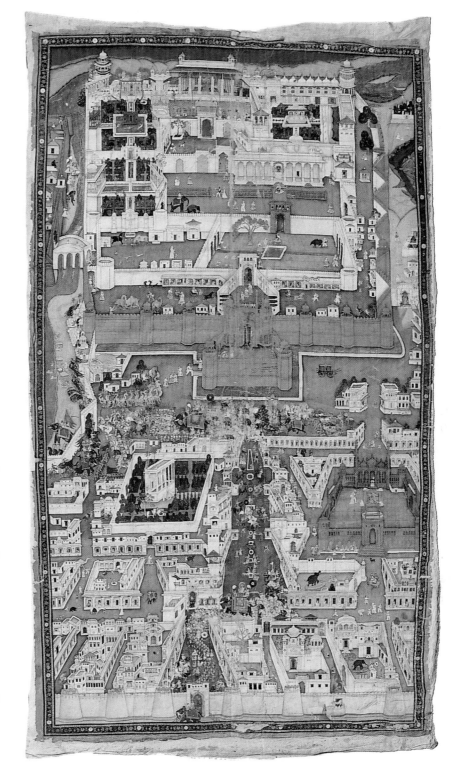

This richly anecdotal and comical "fruitcake" of a work, a virtual panorama of the Mughal fort and environs, is crammed with amusing observations of life and incidental characterizations. Along with dancing goats, pigeons, massed camels, horses, and elephants, there is the full range of Delhi personalities, from its aristocracy to hoi polloi. There are many slightly irreverent portraits, for which — alas — no identifications are given. One would like to know more about the English couple inappropriately holding hands in the courtyard of Shah Jahan's Friday mosque, and also who the prosperous, stout man in the snappy carriage might have been. Of greater moment, of course, are the two principal players in this pictorial drama: the last Mughal emperor, Bahadur Shah II (r. 1837–58), who peeps delightfully through a brass telescope at the second, Maharao Ram Singh of Kotah (r. 1827–66). Even the emperor's comfortably plump and smiling senior wife (*begum*) — on a balcony — was excited by the maharao's "state visit." The Mughal house had long been served by princely Kotah warriors, to whom one of the former presented the giltcopper fish standard (*mahi*) (cat. 68). The significance of Ram Singh's stately and ambitious progress from Kotah to Delhi (Shah Jahanabad) with full retinue, elephants, and horses can be gauged from the scale of this picture, the supreme work of the maharao's ateliers, and one that was repeated as a wall painting.

Although Bahadur Shah appears only once, atop the Shah Burj (Royal Tower), Ram Singh is seen twice: on the far side of a rivulet, near a comically dressed pet monkey, and mounted on a magnificently caparisoned state elephant. Both of these royal appearances are outside the fort walls. Astonishingly, this great picture of a potentially momentous encounter serves as convincing evidence that despite Ram Singh's major expedition to the Red Fort, and despite

the emperor's obvious interest in his Rajput visitor, the two never met.[1]

Fifteen years after Ram Singh's visit to Delhi, his would-be host became the nominal head of the so-called Indian Mutiny. At Kotah, in the British Residency of the emperor's would-be guest, Major Burton and his two sons were murdered. In the Mutiny's aftermath, Bahadur Shah II was tried by the British and

exiled to Rangoon, where he died. Although Ram Singh could not be fully implicated in the killing, he suffered the humiliation of having his official salute reduced by several guns.

SCW

1 See Stuart Cary Welch's essay, above, for details of this event.

Published: M. B. Singh 1985, fig. 40; [=Welch 1985, no. 285; Bautze 1990, figs. 3 and 17 (detail)].

Maharao Ram Singh about to Strike the
Marriage Doorway Decoration (Torana)
in the Presence of Maharawal Gaj Singh
of Jaisalmer

1843
Opaque watercolor, gold
66.5 x 71 cm
Rao Madho Singh Trust Museum, Fort Kotah
Inscribed on recto: "Shri."
Inscribed on verso: "Honorable Ram! [This is] a pic-
ture of the arrival of the procession of the honorable
great king, the king of kings, lord of the earth, Maharao
Ram Singh of Kotah and the honorable Maharawal Gaj
Singh of Jaisalmer at the first decoration (Torana) [or:
on the first day of] the month February/March (Phal-
gun) in the year 1843 C.E. (V.S. 1900)."

Even during serious moments, such as marriage
rituals, Maharao Ram Singh, like his ancestors
and descendants, took pleasure in life. On this
occasion, he and his colorfully decked-out en-
tourage combined rewarding ancient religious
traditions with the delights of a royal house
party. This was a family gala, to which a myriad
of cousins and collateral relatives were invited,
together with mobs of friends, all aglitter in
Rajput finery. Weavers, embroiderers, makers
of gold and silver thread, armorers, jewelers,
shoemakers, and artists all benefited from the
largesse that flowed from princely treasuries to
make this a memorable occasion. The maharao's
marriage to one of the maharawal's daughters
was also a political event, cementing relations
between two Rajput powers. Best of all, it
brought yet another charming young lady into
Ram Singh's zenana.

Large paintings of this sort were frequently
made in Rajputana during the first half of the
nineteenth century. If they commemorate royal
happenings, they also proclaim freedom from
the now-enfeebled Mughals, and the time of
independence before the Indian Mutiny of 1857.
Court artists at Kotah and many other Rajput
kingdoms were kept busy, as were the soldiers,
butlers, chefs, wrestlers, musicians, poets, and
priests. Artistic ways, freed from Mughal naturalism, were beginning to revert to old Rajput
modes. Although the major figures here retain
their individuality, lesser beings are beginning
to lose their identities by being transformed

into formulas. Soldiers and townspeople whose
ancestors were shown as true portraits by such
artists as the Kotah Master or Sheikh Taju are
becoming a refulgent chorus line of geometricized noses, brows, bellies, and rumps. Rajasthani artists, it seems, were enjoying a last
exuberant fling before the onslaught of photography.

SCW

The ceremonial gateway (*torana*: literally, gateway or door) is the decoration above the lintel
of the palace entrance in front of Rawal Gaj
Singh of Jaisalmer, behind whom two attendants wave their fly whisks (*chauris*). Maharao
Ram Singh is about to strike the decoration, an
act he should perform with his sword.[1] The
"striking of the Torana" (*torana torna* or *torana
marna*) still forms a part of Rajput marriage
ceremonies.

Many of the people present in this picture
are also known from other, similarly inscribed
paintings. Raja Arjun Singh, Chaturbhuj Singh
of Gainta, and Pratap Singh Tavar, for example,
accompanied the Kotah maharao during one of
the annual buffalo sacrifices in connection with
the Dashahra festivities.[2] Gainta is an estate
(*jagir*) that formed part of the eight feudatories
(*kotris*) annexed to Kotah in 1761. Nimolia is an
estate that originated with the family of Indargarh, which was founded by Indar Sal, the
younger brother of Rao Shatru Sal of Bundi.[3]
Palaitha was founded by Mohan Singh, second
son of Madho Singh; its ruler at the time of the
painting, Fateh Singh, died issueless in 1858.[4]
Koela was founded by Kaniram (Kanha), the
third son of Madho Singh of Kotah.

The two wrestlers formed an integral part of
the court during Maharao Ram Singh's time.
Like the dancers, they provided entertainment
during darbars and are frequently shown in
darbar paintings.[5]

JKB

1 For a description of such decorations and their
   meaning, see Tod 1920 ed., 317, n. 2.
2 Bautze 1995b, 149f.
3 Chiefs and Leading Families 1894, 57.
4 Ibid., 58.
5 See Bautze 1990, figs. 2, 10, and 14; for an individual
   portrait sketch of the wrestler Guna or Gunji, dated
   1853 C.E. (V.S. 1910), see Bautze 1990, fig. 15. See also
   Bautze 1988/89, Appendix II, no. 7.

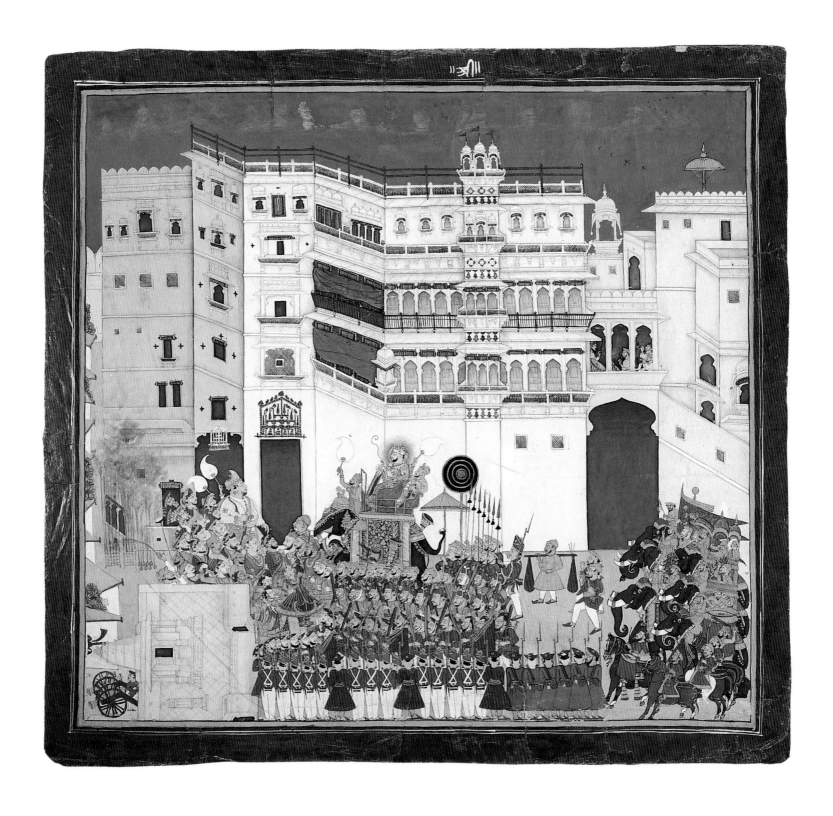

207

67

Thunderous Tryst

c. 1866–89
Opaque watercolor, gold, metallic gray watercolor
34.5 x 25.5 cm
H.H. Maharao Brijraj Singh of Kotah

Painting and drawing at Kotah eased into comparative inactivity during the reign of Shatru Sal II (r. 1866–89), but it did so without losing its ability to inspire smiles, laughter, and occasional burlesques. The most finely carried out of Rao Shatru Sal II's pictures show him and assorted beloveds celebrating erotic love in almost clinical detail, but this *Thunderous Tryst* would never raise an eyebrow. This picture's cheery gusto compensates for its coarse execution: it rings the same bells as such classic moments in film as the scene in which Charlie Chaplin gently dumps ice cream into a dowager's ample décolletage. Inasmuch as Kotah patrons and painters had always enjoyed zestful pictures, it is pleasing to know that this lively tradition was — and is — maintained. Whether or not the anonymous artist knew it, he imbued the impassioned hero's wiggly rope and the tangles of lightning with Turkman verve and ably conveyed the heroine's demure insouciance.
SCW

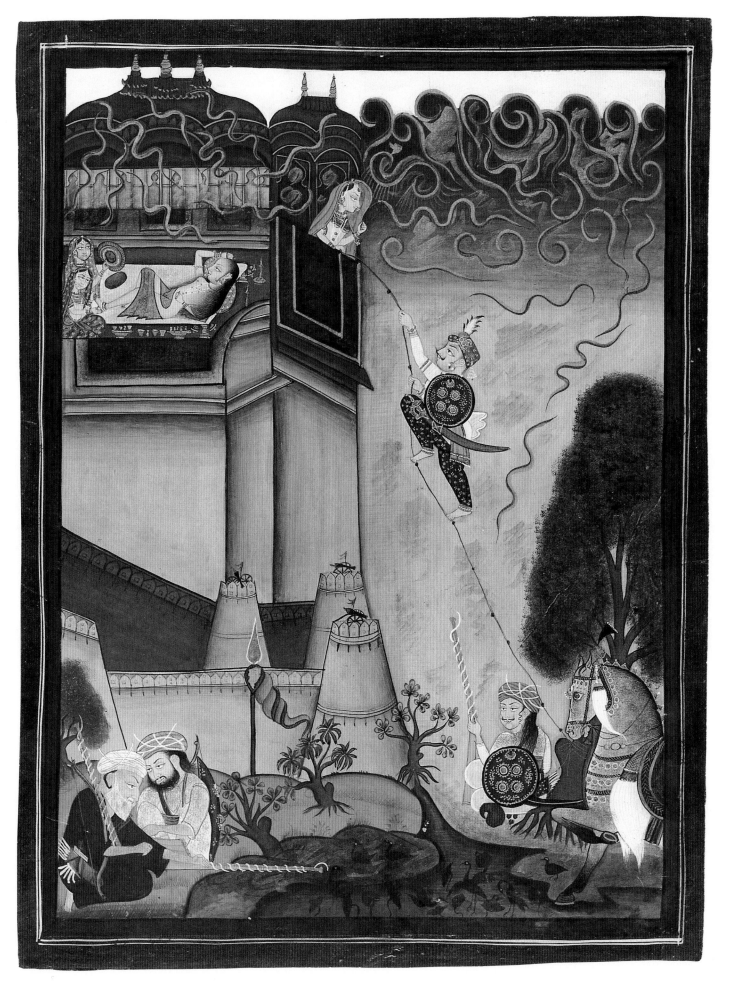

68

Fish Standard (Mahi)

c. late eighteenth century
Gilt copper, cloth
12.8 (diam.) x 16 (length) x 5 (height) cm
Rao Madho Singh Trust Museum, Fort Kotah

This standard — the fish was considered a symbol of success — was fixed to the top of a pole and carried in important processions and into battle on the back of an elephant, together with two gilded copper balls, also fixed on poles. Wind blowing through the mouth of the fish inflated the textile streamer. When appearing in the company of two gilded balls, it is called the "fish and dignities" (*mahi-o-maratib*).[1]

From a distance, this fish looks more like the head of a dragon — not surprisingly, since the dragon standard was the forerunner of the fish standard, as is shown by a number of contemporary paintings[2] and descriptions.[3] A closer examination, however, reveals the typical scales and fins. The first fish standard of the present shape did not appear before the late seventeenth century, when it was used by the Mughal emperor Aurangzeb (r. 1658–1707) during the siege of Golconda.[4] The standard as such, however, is already mentioned during the fourth regnal year of the emperor Shah Jahan (r. 1628–58), and it was said that in former times the sovereigns of Delhi "bestowed them on the rulers of the Deccan, where they are even more highly esteemed and are only conferred on such as are deserving of the highest consideration."[5] The fish standard was one of the highest honors the Mughals could bestow on their allies during the eighteenth century, and it was often accompanied into battle by drums (*nobut*).

The fish standard shown here, of which the two gilded balls marking the more complete "fish and dignities" seem no longer to exist,

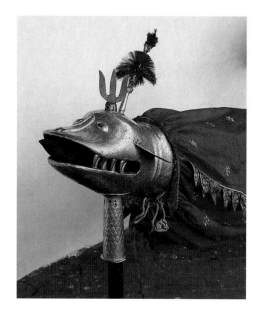

was conferred on Maharao Bhim Singh I (r. 1707–20), the greatest of all Kotah kings. The contemporary Mughal historian Khafi Khan reports on this:

> Hussein Ali Khan (the Bakshi [paymaster]) made an agreement (on behalf of the Mughal emperor Muhammad Shah) with Maharao Bhim Singh (of Kotah) that after punishing Salim Singh zamindar of Bundi and settling the affairs of Nizam-ul-Mulk, he would be given the title of "Maharajah" and his rank would be higher than all the other Rajahs except that of Maharajah Ajit Singh (of Jodhpur). He was then granted a Mansab [rank] of 7,000 (zat [infantry]) and 7,000 sawars [cavalry] and the honour of the Mahi-Maratib and along with Rajah Gaj Singh of Narwar and Dilawar Khan etc. was given a strong force of 18,000 cavalry to remove Salim Singh and watch the movements of Nizam-ul-Mulk.[6]

This is why the "fish and dignities" is seen for the first time in Kotah painting in a large painting on cloth in which Maharao Bhim Singh I rides with Raja Gaj Singh against Nizam-ul-Mulk. Nizam-ul-Mulk, Maharao Bhim Singh's enemy, displays a different standard — the "lion dignity" (*sher-maratib*), which appeared in the Deccan only as shown in this painting.
JKB

1 Irvine 1896, 537f.
2 Hickmann 1979, pl. 31. The dragon standard is the third from the right at the right-hand border.
3 Mundy 1914, 199.
4 Sanderson and Hasan 1911, pl. XLIX.
5 'Inayat Khan 1990 ed., 72.
6 Khafi Khan, in his *Muntakhabal Lubab*, following the translation of this part of the text in the Rao Madho Singh Trust Museum, Fort Kotah.

Published: M. B. Singh 1985, fig. 42

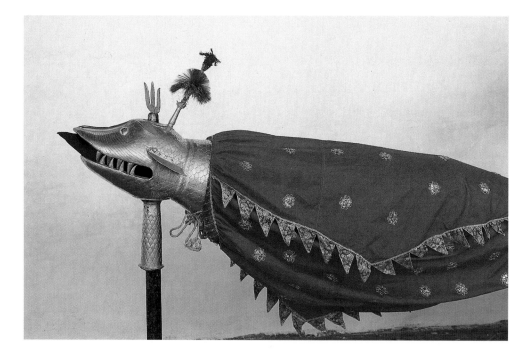

69

Sword with Friezes of Animals on Blade

Relief perhaps designed by Sheikh Taju
Mid eighteenth century
Steel and bronze
99 x 10 x 8 cm
Rao Madho Singh Trust Museum, Fort Kotah

70

Two Matchlocks

Eighteenth century
Steel with gilt decoration and wood
a: 174 x 4.5 x 7 cm; b: 145.5 x 10 x 4.3 cm
Rao Madho Singh Trust Museum, Fort Kotah

71

Globular Mace

Eighteenth century
Steel with gilt decoration
18 (diam.) x 75 (length) cm
Rao Madho Singh Trust Museum, Fort Kotah

72a

Mace

Eighteenth century
Steel
73.5 x 11.3 x 1.3 cm
Rao Madho Singh Trust Museum, Fort Kotah

72b

Battle-Ax

Eighteenth century
Steel and wood
67 x 10.3 x 2.5 cm
Rao Madho Singh Trust Museum, Fort Kotah

73

Katar with Vegetable Ornament

Eighteenth century
Steel with gilt decoration
38 x 8.6 x 2 cm
Rao Madho Singh Trust Museum, Fort Kotah

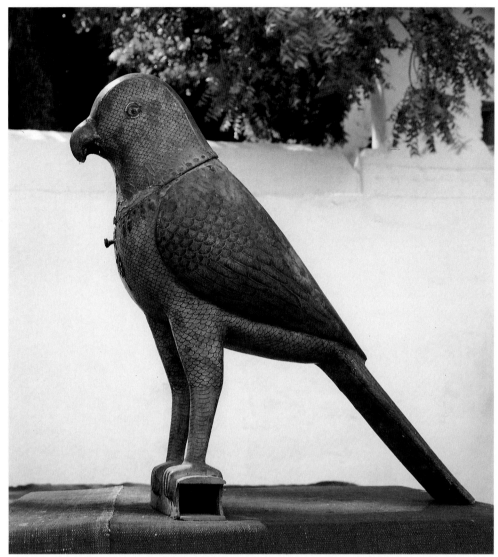

74

74

*Lacquered Case for Gunsmith's Tools,
in the Form of a Bird*

Nineteenth century
Wood, lacquer
Approx. 42 x 42 x 19 cm
Rao Madho Singh Trust Museum, Fort Kotah

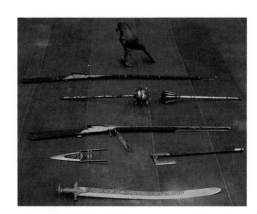

69–74

73

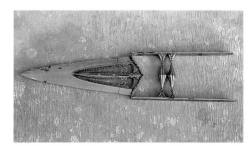

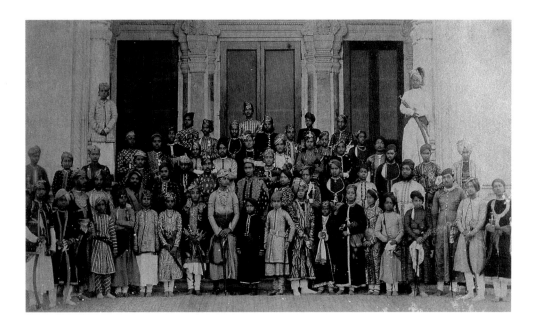

75

Boys Group, Mayo College, Ajmer

Bourne and Shepherd
c. 1885
Photograph
Mount: 21.5 x 30.3 cm; photograph: 18.7 x 28.9 cm
Rao Madho Singh Trust Museum, Fort Kotah

Among the most characteristic Rajput works of art gathered here are the tools of the Rajputs' soldierly trade. Functional, elegant, tactile, and sometimes eye-catchingly enriched with gold, they lent sieges, battles, parades, and festivals the look of grand opera or ballet. However blood-chillingly utilitarian, many of them are superbly designed works of art. Occasionally, they seem witty, or even whimsical. Perhaps to sweeten the lethal blows it delivered, a powerful steel mace in the form of an orb bristling with daggerlike spikes is adorned with cheery golden grapevines (cat. 72a). Along with a Rajput prince's sumptuous clothing, splendid turban, and jewels, such objects represent the hardy military man's streak of aestheticism. Like eminent fighting men in the West, whose shields, suits of armor, maces, and edged weapons now grace museums and armories, Rajputs took pride in their military paraphernalia, parts of which sometimes were commissioned en suite by especially well-outfitted men of battle.

Outstanding among the pieces in the Kotah armory are several swords adorned with friezes of figures and animals in low relief. One such is the hunting sword (cat. 69) bearing designs of huntsmen, elephants, cheetahs, lions, and black buck, perhaps endowing it with "hunting magic" to attract the prey it depicts. Like several other pieces here, it was created from Wootz (or "watered") steel, both to strengthen the metal and to please the eye with its organically free patterns, which resemble rippling water, sky, or smoke. To make this, iron ingots of higher and lower carbon content were artfully mingled by being hammered together on an anvil under intense heat. Wootz steel was also employed in making gun barrels, as is seen here in a particularly brilliant example (cat. 70). After being roughly shaped by hammering, the blade was fastened with a waxlike compound, perhaps containing bitumen,[1] into a stone form, perhaps slate, specifically grooved to hold it firmly during the lengthy process of refining the shape and thickness or thinness of the blade and creating the animal frieze with files and abrasives.

But was this blade created at Kotah? Although its figures wear the characteristic flat-crowned Kotah turban, and the lively reliefs might have been designed by one of the Kotah artists — perhaps Sheikh Taju[2] — no records have been found of the provenances either of this object or of the other pieces seen here. In India under the Mughals and Rajputs, specialized crafts developed at many centers. Bidar, for instance, was renowned for its "Bidri-work" hookah bases, vases, cups, dishes, boxes, and salvers in which inlays of brass, copper, silver, or gold arabesques, flowers, figures, and many other motifs were set into an alloy of zinc, lead, and copper. Bidri was sold to courtly and other clients all over India and beyond. Even if this hunting sword was not manufactured at Kotah, it represents a maharao's taste early in the eighteenth century and relates harmoniously to Kotah paintings and drawings.
scw

1 This brownish black gum is similar to that employed to fasten blades into hilts. Lest blades pop unmanningly from their hilts on hot days in the battle or hunting field, it possessed a high melting point.
2 Several of Sheikh Taju's designs for weapons have survived.

Bibliography,
Authors,
and
Appendix

Bibliography

ABU'L FAZL 'ALLAMI

1973 *The Akbar Nama of Abu-l-Fazl: History of the Reign of Akbar Including an Account of His Predecessors.* 3 vols. Translated from Persian by Henry Beveridge. New Delhi: Ess Ess Publications.

1977 *A'in-i Akbari.* Translated from Persian by H. Blochmann. Edited by D. C. Phillott. 2d ed., rev. New Delhi: Oriental Books Reprint Corporation.

AGRAWAL, LALA CHIRANJI LAL

n.d. *Status of Uniara: A Reply to Mr. C. U. Will's Report on the Land Tenures and Special Powers, on Certain Thikanedars of the Jaipur State.* Jaipur: Vakil Chief Court.

AGRAWAL, O. P.

1969 A Study in the Techniques and Materials of Indian Illustrated Manuscripts. In *Problems of Conservation in Museums: International Council of Museums Committee for Museum Laboratories and the Committee for the Care of Paintings.* New York: Humanities Press.

1972 A Study of the Technique and Materials of Indian Illustrated Manuscripts. *Bulletin of the National Museum of India,* no. 3.

AHMAD, KHWAJAH NIZAMUDDIN

1939 *Tabaqat-i-Akbari: A History of India from the Early Musalman Invasions to the Thirty-Eighth Year of the Reign of Akbar.* Vol. 3, pt. 2. Translated and annotated by Brajendranath De. Revised and edited by Baini Prashad. Bibliotheca Indica, no. 225. Calcutta: Royal Asiatic Society of Bengal.

AHMAD, QADI

1959 *Calligraphers and Painters.* Translated by Tatiana Minorsky. Freer Gallery of Art Occasional Papers, vol. 3, pt. 2. Washington, D.C.

AITCHISON, C. U.

1909 *A Collection of Treaties, Engagements, and Sanads Relating to India and Neighbouring Countries,* vol. 3, *Containing the Treaties . . . Relating to the States in Rajputana, Revised and Continued up to June 1st, 1906.* Calcutta: Office of the Superintendent of Government Printing.

AKIMUSHKIN, O.F., I. IWANOW, AND S.C. WELCH

1996 *The St. Petersburg Muraqqa': Album of Indian and Persian Miniatures from the 16th through the 18th Century and Specimens of Persian Calligraphy by 'Imad al-Hasani.* Lugano and Milan: ARCH Foundation and Leonardo Arte SRL.

AL-BADAONI ('ABDU-L-QADIR IBN-I-MULUK SHAH)

1973 *Muntakhabu-t-Tawarikh.* 3 vols. Translated from Persian and edited by George S. A. Ranking. Revised and enlarged by Brahmadeva Prasad Ambashthya. Reprint, Patna: Academica Asiatica.

AMBALAL, AMIT

1987 *Krishna as Shrinathji.* Ahmedabad: Mapin Publishing.

ANAND, UMA

1975 *Guide to Rajasthan.* New Delhi: India Tourism Development Corporation.

ANDHARE, B. R.

1984 *Bundelkhand under the Marathas (1720–1818 A.D.): A Study of Maratha-Bundela Relations.* Nagpur: Vishwa Bharati Prakashan.

ANDHARE, SHRIDHAR

1973 An Early Ragamala from the Kankroli Collection. *Bulletin of the Prince of Wales Museum of Western India* 12:58–64 + plates.

APPADURAI, ARJUN, ED.

1986 *The Social Life of Things: Commodities in Cultural Perspective.* Cambridge, England: Cambridge University Press.

APTE, V. S.

1986 *The Practical Sanskrit-English Dictionary.* Kyoto: Rinsen.

ARCHER, M.

1833 *Tours in Upper India, and in Parts of the Himalaya Mountains; with Accounts of the Courts of Native Princes &c.* London: Richard Bentley.

ARCHER, WILLIAM GEORGE

1959 *Indian Painting in Bundi and Kotah.* London: Her Majesty's Stationery Office.

ASHTON, L., ED.

1950 *The Art of India and Pakistan: A Commemorative Catalogue of the Exhibition Held at the Royal Academy of Arts, London, 1947–8.* London: Faber and Faber Ltd.

ATHAR ALI, M.

1966 *The Mughal Nobility under Aurangzeb.* London: Asia Publishing House.

1985 *The Apparatus of Empire: Awards of Ranks, Offices, and Titles to the Mughal Nobility, 1574–1658.* Delhi: Oxford University Press.

BABUR, ZAHIRU'D-DIN MUHAMMAD GHAZI PADSHAH

1979 *Babur-Nama (Memoirs of Babur).* Translated from Turki by Annette Susannah Beveridge. New Delhi: Oriental Books Reprint Corp.

BAER, NORBERT, N. INDICTOR, AND A. JOEL

1971 *The Chemistry and History of the Pigment Indian Yellow.* Lisbon: Conservation of Paintings and the Graphic Arts.

BAHADUR, K. P.

1972 *The Rasikapriya of Keshavadasa.* Delhi: Motilal Banarsidas.

BAILEY, JULIA

1985 Royal and Provincial Persian Painting of the Sixteenth Century. Unpublished paper. Cambridge, Mass.: Harvard University.

BAKHTIN, M. M.

1981 *The Dialogic Imagination: Four Essays.* Translated by Caryl Emerson and Michael Holquist. Edited by Michael Holquist. Austin: University of Texas Press.

BANERJEE, A. C.

1983 *Aspects of Rajput State and Society.* New Delhi: Rajesh Publications.

BANERJI, ADRIS

1972 The Saga of Chittorgarh: A Study. *Journal of the Asiatic Society* 14(2–4):9–20.

BAPNA, PRAKASH

1976 List of Inscriptions of Hadoti. In *Cultural Heritage of Hadoti: Cultural Glimpses of Kota, Bundi, and Jhalawar,* edited by Mahavirsingh Gahlot, Sukhvirsingh

Gahlot, and Vijaysingh Gahlot. Jodhpur: Hindi Sahitya Mandir, 23.

BARRETT, DOUGLAS, AND BASIL GRAY

1963 *Indian Painting.* Geneva: Editions d'Art Albert Skira.

BARRO, LISA

1993 A Technical Analysis of Five Kota Sketches. Unpublished paper. Cambridge, Mass.: Harvard University.

BARZ, RICHARD K.

1992 *The Bhakti Sect of Vallabhacharya.* New Delhi: Munshiram Manoharlal Publishers.

BAUTZE, JOACHIM K.

1985a Zuordnungsfragen bei Kota-Malereien. *Zeitschrift der Deutschen Morgenländischen Gesellschaft* (Supplement 6) 22:438–44.

1985b Drei Miniaturmalereien aus Kota im Linden-Museum. *Tribus: Jahrbuch des Linden-Museums Stuttgart* 35 (December): 89–120.

1986a A Contemporary and Inscribed Equestrian Portrait of Jagat Singh of Kota. In *Deyadharma: Studies in Memory of Dr. D. C. Sircar,* edited by Gouriswar Bhattacharya. Sri Garib Das Oriental Series, no. 33. Delhi: Sri Satguru Publications.

1986b Mughal and Deccani Influence on Early 17th-Century Murals of Bundi. In *Facets of Indian Art: A Symposium Held at the Victoria and Albert Museum,* edited by Robert Skelton, Andrew Topsfield, Susan Stronge, and Rosemary Crill. London: Victoria and Albert Museum, 168–75.

1986c Sporting Pastimes of the Hara Kings: Murals of Bundi and Kota. *India Magazine* 6 (November): 64–71.

1986d Eine Garudastandarte aus Kota im Linden-Museum. *Tribus: Jahrbuch des Linden-Museums Stuttgart* 35 (December): 57–82.

1986e Portraits of Rao Ratan and Madho Singh Hara. *Berliner Indologische Studien* 2:87–106.

1987a Drei "Bundi"-Ragamalas. In *Ein Beitrag zur Geschichte der rajputischen Wandmalerei.* Monographien zur indischen

Archäologie, Kunst und Philologie, vol. 6. Stuttgart: Franz Steiner.

1987b Zur Darstellung der Hauptgottheiten Kotas in der Malerei der zweiten Hälfte des 18. und der ersten Hälfte des 19. Jahrhunderts. *Berliner Indologische Studien* 3:253–78.

1988 Zwei Entwurfsskizzen aus Kota im Linden-Museum. *Tribus: Jahrbuch des Linden-Museums Stuttgart* 37 (December): 83–117.

1988–89 Porträtmalerei unter Maharao Ram Singh von Kota. *Artibus Asiae* 49(3–4):316–50.

1989a Shri Brijnathji and the Murals in the Chattar Mahal, Kota. In *Praci-Prabha, Perspectives in Indology: Essays in Honour of B. N. Mukherjee*, edited by D. C. Bhattacharya and Devendra Handa. New Delhi: Harman Publishing House, 319–26.

1989b Deckenmalereien Ost-Rajasthans im 17. Jahrhundert am Beispiel des "Badal Mahal" in Bundi. *Zeitschrift der Deutschen Morgenländischen Gesellschaft* (Supplement 7): 666–81.

1989c Dating the Murals in the Arjun Mahal, Kota. In *Ratnachandrika: Panorama of Oriental Studies (Shri R. C. Agrawala Festschrift)*, edited by Devendra Handa and Ashvini Agrawal. New Delhi: Harman Publishing House, 377–94 and pl. 44.1–44.7.

1990 The Ajmer Darbar of 1832 and Kota Painting. *South Asian Studies* 6:71–91.

1991 Lotosmond und Löwenritt. In *Indische Miniaturmalerei*. Stuttgart: Linden-Museum Stuttgart.

1991–92 Some Notes on the "Shoulder Ornament" in the Art of Northern India. In *Silk Road Art and Archeology: Journal of the Institute of Silk Road Studies* (Kamakura) 2:215–38.

1992a Amsterdam and the Earliest Published Kota Painting. In *Indian Art and Archaeology*, edited by Ellen M. Raven and Karel R. van Kooij. Panels of the 7th World Sanskrit Conference, Kern Institute, Leiden, vol. 10. Leiden: E. J. Brill, 78–93.

1992b Victory and Death of Maharao Bhim Singh of Kota. In *South Asian Archaeology 1989: Papers from the Tenth International Conference of South Asian Archaeologists in Western Europe*, edited by Catherine Jarrige. Paris and Madison, Wis.: Musée National des Arts Asiatique-Guimet and Prehistory Press, 309–16.

1993a German Private Collections of Indo-Islamic Paintings. In *Oriental Splendour: Islamic Art from German Private Collections*, edited by Claus-Peter Haase, Jens Kröger, and Ursula Lienert. Hamburg: Museum für Kunst und Gewerbe, 247–83, 289–94.

1993b Gott und König in Kotah. *Tribus: Jahrbuch des Linden-Museums Stuttgart* 42 (November): 79–96.

1994 Jhala Zalim Singh of Kotah: A Great Patron of Rajput Painting. In *Festschrift Klaus Bruhn*, edited by Nalini Balbir and Joachim K. Bautze. Reinbek: Inge Wezler, 105–25.

1995a A Second Set of Equestrian Portraits Painted during the Reign of Maharao Umed Singh of Kota. In *Indian Painting: Essays in Honour of Karl J. Khandalavala*, edited by B. N. Goswamy with Usha Bhatia. New Delhi: Lalit Kala Akademi, 35–51.

1995b Die Welt der höfischen Malerei. In *Rajasthan: Land der Könige*, edited by Gerd Kreisel. Stuttgart: Linden-Museum Stuttgart, 123–80, 287–92, and 295–306.

1995c Portraits of Maharao Shatru Sal of Kota. In *Rupankan, Sampadak: Vijay Shankar Shrivastav and Mohan Lal Gupta*. Jaipur: Printvail, 84–91.

BAYLY, C. A.

1983 *Rulers, Townsmen, and Bazaars: North Indian Society in the Age of British Expansion, 1770–1870*. Cambridge, England: Cambridge University Press.

BEACH, MILO C.

1966 Rajput and Related Paintings. In *The Arts of India and Nepal: The Alice and Nasli Heeramaneck Collection*. Boston: Museum of Fine Arts, 120–34.

1972 Painting of the Later Eighteenth Century at Bundi and Kota. In *Aspects of Indian Art*, edited by Pratapaditya Pal. Leiden: E. J. Brill, 124–29.

1974 *Rajput Painting at Bundi and Kotah*. Artibus Asiae Supplementum, 32. Ascona, Switzerland: Artibus Asiae Publishers.

1981 *The Imperial Image: Paintings for the Mughal Court*. Washington, D.C.: Freer Gallery of Art, Smithsonian Institution.

1983 *The Adventures of Rama*. Washington, D.C.: Freer Gallery of Art, Smithsonian Institution.

1985 *The Art of India and Pakistan*. Durham, N.C.: Duke University Institute of the Arts.

1992 *Mughal and Rajput Painting*. Vol. 1.3, *The New Cambridge History of India*. Cambridge, England: Cambridge University Press.

BEALE, THOMAS WILLIAM

1894 *An Oriental Biographical Dictionary*. New edition revised and enlarged by Henry George Keene. London: W. H. Allen & Co.

BELTING, HANS

1994 *Likeness and Presence: A History of the Image before the Era of Art*. Chicago: University of Chicago Press.

BERNIER, FRANÇOIS

1916 *Travels in the Mogul Empire, A.D. 1656–1668*. Translated and annotated by Archibald Constable. 2d ed. London: Humphrey Milford/Oxford University Press.

BHARGAVA, V. S.

1979 *Rise of the Kacchawas in Dhundhar (Jaipur): From the Earliest Times to the Death of Sawai Jai Singh, 1743 A.D.* Ajmer: Shabd Sanchar.

BHATIA, USHA

1986 *Indian Miniature Painting Series 11*. New Delhi: Lalit Kala Akademi.

BHATNAGAR, V. S.

1974 *Life and Times of Sawai Jai Singh, 1688–1743*. Delhi: Impex India.

BHATT, S. K.

1971 Holkar-Rajput Relations. In *Maratha History Seminar, May 28–31, 1970: Papers*. Kolhapur: Dr. Usha Ithape, 197–203.

BHATTACHARYA, ASOK K.

1976 *Technique of Indian Painting: A Study Chiefly Made on the Basis of the Silpa Texts*. Calcutta: Saraswat Library.

BHIMSEN SAKSENA

1972 *Tarikh-i-Dilkasha: Memoirs of Bhimsen Relating to Aurangzib's Deccan Campaigns*. Translated and edited by V. G. Khobrekar. Bombay: Department of Archives, Maharashtra.

BINNEY, EDWIN

1973 *Indian Miniature Painting from the Collection of Edwin Binney, 3rd*, vol. 1, *The Mughal and Deccani Schools with Some Related Sultanate Material*. Portland: Portland Art Museum.

BINYON, LAURENCE

1921 *The Court Painters of the Grand Moguls*. London: Humphrey Milford/Oxford University Press.

BRIJBHUSHAN, JAMILA

1979 *The World of Indian Miniatures*. Tokyo: Kodansha International Ltd.

BROOKES, J. C.

1851 *History of Meywar*. Calcutta: Baptist Mission Press.

BROUGHTON, THOMAS DUER

1892 *Letters Written in a Mahratta Camp during the Year 1809: Descriptive of the Character, Manners, Domestic Habits, and Religious Ceremonies of the Mahrattas*. Archibald Constable & Co.'s Oriental Miscellany of Original and Selected Publications, vol. 4. Westminster: Archibald Constable and Co.

CANBY, SHEILA R.

1996 *The Rebellious Reformer: The Drawings and Paintings of Riza-yi 'Abbasi of Isfahan*. London: Azimuth Editions.

CAT. BERLIN

1971 *Museum für Indische Kunst Berlin. Katalog 1971. Ausgestellte Werke*. Berlin: Staatliche Museen Preußischer Kulturbesitz.

1976 *Museum für Indische Kunst Berlin. Katalog 1976. Ausgestellte Werke*. Berlin: Staatliche Museen Preußischer Kulturbesitz.

CHAITANYA, KRISHNA

1982 *A History of Indian Painting: Rajasthani Traditions*. New Delhi: Abhinav Publications.

CHANDRA, MOTI

1949 *The Technique of Mughal Painting*. Lucknow: U. P. Historical Society.

CHANDRA, PRAMOD

1960 Ustad Salivahana and the Development of Popular Mughal Art. *Lalit Kala*, no. 8 (October): 25–46.

1971 *Indian Miniature Painting: The Collection of Earnest C. and Jane Werner Watson*. Madison, Wis.: Elvehjem Art Center and University of Wisconsin Press, Madison.

CHANDRA, SATISH

1979 *Parties and Politics at the Mughal Court, 1707–1740*. 3d. ed. New Delhi: People's Publishing House.

CHIEFS AND LEADING FAMILIES

1903 *Chiefs and Leading Families in Rajputana*. Calcutta: Office of the Superintendent of Government Printing.

1916 *Chiefs and Leading Families in Rajputana*. Calcutta: Office of the Superintendent of Government Printing.

CHRISTIE'S INC.

1980 *Indian Miniatures and Watercolours*. London: sale catalogue, July 3.

CLUNES, JOHN

1833 *An Historical Sketch of the Princes of India, Stipendiary, Subsidiary, Protected, Tributary, and Feudatory ... *Edinburgh and London: Smith, Elder & Co.

COHN, MARJORIE B.

1977 *Wash and Gouache: A Study of the Development of Watercolor*. Cambridge, Mass.: Fogg Art Museum, Harvard University Art Museums.

COMPTON, H.

1893 *A Particular Account of the European Military Adventurers of Hindustan: From 1784 to 1803*. London: T. Fisher Unwin.

COOMARASWAMY, ANANDA K.

1914 The Eight Nayikas. *Journal of Indian Art and Industry* 128 (October): 99–116 + plates.

1934   The Technique and Theory of Indian Painting. *Technical Studies in the Field of the Fine Arts* 3(2):59–89.
1957   *The Dance of Siva.* New York: Noonday Press.

CROFTON, O. S.
1934   *List of Inscriptions on Tombs or Monuments in Rajputana and Central India, with Biographical Notes.* Delhi: Manager of Publications.

CZUMA, STANISLAW
1975   *Indian Art from the George P. Bickford Collection.* Cleveland: Cleveland Museum of Art.

DANA, JAMES DWIGHT
1944–62   *The System of Mineralogy of James Dwight Dana and Edward Salisbury Dana, Yale University, 1837–1892: 7th Edition, Entirely Rewritten and Greatly Enlarged by Charles Palache, Harry Berman, and Clifford Frondel.* New York and London: J. Wiley and Chapman and Hall, Ltd.

DANIEL, E. VALENTINE
1984   *Fluid Signs: Being a Person the Tamil Way.* Berkeley: University of California Press.

DANIEL, SHERYL B.
1983   The Tool Box Approach of the Tamil to the Issues of Moral Responsibility and Human Destiny. In *Karma: An Anthropological Inquiry,* edited by Charles F. Keyes and E. Valentine Daniel. Berkeley: University of California Press, 27–62.

DAS, A. K.
1995   Activities of the Jaipur Suratkhana, 1750–1768. In *Indian Art and Connoisseurship: Essays in Honour of Douglas Barrett,* edited by John Guy. Middleton, N.J., and Ahmedabad: Grantha Corp. and Mapin Publishing, 200–11.

DAY, UPENDRA NATH
1978   *Mewar under Maharana Kumbha, 1433 A.D.–1468 A.D.* New Delhi and Allahabad: Rajesh Publications.

DE LAET, JOANNES
1928   *The Empire of the Great Mogol: A Translation of De Laet's "Description of India and Fragment of Indian History."* Translated by J. S. Hoyland. Annotated by S. N. Banerjee. Bombay: D.B. Taraporevala Sons & Co.

DESAI, VISHAKHA N.
1985   *Life at Court: Art for India's Rulers, 16th–19th Centuries.* Boston: Museum of Fine Arts.

DESAI, VISHAKHA N., AND DENISE PATRY LEIDY
1989   *Faces of Asia: Portraits from the Permanent Collection.* Boston: Museum of Fine Arts.

DESCRIPTIVE LIST
1974   *A Descriptive List of the Vakil Reports Addressed to the Rulers of Jaipur (Rajasthani).* Bikaner: Rajasthan State Archives, Government of Rajasthan.
1978   *A Descriptive List of the Arzdashtas Addressed to the Rulers of Jaipur (Rajasthani).* Bikaner: Rajasthan State Archives, Government of Rajasthan.

DEVKAR, V. L.
1955–56   Some Recently Acquired Miniatures in the Baroda Museum. *Bulletin of the Museum and Picture Gallery Baroda* 12:19–24.

DICKINSON, ERIC, AND KARL KHANDALAVALA
1959   *Kishangarh Painting.* New Delhi: Lalit Kala Akademi.

DICKSON, MARTIN BERNARD, AND STUART CARY WELCH
1981   *The Houghton Shahnameh.* 2 vols. For the Fogg Art Museum, Harvard University. Cambridge, Mass., and London: Harvard University Press.

DIRKS, NICHOLAS B.
1987   *The Hollow Crown: Ethnohistory of an Indian Kingdom.* Cambridge, England: Cambridge University Press.

DOW, ALEXANDER
1792   *The History of Hindoostan.* 3 vols. 3d ed. London: John Murray.

DWIVEDI, VINOD PRAKASH
1980   *Barahmasa: The Song of Seasons in Literature and Art.* Delhi: Agam Kala Prakashan.

EBELING, KLAUS
1973   *Ragamala Painting.* New Delhi: Ravi Kumar.

EHNBOM, DANIEL JAMES
1985   *Indian Miniatures: The Ehrenfeld Collection.* With essays by Robert Skelton and Pramod Chandra. New York: Hudson Hills Press.

ELLIOT, H. M., AND JOHN DOWSON
1873   *The History of India as Told by Its Own Historians: The Muhammadan Period.* Vol. 5. London: Trübner and Co.
1875   *The History of India as Told by Its Own Historians: The Muhammadan Period.* Vol. 6. London: Trübner and Co.
1877   *The History of India as Told by Its Own Historians: The Muhammadan Period.* Vol. 7. London: Trübner and Co.

ENDERLEIN, VOLKMAR, AND REGINA HICKMANN
1995   *Meisterwerke der Moghul-Zeit: Indische Miniaturen des 17. und 18. Jahrhunderts aus dem Museum für Islamische Kunst der Staatlichen Museen zu Berlin.* Stiftung Preußischer Kulturbesitz. Lachen am Zürichsee: Corom Verlag.

FALK, TOBY
1978   Mughal and Rajput Painting. In *Indian Painting: Mughal and Rajput and a Sultanate Manuscript.* London: Colnaghi, 11–108.

FELLER, ROBERT L.
1986   *Artists' Pigments: A Handbook of Their History and Characteristics.* Washington, D.C.: National Gallery of Art.

FERISHTA, MAHOMED KASIM
1829   *History of the Rise of the Mahomedan Power in India, till the Year A.D. 1612.* 4 vols. Translated from Persian by John Briggs. London: Longmans.

FRANCCLIN, WILLIAM
1805   *Military Memoirs of Mr. George Thomas; Who, By Extraordinary Talents and Enterprise, Rose from an Obscure Situation to the Rank of a General, in the Service of the Native Powers in the North-West of India …* London: Reprinted for John Stockdale.

FRYER, JOHN
1909–15   *A New Account of East India and Persia: Being Nine Years Travels, 1672–1681.* 3 vols. Edited by William Crooke. Hakluyt Society, Second Series, nos. 19, 20, and 39. London: Hakluyt Society.

FULLER, C. J.
1992   *The Camphor Flame.* Princeton: Princeton University Press.

GAHLOT, JAGDISHSIMH
1960   *Rajputane ka Itihas (pamc hagom mem).* Jodhpur: Hindi Sahitya Mandir.

GETTENS, RUTHERFORD J., AND GEORGE STOUT
1966   *Painting Materials: A Short Encyclopedia.* New York: Dover.

GOETZ, HERMANN
1950   *The Art and Architecture of Bikaner State.* Oxford: Bruno Cassirer.

GORAKSHKAR, SADASHIV, AND M. L. NIGAM
1988   *Mriga, Animal in Art.* Tokyo: Yomiuri Shimbun/Japan Association of Art Museums.

GORDON, STUART
1977   The Slow Conquest: Administrative Integration of Malwa into the Maratha Empire, 1720–1760. *Modern Asian Studies* 11(1):1–40.

GOSWAMY, ACHARYA G. S. MAHARAJ, AND S. K. GOSWAMY MAHARAJ
1975   *Sri Vitthales Kirtan Ratnakara.* Indore: Sri Govardhanthji ka Mandir.

GOSWAMY, B. N.
1986   *Essence of Indian Art.* San Francisco: Asian Art Museum.

GRANT DUFF, JAMES
1863   *History of the Mahrattas.* 3 vols. Bombay: Exchange Press.

GRAY, BASIL
1949   *Indian Miniatures: Catalogue of an Exhibition of Works from the Collection of H.H. the Maharaja of Bikaner.* London: Arts Council of Great Britain.
1955   *Treasures of Indian Miniatures in the Bikaner Palace Collection.* Oxford: Bruno Cassirer.

GUPTA, BENI
1979   *Maratha Penetration into Rajasthan through the Mukandara Pass.* New Delhi: Research Publications in the Social Sciences.

GUPTA, K. S.
1971   *Mewar and the Maratha Relations, 1735–1818 A.D.* New Delhi: S. Chand & Co.

GUY, JOHN, AND DEBORAH SWALLOW
1990   *Arts of India, 1550–1900.* London: Victoria and Albert Museum.

HALBWACHS, MAURICE
1992   *On Collective Memory.* Translated and edited by Lewis A. Coser. Chicago: University of Chicago Press.

HARLAN, LINDSEY
1992   *Religion and Rajput Women: The Ethic of Protection in Contemporary Narratives.* Berkeley: University of California Press.

HARLEY, R. D.
1970   *Artist's Pigments c. 1600–1835: A Study in English Documentary Sources.* London: Butterworths.

HATANAKA, KOKYO
1994   *Indian Court Miniature Painting.* Kyoto: Kyoto Shoin Co.

HEBER, BISHOP REGINALD
1828   *Narrative of a Journey through the Upper Provinces of India, from Calcutta to Bombay, 1824–25 (with Notes upon Ceylon), an Account of a Journey to Madras and the Southern Provinces, 1826, and Letters Written in India.* 2 vols. London: John Murray.

HEERAMANECK, ALICE N.
1984   *Masterpieces of Indian Painting from the Former Collections of Nasli M. Heeramaneck.* Verona: Alice N. Heeramaneck.

HENCHY, PATRICK
n.d.   *The Chester Beatty Library and Gallery of Oriental Art Dublin.* Dublin: Chester Beatty Library.

HENDLEY, THOMAS HOLBEIN
1897   *The Rulers of India and the Chiefs of Rajputana, 1550 to 1897.* London: W. Griggs.

HICKMANN, REGINA
1979   *Indische Albumblätter: Miniaturen und Kalligraphien aus der Zeit der Moghul-Kaiser.* Leipzig/Weimar: Gustav Kiepenheuer Verlag.

HILL, ALLISON A.

1993 A Pigment and Technical Analysis of Durjan Sal Plaiting Krishna's Hair. Unpublished paper. Cambridge, Mass.: Harvard University.

HILTEBEITEL, ALF

1976 The Ritual of Battle: Krishna in the Mahabharata. Ithaca, N.Y.: Cornell University Press.

HODGKIN, HOWARD, AND TERENCE MCINERNEY

1983 Indian Drawing. London: Arts Council of Great Britain.

HOTEL DROUOT

1983 Miniatures orientales, miniatures mogholes et indiennes. Paris: sale catalogue, June 28.

HUNTER, WILLIAM

1801 Narrative of a Journey from Agra to Oujein. Asiatick Researches 6:47–67.

HUSAIN, YUSUF

1963 The First Nizam: The Life and Times of Nizam'ul-Mulk Asaf Jah I. Bombay: Asia Publishing House.

HUSSEIN [HOSSEIN]-KHAN, MIR GHOLAM

1832 The Siyar-Mutakherin: A History of the Mahomedan Power in India during the Last Century, by Mir Gholam Hussein-Khan. Revised by John Briggs. London: Oriental Translation Fund of Great Britain and Ireland.

1986 The Seir Mutaqherin, or Review of Modern Times: Being a History of India Containing in General the Reigns of the Seven Last Emperors of Hindustan. Vol. 1. Reprint, New Delhi: Inter-India Publications.

HUTCHINS, FRANCIS G.

1980 Young Krishna. Translated from the Sanskrit Harivamsa and illustrated with paintings from historic manuscripts. West Franklin, N.H.: Amarta Press.

IMPERIAL GAZETTEER

1908 The Imperial Gazetteer of India, Provincial Series: Rajputana. Calcutta: Office of the Superintendent of Government Printing.

INDEN, RONALD B.

1990 Imagining India. Oxford: Basil Blackwell.

IPSIROGLU, MAZHAR S.

1976 Siyah Qalem. Graz, Austria: Akademische Druck- u. Verlagsanstalt.

IRVINE, WILLIAM

1896 The Army of the Indian Moghuls: Its Organization and Administration. Journal of the Royal Asiatic Society (July) 509–70.

1971 Later Mughals, vol. 1, 1707–1720; vol. 2, 1719–1739. Edited and augmented by Jadunath Sarkar. Reprint, New Delhi: Oriental Books Reprint Corp.

ISER, WOLFGANG

1989 Prospecting: From Reader Response to Literary Anthropology. Baltimore: Johns Hopkins University Press.

IYER, K. BHARATA

1970 The Naga in Art and Lore. Times of India Annual 1970: 71–80.

JAGATNARAYAN

1983 Kota ke Maharav Ummedsimh Dvitiya Evam Unka Samay. Kotah: Neha Vikas Pakashan.

JAHANGIR

1978 The Tuzuk-i-Jahangiri, or Memoirs of Jahangir. 2 vols. Translated by Alexander Rogers. Edited by Henry Beveridge. Reprint, New Delhi: Munshiram Manoharlal Publishers.

Forthcoming The Tuzuk-i-Jahangiri (Memoirs of Jahangir). Translated by Wheeler M. Thackston. Washington, D.C.: Freer Gallery of Art, Smithsonian Institution.

JOSHI, NILAKANTH PURUSHOTTAM, AND MUKANDILAL, EDS.

1973 Vishnudas krita rukminimangala. Lakhnau: Rajya Lalit Kala Akadami.

KAYE, SIR JOHN WILLIAM

1858 The Life and Correspondence of Charles, Lord Metcalfe. 2 vols. London: n.p.

KEENE, H. G.

1891 Mádhava Ráo Sindhia Otherwise Called Madhoji. Oxford: Clarendon Press.

1907 Hindustan under Free Lances 1770–1820: Sketches of Military Adventure in Hindustan during the Period Immediately Preceding British Occupation. London: Brown, Langham and Co.

KEWAL RAM

1985 Tazkiratul-Umara of Kewal Ram: Biographical Account of the Mughal Nobility, 1556–1707 A.D. Translated from Persian by S. M. Azizuddin Husain. New Delhi: Munshiram Manoharlal Publishers.

KHAJANCHI CAT.

1960 Miniature Painting: Catalogue of the Exhibition of the Sri Motichand Khajanchi Collection Held by the Lalit Kala Akademi 1960. New Delhi: Lalit Kala Akademi.

KHAN, 'INAYAT

1990 The Shah Jahan Nama of 'Inayat Khan: An Abridged History of the Mughal Emperor Shah Jahan, Compiled by His Librarian. Translated by A. R. Fuller. Edited and completed by W. E. Begley and Z. A. Desai. Delhi: Oxford University Press.

KHAN, NAWWAB SAMSAM-UD-DAULA SHAH NAWAZ, AND 'ABDUL HAYY

1952 The Maathir-ul-Umara: Being Biographies of the Muhammadan and Hindu Officers of the Timurid Sovereigns of India from 1500 to about 1780 A.D. Vol. 2. Translated by Henry Beveridge. Revised and completed by Baini Prashad. Bibliotheca Indica, no. 202. Calcutta: Asiatic Society.

1979 The Maathir-ul-Umara: Being Biographies of the Muhammadan and Hindu Officers of the Timurid Sovereigns of India from 1500 to about 1780 A.D. Vol. 1. Translated by Henry Beveridge. Revised and completed by Baini Prashad. Reprint, Patna: Janaki Prakashan.

KHAN, SAQI MUST'AD

1947 Maasir-i-'Alamgiri: A History of the Emperor Aurangzib-'Alamgir, Reign 1658–1707 A.D. Translated and annotated by Jadunath Sarkar. Bibliotheca Indica, no. 269. Calcutta: Royal Asiatic Society of Bengal.

KHANDALAVALA, KARL, AND MOTI CHANDRA

1974 An Illustrated Aranyaka Parvan in The Asiatic Society of Bombay. Bombay: The Asiatic Society of Bombay.

KHOURY, NUHA

1985 Technical Analysis of Pigments in Royal Persian Miniatures. Unpublished paper. Cambridge, Mass.: Harvard University.

KINCAID, C. A., AND D. B. PARASNIS

1931 A History of the Maratha People. London: Humphrey Milford/Oxford University Press.

KOCH, EBBA

1986 Notes on the Painted and Sculptured Decoration of Nur Jahan's Pavilions in the Ram Bagh (Bagh-i Nur Afshan) at Agra. In Facets of Indian Art: A Symposium Held at the Victoria and Albert Museum, edited by Robert Skelton, Andrew Topsfield, Susan Stronge, and Rosemary Crill. London: Victoria and Albert Museum, 51–65.

KOLFF, D. H. A.

1990 Naukar, Rajput, and Sepoy: The Ethnohistory of the Military Labour Market in Hindustan, 1450–1850. Cambridge, England: Cambridge University Press.

KRAMRISCH, STELLA

1986 Painted Delight: Indian Paintings from Philadelphia Collections. Philadelphia: Philadelphia Museum of Art.

KRISHNA, KALYAN, AND KAY TALWAR

1979 Indian Pigment Paintings on Cloth. Ahmedabad: Calico Museum.

KÜHNEL, ERNST

1937 Indische Miniaturen aus dem Besitz der Staatlichen Museen zu Berlin. Berlin: Gebrüder Mann.

LAKSHMANDAN, THAKURA

n.d. Maharao Shatru Salji ki Vamsa Prashasti (or: Kota Rajya ke Hastalikhita Itihas ki Pratilipi). Unpublished manuscript, ca. 1868, in the possession of Kaviraja Mahipat Singh.

LEACH, LINDA YORK

1986 Indian Paintings: The Cleveland Museum of Art, Catalogue of Oriental Art, Part One. Cleveland: Cleveland Museum of Art in Cooperation with Indiana University Press.

1995 Mughal and Other Indian Paintings from the Chester Beatty Library. 2 vols. London: Scorpion Cavendish, World of Islam Festival Trust.

LEE, SHERMAN, AND GEORGE MONTGOMERY

1960 Rajput Painting. New York: The Asia Society.

LOWRY, GLENN D. AND MILO C. BEACH

1988 An Annotated and Illustrated Checklist of the Vever Collection. Washington, D.C. and Seattle: Smithsonian Institution and University of Washington Press.

LYONS, TRYNA

1995 The Artists of Nathadwara. Ph.D. diss., University of California, Berkeley.

MALCOLM, JOHN

1826 The Political History of India: From 1784 to 1823. 2 vols. London: John Murray.

MALLESON, G. B.

1875 An Historical Sketch of the Native States of India in Subsidiary Alliance with the British Government, with a Notice of the Mediatized and Minor States. London: Longmans, Green, and Co.

1889 Kaye's and Malleson's History of the Indian Mutiny of 1857–8. Vol. 4. Edited by Colonel Malleson. London: W. H. Allen & Co.

MARRIOTT, MCKIM

1976 Hindu Transactions: Diversity without Dualism. In Transaction and Meaning: Directions in the Anthropology of Exchange and Symbolic Behavior, edited by Bruce Kapferer. Philadelphia: Institute for the Study of Human Issues, 109–42.

MARTIUS, RALF

1995 Die Herkunft der Rajputs. In Rajasthan: Land der Könige, edited by Gerd Kreisel. Stuttgart: Linden-Museum Stuttgart, 40–49.

MARWAR DARBAR

1894 Marwar Darbar: Report on the Census of 1891, vol. 2, The Castes of Marwar. Jodhpur: Published by Order of the Marwar Darbar.

MATHUR, R. S.
1986   *Relations of Hadas with Mughal Emperors, 1568–1720 A.D.* Delhi: Deputy Publications.

MEISTER, MICHAEL W.
1981   Darra and the Early Gupta Tradition. In *Chhavi–2: Rai Krishnadasa Felicitation Volume.* Banaras: Bharat Kala Bhavan, 192–205.

MISHRA, N. L.
1987   *Geography behind Political History: A Study of Harauti Region.* Jaipur: R.B.S.A. Publishers.

MISHRA, R. L.
1985   *The Forts of Rajasthan.* Mandawa (Jhunjhunu): Kutir Prakashan.

MISHRAN, SURYAMALLA
c. 1899   *Vansh Bhaskar.* 8 vols. Edited by Ramakarna Asopa. N.p.: n.p.

MITCHELL, W. T. J.
1994   *Picture Theory.* Chicago: University of Chicago Press.
1996   What Does a Picture Want? Unpublished lecture, forthcoming in *October.*

MITTAL, JAGDISH
1989   *Indian Drawings, 16th–19th Century.* Hyderabad: Jagdish & Kamla Mittal Museum of Indian Art.

MODAVE, COMTE DE
(LOUIS LAURENT DE FÉDERBE)
1971   *Voyage en Inde du Comte de Modave, 1773–1776: Nouveaux mémoires sur l'état actuel du Bengale et de l'Indoustan,* edited and annotated by J. Deloche. Paris: L'Ecole Française d'Extrême-Orient.

MORELAND, W. H.
1936   Rank (*mansab*) in the Mogul State Service. *Journal of the Royal Asiatic Society* (October): 641–65.

MUNDY, G. C.
1858   *Pen and Pencil Sketches in India: Journal of a Tour in India.* London: John Murray.

MUNDY, PETER
1914   *The Travels of Peter Mundy, in Europe and Asia, 1608–1667,* vol. 2, *Travels in Asia, 1628–1634.* Edited by R. C. Temple. Hakluyt Society, Second Series, no. 35. London: Hakluyt Society.

NATH, AMAN,
AND SAMAR SINGH JODHA
1994   *Jaipur, the Last Destination.* Bombay: India Book House.

NOEY, CHRISTOPHER,
AND JANET TEMOS
1994   *Art of India from the Williams College Museum of Art (From the Mildred Kip Frost Collection).* Williamstown, Mass.: Williams College Museum of Art.

O'FLAHERTY, WENDY DONIGER
1980   Karma and Rebirth in the Vedas and Puranas. In *Karma and Rebirth in Classical Indian Traditions,* edited by Wendy Doniger O'Flaherty. Berkeley: University of California Press, 337.

OJHA, GAURISHANKAR HIRACAND
1939   *Bikaner Rajya ka Itihas (rajputane ka itihas, pahla bhag).* Ajmer: Gaurishankar Hiracand Ojha.

PAL, PRATAPADITYA
1976   *The Flute and the Brush: Indian Paintings from the William Theo Brown and Paul Wonner Collection.* Newport Beach, Calif.: Newport Harbor Art Museum.

PAL, PRATAPADITYA,
AND CATHERINE GLYNN
1976   *The Sensuous Line: Indian Drawings from the Paul F. Walter Collection.* Los Angeles: Los Angeles County Museum of Art.
1980   In Her Image: Indic Culture. In *In Her Image: The Great Goddess in Indian Asia and the Madonna in Christian Culture.* Santa Barbara: UCSB Art Museum, 29–94.

PARIHAR, G. R.
1985   *Marwar and the Marathas (1724–1843 A.D.).* Jodhpur: Hindi Sahitya Mandir.

PATNAIK, NAVEEN,
AND STUART CARY WELCH
1985   *A Second Paradise: Indian Courtly Life, 1590–1947.* London: Sidgwick & Jackson.

PEABODY, NORBERT
1991a   In Whose Turban Does the Lord Reside? The Objectification of Charisma and the Fetishism of Objects in the Hindu Kingdom of Kota. *Comparative Studies in Society and History* 33:726–54.
1991b   Kota Mahajagat, or The Great Universe of Kota: Sovereignty and Territory in 18th-Century Rajasthan. *Contributions to Indian Sociology* 25:29–56.
1996   Tod's *Rajast'han* and the Boundaries of Imperial Rule in Nineteenth-Century India. *Modern Asian Studies* 30: 185–220.

PELSAERT, FRANCISCO
1972   *Jahangir's India: The Remonstrantie of Francisco Pelsaert.* Translated from Dutch by W. H. Moreland and P. Geyl. Reprint, Delhi: Idarah-i Adabiyat-i Delli.
1979   *De Geschriften van Francisco Pelsaert over Mughal Indie, 1627: Kroniek en Remonstrantie.* Edited by D. H. A. Kolff and H. W. van Santen. Werken uitgegeven door de Linschoten-Vereeniging, no. 81. 'S Gravenhage: Martinus Nijhof.
1982   *Petals from a Lotus: An Introduction to the Arts and History of the Indian Subcontinent.* Bradford: Bradford Art Galleries and Museums.

PFEIFFER, IDA LAURA
c. 1852   *A Woman's Journey Round the World, from Vienna to Brazil, Chili, Tahiti, China, Hindostan, Persia, and Asia Minor.* London: Office of the National Illustrated Library.

POWLETT, P. W.
1880   1880 Kotah Agency Report, no. 150, dated Kotah, 28th April 1879. In *Report on the Political Administration of the Rajputana States for 1878–79.* Selections from the Records of the Government of India, Foreign Department, no. 162. Calcutta: Office of the Superintendent of Government Printing, 85–113.

PRASAD, BENI
1973   *History of Jahangir.* Allahabad: Indian Press.

PRASAD, RAJIVA NAIN
1966   *Raja Man Singh of Amber.* Calcutta: World Press.

PURINTON, NANCY,
AND RICHARD NEWMAN
1985   A Technical Analysis of Indian Painting Materials. In *Pride of the Princes: Indian Painting of the Mughal Era in the Cincinnati Art Museum,* edited by Ellen S. Smart and Daniel Walker. Cincinnati: Cincinnati Art Museum, 107–13.

RANDHAWA, MOHINDER SINGH
1962   *Kangra Paintings on Love.* New Delhi: National Museum.

RAY, NIHARRANJAN
1975   *Mughal Court Painting: A Study in Social and Formal Analysis.* Calcutta: Indian Museum.

REDINGTON, JAMES
1983   *Vallabhacharya on the Love Games of Krishna.* Delhi: Motilal Banarsidass.

RIZVI, ATHAR ABBAS,
AND VINCENT JOHN ADAMS FLYNN
1975   *Fathpur-Sikri.* Bombay: D.B. Taraporevala Sons & Co.

ROE, SIR THOMAS,
AND JOHN FRYER
1873   *Travels in India in the Seventeenth Century.* Reprinted from *Calcutta Weekly Englishman.* London: Trübner & Co.

ROUSSELET, LOUIS
1877   *L'Inde des Rajahs: Voyage dans l'Inde centrale et dans les Présidences de Bombay et du Bengale.* Paris: Librairie Hachette et Cie.
1878   *India and Its Native Princes: Travels in Central India and in the Presidences of Bombay and Bengal.* London: Bickers and Son.

ROY, ASHOK
199   *Artists' Pigments: A Handbook of Their History and Characteristics.* Vol. 2. Washington, D.C.: National Gallery of Art.

ST. LAURENT-LOCKWOOD, BEATRICE
1985   Comparative Analysis of Sixteenth Century Persian and Indian Miniatures: Pigment Analysis. Unpublished paper. Cambridge, Mass.: Harvard University.

SANDERSON, GORDON,
AND ZAFAR HASAN
1911   *Delhi Museum of Archaeology: Loan Exhibition of Antiquities, Coronation Durbar, 1911: An Illustrated Selection of the Principal Exhibits.* Delhi: Archaeological Survey of India.

SARKAR, JADUNATH
1919   *History of Aurangzeb,* vol. 4, *Southern India, 1645–1689.* Calcutta: M. C. Sarkar & Sons.
1924   *History of Aurangzeb,* vol. 5, *The Closing Years, 1689–1707.* Calcutta: M. C. Sarkar & Sons.
1932   *Fall of the Mughal Empire,* vol. 1, *1739–1754.* Calcutta: M. C. Sarkar & Sons.
1934   *Fall of the Mughal Empire,* vol. 2, *1754–1771.* Calcutta: M. C. Sarkar & Sons.
1937   Aurangzib, 1658–1681. In *The Cambridge History of India,* vol. 4, *The Mughal Period,* edited by Richard Burn. Cambridge, England: Cambridge University Press, 222–59.
1938   *Fall of the Mughal Empire,* vol. 3, *1771–1788.* Calcutta: S. N. Sarkar.
1984   *A History of Jaipur, c.1503–1938.* Revised and edited by Raghubir Sinh. Jaipur: Maharaja Sawai Man Singh II Museum.

SCHIMMEL, ANNEMARIE
1987   Khankhanan 'Abdur Rahim: Ein Kunstmazen zur Moghulzeit. In *Wege zur Kunst und zum Menschen: Festschrift für Heinrich Lützeler zum 85. Geburtstag,* edited by Frank-Lothar Kroll. Bonn: Bouvier Verlag Herbert Grundmann.

SEN, GEETI
1984   *Paintings from the Akbar Nama: A Visual Chronicle of Mughal India.* Calcutta: Lustre Press.

SHAKTAWAT, THAKUR LALSINGH
1966   *The Immortal Chittor Fort.* Udaipur: Kunwar Mohan Singh Shaktawat.

SHARMA, BRAJBHUSAN,
AND DVARKADAS PARIKH, EDS.
1951–53   *Do sau bavan vaisnavan ki varta.* 3 vols. Kankaroli: Suddhadvaita Academy.

SHARMA, G. N.
1962   *Mewar and the Mughal Emperors, 1526–1707 A.D.* Agra: Shiva Lal Agarwala & Co.
1970   *Rajasthan Studies.* Agra: Lakshmi Narain Agarwal.

SHARMA, M. L.
1939   *Kota Rajya ka Itihas.* 2 vols. Kota: Kota Printing Press.

SHARMA, O. P.
1973   *Indian Miniature Painting.* Tokyo: Asahi Shimbun.

SHASTRI, MADANMOHAN
1961   *Catalogue to Government Museum, Kota.* Jaipur: Department of Archaeology and Museums.

SHASTRI, R. P.
1971   *Jhala Zalim Singh (1730–1823): The De-Facto Ruler of Kota, Who Also Dominated Bundi and Udaipur: Shrewd Politician, Administrator and Reformer.* Jaipur: Raj Printing Works.

SHERWANI, H. K.
1974   *History of the Qutb Shahi Dynasty.* New Delhi: Munshiram Manoharlal Publishers.

SHIMIZU, TADASHI
1993   *The Bhagavata Purana Miniature Paintings from the Bhandarkar Oriental Research Institute Manuscript Dated 1648.* Tokyo: Toyo Bunko/Centre for East Asian Cultural Studies for UNESCO.

SHYAMALDAS, KAVIRAJA
1886   *Vir Vinod.* 2 vols. Udaipur: Rajayantralaya.

SIMPSON, M. S.,
AND STUART CARY WELCH
1980   *Arab and Persian Painting in the Fogg Art Museum.* Cambridge, Mass.: Fogg Art Museum, Harvard University.

SINGH, DILBAGH
1990   *The State, Landlords, and Peasants.* Delhi: Manohar.

SINGH, HARNATH
1965   *Genealogical Table of Kachawahas.* Jaipur: Dundlod House.

SINGH, KISHOR
n.d.a   *Shri Brajrajji ka Ghar ki Utsav Malika* (Garland of Festivals from the House of Lord Brijrajji) or *Shri Brajrajji ki Nitiprati Sevaprakar* (Manual for the Daily Worship of Lord Brijrajji). Manuscript written and illustrated for Kishor Singh when he was crown prince (*maharajkumvar*). Kota: Government Museum (see also *Vallabhotsava Chandrika* in M. Shastri 1961, 46–47).
n.d.b   *Shri Brajrajji ka Ghar ki Utsav Malika.* Artist's mock-up. Kota: Rajasthan Prachyavidya Pratishthan, MS 3447.
n.d.c   *Utsavan ki Bhavana ke Kirtan.* In *Chaupai Janmashtami ka Utsav ka Radhashtami ka Kirtan ki.* Kota: Rajasthan Prachyavidya Pratishthan, MS 3474.
n.d.d   *Nitya ke Kirtan.* In *Chaupai Janmashtami ka Utsav ka Radhashtami ka Kirtan ki.*

Kota: Rajasthan Prachyavidya Pratishthan, MS 3474.
n.d.e   *Shri Brajnathasya Svarupa Bhavana.* Kota: Rajasthan Prachyavidya Pratishthan, MS 7071/3.

SINGH, KUMAR SANGRAM
1965   *Catalogue of Indian Miniature Paintings: Collection of Kumar Sangram Singh of Nawalgarh.* Jaipur: Rajasthan University Library and Lalit Kala Akademy.

SINGH, M. BRIJRAJ
1985   *The Kingdom That Was Kotah: Paintings from Kotah.* New Delhi: Lalit Kala Akademi.
1991   Kota und Umgebung. In *APA Guides: Rajasthan.* Berlin: APA Guides, RV Reise- und Verkehrsverlag, 244–58.

SINGH, NARENDRA
1939   *Thirty Decisive Battles of Jaipur.* Jaipur: J.E.P. Works.

SINGH, THAKUR JASWANT
1990   *Rajasthan ke Rajavadi Git.* 3 vols. Jaipur: Sanghi Prakashan.

SKELTON, ROBERT
1973   *Rajasthani Temple Hangings of the Krishna Cult.* New York: American Federation of Arts.
1981   Shaykh Phul and the Origins of Bundi Painting. In *Chhavi–2: Rai Krishnadasa Felicitation Volume.* Banaras: Bharat Kala Bhavan, 123–29.

SMITH, EDMUND W.
1897   *The Moghul Architecture of Fathpur-Sikri, Described and Illustrated.* Archaeological Survey of India, New Imperial Series, vol. 18.3. Allahabad: Superintendent, Government Press, Northwest Provinces.

SNELL, RUPERT
1991   *The Hindi Classical Tradition: A Braj Bhasa Reader.* London: School of Oriental and African Studies.

SOMANI, RAM VALLABH
1976   *History of Mewar: From Earliest Times to 1751 A.D.* Jaipur: C.L. Ranka & Co.
1985   *Later Mewar.* Jaipur: Shantidevi Somani and Mahesh Prakashan.

SOTHEBY'S, INC.
1972   *Fine Indian and Persian Miniatures and a Manuscript Selected from the Well-Known Collection . . .* London: sale catalogue, December 12.
1973   *Fine Oriental Miniatures and Manuscripts.* London: sale catalogue, July 11.
1981   *Fine Oriental Miniatures, Manuscripts, and Works of Art.* New York: sale catalogue, December 10.
1989   *Indian, Himalayan, and Southeast Asian Art.* New York: sale catalogue, March 22.

1992   *Indian and Southeast Asian Art.* New York: sale catalogue, December 5.
1994   *Indian Miniatures.* London: sale catalogue, April 26.
1996   *Persian and Indian Manuscripts and Miniatures from the Collection Formed by the British Rail Pension Fund.* London: sale catalogue, April 23.

STOOKE, H. J.,
AND KARL KHANDALAVALA
1953   *The Laud Ragamala Miniatures: A Study in Indian Painting and Music.* Oxford: Bruno Cassirer.

SURJANACHARITAMAHAKAVYAM
1952   *Surjanacharitamahakavyam: Gaudiyamahakavi shri candrashekhara viracitam surjanacarita mahakavyam.* Translated into Hindi and edited by Candradhar Sharma. Kashi: Candradhar Sharma.

SYED, ANEES JAHAN
1977   *Aurangzeb in Muntakhab-al Lubab.* Bombay and New Delhi: Somaiya Publications.

TAGARE, GANESH VASUDEO
1978   *The Bhagavata Purana.* Pt. 4. Delhi: Motilal Banarsidas.

TAVERNIER, JEAN-BAPTISTE
1925   *Travels in India by Jean-Baptiste Tavernier, Baron of Aubonne (1676).* 2 vols. Translated from French by V. Ball. Edited by William Crooke. 2d ed. Oxford: Oxford University Press/Humphrey Milford.

TAYLOR, WOODMAN
1991   The Post-Production Life of Visual Forms: Performance, Audiences, and the Generation of Meanings. Paper delivered at the fifth ACSAA South Asian Art Symposium.

THORN, WILLIAM
1818   *Memoir of the War in India, Conducted by General Lord Lake, Commander-in-Chief, and Major-General Sir Arthur Wellesley, Duke of Wellington: From Its Commencement in 1803 to Its Termination in 1806.* London: T. Egerton, Military Library.

THORNTON, EDWARD
1854   *A Gazetteer of the Territories under the Government of the East-India Company, and of the Native States on the Continent of India.* 4 vols. London: W. H. Allen & Co.

TOD, JAMES
1829   *Annals and Antiquities of Rajast'han, or The Central and Western Rajpoot States of India.* Vol. 1. London: n.p.
1832   *Annals and Antiquities of Rajast'han, or The Central and Western Rajpoot States of India.* Vol. 2. London: n.p.
1920   *Annals and Antiquities of Rajasthan, or The Central and Western Rajput States.* 3 vols. Edited by William Crooke. London:

Humphrey Milford/Oxford University Press.
1983   *Annals and Antiquities of Rajasthan.* 2 vols. New Delhi: Oriental Books Reprint Corp.

TOPSFIELD, ANDREW
1980   *Paintings from Rajasthan in the National Gallery of Victoria.* Melbourne: National Gallery of Victoria.
1990   Eugene Impey at Mount Abu and Jodhpur. *History of Photography* 14(3):251–74.
1995   The Royal Paintings Inventory at Udaipur. In *Indian Art and Connoisseurship: Essays in Honour of Douglas Barrett,* edited by John Guy. Middleton, N.J., and Ahmedabad: Grantha Corp. and Mapin Publishing, 188–99.

TOPSFIELD, ANDREW,
AND MILO C. BEACH
1991   *Indian Paintings and Drawings from the Collection of Howard Hodgkin.* London: Thames and Hudson.

VARMA, BADRI NARAYAN VARMA
1989   *Kota bhitti citramkan parampara (hadoti bhitti citra kala ki pasthabhumi).* Nai Dilli: Radha Pablikeshans.

VATSYAYANA, KAPILA
1982   *Dance in Indian Painting.* New Delhi: Abhinav Publications.

WALDSCHMIDT, ERNST,
AND ROSE LEONORE
1971   Indische Malerei. In *Indien und Südostasien,* edited by Herbert Härtel and Jeannine Auboyer. Berlin: Propyläen Verlag, 179–97 + plates.

WATTERS, MARK P.,
AND NANCY PURINTON
1989   A Preliminary Study of the Materials Used by Medieval Persian Painters. Unpublished paper. Newark, Del.: Winterthur Program in Art Conservation/University of Delaware.

WELCH, STUART CARY
1976   *Indian Drawings and Painted Sketches: Sixteenth through Nineteenth Centuries.* New York: The Asia Society.
1978   *Imperial Mughal Painting.* New York: Braziller.
1983   Return to Kotah. In *Essays on Near Eastern Art and Archaeology in Honour of Charles Kyrle Wilkinson,* edited by Prudence Harper and Holly Pittman. New York: Metropolitan Museum of Art, 78–93.
1985   *India: Art and Culture, 1300–1900.* New York: Metropolitan Museum of Art/Holt, Rinehart and Winston.
1994   A Matter of Empathy: Comical Indian Pictures. *Asian Art and Culture* (Fall 1994): 76–103.

WELCH, STUART CARY,
AND MILO C. BEACH
1965   *Gods, Thrones, and Peacocks.* New
York: The Asia Society.

WHITE, SUSAN M.
1984   Orpiment on Persian Miniatures.
Unpublished paper. Newark, Del.:
Winterthur Program in Art Conserva-
tion/University of Delaware.

WILLIAMS, JOANNA
1990   From the Fifth to the Twentieth
Century and Back. *Art Journal* 49(4):
363–69.

WOODS, JOHN E.
1976   *The Aqquyunlu: Clan, Confederation,
Empire.* Minneapolis and Chicago:
Bibliotheca Islamica.

YOUNG, D.
1959   *Fountain of the Elephants.* London:
Collins.

ZEIGLER, NORMAN P.
1973   *Action and Power in Rajasthani Culture: Social History of Rajputs of Middle Period
Rajasthan.* Ph.D. diss., University of
Chicago.

ZETTERSTEEN, K. V.,
AND C. J. LAMM
1948   *Mohammed Asafi: The Story of Jamal
and Jalal, an Illuminated Manuscript in the
Library of Uppsala University.* Uppsala:
Almqvist and Wiksells Boktryckeri A B.

Authors

STUART CARY WELCH, curator of the exhibition, author of the introductory catalogue essay, and coordinator of the catalogue entries, is curator emeritus of Islamic and later Indian Art at the Harvard University Art Museums. Major exhibitions he has curated include *India, Art and Culture 1300–1900* (Metropolitan Museum of Art, New York, 1985) and *Wonders of the Age* (British Museum, London; National Gallery of Art, Washington, D.C.; and Fogg Art Museum, Cambridge, Mass., 1979–80). Mr. Welch has also authored or edited numerous publications, among them *The Emperors' Album: Images of Mughal India* (Metropolitan Museum of Art, New York, 1987, with A. Schimmel, M. Swietochowski, and W. Thackston) and *India, Art and Culture 1300–1900* (Metropolitan Museum of Art, New York, 1985).

JOACHIM K. BAUTZE, in charge of the chair of art history of South Asia at the South Asia Institute of Heidelberg University, is a specialist in the Hara dynasty and its major schools of painting at Bundi and Kotah. Dr. Bautze, who received his Ph.D. from the Free University, Berlin, has published over forty articles on Rajasthani painting and Rajput history, as well as articles and catalogues on other aspects of Indian art.

WOODMAN TAYLOR is Assistant Professor of Asian Art at the University of Illinois, Chicago. He has organized many exhibitions of South Asian art, particularly while Assistant Curator of Islamic and Later Indian Art at the Harvard University Art Museums. Current projects include studying the performative uses of visual culture in the Vallabha Sampraday religious community based on dissertation research conducted at Kota, problematizing hybridity in premodern South Asian visual cultures focusing on Abdur Rahim's illustrated *Ramayana*, and curating an exhibition on the religious uses of backdrop cloth paintings (*pichhvais*) for the Smithsonian's Sackler and Freer Galleries.

NORBERT PEABODY is a fellow of Wolfson College, Cambridge, and holds the Graduate Office in Research at the Centre of South Asian Studies at the University of Cambridge. Dr. Peabody was curator for *Leaves from the Jungle: An Exhibition of Folk and Tribal Art from India* (Harvard University Art Museums, 1984). His doctoral dissertation was a study of changes in the institution of Hindu kingship in Kotah under precolonial and colonial rule. His publications on kingship in Kotah include a forthcoming book, *Hindu Kingship and Polity in Kota, 1719–1990* (Cambridge University Press).

CRAIGEN W. BOWEN is deputy director and Philip and Lynn Straus conservator of works on paper at the Straus Center for Conservation, Harvard University Art Museums. Ms. Bowen is a specialist in the materials and painting techniques of the Kotah school and has traveled to Kotah to work as conservator for the Rao Madho Singh Fort Trust Collection.

Appendix

Following are transliterations of inscriptions found on the paintings included in this catalogue. The original inscriptions are in Devanagari script unless otherwise noted.

14

Maharao Bhim Singh 1 Received by Emperor Farrukh Siyar ("Emperor Aurangzeb [sic] in Darbar")

Inscribed on recto:
pātasyahā noraṃg/jeb kī chabī.

17

Siege of a Strong Fort

Inscribed in the left half:
sekh taju ko.

18

The Mughal Emperor Farrukh Siyar Carried in a Palanquin

Inscribed on verso:
pātsā phurak syāha.

This seems to be the Hindusthani rendering of another inscription, apparently in Nastaliq, below.

19

Brijnathji and Maharao Arjun Singh aboard a Hunting Barge on the Chambal River

Inscribed on verso, in a later hand:
māhārāvjī śrī arjan sīghjī.

Inscribed below on verso, in the typical hand of a Kotah scribe:
savī śrī vrajnathjī kī māhārā/vjī
śrī arjan sīghjī kī sīkār / karā — kī.

20

Maharao Arjun Singh as Brijnathji on a War Chariot

Inscribed on verso:
savī māhārāvjī śrī arjan sīghjī.

21

Maharao Arjun Singh Celebrating Krishna's Birthday (Janmashtami) in the Audience Hall (Darikhana) of the Raj Mahal at Kotah

Inscribed on recto:
māhārāvjī śrī arjan sīghjī janma astamī darīkhāno rājmahal ko.

Inscribed on verso, in a later hand:
māhārāvjī śrī arjan sihjī.

A shorter inscription below the first line on the recto is partly obliterated by the black rule and hence unreadable.

22

Maharao Arjun Singh Celebrating Krishna's Birthday (Janmashtami) in the Audience Hall (Darikhana) of the Raj Mahal at Kotah

Inscribed on verso:
māhā[rā]vjī śrī dīvān ar[ja]/n sīghjī janmastamī ko / darīkhāno.

27

Maharao Durjan Sal's Elephant, Kisanprasad

Inscribed on recto:
māhārāvj[ī śrī du]rjan sāljī kī / hāthī kīsan[p]rasād.

29

Brijnathji and Durjan Sal Sight a Pride of Lions

Inscribed on verso:
chavī śrī vrajnāthjī kī vā māhā/rāvjī durjan sāljī kī jā— aso sī/ghjī kī sakār [sikār] jora / kī kaṭaḍa nāhā/rā kī hāthā [hāthī] kī śondār [kondār?] / gaṃgaijī hāthī / kī.

32

Rao Madho Singh of Kotah Hunting Boar from Horseback

Inscribed on recto, at top border:
māhārāv śrī mādho sīghjī māḍā / suar—.

Inscribed on verso:
rāmjī / mhārājadhīrāj mhārāj mhārāvjī śrī mādho sīghjī / kī katār — smīkho[?] ghoḍā ka che[?].

Some passages are illegible, but it is clear that this inscription captions the painting.

35

Brijnathji and Durjan Sal Hunting Deer

Inscribed on verso:
chavī śrī vrajnāthjī kī māhārā/v durjan sāljī kī sakār haranā / kī — kī.

36

Maharao Durjan Sal and Maharana Jagat Singh in a Palanquin, Surrounded by Royal Courtiers

Inscribed on verso:
rā° [rāmjī!] / māhārājādharājī māhārājā māhārānā śrī jagat sīghjī māhārāv/jī śrī durjan sāljī — ka takhat ma va rājā sīrdār asavārī ma māhā/rājā takhat sīghjī, māhārājā nāthjī, māhārājā vakhat sīghjī, ka/varjī prathīrājjī, chītra sīghjī rājāvāt, dhābhāī uderām pāno / vanā dhyo kalamī sekh cuterā tājūn śrī hajur najar kī dhyo.

A one-line Nastaliq inscription runs parallel to the second line of the Nagari inscription.

40

May/June (Jeth Masa)
Folio from a *Twelve Months (Barahmasa)* Series

Inscribed:
mās jeṭh.

41

August/September (Bhadon Masa)
Folio from a *Twelve Months (Barahmasa)* Series

Inscribed:
mās bhādavo.

44

Camp of Maharao Shatru Sal 1

Inscribed on recto:
bhānaja jagat / sīghjī; bhuvānī sīghjī; phate sīghjī rājāvat / jā° jalvāḍā; nāvāv nāmdār [hāyḍar?] khājī; jagat sīghjī kī cau[?] / uma— rājgaḍh ko; surjalaljī rājā / [illegible]; ḍerī cā[ṃ]d sīghjī / ramkot ko; ḍerī bhāī nāthjī har/dāvat pīpaldāv ko; ḍerī bhāī samār sīghjī / palāīthā vālā ko; bhaṭ jorāvār / sīghjī khāto/lī kā; śrī bhaṭjī śrī burj/ānaṃdjī ko—; modī kanīrā/m kobār ko ḍerī; ḍerī naga/r khānā ko; pasārya ko / vājār; pāsvānā ko ḍero; shā govaṃdrāmjī; sā° nānū rāmjī; shā samaṃd rāmjī; vāgsī sakhrā/m dev ko; ḍero śrī māmājī sāhī/v ko; śrī māmājī sāhāb / kā kāsā ghoḍā kī pāī/gā; jeṭhī hāthī rām; duvān khānā kā ḍerā; pīlkhānā / ko ḍerā; ḍerī bhāī sobhāg sī/ghjī ratlāmvālā kā; bhāī magh sīghjī ko ḍero; darīkhānā ko ḍero; gāḍīkhānā; surajmaljī, rājā/vat bathalī kā [line below illegible]; ḍero jadvā[?] ko; tosākhānā kī ḍerā; rughanāth sīgh/jī jhālā kā ḍerā; sāva[ṃ]t sīghjī /mān sīghvot; mālārāmjī jeṭhī ko; darīkhānā ko ḍerā; ḍero jamāndār thanu / khājī ko; ḍerī ghātyajī yadāgo[?] ko; śrī dārbār kā kāsā ghoḍā / kī pāīgā; ḍero pojhā gaṃgā/datjī ko; kuver jeṭhī ko; bhāī gīrvār sīghjī / ko ḍero; son sīgh/jī rāmkot.

45

Maharao Umed Singh I and His Chief Minister, Zalim Singh Jhala, Tiger Shooting

Inscribed on verso:

rāmjī / sa° 1827 basākh budī 11 somvār / ḍolya ka kuv kan jyarka aḍ[a?]/da nāhār sodyarī 1 māhārāv/jī śrī umed sīghjī [followed by about three syllables blacked out] / [about 10 syllables blacked out] — onamāda / nār sodyarī kana jāra vākedār jhara / ma ahāḍī samḍārām bīṃḍa ka aja/ḍa jāgīrī ḍolo derā rāypur kā — / sīkār khela rāypur dākhalī huvā / lār sīrdār māmājī śrī hajur sevānī[?] / mā[hā]rājā nāthjī khā[ṃ]jī anur khā[ṃ]jī / yād sīghjī kavar bhuvānī sīghjī bara/t[?] sīghjī arjan poto josī devkara/njī pyardān ṭhākurā puran samghjī vā / bagsī akharām hākam pāno baṃnā/yo sekh tāju cuterā kā hāth ko / kī do.

46

Maharao Umed Singh I and His Chief Minister (Divan), Zalim Singh Jhala, Tiger Hunting

Inscribed on verso:

rā° / samvat 1831 kā jeth vudī 11 dītvār — / ālnyā ka ajāḍa nāhār nāhārī ko joḍī / mārī / 2.

Inscribed below, in a different hand and partly obliterated:

sa° 1836 ko — sud 3 mā/hārāvjī śrī umed sīghjī rāje śrī jā/lem sīghjī alainyā kī nadī ma nā/hār nārī mārī [rest of this line illegible] / hāḍi kī [?] / nāhār tomāḍa nāhārī hākam / nārī 1 nār 1.

Inscribed below, in a third hand:

josī hamsrājan kī do.

48

Maharao Umed Singh I and Nobles Shooting Lions in Alnia

Inscribed on verso:

rā° / samvat 1841 kā pra° cet sud 13 [the rest of this line is lost] / ha ālnyā ka ajāḍa nāhār uṭḍa mā/rā / 3.

Inscribed below, in a different hand:

josī hatuvārāt — ko kī do.

Inserted between the first and second line, in a later hand:

māhārāvjī śrī ume—.

49

Maharao Umed Singh I and Zalim Singh Jhala with the Zenana Shooting Lions

Inscribed on verso:

rā° / samvat 1841 kā phāgun budī 1 bu° / hamahalajhāmar ajāḍa huvo ka nā/hār nāhārī mārya uṭḍa / 3 / nahar uṭḍa: 1 naharya uṭḍa: 2.
The numerals are written below the respective sex of the lion.

Inscribed below, in a different hand:

cuterā gumānī ka hāt / ko kī do.

Inscribed, again in a different hand, below the central top part of the verso of the painting:

śrī / māhārāvjī śrī umed sīghjī sakār padhārya lār jhā/lā jālam sīghjī ko janāno sakār ma.

50

A Tiger Shoot in the Jungle at Raipur

Inscribed on verso:

rā° / samvat 1843 kā pos sudī 1 / gurvār ma rāīpur kīrāḍī paṭal / rupā ka ajāḍa nāhār sodha/rī mārī: / 1.

Inscribed below, in a different hand:

pāṃdugarsī ko beṭo sītā/rām kā hāth ko kī do.

Inscribed beside the first inscription, in the same hand:

rā° / samvat 1844 kā āghan bu/dī 1 maṃ°ha rāīpur kīrāḍī paṭal ru/pā ka ajāḍa 1 nāhār sodhārī mārī / 1.

51

A Tigress Shoot in Open Landscape

Inscribed on verso:

rā° / samvat 1845 kā phāgun sudī / 3 sukravār takanjya kā hakā/m sadārām rāvat ko ajāḍa ma / nāhārī sodharī mārī: / 1.
The numeral is written below the middle word of the second-to-last line.

53

Shrimant Patelji Mahadji Sindhia on Horseback out Hawking

Inscribed on verso:

śrīmant paṭal māhājī sī[ṃ]dhyā.

55

Shri Nathji and Navanitapriyaji during the Flower Swing Festival (Phuldol)

Inscribed on top border:

śrī nāthjī ko ḍol ko ucchav he.

56

Maharao Kishor Singh Performing the Lamp-Waving (Arati) Ceremony of Brijrajji during the Holi Festival

Inscribed on top margin:

śrī vrījrājjī ko horī ke ucchav [rubbed, illegible] ārtī ko.

57

Maharao Kishor Singh Performing the Lamp-Waving (Arati) Ceremony of Brijrajji during the Festival for Religious Merit (Akshatritiya)

Inscribed on top margin:

śrī vrajrāyjī ko āṣatīj ko ucchav hai.

58

Maharao Kishor Singh Bathing Brijrajji during the Bathing Festival (Snan Yatra)

Inscribed on top margin:

śrī vrījrāyjī ko asnān yātrā ko cītra.

59

Maharao Kishor Singh Performing the Lamp-Waving (Arati) Ceremony of Brijrajji during the Festival of Water Sports (Jalakrida)

Inscribed on top margin:

jaiṭh sud 2 jalakrīḍā ko cītra hai.

60

Maharao Kishor Singh Bathing Govardhanji with Milk during the Festival of Awakening (Prabodhini)

Inscribed on top margin:

śrī kātī sud 11 pramodni ko utsa hai.

61

Maharao Kishor Singh Performing the Lamp-Waving (Arati) Ceremony during Brijrajji's Throne (Pat) Festival

Inscribed on top margin:

śrī vrajrāyjī pat uchav vesāṣ sud 5.

62

Maharao Kishor Singh Performing the Lamp-Waving (Arati) Ceremony of Brijrajji during the Festival Honoring Vyas

Inscribed on top margin:

asāḍh sud 15 punyo ko uchav hai.

63

Maharao Ram Singh Playing Polo near Gagraon

Inscribed on recto on the top margin:

śrī.

Inscribed on verso:

rā° / mhārājdhīrāj mhī mhed mhārāvjī śrī rām sīghjī gāgroṇ padharya / mukām derā ma*the*va*rī*ka*ja*the*ga*da khelya umrāvāṃ s°1895.

66

Maharao Ram Singh about to Strike the Marriage Doorway Decoration (Torana) in the Presence of Maharawal Gaj Singh of Jaisalmer

Inscribed on recto:

śrī [śrī darbār, here in the meaning of "royalty" or "His Highness".

Inscribed on verso:

śrī rāmjī / śrī mhārājādhīrāj mhāhārāj mhīmhemdra mhārāvrājājī śrī rām sīhjī bāhādur hīs koṭā kā jasalmer kā mhārāvaljī śrī gaj sīghjī kapraṇ[?] bā padhyārav samat 1900 / ka sāl mās phālgunaṃ pratham torana pha[?] padhāryajī kī savārī kī chavi / 1 / lārā sardār umrāv kārava rīvāgar[?] / umrāv sīrdār / rāja arjan sī/ghjī; ratan sīghjī; caṃdrāvat; nīmolāyā / acal sīghjī; gatāmabhā ca/trabhuj sīghjī; palāitha āpjī sa° / phate sīghjī; sārthal kā / narpat sīghjī; mhārāja ude/sīghjī; koelā sār/dār sīghjī; / lāljī rāmjī; —rasthal[?]jī [illegible] ratanlāl kau; vaichodurām; paimavorāmdaśtra[?]; sohān [text breaks off here]; / vāgsī manakrāmjī; jeṭhī gunjī; jeṭhī kanīrāmjī; pāsvān nāthujī / phate sīghjī go/ḍ; pratāp sīghjī ta/var; jmādar mhamad / mustaphā ṣā; bhuvānidānjī / caran; jmādār abdal / edīm ṣajī; rāv bujlāl/jī; bābārām pralā/djī; hotī govaṃd gaj pas savār.